Bt
5.56

MARK TWAIN *and* BRET HARTE

MARK TWAIN
AND
BRET HARTE

BY MARGARET DUCKETT

UNIVERSITY OF OKLAHOMA PRESS : NORMAN

LIBRARY OF CONGRESS CATALOG CARD NUMBER: 64–21709

Copyright 1964 by the University of Oklahoma Press, Publishing Division of the University. Composed and printed at Norman, Oklahoma, U.S.A., by the University of Oklahoma Press. First edition.

To R. C. H.

PREFACE

THIS IS AN EXAMINATION of a strange and finally painful relationship between two very different human beings. Both were extremely sensitive. One freely and often violently articulated his emotional responses to personal experience. The other was extraordinarily reticent. Although a writer's work must stand or fall on its intrinsic merit, in a study of the relationship between Mark Twain and Bret Harte, a complete separation of the individuals from their literary productions is impossible for several reasons. First, there is the matter of literary influence of each man on the other. The second reason is the crucial experience of collaboration. And a third reason is that Twain's sweeping indictments of Harte included not only the man, whom Twain loved and hated, but also the man's writings, which Mark Twain admired and damned.

For many years I have been interested in Bret Harte as a nineteenth-century liberal interpreting the social scene for readers of popular fiction in England and America. Except for three or four anthology-stale stories, Harte's writings—produced over a period of more than forty years and filling more than twenty volumes—are little known today. An examination of these writings in relation to the struggle for social justice and civil rights developed in me a sincere respect for the perceptiveness and consistency of this currently denigrated author. However, for many more years I have maintained a decided preference for Tom Sawyer and Huckleberry Finn to M'liss, Colonel Starbottle, or the pathetic infant of Roaring Camp. As my search proceeded and data accumulated, it seemed to me increasingly evident that more than a little truth has been crushed to earth—truth not only about the relationships of the two men but also about the relationships of their works. Finally, in my observations of the parallels and contradictions of these extraordinary friends, my sympathies mounted on the side of the man who remained silent in the face of considerable provocation. But sympathy for Bret Harte has increased rather than diminished my appreciation of Mark Twain's masterpiece, *The Adventures of Huckleberry Finn*.

In a work of this sort, it is impossible to name—or even to know—all those to whom the worker is indebted. The idea for this book originated with Miss Gertrude Ruhnka, who while reading some of Mark Twain's letters when they were in the Huntington Library, found her sympathies aroused for Bret Harte. My investigation of the Mark Twain–Bret Harte relationship, begun as an article, was encouraged by Professor James D. Hart and Professor George R. Stewart, who pointed out that though the break in the friendship has frequently been alluded to by critics hostile to Harte, there is another side of the story which has never been told. Footnotes in this volume acknowledge only part of my indebtedness to Professor Stewart, on whose biography, bibliographies, articles, notes, and editions of Bret Harte I have frequently relied. Professor Harry R. Warfel, who first stimulated my interest in Harte, suggested some years ago that I enumerate some of the familiar charges against Harte and present pertinent evidence.

To Professor Henry Nash Smith, literary editor of the Mark Twain Papers, and to his assistant, Mr. Frederick Anderson, I am indebted for access to materials in the collection in their care. Furthermore, I am indebted to Professor Smith, Mr. Anderson, and Professor William M. Gibson for the meticulous and comprehensive editing and annotating of the correspondence of Mark Twain and William Dean Howells, published by the Belknap Press of the Harvard University Press in 1960. For permission to use material in the Mark Twain Papers in Berkeley, I am indebted to the Mark Twain Estate.

The Bret Harte family, represented by Mr. Lawrence K. Bret Harte, gave me generous permission to publish some hitherto unpublished letters of Bret Harte, including the letters to Mark Twain preserved in the Mark Twain Papers in Berkeley. Mrs. Geoffrey Bret Harte kindly permitted me to quote from a letter of her late husband.

Most of my research was done in the Henry E. Huntington Library of San Marino, California; the William Andrews Clark Memorial Library of Los Angeles; the University of California Library and the Bancroft Library of Berkeley. I am grateful for the cheerful assistance —often beyond the call of duty—of members of the staff in each library, particularly to Mr. Lyle Wright and Miss Mary Isabel Fry of Huntington and Mr. George P. Hammond, Mr. John Barr Tompkins, Mrs. Julia McCleod, Mrs. Helen Bretnor, and Miss Estelle Rebec of Bancroft. To the Houghton Library, Harvard University, I am indebted for sending me, at the suggestion of Mr. Jacob Blanck, a rare copy of *Three Aces, Jim Todd's Episode in Social Euchre, A Poem and a Denial, by Mark Twain,* which I was permitted to photograph. To the Yale University Library I am indebted for permission to publish Bret Harte's letter to James R. Osgood of April 15, 1874.

To Mr. Clifton Waller Barrett and the Alderman Library of the University of Virginia I am indebted for permission to publish and quote excerpts from Bret Harte's letters to Mrs. Henniker, now in the "Barrett Library Bret Hartes." In August, 1958, before Mr. Barrett acquired the prompt book of *Ah Sin* (edited by Mr. Frederick Anderson and published by the Book Club of California in 1961), Mr. Marston E. Drake of James F. Drake, Incorporated, of New York, very generously sent the manuscript to San Francisco so that I could read it in the apartment of Mr. Drake's son-in-law and daughter, Mr. and Mrs. Robert M. Strong. Mr. David Magee of San Francisco kindly permitted me to examine Madame Van de Velde's copy of Bret Harte's Diary, 1881–1888, now in The New York Public Library. To this library I am indebted for further use of the diary. In the University of Washington Library, my home base, I am indebted to Mr. George Piternick, Mr. J. Ronald Todd, and Mr. Robert D. Monroe, and Mrs. Ione Redford for assistance, advice, and moral support. The index was made by Mrs. Mary Demery.

To the Graduate Studies Committee of the University of Washington, I am indebted for grants-in-aid for research, typing, and indexing, as well as for two leaves of absence from teaching. But most of all I am indebted to Professor Robert B. Heilman who, as executive officer of the English Department of the University of Washington, was chiefly responsible for my being given time and encouragement for my tortoise-pace travels along the historical approach.

Professor Bradford Booth of the University of California in Los

Angeles, Professor Harry Burns and the late Professor Merrell Davis of the University of Washington were good enough to read earlier manuscript versions of this book. Its present weaknesses are all my own, Mark Twain's, and Bret Harte's.

MARGARET DUCKETT

Seattle, Washington
July 8, 1964

CONTENTS

ILLUSTRATIONS

MARK TWAIN *and* BRET HARTE

There the torches blazed the brightest, there the moon shone out like day, and there, in tar-and-feathery dignity, sat his kinsman, Major Molineux!

NATHANIEL HAWTHORNE

1

> Lawyers always construct theories when they cannot discover facts.
> A good lawyer examines his theory closely and rejects it if not consist-
> ent with facts as they appear. A bad lawyer clings to his pet theory even
> after investigation shows that it is founded on an imperfect knowledge
> of facts.
>
> BRET HARTE[1]

AMONG MARK TWAIN'S MANY TALENTS was the ability to fabricate
a story and tell it so many times that he believed it himself. A blurb
for the dust jacket of his *Autobiography*, published in 1959, called attention to Mark Twain's "magnificent and priceless" portraits of his
contemporaries and headed a list of those contemporaries with the name
Bret Harte. Although Charles Neider, the editor of this autobiography,
included a final, hitherto unpublished comment by Mark Twain about
this former friend, most of Twain's dictations about Harte distributed
through several chapters of the Neider edition are repetitions of reminiscences and criticisms edited earlier by the late Bernard De Voto
and published in 1940 in a book entitled *Mark Twain in Eruption:
Hitherto Unpublished Pages about Men and Events*. De Voto cautioned readers against accepting every page as history, yet he considered
the passages about Harte "privileged as a part of the history of American literature." In 1960 an excellent "Pictorial Biography," *Mark
Twain Himself*, quoted some of Mark Twain's most devastating eruptions and with no encouragement of skepticism entitled the passages
"Portrait of Bret Harte."

That Mark Twain himself came almost to believe what he said
about Bret Harte is not so surprising as the extent to which literary

[1] Quoted by Jacob Blanck in "The Question of Bret Harte's Mliss," *Publisher's
Weekly*, Vol. CXXX, Pt. 2 (Nov. 28, 1936), 2102–2103.

historians and contemporary critics have been influenced by his words. One example of this influence can be found in a valuable study of Bret Harte as one of eight "major interpreters in American literature of Spanish and Spanish-American culture." In *The Spanish Background of American Literature*, Stanley Williams cited as evidence of "recent confirmation" of Harte's "serious defects of character" pages in *Mark Twain in Eruption* charging Harte with lack of conscience, lack of sensitivity, and lack of sincerity.[2] Though fairly comprehensive, these accusations dictated four years after Bret Harte's death by no means exhaust Mark Twain's charges against the man who, he once testified, "trimmed and trained and schooled" him "patiently," changing him from an "awkward utterer of coarse grotesquenesses to a writer of paragraphs and chapters that have found a certain favor in the eyes of even some of the very decentest people in the land."[3]

That Mark Twain, a man of many contradictions, violently labeled numerous individuals liars, thieves, and rascals is well known. His sweeping damnations excluded neither former friends nor relatives.[4] Once Twain wrote of John T. Raymond, the actor whose comic portrayal of Colonel Sellers brought Twain's only financial success in the theater: "He would stand with his foot on the steps of the throne of God & lie. . . . He knows that I know that as a liar he has not his equal, either in hell or out of it." Of this charge, Mark Twain's nephew and namesake, Samuel Charles Webster, observed: "I think Uncle Sam is too modest here."[5]

Most of Twain's verbal extravagancies (such as his criticisms of Jane Austen, George Eliot, Henry James, and Edgar Allan Poe) have been recognized as extravagancies and discounted by even the most enthusiastic admirers of Tom Sawyer and Huckleberry Finn, including that eminently human being Samuel L. Clemens. Yet Mark Twain's words about Bret Harte, marked by a lack of restraint extreme even for the man from Hannibal, Missouri, have acquired the authority of dicta and

---

[2] II, 209, 351. See *Mark Twain in Eruption* (hereinafter cited as *MTE*), edited by Bernard De Voto, 264–65, 272, 274–75, 280–82.

[3] *Mark Twain's Letters* (hereinafter cited as MTL), edited by Albert Bigelow Paine, I, 182–83.

[4] Bernard De Voto, "The Other Side of Some Mark Twain Stories," *The New York Herald Tribune Weekly Book Review* (Feb. 10, 1946), 3.

[5] *Mark Twain: Business Man*, 228n.

have become in some strange fashion "the truth about Bret Harte." That Mark Twain's words inestimably damaged the reputation of Bret Harte as a man and as a writer is illustrated not only in their citation by so eminent a scholar as Professor Williams but also by an editorial preface to a Bret Harte story in *Jubilee*, an anthology of *Atlantic* contributions published by the *Atlantic Monthly* in 1957.[6]

As is generally known, the final break in the friendship between the two writers came in 1877, when Mark Twain and Bret Harte were ending their collaboration on a play called *Ah Sin*, which attempted to exploit the phenomenal popularity of Bret Harte's doggerel "Plain Language from Truthful James," known throughout the world as "The Heathen Chinee." A letter which Twain wrote to Thomas Bailey Aldrich on January 28, 1871, mentions an earlier disaffection between Twain and Harte in 1870, the year Ah Sin turned his first "pensive and childlike" smile upon a delighted world. Another Chinese character, named Hop Sing, in 1876 was responsible for bringing the two writers together for the disastrous collaboration. In *Mark Twain in Eruption* the bitter charges against Harte are prefaced by a long account of Twain's own early writing about Chinese in San Francisco. Was the Chinaman's ubiquity in this relationship mere coincidence? That the manuscript of *Ah Sin* was for many years believed lost increased the mystery.

On the opening night of *Ah Sin* in Daly's Fifth Avenue Theatre in New York, Bret Harte was absent, but Mark Twain responded to a curtain call for both authors with a rambling speech in which he alluded to "plagiarism" in the play he and Harte had written.[7] The word might have been considered facetious had not Twain vehemently and directly repeated this charge against Harte on August 3, 1877, in a personal letter to William Dean Howells.[8] Was "plagiarism" the cause of the break?

The calendar of Pudd'nhead Wilson, seer of Dawson's Landing, includes the aphorism: "The holy passion of Friendship is of so sweet and steady and loyal and enduring a nature that it will last through a whole

---

[6] Bernard De Voto, *Mark Twain's America*, 162f., 219.

[7] See Joseph Francis Daly, *The Life of Augustin Daly*, 234.

[8] *Mark Twain–Howells Letters* (hereinafter cited as *MTH*), edited by Henry Nash Smith and William M. Gibson with the assistance of Frederick Anderson, 192.

lifetime, if not asked to lend money."[9] Did Twain, as some believe, turn against Harte because Harte borrowed money from him?

In the narrative *Pudd'nhead Wilson*, Mark Twain invested the Negro changeling, Chambers, with many unpleasant traits which he also ascribed to Bret Harte. For example, the boy thought to be Tom Driscoll was "rather pleasantly soft and smooth" when he returned from Yale; he was "furtively and sometimes openly ironical of speech, and given to gently touching people on the raw." Did Bret Harte perhaps exercise this faculty of "gently touching people on the raw" once too often in conversations with Mark Twain? Many literary historians accept the explanation that Twain finally broke with Harte because of a "slight and vague and veiled satirical remark" which Twain thought Harte made about Mrs. Clemens and the Clemens' house furnishings.[10] According to the late Dixon Wecter, Harte's "trickiness, shabby sponging, and flair for plagiarism—which led Mark to brand him to Howells as 'the most abandoned thief that defiles the earth'—were more venial in Mark's eyes than Harte's sarcasms against the household in which he was a guest, and against Livy herself."[11] That he had insulted or intended to insult Mrs. Clemens in any way Bret Harte denied, and Mark Twain himself said, "I might have accepted the denial if I had been in a friendly mood but I was not, and was too strongly moved to give his reasonings a fair hearing."[12]

Jubilee shows strongly the influence of a paragraph in *Mark Twain's America* in which Bernard De Voto asserted that it was Harte's "acetic malice" which "finally ended all his friendships." The editors of the *Atlantic* introduce Bret Harte's sentimental Christmas story "How Santa Claus Came to Simpson's Bar" with a paragraph mainly about Mark Twain. The paragraph concludes with this sentence: "As Mark Twain's star rose and Harte's fell, the latter became jealous and vindictive."[13] According to this paragraph, when Sam Clemens offered character references to Jervis Langdon, whom he wished to make his father-in-law, the young man included "the name of Schuyler Colfax of the Pacific Coast and his secretary Frank B. Harte." Schuyler Colfax was Vice-President of the United States from 1869 to 1873. Although

---

[9] *Pudd'nhead Wilson and Those Extraordinary Twins*, 68.   [10] *MTE*, 278.
[11] *The Love Letters of Mark Twain* (hereinafter cited as *LL*), 194.
[12] *MTE*, 278   [13] Page 88.

6

he visited the West Coast and his visit was alluded to in one of Harte's letters as San Francisco correspondent for the Springfield *Republican,* Colfax was not *of* the Pacific Coast. Twain did not say he was. Bret Harte was never Schuyler Colfax's secretary. As for the *Atlantic's* charge that Harte was jealous and vindictive, Anna Dickinson, noted lecturer of the nineteenth century, who knew both Harte and Twain well and who had visited in Twain's home, was convinced that it was Twain's jealousy rather than Harte's which caused trouble between the two men.[14]

Here are many contradictions. What was the real cause of the broken friendship? Why did Mark Twain make such obsessively violent charges against Bret Harte? More important, what precisely were the factual bases of these charges?

In Twain's memory, the evil that Harte did lived after him and the good was interred long before his bones. Yet aside from Mark Twain's words dictated in 1906 and 1907, the quarrel has been recorded only by scattered generalizations and allusions. It is doubtful that the full story of the truncated friendship between Mark Twain and Bret Harte can ever be known, but existing evidence affords enough contradictions to Twain's widely accepted appraisal of Harte to make a review of the relationship between the two men and a re-examination of Twain's charges a matter of simple justice. Furthermore, to suppress or indulgently to explain away a serious consideration of aspects of Twain's character exhibited in his relationship with Harte is to modify and sentimentalize the truth about one of America's greatest writers.

[14] See James H. Young, "Anna Dickinson, Mark Twain, and Bret Harte," *Pennsylvania Magazine of History and Biography*, Vol. LXXVI (Jan., 1952), 45.

2

HOW THE MARK TWAIN–BRET HARTE
FRIENDSHIP BEGAN

Though I am generally placed at the head of my breed of scribblers
in this part of the country, the place properly belongs to Bret Harte,
I think, though he denies it, along with the rest.

MARK TWAIN, 1866

As MARK TWAIN REPORTED in his *Autobiography*, he and Bret Harte
first became acquainted in San Francisco in 1864, when Harte was secretary to R. B. Swain, superintendent of the San Francisco branch of the
United States Mint, and Twain, recently arrived from Virginia City,
Nevada, was reporting for the *Morning Call*, a San Francisco newspaper with offices on three floors of the same building that housed the
Mint.

Harte was immediately impressed by the appearance of the newcomer: the curly hair, the aquiline eye ("an eye so eaglelike that a second lid would not have surprised me," said Harte), the thick, bushy
eyebrows, and the "general manner . . . of supreme indifference to
surroundings and circumstances."[1] As time passed, Harte was even
more impressed with the originality of his new acquaintance, and
he found "irresistible" Twain's satirically drawling account of a town
he had visited where "unearthly laziness" prevailed and where men
sat around a barroom stove all day spitting and swapping lies. A favorite with Harte was Twain's report of a jumping frog yarn which he
had heard in one of these sessions. Many years later Bret Harte in
England would tell his friend T. Edgar Pemberton: "[The story] is
known and laughed over, I suppose, wherever the English language
is spoken; but it will never be as funny to any one in print as it was
to me, told for the first time by the unknown Twain himself on that
morning in the San Francisco Mint."

[1] T. Edgar Pemberton, *The Life of Bret Harte*, 74–75.

8

Although Harte's account of Twain's telling the jumping frog yarn in the mint office was corroborated by "a well-known citizen of San Francisco,"[2] who said he was in the office on business with Swain when the incident occurred, there is a minor contradiction between Harte's and Twain's accounts of the publication of this story. As Harte remembered it, after hearing the story, he had asked Twain to write his version of "The Jumping Frog of Calaveras County" for the *Californian* (edited by Charles H. Webb and Harte), and the story was an "emphatic success." As Twain remembered it, the story of the jumping frog was written at the suggestion of Artemus Ward, then the world's most famous humorist. The story was sent to Ward's publisher, G. W. Carleton, in New York, where—to Carleton's subsequent chagrin—it was rejected and turned over to the *Saturday Press* to be included in its "deathbed issue."

Albert Bigelow Paine seems to have entertained some doubt about the reliability of Mark Twain's memory of this incident, for the biographer reports that although Twain gave him a word-for-word account of the conversation in San Francisco when Ward suggested he write "The Jumping Frog" and submit it to Carleton, Paine could find no positive evidence that Ward was in San Francisco at the time when Twain said the conversation was held.[3] Paine believed that Twain did not submit the story first to the *Californian* because he thought the yarn not good enough for that weekly, whose literary standards Twain held in very high esteem. According to the record, after publication in the *Saturday Press* for November 18, 1865, the jumping frog story was republished in the *Californian* on December 16, "less than a month after its original publication,"[4] and was quickly picked up by many other journals in California and elsewhere.

In understanding a relationship between two human beings, the emotional tones or moods of memory may reveal more than factual details. T. Edgar Pemberton's two biographies of Bret Harte rely too

[2] See "The Jumping Frog of Calaveras, By Mark Twain. With an Introductory and Explanatory Note by J. G. H.," *Overland Monthly*, Vol. XL (Sept., 1902), 287–88. This further supports Harte's account reported by Pemberton, for Harte said he liked the story so much that he asked Twain to "tell it again to a friend who came in."

[3] *Mark Twain: A Biography*, 277.

[4] Oscar Lewis, *The Origin of the Celebrated Jumping Frog of Calaveras County*, 17–19.

much on an old man's memories and consequently, like the autobiographical dictations of Mark Twain, they include inaccuracies. Yet the tones of the reminiscences unmistakably reflect the contrasting emotions with which the two old men looked back upon the early friendship. Bret Harte's recollections of the appearance and manner of Mark Twain are mellow, affectionate, admiring. Mark Twain's memories of the appearance and manner of Bret Harte are steeped in bitterness and scorn.

Mark Twain had a particularly vivid recollection of Bret Harte's necktie: "Most frequently . . . it was crimson—a flash of flame under his chin; or it was indigo blue and as hot and vivid as if one of those splendid and luminous Brazilian butterflies had lighted there." He asserted that Harte was "showy, meretricious, insincere; and he constantly advertised these qualities in his dress." The word "showy" comes strangely from the wearer of the famous white serge suits and that sealskin coat which, in spite of Mark Twain's own warmth in it, sent cold chills through William Dean Howells when he "accompanied it down Broadway and shared the immense publicity it won him."[5] Mark once told Paine: "I should like to dress in a loose and flowing costume made all of silks and velvets resplendent with stunning dyes, and so would every man I have ever known; but none of us dares to venture it."[6] Twain's report that Harte was "distinctly pretty, in spite of the fact that his face was badly pitted with smallpox," and his descriptions of Harte's "dainty self complacencies" extending to his carriage and gait, which Mark described as "of the mincing sort," suggest effeminacy, even homosexuality. Twain could hardly have been unaware of the implications of his words, for he was acquainted with nineteenth-century England where he had met Joaquin Miller's Pre-Raphaelite friends[7] and where the subject of homosexuality had been dramatized by the trial of Oscar Wilde, whom Mark Twain also knew.[8]

Stories persist of Harte's Bohemianism in San Francisco. To more than one Westerner besides Mark Twain, Harte seemed a complacent,

[5] *My Mark Twain*, 4.

[6] Paine, *Biography*, 1342. See also Edward Wagenknecht, *Mark Twain: The Man and His Work*, 87–88.

[7] See M. M. Marberry, *Splendid Poseur: Joaquin Miller—American Poet*, 88, 114. See also *MTH*, I, 60n.

[8] Clara Clemens, *My Father, Mark Twain*, 113–14.

opinionated product of the effete East. Actually, at the time of his meeting Twain in 1864, Harte was a relatively industrious, rather conventional family man who had been living in California for ten years.

In 1854 the seventeen-year-old Francis Brett (Frank) Harte and his younger sister Margaret had traveled from New York to California to be with their mother, who had married Colonel Andrew Williams, onetime mayor of Oakland. After trying his hand at various jobs for several years without success, Frank had rejoined Margaret, who in the meantime had married B. H. Wyman and in 1857 was living in a small frontier town in northern California. In Uniontown (now Arcata), Frank Harte in his early twenties worked on a newspaper and decided to dedicate his life to literature because, he concluded with a characteristically whimsical mask for earnestness, he was "fit for nothing else."[9]

Colonel S. G. Whipple, editor of the *Northern Californian*, described his young reporter and "junior editor" as a "good writer . . . a warm-hearted, genial companion, and a gentleman in every sense of the word."[10] Like the later Mark Twain, however, some of the frontiersmen—the cattlemen, "the pack-train drivers, the red-shirted miners down from Trinity River"—resented the fastidiousness of the young writer's dress and manner.[11] Frank Harte was never hail-fellow-well-met at the local bars, and sometimes he exercised his wit at the expense of high and low alike. But most of all, the frontiersmen of Uniontown resented the young man's sympathy for the local Indians and his sense of outrage when the Diggers were made victims of the white men's casual brutalities. Finally, it was Harte's forthright reporting of the white men's massacre of Indian women and children on an island in Humboldt Bay which cost Frank his job and sent him back to San Francisco.[12]

In San Francisco, Frank Harte secured a job as compositor and oc-

[9] George R. Stewart, *Bret Harte, Argonaut and Exile* (hereinafter cited as *BHAE*), 68.

[10] "Three Lost Years in the Life of Bret Harte," San Francisco *Examiner* (Jan. 24, 1926), Pt. II, 1. Clipping in Bancroft Library, Berkeley, California (hereinafter cited as Bancroft).

[11] *Ibid.* See also *BHAE*, 73.

[12] *BHAE*, 83–90. See also my article "Bret Harte and the Indians of Northern California," *Huntington Library Quarterly*, Vol. XVIII (Nov., 1954), 59–83.

casional contributor to the *Golden Era*. He began to sign his work "Bret" (an abbreviated spelling for his grandmother's family name). One of his sketches attracted the attention of Jessie Benton Frémont, wife of the famous John Charles Frémont. Mrs. Frémont—a gracious, perceptive, and extraordinarily intelligent lady—sought out the young author and before long invited him regularly as a Sunday guest in the Frémont home. There Bret Harte met Thomas Starr King, eloquent Unitarian minister of San Francisco, who became one of the strongest influences on Harte's life. Harte married Anna Griswold, the contralto in the choir of Starr King's church. The couple's eldest son was named Griswold, for his mother's family, but the second son—Francis King Harte, born March 5, 1865—was named for the San Francisco minister whose actively expressed opposition to race prejudice and discrimination reinforced Harte's own.

By 1863, Harte was earning $180 a month at the Mint, thereby arousing the envy of other San Francisco journalists who did not hesitate to publish good-natured jibes about Harte's "sinecure." For, prompted by Mrs. Frémont, Swain had given Frank Harte a job in the Mint with the understanding that he would devote considerable time to his writing. The young author continued to publish sketches and poems in California journals. Many of his poems were abolitionist verses attacking slave-owning Jefferson Davis, or patriotic odes in impassioned support of Lincoln and the Union. In a San Francisco somewhat nervous about subversive Confederate sympathizers among its citizens, Harte's lyrics attracted particular attention. Frank was appointed "Poet-of-the-Day" for the Fourth of July celebration in 1863. Always diffident, he was too shy to read his own work, but his poem for the occasion, read by Thomas Starr King, brought wild applause. Thus, Bret Harte at twenty-seven "found himself an established man with a family, a local reputation and a good income." Nevertheless, he was frequently short of cash and he had a bad habit of borrowing from his friends.[13]

When Anna Griswold and Francis Brett Harte were married in the Methodist Church of San Rafael on August 11, 1862, families and

---

[13] Henry Childs Merwin, *The Life of Bret Harte*, 214. See also *BHAE*, 170–71, 352. Stewart's sources here include Mark Twain, William Gillis, and W. A. Kendall, all of whom developed extraordinary antipathy toward Harte.

friends of both the bride and the groom believed the marriage a mistake.[14] For one thing, Anna Griswold was some years older than Frank Harte. Furthermore, the groom's mother remained convinced that this was not the girl for her son. On the other side, family and friends of the promising singer felt that she was throwing herself away on a young man who at that time was working as a minor clerk in the surveyor general's office.

After Anna and Frank married, they lived in a house at 524 Sutter Street. Almost from the beginning, the wife found a good deal to complain about. In particular, she complained that they did not have enough money to live on. And when a baby was expected, she had for a time to stop singing in the choir of the Unitarian Church. This was a sacrifice not only of money but of her career as a musician.

Before long, the young husband changed from a nobody to a somebody in San Francisco. Starr King and Mrs. Frémont predicted for him a great future in literature. Many promising young writers became his friends, delighted in his wit, respected his literary judgments, and did not let their jibes about his easy job keep them from dropping by his office for stimulating talk. Among his most loyal friends and literary associates were Ina Coolbrith and Charles Warren Stoddard. Sometimes Bret and Charley Stoddard spent a gay evening in Ina Coolbrith's home on Russian Hill. She treated them like brothers. Sometimes the three, who came to be known as the "Golden Gate Trinity," entertained themselves by making limericks. On at least one occasion, Harte—by that time an editor—tied an apron over his suit and helped prepare vegetables for dinner.[15]

Such gay goings on were frowned upon in the more decorous Harte household, which now included two servants. Mrs. Harte resumed singing in the church choir. According to gossips, she was jealous of her husband's growing popularity and prestige. "It is said on good authority," wrote one Californian, "that . . . she was not willing to accept submissively the position of being the wife of a genius nor to be absorbed in his greater light."[16]

Although the young men who were Harte's friends found Mrs.

[14] *BHAE*, 113.

[15] *Ibid.*, 169–70. See also Franklin Walker, *San Francisco's Literary Frontier*, 268–70.

[16] Ella Sterling Cummins (Mrs. Mighels), *The Story of the Files*, 127.

Harte somewhat forbidding, women were her severest critics. Bret Harte's mother complained to sympathetic listeners that when her son wanted to write at night, he had to wait until after his wife decided to go to bed, and then when he began to work, the wife protested that his light kept her awake. Young women employed in the *Overland* office indignantly observed that sometimes when Harte was busiest, his wife would enter and insist that the editor stop his work to go shopping with her. According to these fiercely partisan young women, it was his wife's fault that he sometimes failed to produce a manuscript or pay a debt on time. One outspoken contributor and proofreader, whose common sense Harte habitually respected, told him bluntly that he let himself be ruled too much by his wife, but this Bret Harte firmly denied.[17]

Other friends testified that Harte often spoke of his wife with great affection, took pride in her cleverness, and dotingly recounted funny doings and sayings of his two little boys.[18] Many years later Harte himself liked to remember a beautiful drive which he and his wife had taken in the mountains near Santa Cruz and another very special time when he had read aloud to her "The Luck of Roaring Camp" and she had been the first to respond with sympathy and support.[19]

Notwithstanding jokes about his easy job at the Mint, Bret Harte in San Francisco worked harder than is generally supposed. That he did not neglect his official duties is evidenced by the steady increase of his salary and his promotion to head a department with twelve men under his immediate supervision. The record that he made at the Mint would stand him in good stead in the future. But his chief interest was literature. While he was still employed by the Mint, he began editing the *Overland Monthly,* and the combination of editorial duties and business responsibilities kept him very busy indeed.

When he returned home in the evening, instead of the two hours of writing he hoped for, Harte was apt to be assigned household chores including painting or papering the house, watering the garden, or baby-

[17] Josephine Clifford McCrackin, "A Letter from a Friend," *Overland Monthly,* Vol. XL (Sept., 1902), 222–23. This proofreader, Miss Dolson, should not be confused with the proofreader shocked by "The Luck of Roaring Camp."

[18] Merwin, *The Life of Bret Harte,* 52.

[19] *The Letters of Bret Harte* (hereinafter cited as *BHL*), edited by Geoffrey Bret Harte, 151, 152–53. Harte was very angry when Mrs. Roman in 1879 claimed to have been the story's sponsor.

sitting. He was not very skillful at any of them, even baby-sitting. The children loved it, but Mrs. Harte objected that her husband frolicked in too free and undignified a manner with his sons.[20] On some evenings Harte attended plays or accompanied his wife to the opera. Somehow he found time to read many books. That he read with critical and discriminating attention is apparent not only in his book reviews for the *Overland* but also in his *Condensed Novels,* which began appearing in the *Golden Era* and the *Californian* while Mark Twain was still a restless reporter and practical joker in Nevada.

Charles A. Murdock, who had known Harte in Uniontown and who at this time worked in San Francisco in the office of the superintendent of Indian affairs, gives us a glimpse of Bret Harte and Mark Twain not long after the two met. On an imaginary tour of the city, Murdock points out Harte, "a well-dressed young man with Dundreary whiskers and an aquiline nose" walking via Commercial Street to his office in the Mint. "At Clay," wrote Murdock, "we pass a saloon with a cigarstand in front and find a group listening to a man with bushy hair and a reddish mustache, who in an easy attitude and in a quaintly drawling voice is telling a story. We await the laugh and pass on, and I say that he is a reporter, lately from Nevada, called Mark Twain."[21]

By 1864, Samuel L. Clemens had come much farther than from Nevada. From his birthplace in Florida, Missouri, he had moved to Hannibal; from Hannibal, he moved to St. Louis; and from St. Louis, he moved on to New York, Philadelphia, Muscatine, and Keokuk. He had been a job printer in Cincinnati, briefly. He had set out for South America, but changed his course to become a river-boat pilot on the Mississippi. In June, 1861, when Bret Harte in San Francisco was already writing fiction with a California background and joining Thomas Starr King in support of the Union and abolition, Sam Clemens enlisted as a second lieutenant in the "Marion Rangers," an undisciplined group of militia organized in Hannibal to fight for the Confederacy. After a brief period of "retreating for the secesh" Clemens at twenty-six declared a personal armistice with the Union and went for a visit to his brother Orion in Keokuk. Orion Clemens in Missouri—like Bret Harte in California—had staunchly supported the cause of abolition. When, in the same year that Sam Clemens enlisted in the Marion Rangers, a member

[20] *BHAE,* 118–19, 140–41.   [21] *A Backward Glance at Eighty,* 110–12.

15

of Lincoln's cabinet secured for Orion Clemens an appointment as secretary to the new Territory of Nevada, Sam accompanied his brother West.[22] In "The Private History of a Campaign That Failed" (written many years later when Twain's publishing firm was issuing General Grant's *Memoirs*), Mark Twain's report that people in border states leaned "first this way and then that, then the other way" accurately described his own reactions to the Union and the Confederacy for many years after he left the Marion Rangers and even after William Dean Howells formed the opinion that Mark Twain was the "most Reconstructed" Southerner Howells had ever known.

In Nevada, the younger Sam Clemens tried his hand at mining for a while and saw men strike it rich all about him while he remained poor. He was determined not to return to his mother and sister in Missouri until he could return with money. Fifteen months after his arrival in Nevada he showed up in Virginia City, where for a year and nine months he served as a reporter on Virginia City's *Territorial Enterprise*, edited by twenty-four-year-old Joseph Goodman, a strong pro-Union man.

In Virginia City, Sam Clemens began to use the name "Mark Twain" for his by-line. About his manner of acquiring the nom de plume, speculation continues. Albert Bigelow Paine believed that Clemens appropriated the name from Captain Isaiah Sellers, an old Mississippi River pilot who signed "Mark Twain" to his own contributions to the New Orleans *Picayune*. According to this account, the old man had been so wounded by Clemens' ridicule that he stopped writing altogether, and because Sam Clemens had a guilty conscience about this, he took the old man's pen name to make amends.[23] Later research showed that Sellers submitted his work to the *True Delta* rather than to the *Picayune* and that, contrary to Clemens' story, Isaiah Sellers was still alive when Sam Clemens began using the name Mark Twain in Nevada.[24] More recently, Paul Fatout has convincingly theorized that when Mark Twain became intensely desirous of respectability long after he left Virginia City, he made up his story about Isaiah Sellers and stuck

[22] Paine, *Biography*, 168.

[23] *Ibid.*, 149–50, 221–22.

[24] Carl J. Weber, *The Rise and Fall of James Ripley Osgood: A Biography*, 196; see also *Eighteenth Year Book, 1919*, printed for members of the Bibliophile Society, Boston, 124, for facsimile of a letter from Saml L. Clemens giving the origin of the pen name of Mark Twain.

to it in order to obscure the truth, that Sam Clemens acquired the name Mark Twain in Western saloons where it was his custom to sing out the riverman's cry as a means of telling the bartender to charge him for another drink or two when he was short of cash. Fatout comments: "Indicative of [Mark Twain's] tendency either to believe something that was not so or to gloss over is his remark in 1882: 'I have not had a large experience in the matter of alcoholic drinks.'" According to Fatout, "Western friends, western newspapers, and the Mark Twain of Nevada tell a contrary tale."[25] These observations are particularly pertinent to accusations which Mark Twain would make about Bret Harte in 1879.

Whatever its origin, the new pen name adopted in Nevada suited Clemens to a T, and before long, humorous and satirical writings under Mark Twain's by-line were read with such lively interest in Nevada and quoted so widely that people began calling Sam Clemens himself "Mark Twain" just as they called Charles Farrar Browne "Artemus Ward," forgetful or ignorant that either humorist had another name.

This split-fused Sam Clemens–Mark Twain personality had decided advantages. For a time, the politically influential reporter Sam Clemens and the "irresponsibly imaginative" Mark Twain could exist as carefully distinct entities.[26] And as a person, Sam Clemens could enjoy Mark Twain's fame with considerable immunity from responsibility for Mark Twain's words. In the familiar tradition of the teller of tall tales in the West, Mark Twain's words were apt to show more regard for effect than for truth. His newspaper cronies and frontier friends, enjoying the current practice of public exchange of personal ridicule, listened with rapt attention to the range and precision of Mark's epithets against anyone who aroused his displeasure. As an alter ego, Mark Twain was satisfying to his friends and readers as well as to Clemens, for he could serve (and sometimes still serves) as a fairly safe agent for vicariously discharging the reader's own angers and aggressions. If those at whom Mark Twain aimed his fire sometimes proved more actively impenitent than the proverbial mule, it was all part of the fun

[25] Paul Fatout, "Mark Twain's Nom de Plume," *American Literature*, Vol. XXXIV (Mar., 1962), 6–7.

[26] *Mark Twain of the* Enterprise, edited by Henry Nash Smith with the assistance of Frederick Anderson, 8–9.

in this Western life which the *Enterprise* staff seemed at times to regard as one huge practical joke.

Mark Twain's vitality, however, was not altogether a symptom of robust good health. With all his foolery, Sam Clemens at twenty-eight was "high-strung and neurotic," subject to bronchial ills.[27] He continued to be plagued by a sense of sin. Yet he was a dutiful son and brother, and his letters to his mother and sister in St. Louis frequently enclosed twenty dollars.

According to Henry Nash Smith, Mark Twain for a time "immensely" enjoyed his life in Virginia City. He and other reporters of the *Enterprise* "played billiards and had passes to the theaters; they smoked cigars and drank a special 'reporter's cobbler': they received presents of 'feet' in mines which they could sell for enough money to finance vacations in San Francisco."[28] When Mrs. Jane Clemens wrote her son that if he worked hard and attended to business, he might aspire to a place on a big San Francisco paper some day, Mark boasted that he could get such a situation any time he asked for it, but he didn't want it, for "No paper in the United States can afford to pay me what my place on the *Enterprise* is worth." "How I hate everything that looks or tastes or smells like California," Twain wrote about this time. Less than a year later he would be "glorifying California."[29]

Mark Twain was always a man of many contradictions. Smith believes that Twain began to "identify himself with the Union Cause" soon after he came to Nevada. In Virginia City during the Civil War, Twain wrote his sister Pamela that he took no interest in politics or Eastern news and refused to write editorials about political issues.[30] As the *Enterprise* reporter of legislative activities in Carson City, however, Twain exercised considerable influence, and it was believed that he and his friends could determine the success or failure of any bill. Many of his closest friends were Southern sympathizers.

Among these close friends was Steve Gillis, a compositor on the *Enterprise*. For Steve and his brother Jim, Mark Twain would maintain a lifelong loyalty. The Gillis family was from Mississippi. James Gillis, who had a cabin on Jackass Hill in Calaveras County, had reportedly

[27] Paine, *Biography*, 238.
[28] *Mark Twain of the* Enterprise, 5.
[29] Paine, *Biography*, 229, 238–39.
[30] *Mark Twain of the* Enterprise, 19.

provided lodging for a night to Frank Harte shortly after the young New Yorker arrived in California. Frank had been looking for work, journeying through an area later to become famous as "the Bret Harte country." At nightfall he had arrived footsore and penniless at the Gillis door. Jim had taken him in and spent the evening listening to the young man's talk about his hopes and plans for the future. Gillis said that when Harte left the next morning, Jim gave him some money.[31] Later Albert Bigelow Paine and many others, including Harte's biographer T. Edgar Pemberton, would say that Jim Gillis was the prototype for that Truthful James whose account of the dark ways of Ah Sin in a euchre game brought Bret Harte world renown. And those who knew Harte and understood the poem would recognize that the author was poking fun not so much at the Heathen Chinee as at the race prejudice of Truthful James.

Mark Twain liked to remember that the father and a brother of Jim and Steve Gillis had fought with William Walker, that "grey-eyed man of destiny" whose military invasions of Sonora and Nicaragua provided banner headlines for American newspapers from 1854 to 1860. The contrasting atttiudes of Mark Twain and Bret Harte toward this historic figure provide clues to significant differences in the characters of the two writers. Harte wrote a pseudohistorical novelette burlesquing the strutting little man's violations of international law, and in a letter referred to him as the "wild filibuster."[32] Mark Twain, on the other hand, maintained all his life an uncritical admiration of Walker, exponent of manifest destiny, who to gain support from the slave states argued for and re-established slavery in Nicaragua. "To say that a man was a major under Walker, and came out of that struggle ennobled by Walker's praise," dictated Mark Twain in 1906 about the father of Steve and Jim Gillis," is to say that the major was not merely a brave man, but that he was brave to the very utmost limit of that word. All of Walker's men were like that."[33] (A twentieth-century historian

31 *BHAE*, 52–53.
32 *BHL*, 321. Harte's fictional use of William Walker has been discussed more fully in my article "The 'Crusade' of a Nineteenth-Century Liberal," *Tennessee Studies in Literature*, Vol. IV (1959), 109–20.
33 Albert Bigelow Paine, editor, *Mark Twain's Autobiography*, I, 351–52; *Autobiography*, edited by Charles Neider, 113.

describes Walker's "Immortals" as the "rag-tag and bob-tail" of the West Coast.)[34] Certainly the physical courage and bravado exhibited by them and their leader represented a different kind of courage from that exhibited by Orion Clemens as an abolitionist in Hannibal, or by Bret Harte in attempts to defend California Indians from their manifest destiny at the hands of frontiersmen near Uniontown.

In the complex personality of Mark Twain this admiration for the individual strong enough to seize what he desires and to dominate by sheer will power and physical force has not been sufficiently recognized. All his life, Mark Twain wanted to be this kind of Strong Man. The dictatorial power of a pilot on a Mississippi river boat had been one of the strongest attractions to piloting. In Nevada, where Mark Twain boasted that he "fared like a prince," he could assume the role of a strong man not only with politicians in Carson City but also with his older brother. Henry Nash Smith reports that many of Sam's letters to Orion during these months had "the tone of the master of a household addressing a servant."[35]

There was, of course, another side of Mark Twain. He could "put his soul" into entertaining Artemus Ward, who visited Virginia City at the height of his fame. And so successful was Twain that after Ward left, he received from the world celebrity a thank-you letter beginning "My dearest love."[36] If Mark Twain could be ruthless to those whom he disliked or whom he felt to be weak and ineffectual, his partly saving grace was his ability to write to his mother and sister: "I am proud to say I am the most conceited ass in the Territory."[37]

Although Steve Gillis weighed only ninety-five pounds, Mark wrote that it was "well known throughout the Territory that with his fists he could whip anybody that walked on two legs, let his weight and science be what they might."[38] When it came to a fight, Steve was on Mark's side. And vice versa. Mark Twain's last days in Virginia City were enlivened by challenges, charges, and countercharges about a duel that never occurred. The flurry followed a Twain editorial intimating that money raised at a fancy-dress ball given by ladies in Carson City for

[34] Laurence Greene, *The Filibuster*, 30. For a more flattering description of Walker's "Immortals," see Edward S. Wallace, *Destiny and Glory*, 107.
[35] *Mark Twain of the* Enterprise, 23.   [36] *MTL*, I, 93.
[37] *Mark Twain of the* Enterprise, 23.   [38] Paine, *Biography*, 213.

the Sanitary Fund had, in fact, been "sent to aid a Miscegenation Society somewhere in the East." Later Twain told Orion's wife that he had written the editorial while he was drinking.[39] Whether written when he was drinking or sober, this editorial casts some doubt on the explanation that Twain's sympathy for a racial minority influenced his withdrawal from the Marion Rangers to associate himself with his abolitionist brother. As for the duel, reportedly Steve Gillis had egged Mark on to a challenge and then, since he was an expert marksman and Twain was not, Steve had tried to take the other's place. Both of Mark Twain's accounts of the incident are apocryphal.

When Mark Twain and Steve Gillis left Virginia City for San Francisco on May 29, 1864, they carried with them the good will of their associates on the *Enterprise*. There were, of course, some citizens and officials of that Nevada community who were not sorry to see them go. Not everyone appreciated the personal invective of Twain's journalism, and some were convinced that Mark Twain was merely a " 'smart Alec,' always showing-off and trying to make others appear ridiculous."[40] This appraisal was transmitted orally in Nevada for many years. But others who had known Mark Twain intimately would remember his vitality, his great personal magnetism, and his warmhearted loyalty to those whom he liked.

In San Francisco, Mark Twain became a reporter and Steve Gillis a compositor on the *Morning Call*, a newspaper of which Twain would later express a very low opinion. He developed an even lower opinion of the San Francisco police, whom he seldom missed an opportunity to criticize. For social occasions, Mark and Steve arrayed themselves with "considerable elegance."[41]

During the first four months, Mark Twain changed his lodging five times. At one place where he and Steve shared a room in California Street, they amused themselves on Sundays by hurling empty beer bottles down on the "tin-can houses" of neighboring Chinese in order to see the Orientals swarm out, shake their fists, and "pour out Chinese vituperations" at their two "tormentors" on the bluff above. After

---

[39] *Mark Twain of the* Enterprise, 26, 196–98. See also DeLancey Ferguson, *Mark Twain: Man and Legend*, 93–94.

[40] *Ibid.*, 23–29, 215–16.

[41] Paine, *Biography*, 253. See also Mark Twain, *Roughing It*, 419.

the Chinese quieted down and went back into their houses, Steve and Mark would throw another bottle.[42]

Soon after Mark Twain arrived in San Francisco, his employer, George Barnes of the *Call*, took him to the Mint offices and introduced him to Bret Harte. Notwithstanding the bitterness of Twain's later words, he was at that time much attracted to Harte, and before long the two young men with all their differences in temperament and background became close friends. Mark spent much time in Bret's office. Not long thereafter, Mark Twain left the *Morning Call*. As Twain would remember it, he was dismissed after Barnes had suppressed an article which Twain had written in impassioned defense of a Chinese laundryman whom he had seen stoned in the streets of San Francisco one Sunday while a policeman looked on with "amused interest."[43]

By 1864, when the twenty-nine-year-old Mark Twain came as a reporter to San Francisco, the twenty-eight-year-old Bret Harte had already served his literary apprenticeship and demonstrated his liberal sympathies, most obviously and consistently in his attitude toward discrimination in theory or practice against racial minorities. Harte's many contributions to San Francisco's *Golden Era* and *Daily Evening Bulletin* included "The Work on Red Mountain" (to become phenomenally popular as "M'liss") as well as abolitionist verses among which was a clear-headed reply to Thomas Carlyle, who had advised Northerners to mind their own business and let the South handle its problem of slavery.[44] In a San Francisco of divided sympathies, Harte had demonstrated by deed as well as by words unwavering support of Lincoln and the Union. He had published in the *Atlantic Monthly* an eight-page sketch showing that early interest in the history of Hispanic America noted by Stanley Williams. This sketch, entitled "A Legend of Monte del Diablo," also made clear his sympathy for the dispossessed Spanish Californians and Mexican Indians. Most significantly, Harte had written enough in defense of the Chinese to make his influence felt among the group of San Francisco's literary men, who were "almost unanimously opposed" to the verdict of popular sentiment and popular

---

[42] Paine, *Biography*, 255–56.

[43] *MTE*, 256. George Barnes insisted that Mark Twain had resigned of his own accord, and Paine believed Barnes. See *MTL*, I, 101; Paine, Biography, 262.

[44] *The Writings of Bret Harte*, XX, 361.

journalism of the nineteenth century which decried the "yellow peril" and insisted that Chinese "cheap labor" must be deported.[45] Mark Twain's dawning sympathy for the Chinese coincided with his transfer from the group of roistering journalists of Virginia City to the consciously literary group in San Francisco.

The lively young writers on "San Francisco's Literary Frontier" who frequently gathered in the office of the secretary of the Superintendent of the San Francisco branch of the United States Mint included Ambrose Bierce, Charles H. Webb, Prentice Mulford, Charles Warren Stoddard, and Orpheus C. Kerr (Robert Henry Newell).[46] This group acknowledged Harte as its leader and recognized in him an uncompromising critic of his own work as well as of the work of his companions. Though shy, sensitive, sometimes moody, Harte was not cold. That he was able to inspire strong personal affection is indicated by a poem in the *Era* which the very young Stoddard addressed "To Bret" beginning: "Oh, Bret, sweet rhymer and most pleasant friend."[47] That he could attract a very different kind of person is evidenced by the fact that Ambrose Bierce was also "on the best of terms with Harte."[48] Joaquin Miller came down from Oregon hoping to be included in this San Francisco group whose renown was growing. Although Miller was welcomed by some members of Harte's coterie and later proved one of the most generous and loyal of Harte's friends, his writing was too undisciplined to win complete approval from Harte, the literary critic. But Mark Twain promptly found his rightful place at the heart of this gay company of young writers with a strong sense of their role in the production of a new and robust American literature.

Of Twain's many friends in this group, the closest was Harte. According to Albert Bigelow Paine, their associates recognized Bret Harte and Mark Twain as "belonging in a class by themselves."[49] In time, Western legends about the two men included a report that Mark Twain was much attracted to Ina Coolbrith and once called Bret Harte "a dirty name" because Miss Coolbrith showed some predilection for

---

[45] William Purviance Fenn, *Ah Sin and His Brethren in American Literature*, 45; Roger Rilus Walterhouse, *Bret Harte, Joaquin Miller, and the Western Local Color Story*, 53.

[46] For the fullest and most reliable account of this group, see Walker, *Literary Frontier*, 59.

[47] *BHAE*, 120.   [48] Walker, *Literary Frontier*, 240.   [49] Paine, *Biography*, 260.

Harte. This report is tempting because it affords modern analysts a latent cause for the extreme bitterness of Mark Twain's later accusations, but the source of the story of romantic rivalry is questionable, and biographers agree that Ina Coolbrith's actual relationship with Bret Harte in San Francisco was of the "sisterly sort."[50]

Charles H. Webb, better known as "Inigo," had come from New York to serve as literary editor of the San Francisco *Bulletin*. In May, 1864, a new weekly publication entitled the *Californian* appeared in San Francisco as a practical demonstration of journalistic principles and practices about which Webb and Harte had been holding prolonged—sometimes facetious—discussions. Initially, Webb was the owner and editor, while Harte was the star contributor. However, by September —when Bret Harte and Mark Twain had become friends—Harte also functioned as the editor. One of Harte's first editorial acts was to offer Mark Twain fifty dollars a month for an article every week, an offer which Twain was glad to accept because, he wrote his mother and sister, the " 'Californian' circulates among the highest class of the community, and is the best weekly literary paper in the United States."[51]

In this letter Twain said he had quit the *Golden Era* because it "wasn't high-toned enough" and had told the *Morning Call* "folks" to pay him twenty-five dollars a week and let him "work only in daylight." He did not mention the stoning of a Chinese laundryman in San Francisco or his disappointment about Mr. Barnes's failure to publish his article of protest, but in reporting that the new census showed San Francisco had a population of 130,000, Mark commented: "They don't count the hordes of Chinamen." He also mentioned that Steve Gillis had married a very pretty girl, "worth $130,000 in her own right." The letter was dated September 25, 1864.

Before long, Mark Twain's reputation mounted. If his criticism of the San Francisco police was restricted or suppressed by the *Morning Call*, Joe Goodman gave him a free hand as San Francisco correspondent for the *Territorial Enterprise*. Mark made the most of this freedom, and though he published nothing more about the Chinese while he was in San Francisco, his continued attacks on the San Francisco police increased the circulation of the *Enterprise* and the fame of

[50] Walker, *Literary Frontier*, 225, 270, 398n.
[51] *BHAE*, 126–27; *MTL*, I, 100, See also Paine, *Biography*, 261.

Mark Twain. When Steve Gillis' gamecock activities in a local bar gave the police an opportunity to retaliate against the reporter, who was Steve's friend, Mark found it expedient to take refuge with Jim Gillis in his cabin on Jackass Hill.[52] During the period of his withdrawal from San Francisco in the winter months of 1864, Mark spent many pleasant evenings before an open fire listening to tall tales, some of which—like "The Burning Shame"—would appear later in Mark's books. And while prospecting with Jim Gillis near Angel's Camp, Mark heard from Ben Coon the story of the jumping frog, which he told to Harte after Twain returned to San Francisco.

Mark Twain's published version of this story received in 1865 an enthusiastic reception in the East and in the West. Wrote the New York correspondent for San Francisco's *Alta California*: "Mark Twain's story in the *Saturday Press* of November 18th, called 'Jim Smiley and His Jumping Frog,' has set all New York in a roar, and he may be said to have made his mark. I have been asked fifty times about it and its author, and the papers are copying it far and near. It is voted the best thing of the day."[53] Then the correspondent asked a pointed question: "Cannot the *Californian* afford to keep Mark all to itself? It should not let him scintillate so widely without first being filtered through the California press." We have already noted that Harte believed he had asked Mark to submit the story to the *Californian* and that Paine believed Mark did not do so because Mark considered the yarn not good enough.

A clipping of this praise from the *Alta California* was pasted in a letter which Mark Twain wrote to his mother, Mrs. Jane Clemens, and his sister, Mrs. Pamela Moffett, in St. Louis on January 20, 1866. This is the first of the Mark Twain letters collected by Albert Bigelow Paine in which the name of Bret Harte appears.

Mark Twain expressed some embarrassment that "those New York people" should compliment him on "Jim Smiley and His Jumping Frog" which he now described as "a villainous backwoods sketch," "a squib" that would "never have been written but to please Artemus Ward."[54] Smarting from Carleton's rejection of the work, Twain told his mother and sister that Ward's book for which the sketch had been

---

[52] Ferguson, *Man and Legend*, 100–101.   [53] Paine, *Biography*, 271, 279.
[54] *MTL*, I, 101.

submitted was "a wretchedly poor one, generally speaking" and "it would be no credit to either of us to appear between its covers."[55] Yet, notwithstanding Twain's depreciation of the New York compliments, the popularity of the sketch boosted his ego.[56]

In this letter Mark Twain showed obvious pride in his association with Bret Harte. He also revealed a sense of professional rivalry. Harte, he said, wanted him to "club a lot of old sketches together with a lot of his, and publish a book." With a bit of verbal swagger, Twain told his womenfolk that he would not do it except that Harte "agrees to take all the trouble" and Harte had already written to a New York publisher. If the publisher offered a "bargain" that "would pay for a month's labor," Twain reported, he and Harte would go to work and prepare the volume for the press. Particularly noteworthy is a sentence praising Harte but beginning and ending with emphasis on Twain's own eminence: "Though I am generally placed at the head of my breed of scribblers in this part of the country, the place properly belongs to Bret Harte, I think, though he denies it, along with the rest."[57]

This letter is helpful to an understanding of later conflicts between Bret Harte and Mark Twain. In his consideration of the proposed collaboration on a book of sketches, Twain's determination "to know whether we are going to make anything out of it, first" shows his approach to writing more businesslike than Harte's. Moreover, the early development of Twain's practice of measuring his achievements in terms of Harte's presages that desire "to shine . . . to make money, to rival and outrival those whom the public most admired" which Van Wyck Brooks believed in time became Mark Twain's ruling passion.[58]

[55] *MTH*, I, 132.

[56] See *"My Dear Bro:" A Letter from Samuel Clemens to His Brother Orion*, with a foreword by Frederick Anderson.

[57] *MTL*, I, 102.

[58] See also Van Wyck Brooks, *The Ordeal of Mark Twain*, 135, 145, 167–68.

3

A CRITIC'S VIEW OF A NEW STAR

I think I recognize a new star rising in this western horizon.

BRET HARTE, 1866

AFTER THE SUCCESS of his jumping frog story, San Francisco showed Mark Twain considerable deference as a "national literary figure."[1] In March, 1866, the Sacramento *Union* engaged him to go to Hawaii and send back to California reports of life on the islands, then known as the Sandwich Islands. These reports as well as Mark Twain's dramatic account of the *Hornet's* survivors were much admired. The *Hornet* was a ship from New York which had caught fire at sea. After forty-three days in an open boat, its fifteen starving passengers had finally been rescued. Even though Twain was suffering so severely from saddle boils that he was forced to stay in bed, arrangements were made to carry him from his Honolulu hotel to the ship to interview the survivors and send the story of their ordeal back to the States. This story, for which the *Union* paid Twain ten times the usual rates, was copied throughout America, and even in New York proved a sensation. At this time Mark Twain's genius was recognized by Anson Burlingame, minister to China, and General Robert B. Van Valkenburg, minister to Japan. "California is proud of Mark Twain," said the General, "and some day the American people will be, too, no doubt."[2]

Like the rest of California, Bret Harte was proud of his friend and "boomed Clemens with ardor."[3] In 1866, Harte was special San Francisco correspondent for the *Christian Register* of Boston and the Spring-

[1] Paine, *Biography*, 281.   [2] *Ibid.*, 285.

[3] Noah Brooks, Letter to the Editor, June 27, 1902, *Overland Monthly* (Sept., 1902), 225. However, Brooks said that Mark Twain owed more to John McComb, who as editor of the *Alta California* was chiefly responsible for Twain's being given the assignment to write the *Quaker City* letters.

field *Republican,* the latter one of the more widely read and respected newspapers of the day. Harte publicized Twain in both these journals. A letter dated August 30, 1866, published in the *Christian Register* of September 29, dealt at some length with the "Royal Hawaiian Established Reformed Catholic Church." This remarkable establishment is thus described by 'Mark Twain,' a great humorist, as well as a thoughtful and discriminating observer, who has lately visited the island," wrote Harte, quoting copiously from Twain's reports of missionary activities. Bret Harte's eleventh letter to the Springfield *Republican* also praised Mark Twain and referred to his report of the *Hornet* tragedy: "The story of the ill-fated *Hornet,* and the sufferings of her crew in their long voyage in an open boat, has been told, and the world has been thrilled at the recital."[4]

Bret Harte was the first literary critic to recognize that far from being a mere "phunny man," Mark Twain was capable of shrewd and effective social criticism. In 1866, soon after Mark Twain returned from Hawaii to San Francisco, Harte called attention to this element in Twain's humor. Reporting for the Springfield *Republican* Twain's "most interesting lecture upon the Sandwich Islands," Harte editorialized: "He had already acquired, here and abroad, considerable fame as an original and broadly humorous writer, but he took his audience by storm. . . . He has shrewdness and a certain hearty abhorrence of shams which will make his faculty serviceable to mankind. His talent is so well based that he can write seriously and well when he chooses, which is perhaps the best test of true humor."

As San Francisco's leading critic, Harte did not hesitate to point out faults of "crudeness" and "coarseness" in Twain's writing at this period, but Harte concluded: "I am particular in these details, for I believe he deserves this space and criticism, and I think I recognize a new star rising in this western horizon."[5]

[4] *San Francisco in 1866 by Bret Harte, Being Letters to the* Springfield Republican, edited by George R. Stewart and Edwin S. Fussell, 83.

[5] *Ibid.* Mark Twain's lecture was delivered in San Francisco on October 2, 1866. Arthur L. Scott, introducing his valuable compilation *Mark Twain: Selected Criticism,* 3, suggests that Charles H. Webb, in an introduction to Mark Twain's first book of sketches (1867), was the first to recognize the "moralistic basis of Twain's humor." Scott comments: "Few people recall that Bret Harte, in a long review, extolled [*The Innocents Abroad*] not only for its power, originality, and humor, but also for its

If Bret Harte recognized in the new star a challenge to the brilliance of his own, there is very little evidence to support a hypothesis that seeds of jealous rivalry were germinating in the mind of Harte as well as of Clemens in those halcyon days of reciprocal praise. The same letter to the Springfield *Republican* noted that Twain's humor, "peculiar to himself" yet in the Western tradition, "surpassed Artemus Ward's with the advantage of being of a more legitimate quality" and was "perhaps more thoroughly national and American than even the Yankee delineations of Lowell." In 1866 this was high praise indeed. And when Bret Harte reported to his Massachusetts readers that Mark Twain's friends were urging him to repeat the lecture in the East as well as in California, it is safe to assume that Harte was among those friends.

In his detailed study of *Mark Twain on the Lecture Circuit*, Paul Fatout, in 1960, called attention to the fact that Harte's essay (the "most judicious" of all the enthusiastic press notices) included an analysis which "testifies to keen perception exercised a generation before many critics discovered that Mark Twain was more thoroughly American than Lowell or any other."[6]

On May 7, 1867, Mark Twain gave his famous lecture at Cooper Union in New York. On June 7 of the same year he joined other passengers of the *Quaker City* for a pleasure cruise from the New World to the Holy Land, with Twain's passage to be financed by the *Alta California*, whose editors, Noah Brooks and John McComb, agreed to pay him an additional twenty dollars apiece for firsthand reports of the excursion.

On June 22, 1867, Bret Harte published in the *San Francisco News Letter and California Advertiser* a satire entitled "Our Foreign Correspondence." "Our Own Californian Abroad" wrote from Paris of a trip to Venice. The streets reminded him of Sacramento during the flood. The architecture was described in terms of some of the principal buildings of San Francisco. For example, the doge's palace strikingly resembled a building on the corner of Bush and Montgomery. The lions

---

'really admirable rhetoric, vigorous and picturesque.' " Scott refers to Harte's review in the *Overland Monthly*, Vol. IV (Jan., 1870), 100–101. Harte's *Springfield Republican* essay appeared one year before Webb's appraisal and may have influenced Webb's judgment.

[6] Pages 40–41.

of "St. Mark" were larger than "Dr. Rabe's old lions on Clay Street," but in the writer's judgment not so "finely cast." The houses in Venice, he said, had "what is called a water base." "I have seen some in San Francisco with the same peculiarity, but without the water which makes Venice so unpleasant."[7] This satire was written before Mark Twain began his series of letters to the *Alta California,* later collected in *The Innocents Abroad.* And as George Stewart pointed out, in 1867 there was no lack of foreign correspondents who, in writing back to San Francisco papers their impressions of Europe, frequently displayed "a fine provincialism in the sometimes naive preference for the scenery and products of the Pacific Coast."[8] Nevertheless, the proximity of the date of Twain's sailing and references in the satire to Hank Monk and the "Washoe Line" suggest that Harte may have been indulging in typical Western raillery of a fellow journalist.

If the satirist was making fun of the way Mark Twain could be expected to cover the assignment and Mark gained thereby an idea for the tone of *The Innocents Abroad,* Bret Harte was well pleased with the result. When the *Quaker City* letters appeared in the *Alta,* Harte showed immediate recognition of their value by asking to republish four of the best of them in the *Overland Monthly.*[9] Moreover, in reviewing *The Innocents Abroad* for the *Overland* in January, 1870, Harte described Twain's book as "a joyous revelation—an Indian spring in an alkaline literary desert" and reaffirmed his belief that Twain "deserved to rank foremost among Western humorists."[10] The review called the book "six hundred and fifty pages of open and declared fun" and assured prospective buyers that they would enjoy reading every line. It noted that the title provided a clue to the "lawlessness and audacity" with which the rather trite subject of a trip to the Holy Land would be treated, and though admitting that some critics might question the propriety of humorous exploitation of a religious subject, the

[7] George R. Stewart, "Some Bret Harte Satires," *Frontier,* Vol. XIII (Jan., 1922), 94.

[8] *Ibid.,* 99. See also Walter Blair, *Native American Humor,* 155.

[9] See *Mark Twain: Representative Selections,* edited by Fred Lewis Pattee, xxv.

[10] See also Scott, *Selected Criticism,* 13–16. The tone of Harte's criticism here seems incompatible with the conclusion of Ivan Benson that "Harte had no enthusiasm for the success of others; he was envious, covetous of honors bestowed upon those who considered themselves to be his friends." See *Mark Twain's Western Years,* 158.

reviewer pointed out that the humor of *The Innocents Abroad* was largely based on the presence of "Mark Twain" among the pilgrims. In this character's "mock assumption of a righteous indignation" lay the real power of the book, for it enabled Mr. Clemens as a humorist "to say his most deliberately funny things with all the haste and exaggeration of rage." But Bret Harte cautioned all readers to distinguish between Sam Clemens and Mark Twain, and he insisted that Mr. Clemens could no more fairly be held responsible for Mark Twain's irreverence than could the late Charles Farrar Browne be held accountable for Artemus Ward's meanness and humbuggery.

The *Californian* had ceased publication by February 1, 1868. When the *Overland Monthly* was founded in the same year, Bret Harte had been the obvious choice as editor for this journal designed to become the West's *Atlantic*. For five years Harte had been recognized as San Francisco's leading literary arbiter even by those who protested his judgments. The publisher of the *Overland* was Anton Roman; the assistant editor, who later said he was seldom called on to assist, was Noah Brooks. A snarling grizzly bear was designed for the cover, but no one liked him very well until Bret Harte, by drawing two straight lines under his feet, gave the beast symbolic significance.[11] According to Mark Twain, the bear thereby became "the ancient symbol of California savagery snarling at the approaching type of high and progressive Civilization, the first Overland locomotive!" Mark Twain considered this "nothing less than inspiration itself."[12]

By July, the first issue of the *Overland* was on the newsstands. Before long, under Harte's guidance, the new journal was read and respected east as well as west of the Rockies. Among its first contributors was Henry George, whose article published in the *Overland* in October, 1868, "anticipated his later thesis, contending that the railroads would bring riches to a few and poverty to many."[13] By 1870, Harte's own unsigned stories published in the *Overland*—"The Luck of Roaring Camp," "Tennessee's Partner," and "The Outcasts of Poker Flat" —had aroused such enthusiasm on the East Coast that Fields, Osgood

[11] Noah Brooks, "Bret Harte in California," *Century Magazine*, Vol. LVIII (July, 1899), 449.

[12] *MTL*, 183–84.

[13] James D. Hart, *The Oxford Companion to American Literature*, 273.

and Company, publisher of the *Atlantic Monthly*, was eager to publish a collection of Harte's fiction. In England, Charles Dickens himself was so moved by "The Luck" that he wrote a personal letter to its author inviting him to contribute to *All the Year Round* and to visit Dickens at Gad's Hill.[14] This invitation reached Harte after the English novelist's death and after Harte, grief stricken at the news, had composed "Dickens in Camp," a verse tribute to the older writer whom Harte acknowledged his master. But to Bret Harte's chagrin as editor and critic, a parody which he had written entitled "Plain Language from Truthful James," better known as "The Heathen Chinee," brought him his greatest acclaim.

Thus by 1870–71 both Bret Harte and Mark Twain had become famous, and both seemed well along the road to financial security. Mark Twain in the East had married a lovely young woman with a fortune considerably exceeding that of the bride of Steve Gillis. With the aid of his father-in-law, Mark had become part owner and editor of the Buffalo *Express*. And enjoying the phenomenal financial as well as critical success of *The Innocents Abroad*, Mark Twain was editing a column for a New York magazine, *The Galaxy*. For about ten pages of "Memoranda" a month, Mark Twain was promised a yearly sum of $2,000, "nearly double the *Galaxy's* highest rate of payment to its other contributors."[15]

Among the many requests for contributions which Bret Harte received after the publication of "The Heathen Chinee" in September, 1870, were repeated offers from *The Galaxy*, where Mark Twain's submissions in fulfillment of his contract were proving considerably fewer and poorer than anticipated. In letters dated September 26 and October 6, and in a telegram on October 4, Bret Harte rejected *The Galaxy's* bids because, he explained with unwonted vehemence, *The Galaxy's* offer was "the lowest and the least advantageous I have had the honor to recieve [sic] from anyone."[16] One can only guess whether

[14] *BHAE*, 172–73; see also T. Edgar Pemberton, *Bret Harte, A Treatise and a Tribute*, 12–17.

[15] Frank Luther Mott, *A History of American Magazines*, III, 364. Mark Twain wrote Mrs. Fairbanks, with whose husband he had been dickering about a job, that he was offered $2,400 a year. See *The Letters of Mark Twain to Mrs. Fairbanks*, edited by Dixon Wecter, 128.

[16] In the T. W. Norris Collection of Bret Harte Manuscripts, Bancroft.

Twain's association with the journal contributed in any way to the size of the offer or to the vehemence of Harte's rejection.

Bret Harte's mounting fame as a writer of short stories and satiric verses as well as national recognition of his able editing of the *Overland Monthly* enhanced his prestige as a literary critic. It was inevitable that Bret Harte, like other reviewers of the day, should compare the humor of Mark Twain with the humor of Artemus Ward, whose reputation in this field had long been supreme.

In October, 1870, the year when—according to Mark Twain—he and Harte first became estranged, the *Overland Monthly* published Bret Harte's review of a rather uncomplimentary biography of Artemus Ward by Ward's manager, Edward P. Hingston.[17] Hingston's biography, entitled *The Genial Showman,* included allegations of insincerity and lack of integrity in Ward similar to allegations which Twain would one day make against Harte.

In defending the dead humorist in 1870, Harte pointed out that Charles F. Browne had been the accuser's "friend and patron." Harte took issue with Hingston's thesis that the individual Charles F. Browne was as much a showman as the public figure Artemus Ward, and Harte vigorously protested Hingston's assertion that Browne was as "insincere in his relations to the public and had the same lack of self respect which distinguished 'Mr. Ward' without 'Mr. Ward's ignorance.' "[18] The reviewer observed that although Artemus Ward was at the height of his fame as a humorist and lecturer when he died in London only three years earlier, Ward's track was already becoming faint among the "crowding footprints" of other humorists "like 'Nasby' and 'Twain.' " The review includes a brief restatement of Bret Harte's consistently held judgment of the high quality of Mark Twain's humor. It points out that whereas Artemus Ward's humor rarely served or was intended to serve any purpose other than that of the showman, Mark Twain—having mastered Ward's technique—used it with a "larger purpose." Nevertheless, Harte warned these "clever young writers" stalk-

[17] Two years later Twain in London publicly cut Hingston for writing an introduction to the hated "John Camden Hottentot's" edition of *The Innocents Abroad.* In his old age Twain deeply regretted his unkindnes to Hingston. See Paine, *Biography,* 464.
[18] "The Genial Showman. By Edward P. Hingston. New York, Harper & Bros.," *Overland Monthly,* Vol. V (Oct., 1870), 388–89.

ing the fame of the dead master that the showman might become in time a part of the show, might yield his individuality and intellectual integrity to a necessity which could drive and control him.

If a break in the personal friendship of Mark Twain and Bret Harte had occurred in 1870, Harte did not permit the break to affect his literary judgment. But in November, 1870, two months after the appearance of "The Heathen Chinee," Harte published in the *Overland* "The Iliad of Sandy Bar," his story of two partners, Scott and York, owners of the "Amity Claim," who though "singularly devoted to each other," "bitterly and inexplicably quarreled." Whether or not the story was suggested by a real quarrel between Mark Twain and Bret Harte, it foreshadowed several aspects of their future estrangement. Citizens of Sandy Bar speculated about the cause of the quarrel, but the only witness was an irrelevant Chinaman, who wouldn't talk.[19]

In the same month, on November 26, 1870, Mark Twain wrote to Charles H. Webb a letter which seems to be an answer to one from Webb commenting on Bret Harte's soaring reputation:

> Indeed Harte *does* soar, & I am glad of it, notwithstanding he and I are "off," these many months. It happened thus. Harte read all the MS of the "Innocents" & told me what passages, paragraphs & chapters to leave out—& I followed orders strictly. It was a kind thing for Harte to do, & I think I appreciated it. He praised the book so highly that I wanted him to review it *early* for the Overland, & help the sale out there. I told my publisher. He ordered Bancroft to send Harte a couple of books before anybody else. Bancroft declined! . . . Well, Sir, Harte *wrote me the most daintily contemptuous & insulting letter you ever read*—& what I want to know, is, where *I* was to blame?[20]

Mark Twain's publisher was Elisha Bliss of Hartford, Connecticut, and Bancroft was the San Francisco distributor for his firm, the American Publishing Company, which issued books by subscription. Because

[19] The only apparent *raison d'être* of this character is to give Harte a chance to satirize the race prejudice of Colonel Starbottle, a professional Southerner, who says of the inscrutable Chinese: "And this yer's the cattle . . . that some thinks oughter be allowed to testify agin' a White Man!" *Writings*, II, 1. Harte seldom missed a chance to attack the California law which excluded from the courts testimony of Chinese, Indians, and Negroes.

[20] *"Ah Sin," A Dramatic Work by Mark Twain and Bret Harte,* edited by Frederick Anderson, vii–viii.

most books issued in this way were badly written and badly made as well as because subscription publishers took no advertising in the press, subscription firms seldom enjoyed the esteem of reviewers.[21] Harte's low opinion of subscription books is indicated in the first paragraph of his *Overland* review of *The Innocents Abroad* in January, 1870, but the point of the paragraph was that fastidious readers would find Mark Twain's book a delightful exception to the general run of subscription offerings.

In July of the preceding year Mark Twain had been so exasperated by his publisher's delay in issuing this book that he had threatened to sue Bliss, whom he accused of holding back *Innocents* in order to publish the works of other authors. This early suspicion of Bliss is pertinent to the decisive quarrel between Mark Twain and Bret Harte seven years later. But in 1870, Bliss was able to mollify Mark Twain by persuading him that the delay in publishing his book had increased sales.[22]

Along with the fact that Bret Harte wrote what seemed to Mark Twain a contemptuous and insulting letter should also be remembered the fact that during a period when Harte was editing a new magazine and struggling to find time to write his own stories, for which New England publishers were clamoring, Bret Harte took time to help his friend Mark Twain with detailed revisions and editing of the manuscript for 650 printed pages of *The Innocents Abroad*.

[21] See Kenneth R. Andrews, *Nook Farm: Mark Twain's Hartford Circle*, 122.
[22] Hamlin Hill, "Mark Twain's Quarrels with Elisha Bliss," *American Literature*, Vol. XXXIII (Jan., 1962), 443–45.

4

THREE ACES AND TWO BOWERS

In the game of euchre, "the right bower is the knave of trumps, and the left bower is the knave of the suit having the same color as the trump suit."

A Dictionary of American English on Historical Principles

MARK TWAIN'S TESTIMONY that Bret Harte trimmed and trained and schooled him patiently has frequently been quoted as evidence of Mark Twain's magnanimity. Unlike most critics of the past twenty years, the late Van Wyck Brooks averred that Mark Twain was correct and that he did, indeed, owe much to Bret Harte, "the most experienced craftsman he had met."[1] But Mark Twain's words are rarely recalled in context. This tribute to Harte was included in a letter which Mark Twain wrote to the editor of *Every Saturday*, Thomas Bailey Aldrich, four days before Bret Harte left San Francisco in 1871 for a "royal progress" to the East, where he would sign with the publishers of the *Atlantic Monthly* and *Every Saturday* a contract, at the time highly publicized as the most lucrative contract ever offered an American writer.

Bret Harte's fame had continued to mount spectacularly, and as Mark Twain would remember it, Harte "crossed the continent through such a prodigious blaze of national interest and excitement that one might have supposed he was the Viceroy of India on a progress, or Halley's comet come again after seventy-five years of lamented absence."[2] Mark Twain's letter to Thomas Bailey Aldrich—the third in a series—was Twain's attempt to modify his earlier reaction to a critical assertion by Aldrich that Mark Twain had tried unsuccessfully to imitate Bret Harte.

[1] *The Times of Melville and Whitman,* 285.   [2] *MTE,* 265.

36

The first letter which Twain wrote to Aldrich was published in Ferris Greenslet's biography of Aldrich.[3] The second and third letters, with a deletion, were published by Albert Bigelow Paine in *Mark Twain's Letters*. In 1963 a paper-bound book entitled *The Forgotten Writings of Mark Twain*, edited by Henry Duskis, included excerpts from the three letters. Although the complete exchange between Aldrich and Twain is not available in any one source, a knowledge of this correspondence together with its biographical and historical backgrounds is crucial in an understanding of the relationship between Mark Twain and Bret Harte.

As indicated earlier, Bret Harte in 1871 owed much of his phenomenal fame and fortune to Ah Sin, "The Heathen Chinee," who seemed to Truthful James peculiarly addicted to "ways that are dark" and "tricks that are vain." Harte and his literary cronies in San Francisco frequently wrote for their own entertainment limericks and parodies never intended for publication. "Plain Language from Truthful James" was a parody of Algernon Charles Swinburne's "Atalanta." According to one story it was retrieved from the wastebasket;[4] according to another, from the San Francisco *News Letter* when Ambrose Bierce persuaded Harte to publish it in the *Overland Monthly*.[5] For the parody, Harte was paid twenty-five dollars.[6]

The immediate and world-encircling popularity of the verses was as astonishing to their author as to twentieth-century critics. Cheap reprints with caricatures of Ah Sin were vended on the streets of cities around the globe. The words were set to music, and their fame considerably exceeded that of the "Jumping Frog of Calaveras County." Appreciation of "The Heathen Chinee" was by no means limited to the uneducated. Among many admirers in the Eastern United States was the editor Thomas Bailey Aldrich, who in *Every Saturday* for January 14, 1871, gave Eastern fans their first photograph of the famous Harte. One of the best indicators of national interest in Harte as well as the personal enthusiasm of Thomas Bailey Aldrich can be found in this Bret Harte Issue of *Every Saturday*, to which Mark Twain would jeer-

[3] *The Life of Thomas Bailey Aldrich*, 95.   [4] *MTE*, 266.

[5] Carey McWilliams, *Ambrose Bierce*, 89. This is the version accepted by Henry Childs Merwin, *The Life of Bret Harte*, 51.

[6] *Overland Monthly* Ledger, Bancroft.

ingly refer in a letter to William Dean Howells a year and a half later.[7]

In addition to W. J. Linton's engraved portrait of the "Author of 'The Heathen Chinee'" on the cover, and a biographical sketch of Harte on the editorial page, an illustration of "Tennessee's Partner" filled another page, and this *Overland Monthly* story itself was reprinted in full on two more pages. Advertisements provided additional evidence that the new writer in California was phenomenally popular with readers and was expected to bring substantial profits to his publisher. James R. Osgood and Company's listing of "New Books" included works by James Russell Lowell, Charles Dudley Warner, John Greenleaf Whittier, and Charles Dickens. But *Bret Harte's Poems* led all the rest and reappeared twice again in the same column, with puffs for Harte from New York's *World* and *Globe*. Above *Every Saturday*'s masthead, Osgood advertised a seventh edition of *The Luck of Roaring Camp and Other Stories and Sketches* and a fifth edition of *Bret Harte's Poems*. This advertisement, devoted completely to "Bret Harte's Books," quoted from the Springfield *Republican*'s review of "Plain Language from Truthful James":

> . . . certainly nothing has been printed of late, if ever, which has run through the newspapers of the country as this has. Part of this effect is owing to the temporary excitement of the public about the Chinese question,—but the combination of delicate humor, and force of expression, both plain and grotesque, seen in these verses would have made them famous at any time.

Mark Twain's first letter of protest to Aldrich was written on January 15, the day following the appearance of Aldrich's Bret Harte Issue of *Every Saturday*.

Many poetasters of the day attempted to imitate "Plain Language from Truthful James" without recognizing that the skill of the parody lay chiefly in the ironic handling of characterization and point of view. Its technique of communicating in the words of an unsophisticated narrator social criticism and comedy of which he himself is totally unconscious is essentially the technique later employed by Mark Twain to convey fairly sophisticated social commentary and humor in the words of the humorless Huck Finn. The language of the unintentionally truthful "Truthful James" plainly revealed more prejudice and hy-

[7] *MTH*, I, 11.

pocrisy in himself and the notorious Nye than peculiarity in Ah Sin. Harte reportedly once described this doggerel as "the worst poem I ever wrote, possibly the worst poem anyone ever wrote," and he developed for "The Heathen Chinee" an inordinate hatred, especially when it was cited to support that very race prejudice which all his life Harte fought. According to Charles Warren Stoddard, Harte's one consolation was the belief that fame based on such work could not last.[8]

As twentieth-century readers may not remember, "Plain Language from Truthful James" includes an account of a three-handed card game started by Caucasians with the idea of cheating an ignorant foreigner. Yet, though the Caucasian Bill Nye's sleeve was stuffed full of aces and bowers, the Chinese Ah Sin beat the two white men at their own game. Most-quoted lines include the description of Ah Sin's "smile that was childlike and bland"; Truthful James's thesis: "That for ways that are dark/ And for tricks that are vain,/ The heathen Chinee is peculiar . . ."; and the complaint of Bill Nye: "We are ruined by Chinese cheap labor."[9] Commentators argued about whether the game played by the notorious three was really euchre, and more than one suspected that the author of "The Heathen Chinee" actually knew very little about card-playing.

Among the alleged imitations of "The Heathen Chinee" was a thing called "Three Aces," signed by "Carl Byng" and published on December 3, 1870, in the Buffalo *Express*, partly owned and edited by Mark Twain.[10] This doggerel, captioned "Written for the Express" and subtitled "Jim Todd's Episode in Social Euchre," told in dialect how an innocent was fleeced in a card game with "three smooth chaps" on board the *Natchez Ranger*, presumably a river boat. The plays were reported in considerable detail by one who knew the game. At one time the narrator, mistakenly convinced that he was winning, said "Cap . . . you air my huckleberry." The doggerel is far less polished and skillful than "The Heathen Chinee"; the dialect sounds more like Lowell's Yankee Biglow than like Truthful James; and unlike the game in "The Heathen Chinee," the cheating does not end in a brawl.

Thomas Bailey Aldrich believed—as did many others—that Carl Byng, the name signed to "Three Aces," was another pseudonym for

[8] *Exits and Entrances*, 251.   [9] *Writings*, XII, 129–31.
[10] Neider, *Autobiography*, 186.

Samuel Clemens. Consequently Aldrich inserted in the middle of a space-filler called "Literary Items" on an inside page of *Every Saturday* for January 7, 1871, these two sentences: "Mark Twain's versified story of 'Three Aces' seems to be a feeble echo of Bret Harte. The 'Truthful James' vein is one that can be worked successfully only by the owner of the 'claim.'"

Reacting, he later said, "on the spur of the moment," Twain wrote Aldrich what was for him an unusually terse denial that he had "written the 'rhymes referred to'" or that he had had "anything whatever to do with suggesting, inspiring, or producing them."[11] Included in the letter was Mark Twain's accurate paraphrase of "Three Aces," showing detailed familiarity with the doggerel which Twain insisted was the work of a "writer who has for years signed himself Hy Slocum." Twain informed Aldrich that "several responsible publishing houses" had asked him to write a "volume of poems" like the "'Truthful James' rhymes" but he had burned the requests unanswered because he was "not in the imitation business." Curtly Twain requested Aldrich to publish a correction of his "mis-statement."

This note was dated January 15. Aldrich's statement about "Three Aces" appeared on January 7. Mark Twain's angry note was a response not to the Aldrich comment about "Three Aces" eight days earlier, but to the Bret Harte Issue of *Every Saturday* of the preceding day.

Under the noncommittal heading "Mark Twain Says He Didn't Do It," Aldrich immediately inserted in the current dummy of *Every Saturday* Mark Twain's complete letter, followed by what is generally termed Aldrich's "apology," with quotation marks suggesting some ambiguity.[12] Actually, Aldrich retracted little when he wrote: "The poem entitled 'The Three Aces,' with Mark Twain's signature attached as author, appeared in several New York exchanges. That was our only authority for attributing the verses to him." But Aldrich's statement concluded with a compliment: "We are very glad that he did not write them, for the rhymes lack that freshness and brilliancy which Mark Twain has taught us to expect in his writing."

[11] The first letter can be found in *Every Saturday* (Feb. 4, 1871), 118, and in Greenslet, *Thomas Bailey Aldrich*, 95.

[12] Greenslet, *Thomas Bailey Aldrich*, 97.

Within a week of his first note, Mark Twain wrote Aldrich a second asking that his first not be published. Instead, he wanted *Every Saturday* to carry a brief statement (*"a line and a half* under 'Literary Notes' ") that Aldrich had mistaken "one Hy. Slocum [after writing it, Mark Twain crossed out the name Hy Slocum] (no, it was one Carl Byng, I perceive)" for Mark Twain.[13] Twain's second note to Aldrich concluded: "It is hard to be accused of plagiarism—a crime I never committed in my life." Then he added a rather astonishing postscript informing Aldrich that Twain had dropped from the *Express's* list of contributors "for their OWN GOOD" because "everything they write is straightway saddled onto me . . . *both* (the underlining is Mark Twain's) Carl Byng, whose name had been attached to the rhymes in the *Express,* and Hy Slocum, whose only apparent association with "Three Aces" was that Mark had ascribed the verses to him in the first note to Aldrich.[14] We can only speculate whether Hy Slocum ever asked Mark Twain to correct his own "mis-statement" in *Every Saturday,* for the names Carl Byng and Hy Slocum both disappeared from publications.

To Mark Twain's second note Aldrich replied by attaching to his "correction" prepared for *Every Saturday* a somewhat exasperated explanation that Mark's first note was already in print and about to be distributed. "My dear Sir," wrote Aldrich, "It is too late to attempt to prevent me doing you justice!" With tongue in cheek, however, he offered to withdraw his apology.[15]

"No indeed, don't take back the apology!" began Twain's third com-

[13] Twain told Aldrich that Charles H. Webb had written him about the matter but he had asked Webb to "suppress" a paragraph about it which Webb intended to publish. Just a year earlier Twain had written Elisha Bliss that he was suing Webb in the New York courts in order to secure copyright and plates of *The Celebrated Jumping Frog of Calaveras County and Other Sketches,* which Webb had collated and published after Carleton had rejected it. Mark Twain intended to break the plates and prepare a new volume of sketches. Letter to Bliss from Elmira (Jan. 23, 1870), in the Mark Twain Papers, University of California Library, Berkeley (hereinafter cited as MTP). In 1871, Webb was irritated on his own account by the Bret Harte Issue of *Every Saturday* because Aldrich had referred to the *Californian* as "an unsuccessful newspaper enterprise" of Harte's. See Letter to the Editor, *Every Saturday* (Jan. 28, 1871), 91.

[14] Greenslet, *Thomas Bailey Aldrich,* 96. MTL, I, 181–82, includes the letter but deletes the postscript.

[15] Greenslet, *Thomas Bailey Aldrich,* 96.

munication to Aldrich, dated January 28. This was the letter which included the oft-quoted acknowledgment of earlier indebtedness to Bret Harte. It also included Twain's apology to Aldrich and an anecdote about a Nevada drinking party where Artemus Ward, Joseph Goodman, Dan de Quille, and Mark Twain showed fervent enthusiasm for Aldrich's famous "Ballad of Baby Bell." DeLancey Ferguson saw in the reported scene evidence that the men named were not frontiersmen but Victorians, even when they were drunk, and "they accepted Victorian literary tender at face value."[16] It is noteworthy that Twain's anecdote was prefaced by the observation: "Well, it *is* funny, the reminiscences that glare out from murky corners of one's memory, now and then, without warning." For Mark Twain's vivid description of the Western writers' appreciation of "Baby Bell" includes ribald parallels of the scene in "Dickens in Camp," where Bret Harte portrayed Western miners' appreciation of "Little Nell." But if Twain's drunken scene burlesqued Harte's sentimental poem, the resemblance was unquestionably due not to conscious intent but to the "murky corners" of memory.

In his third letter to Aldrich, Twain told how Harte by two strokes of his pen had given symbolic significance to the *Overland* grizzly bear, and Mark pronounced the resulting vignette "the prettiest fancy and the neatest that ever shot through Harte's brain."[17] As if aware that his motive in praising Harte might be questioned, Mark Twain commented that his tribute, which he described as a "grateful remembrance," should be "worth its face" because "a year ago" Bret had broken their long friendship "without any cause or provocation that I am aware of." "I am ashamed every time I think of my bursting out before an unconcerned public with that bombastic pow-wow about burning publishers' letters, and all that sort of imbecility," Twain wrote Aldrich, "and about not being an imitator, etc. Who would find out that I am a natural fool if I always kept cool and never let nature come to the surface? Nobody."

The nature which Mark Twain had let come to the surface in his first letter to Aldrich and which his third letter attempted to submerge was his sense of rivalry with Harte and jealous chagrin that in Eastern

[16] Page 90.
[17] *MTL*, I, 183. Not included in Greenslet, *Thomas Bailey Aldrich*.

opinion, as reflected in *Every Saturday,* Harte's score at that time was far ahead.

To Twain's third letter Aldrich responded with unmodified though delayed cordiality. As if reaffirming his admiration for Bret Harte, Aldrich, on April 29, republished "Plain Language from Truthful James," adding eight illustrations of scenes from the poem to fill two pages of *Every Saturday.* In time, Aldrich recognized that he had perhaps admired in Bret Harte what was least commendable, yet Harte remained in his memory "a careless blithe spirit," and like Howells, Aldrich would doubt that the subsequent American reaction against Harte was closer to the truth than the earlier acclaim.[18]

The correspondence about "Three Aces" marked the beginning of a long friendship between Mark Twain and Thomas Bailey Aldrich. In 1900, Aldrich made an after-dinner speech at the Lotos Club welcoming Mark home from abroad and mentioning "nearly thirty years of unclouded friendship,"[19] yet Mark Twain's autobiographical comments about Aldrich, following the section on Bret Harte in *Mark Twain in Eruption* and supplemented in the Neider *Autobiography,* make clear that the relationship between Aldrich and Mark Twain was not so unclouded as Aldrich thought it was.[20] Mark Twain's conversation with Robert Louis Stevenson on a bench in Washington Square affords one of several indications that after the affair of "Three Aces," Aldrich was frequently associated with Bret Harte in Mark Twain's mind. Mark demurred from Stevenson's praise of Harte by insisting that the wit of Aldrich was superior to that of Harte, but finally, as Stevenson recognized with amusement, Mark Twain consigned both Stevenson and Aldrich to hell.[21]

Mark Twain's angry dissociation of himself from "Three Aces" bears some resemblance to his disclaimer of the Thomas Jefferson Snod-

---

[18] *Life in Letters of William Dean Howells,* edited by Mildred Howells, II, 157–58.

[19] Clara Clemens, *My Father,* 104.

[20] Contrary to frequent assumptions, Twain's critical judgment of Aldrich cannot be altogether explained by the fact that Twain never admitted Mrs. Aldrich, whom he detested, to the *entente cordiale* with her husband. See Mrs. Thomas Bailey Aldrich, *Crowding Memories,* 128–30; then see *MTE,* 293–98, and Neider, *Autobiography,* 357–67.

[21] Neider, *Autobiography,* 288–89.

grass letters and his blistering attack on the man who correctly identified the letters as the work of Samuel L. Clemens.[22] In *The Forgotten Writings of Mark Twain,* advertised on the cover as "Mark Twain's writings in the Buffalo EXPRESS," Henry Duskis persuasively defends his inclusion of "Three Aces" and other contributions signed H. Slocum or Carl Byng. A folder labeled "Buffalo Express I" in the Mark Twain Papers in Berkeley, and Jacob Blanck's bibliographical data about a mysterious pamphlet entitled *Three Aces, Jim Todd's Episode in Social Euchre, A Poem and a Denial, by Mark Twain,*[23] add weight to the argument that Thomas Bailey Aldrich was not guilty of a misstatement in attributing the verses to Mark Twain. If the publication of the doggerel in Mark Twain's particular column entitled "People and Things" in the *Express* explains why Twain's name was signed to the verses in New York exchanges, it also indicates that Mark Twain had at least editorial responsibility for accepting work which before long he contemptuously labeled "plagiarism." However, for our present investigation, whether or not Twain wrote "Three Aces" is not so significant as his violent reaction to Aldrich's belief that Mark Twain had unsuccessfully attempted to imitate Bret Harte.

The affair rankled in Mark Twain's memory and contributed to his "brain fever" in the John Camden Hotten controversy a year and a half later, when the name of Carl Byng was linked with Mark Twain's name in London.[24] It may have influenced Twain's charges that Harte "plagiarized" in the play *Ah Sin.* Twain's continued feeling about the incident was known to his friends and alluded to in one of the letters of the famous April Fool's joke which George Washington Cable con-

[22] Fatout, "Mark Twain's Nom de Plume," *loc. cit.,* 6.

[23] Houghton's Library at Harvard University owns this mysterious pamphlet purportedly printed at the Christmas season of 1929 in Westport, Connecticut, for fifty friends of "Robin and Marian MacVicars." See Merle Johnson's *Bibliography of the Works of Mark Twain, Samuel L. Clemens,* 108. This booklet includes the doggerel "Three Aces" together with quotations from the Clemens-Aldrich correspondence and a "certificate of issue" specifically attributing the verses to Mark Twain. The second volume of Jacob Blanck's monumental *Bibliography of American Literature* adds to the mystery by listing the "Westport, Connecticut," publication but reporting (1) that the "certificate of issue" is false; (2) that "Robin and Marian MacVivars" are figments of the imagination; and (3) that the pamphlet was, in fact, printed in New York sometime in 1930 for one person.

[24] Ferguson, *Man and Legend,* 163.

cocted for Mark Twain in 1884.[25] And in the mind of Mark Twain, the affair of "Three Aces" became like the hard core of one of those boils which sometimes afflicted his body. The hardness took thirty-five years to work itself out, and then it left a scar.

[25] Dean Sage requested Mark Twain's autograph for a young woman who considered Twain's "Heathen Chinee" a delightful poem. Paine, *Biography*, 769.

3

WAS GOLDSMITH'S FRIEND A FRIEND OF
BRET HARTE?

I must and will keep shady and quiet till Bret Harte simmers down
a little, and then I mean to go up head again and *stay* there.

SAMUEL L. CLEMENS to ORION CLEMENS, March 11, 1871[1]

IF DURING THEIR SAN FRANCISCO YEARS Bret Harte had boomed
Mark Twain with ardor, Mark Twain on his part had loyally supported his friend Bret Harte. In 1865, when Harte's editing of *Outcroppings,* an anthology of contemporary California verse, aroused considerable sound and fury among California poets in the California press,[2]
Mark Twain staunchly declared that Bret Harte had shown "rare good
taste and ability in all respects save one—he has not put in a single
line of his own poetry."[3] "I am a friend to 'Outcroppings,'" Mark
wrote Albert S. Evans, reporter and editorial writer for San Francisco's
Alta California, "and I do not like to see you and Smythe trying to
bring the book into disrepute." In the last month of 1866, after his triumphs of lecturing and writing about the Sandwich Islands, Twain left
San Francisco to return to New York. He traveled via Nicaragua, re-
versing the route which Harte had taken to the West Coast twelve years
earlier.

In 1867, G. W. Carleton published Bret Harte's *Condensed Novels,
and Other Papers, with Comic Illustrations by Frank Bellew.* Mark
Twain considered Carleton's earlier rejection of his *Jumping Frog*
volume an insult which he could never forgive.[4] After learning of Carle-

---

[1] *"Ah Sin," a Dramatic Work by Mark Twain and Bret Harte,* viii.
[2] For a detailed account of the *Outcroppings* incident, see *BHAE,* 129–38. For
Harte's account, see "My First Book," *Writings,* X, 427–35.
[3] *Mark Twain: San Francisco Correspondent,* 22.
[4] *MTH,* I, 132. For evidence that he *did* forgive Carleton, see Neider, *Autobiography,* 152–54.

ton's acceptance of Harte's work, Mark Twain angrily wrote Charles W. Stoddard on April 23, 1867, that Bret Harte was publishing with a "Son of a Bitch" who would "swindle him." "We of Bohemia keep away from Carleton's," Mark told Stoddard.[5] But a week later Twain wrote Harte a very friendly letter about Twain's own book, *The Celebrated Jumping Frog of Calaveras County, and Other Sketches,* published by Charles H. Webb after it was rejected by Carleton.

Mark Twain was still showing deference to Bret Harte as critic. He told Harte that the book was out, that it was handsome, but that it included "damnable errors of grammar and deadly inconsistencies of spelling in the Frog sketch because I was away and did not read the proofs." Mark urged Bret to "be a friend and say nothing about these things." He promised to autograph a copy and send it to the Harte family to "pisen the children with."

> I am to lecture in Cooper Institute next Monday night. Pray for me.
> We sail for the Holy Land June 8. Try to write me (to this hotel,) and it will be forwarded to Paris, where we remain 10 or 15 days.
> Regards and best wishes to Mrs. Bret and the family.
>
> Truly Yr Friend
MARK[6]

Although the original plan of collaborating on a book of sketches by both Mark Twain and Bret Harte was never realized, a book of *Overland Sketches* including essays by Bret Harte, Mark Twain, Charles W. Stoddard, and other Western writers was issued in August, 1868, by Thomas O'Kane, a bookseller and stationer in New York.[7]

In December of the same year, anxiously courting Olivia Langdon, the "purest woman" he had ever known, for whom he was offering to censor *Gulliver's Travels* for its "coarse and indelicate" parts and to whom he wrote that he would rather she read "Fifty 'Jumping Frogs' than one *Don Quixote*,"[8] Mark sent to the man he hoped to make his father-in-law a list of people who could be consulted about the character of Samuel L. Clemens. The list began with the name of a former gov-

---

[5] *MTH*, I, 133n.   [6] *MTL*, I, 124.

[7] Milton Meltzer, *Mark Twain Himself, A Pictorial Biography,* 118.

[8] *LL*, 76. Earlier Mark had written: "Don't read a word in that Jumping Frog book, Livy—don't . . . I would be glad to know that every copy [of "that infamous volume"] was burned, & gone forever." *Ibid.,* 41.

ernor of California ("now Chief Justice of the Supreme Court of Nevada, if my memory serves me") and included the "present Governor of Nevada," owners and editors of newspapers, a minister, and even the proprietor of the Metropolitan Hotel in New York. Although Mark identified Frank B. Harte as editor of the *Overland Monthly* and one of the "finest writers" in California, he did not include Harte's name among the names of bigwigs with which the list was loaded. Instead, he gave the name of Harte's employer, Robert B. Swain, superintendent of the San Francisco branch of the United States Mint, whom Mark Twain described as "one of the merchant princes" of California. Clemens assured Mr. Langdon, the wealthy coal dealer of Elmira, New York, that Mr. Swain was "the Schuyler Colfax of the Pacific Coast—being regarded by high & low, rich & poor, Tom, Dick & Harry, as a man against whose pure reputation *nothing* can be said."[9] Unlike Schuyler Colfax, against whom a good deal was said later in relation to the Crédit Mobilier scandal and contributions to a campaign fund in a Presidential election year,[10] Mr. Swain was, indeed, widely and worthily respected. Although acknowledging to Mr. Langdon that Mr. Swain did not know him very well, Mark assured Livy's father that the Superintendent of the Mint could learn about him from Swain's secretary, Frank B. Harte, "for *we* have been very intimate for several years."[11]

The people on the list reportedly returned almost unanimously uncomplimentary verdicts, some recalling Mark's turbulent days with Steve Gillis in Virginia City and San Francisco. According to Mark Twain, finally Olivia Langdon's father observed sadly that since Sam Clemens had no friends, he would be one himself. "Take the girl. I know you better than they do."[12] This makes a good story, but like other good stories by Mark Twain it may well have been enriched by the author's fertile imagination. That Bret Harte, via Mr. Swain, was not among those acquaintances who gave unfavorable reports to Jervis Langdon is evident from a letter Mark Twain wrote as special correspondent for the *Alta California* after he had become happily engaged to the woman he would idolize for the rest of his life. For if Bret Harte had failed to support his friend in a crucial moment of that long and

[9] *Ibid.*, 38. [10] See *Dictionary of American Biography*, IV, 297–98.
[11] *LL*, 38–39. [12] *Ibid.*, 62.

difficult courtship, Mark Twain would never have forgotten or forgiven it. And in a report to the *Alta California* from Hartford in July, 1869, Mark assured San Franciscans that the "Eastern press" were "unanimous in their commendation of your new magazine," the *Overland Monthly*:

> Even the *Nation*, that is seldom satisfied with anything, takes frequent occasion to demonstrate that it is satisfied with the Overland. And every now and then, it and the other critical reviews of acknowledged authority, take occasion to say that Bret Harte's sketch of the "Luck of Roaring Camp" is the best prose magazine article that has seen the light for many months on either side of the ocean.[13]

Mark Twain added that but for the fact that the *Overland* did not publish the names of its contributors, "Harte's name would be very familiar in the land."

Thus Twain was generous in his early appraisals of Harte's work. Bradford A. Booth has noted that Mark Twain's first edition of Bret Harte's *The Luck of Roaring Camp, and Other Sketches* contains "approximately 435 words of manuscript marginalia"[14] showing that Twain once had a higher opinion of Harte's early stories than he expressed in *Mark Twain in Eruption*. Repeatedly, Mark Twain found the "Luck of Roaring Camp" "good." It was Harte's "most finished" work, "nearly blemishless." He objected that Harte's gambler gave the baby only a handkerchief, whereas in real life, the gambler would have given more than all the others put together. Twain also objected that Harte used "ace and two bowers" in a way that showed he really knew very little about gambling. Booth estimates that these jottings were made in the early 1870's, which means that they were written before the publication of "The Heathen Chinee" and before Mark Twain's letter to Webb about Harte's soaring reputation.

Of particular interest are Mark Twain's marginalia for "Tennessee's Partner," the first and most famous of Harte's many stories of friendship between two men.[15] Although T. Edgar Pemberton, whose

---

13 *The Twainian*, Vol. VIII (July–Aug., 1949), 4.

14 "Mark Twain's Comments on Bret Harte's Stories," *American Literature*, XXV (Jan., 1954), 494.

15 For a list of these stories, see *Bret Harte: Representative Selections*, edited by Joseph B. Harrison, 408.

source of information here must have been Harte, identifies Tennessee and his partner as Chaffee and Chamberlain,[16] it is possible that the name and certain attributes of Tennessee (who had a "fine flow of humor, which no business preoccupation could wholly subdue") had been suggested to Harte by Twain's interest in the Tennessee land, an "old sore" cankering within Mark Twain during those years when he and Bret Harte were much together in San Francisco. In 1866, the year in which the early friendship between Twain and Harte reached its peak, Mark Twain's sore was opened again when Orion, because of religious scruples, refused to sell the Tennessee land to winegrowers.[17]

In 1870, Mark Twain's marginalia doubted that Harte, "the artist," showed a "clear knowledge of human nature" when he made Tennessee's partner *"welcome back* a man who has committed against him that sin which neither the great nor the little ever forgive." And in the margin of this story Mark Twain also wrote: "It is granted that when old bosom friends get to hating each other, they hate like 'super-vicious devils.' "[18] Not included in this book of sketches, Harte's next story of friendship between two men, "The Iliad of Sandy Bar," *did* show two former friends hating each other "like super-vicious devils," but the story ended in a deathbed reconciliation and a recognition that the cause of the quarrel was trivial.[19]

In the literary world, 1870 and 1871 were Bret Harte years. After bringing out many editions of Harte's works in 1870, Fields, Osgood and Company was replaced on January 2, 1871, by James R. Osgood and Company. The new head of the publishing firm was, like his recent associate James T. Fields, a Bret Harte enthusiast. Osgood had

[16] *Bret Harte, A Treatise and a Tribute,* 67.

[17] Webster, *Mark Twain: Business Man,* 87–88. Sometimes Harte's characters were based on individuals, but more often they were composites of several people he had known. Aware of contributions of Nevada and San Francisco police to Mark Twain's departures, Western humorists of the day would have enjoyed among themselves the idea that Twain had even a small part in the genesis of Tennessee, whose departures from several towns had been speeded and whose partner loved him and forgave him everything.

[18] Booth, "Mark Twain's Comments on Bret Harte's Stories," *loc. cit.,* 493.

[19] Harte's appraisal of this story as well as his growing prestige is reflected in the fact that for "Tennessee's Partner," Harte collected from the *Overland Monthly* $23, but for "The Illiad of Sandy Bar" he was paid the unprecedented sum of $100. *Overland Monthly,* Ledger, Bancroft.

already invited Harte to come to Boston to talk business, it being Osgood's idea that his two magazines, *The Atlantic Monthly* and *Every Saturday*, should have exclusive rights to Harte's work.[20] New York as well as Boston was angling for the author of "The Luck of Roaring Camp." California, no longer disturbed by the publicity it received from Harte's fiction, tried to hold the author by making him "Professor of Recent Literature and Curator of the Library and Museum" of the young university in Berkeley at a salary of $300 a month. Chicago tried to make him editor of *Lakeside Magazine* and felt rudely rebuffed when the proposed editor failed to appear at a dinner in his honor.[21]

In Chicago, Harte, his wife, and two small sons were visiting Mrs. Harte's relatives,[22] but Harte found time to call on Anna Dickinson, the abolitionist lecturer whom he had met two years earlier in San Francisco and who then happened to be in Chicago. Like others at this time, Miss Dickinson commented on the fact that Harte was singularly unspoiled by all the attention he was receiving. She wrote her mother: "He is *satisfying*:—that is the word for him. . . . I was delighted with the little I saw of him in California, & more than delighted here. . . . He is very quiet, & unassuming,—so say people.—In fact as you watch him you see he knows, as genius always knows, in a steady, unpretentious way, its own power."[23]

Soon after his arrival in the East, Bret Harte signed with the publishers of *The Atlantic Monthly* and *Every Saturday* the contract for "exclusive publication of my poems and sketches (not to be less than twelve in number) in your periodicals for the space of one year commencing March 1, 1871."[24] For the privilege of publishing these as yet unwritten poems and sketches, James R. Osgood and Company agreed to pay the unprecedented sum of $10,000. Furthermore, Osgood decided to republish Harte's *Condensed Novels, and Other Papers,* published in London in 1867 by S. Low, Son and Company the same year it was published by Carleton in New York. And loud in the ears

---

[20] Weber, *James Ripley Osgood*, 115, 120.   [21] *BHAE*, 183, 190–91.

[22] Weber, *James Ripley Osgood*, 120.

[23] James H. Young, "Anna Dickinson, Mark Twain, and Bret Harte," *loc. cit.*, 44–45.

[24] *BHL*, 12. The plural should be noted here in relation to later disagreements about whether Harte fulfilled his contract.

of Mark Twain was Harte's acclaim from many of the world's best-known literary men, including the Brahmins of Boston and Cambridge who turned to Mark Twain only cool New England shoulders.

The late Bernard De Voto noted that passages in *Mark Twain in Eruption* are less reliable as evidence of the actions and characters of Mark Twain's former friends and business associates than as revelations of the mental and emotional processes of Mark Twain.[25] In recalling memories of Harte, Mark Twain's mind in 1906 first harked back to his early days in San Francisco and his job as a reporter for the *Morning Call*, a job which it now seemed to Mark Twain he had lost indirectly because of his own writing about the Chinese and his association with Bret Harte. Mark Twain's digressive account of this experience prefaces his devastating criticisms of Bret Harte in *Mark Twain in Eruption*. If, in his reminiscences of Harte, the sequence of topics about which Twain spoke can be taken as a clue to attitudes unconsciously revealed, it appears that Twain's bitter feeling about Harte was associated with both men's writings about Chinese *before* their unhappy collaboration on *Ah Sin* in 1877.

As Mark Twain remembered it, contrasting with his own reward for writing in defense of Chinese whom he had seen stoned in the streets of San Francisco while police looked on, Harte's "Heathen Chinee" had brought "reverberations of delight which reached the last confines of Christendom," and Harte's name "from being obscure to invisibility" in one week had become "as notorious and as visible in the next as if it had been painted on the sky in letters of astronomical magnitude." Four pages later Mark Twain remembered that when "The Luck of Roaring Camp" "burst upon the world," Harte became "instantly famous; his name and his praises were upon every lip." Since "The Luck" was published almost two years before "Plain Language from Truthful James" and was so admired in England that Charles Dickens invited Harte to contribute to a magazine he edited and to visit him in his home, the name of Bret Harte was not in 1870 "obscure to invisibility."

In these passages of his autobiographical dictations, Mark Twain implicitly asked for a comparison of his own writings about Chinese with Harte's. Such a comparison was made in 1933 by William Pur-

[25] *MTE*, ix–xi.

viance Fenn, then head of the Department of Foreign Languages in the University of Peking. Fenn concluded that of the Western writers (Bret Harte, Prentice Mulford, Mark Twain, Ambrose Bierce, and Joaquin Miller) who defended Chinese by showing hatred of blind prejudice and hypocritical insincerity, "Mark Twain had perhaps least to say." Fenn observed that with Mark Twain, the Chinese were only a passing interest, whereas Bret Harte "throughout his life . . . constantly used his satirical powers on behalf of downtrodden races."[26] Although recent research has discovered more writings by Mark Twain about Chinese than Fenn had examined, the new evidence proves mainly that on this subject as on almost all other subjects, Mark Twain contradicted himself.[27] And a paralleling of Mark Twain's writings about Chinese with Harte's writings about Chinese before the two collaborated on a play about a Chinese character affords considerable support for Fenn's thesis.

Roughing It, written when the furor over Harte was at its height, incorporates in Chapter LIV a column which Mark Twain said he first wrote for the Virginia City *Enterprise.* This column, emphasizing the idiosyncrasies of a peculiar people, would hardly diminish or be intended to diminish Western American prejudice against Orientals. It began with John Chinaman "in all his glory," a "soggy creature," among other "yellow, long tailed vagabonds" smoking opium, "their lustreless eyes turned inward from excess of satisfaction." This sample of Mark Twain's early journalism includes besides the popularly humorous clichés about the Chinaman as a mouse-eater, accounts of a Chinese lottery and Chinese prostitutes. The one thing for which Mark Twain showed real respect was the skill of a Chinese bookkeeper in calculating by abacus.

About the time this account of the Chinese in Virginia City was first published by Mark Twain in Nevada, Bret Harte published in the *Golden Era* of San Francisco an essay entitled "John Chinaman." Harte's essay, like Twain's, began by mentioning Chinese peculiarities, but unlike the Virginia City *Enterprise* sketch, it ended by bluntly identifying "conscious hate and fear with which inferiority always regards the possibility of even-handed justice" as the "keynote to the vulgar

---

[26] Fenn, *Ah Sin*, 33, 34, 45.
[27] For example, see Philip S. Foner, *Mark Twain: Social Critic*, 183-92.

clamor about servile and degraded races."[28] Published eight years later, Mark Twain's introduction to his chapter on the Chinese in *Roughing It* reflects an attitude similar to Harte's. Yet Twain's conclusion to this chapter seems an afterthought, a postscript to Harte's repeated attacks on Californian prejudice against Chinese, including the sketch "John Chinaman" just republished in England and America in Harte's widely praised anthology, *The Luck of Roaring Camp, and Other Sketches.* "No California *gentleman or lady,*" wrote Mark Twain (italicizing the words whose significance for him had increased during his courtship of Olivia Langdon), "ever abuses or oppresses a Chinaman, under any circumstances, an explanation that seems to be much needed in the East."[29]

Characteristically Mark Twain concluded this chapter, entitled in later editions "The Gentle, Inoffensive Chinese," with a name-calling attack on San Francisco police, with whom he continued his personal feud of the Steve Gillis days in San Francisco. "Only the scum of the population" abused the Chinese, Twain said, "they and their children; and naturally and consistently the policemen and politicians, likewise, for these are the dust-licking pimps and slaves of the scum, there as well as elsewhere in America." Five years earlier Bret Harte had denounced San Francisco officials for inadequate courtesy to the visiting Queen of Hawaii and attributed their bad manners to race prejudice in "underbred and underpaid nobodies" to whom had been entrusted the "conduct of a great city."[30] But Bret Harte did not believe that racial discrimination against Chinese was limited to "the scum of the population." And in 1870, when Twain wrote about the "Disgraceful Persecution" of a well-dressed boy who, on his way to Sunday school, threw stones at Chinese, neither did Mark Twain.

Chronologically after the *Enterprise* column included in *Roughing It* came Mark Twain's aborted defense of Chinese in San Francisco in 1864. But when Twain was erupting about that article killed by Mr. Barnes, he probably did not recall a bit of doggerel which he had written about the same time for "M.E.G.'s Album," entitled "The Mysterious Chinaman."[31] Clumsily burlesquing Poe, these stanzas narrate in the

[28] "Bohemian Papers / John Chinaman," *Golden Era* (Apr. 4, 1863). *Writings,* XIV, 223.

[29] *Roughing It,* 397.   [30] *San Francisco in 1866,* 72.

[31] A photostat of this doggerel in Mark Twain's handwriting is in my files.

first person experiences of an individual who found at his chamber door no raven but a drunken Chinaman named Ah Chang, with "shorn and shaven" crest. This "leathery wretch," this "ungainly brute," this "Ghastly, grim and long tailed scullion" had wandered from the kitchen door.

Quoth Ah Chang,/ "No shabby door. (hic!)"

Mark Twain's doggerel is a feeble echo not only of Poe's "The Raven" but also of Harte's parodies of poets including Poe, currently appearing in the *Californian.*[32]

Although they were not his first, Mark Twain's best-known writings about Chinese are his three satires published in *The Galaxy.* The first, entitled "Disgraceful Persecution of a Boy," protested that the boy should not have been arrested and imprisoned for stoning Chinese in San Francisco since he was merely following precepts and examples of his elders. Again Mark Twain's fire concentrated on San Francisco reporters and police.[33] The second *Galaxy* satire about Chinese, "John Chinaman in New York," which appeared in September, 1870, the same month "Plain Language from Truthful James" appeared in the *Overland,* describes, instead of a wooden Indian in front of a cigar store, a man dressed like a Chinaman standing in front of a New York tea store. Sentimental sympathy for Chinese is satirized when the "poor" Chinaman turns out to be an Irishman in disguise.[34] Mark Twain's most vigorous and justly celebrated attack on discriminatory laws and practices against Chinese in California, "Goldsmith's Friend Abroad Again," was published in three installments appearing in October and November, 1870, and in January, 1871.[35] Strangely enough, this third and best *Galaxy* satire attacking abuse of Chinese is the only one not republished in the authorized edition of Mark Twain's writings. It is also

---

[32] For a listing of Harte's parodies of the poets, see George R. Stewart, *A Bibliography of the Writings of Bret Harte in the Magazines and Newspapers of California, 1857–1871,* 148.

[33] *The Galaxy,* Vol. IX (May, 1870), 722. This satire refers to the incident which inspired Mark Twain to write the work allegedly suppressed by Barnes. Now available in *Contributions to* The Galaxy *by Mark Twain,* edited by Bruce R. McElderry, Jr., 42–44.

[34] *The Galaxy,* Vol. X (Sept., 1870).

[35] *Ibid.,* Vol. X (1870), 569, 727; Vol. XI (1871), 156.

the only one published after the phenomenal success of "Plain Language from Truthful James."

All three of these *Galaxy* satires appeared at a crucial period in the national struggle against racial prejudice and discrimination. Reportedly the widespread and hilarious reaction to Harte's "The Heathen Chinee" caused President Ulysses S. Grant to omit from his message to Congress a discussion of the problem of Chinese immigration. And a month after the publication of "Goldsmith's Friend Abroad Again," *Harper's Weekly* editorially attacked Tweed's anti-Chinese labor bill for New York state and published a full-page Nast cartoon captioned "Hands off, Gentlemen! America means fair play for all."[36] Yet as Bruce R. McElderry, Jr., pointed out in his admirable introduction to the facsimile reproductions of *Mark Twain's Contributions to* The Galaxy, *1868–1871*, even though Mark Twain regularly depended upon "staple themes" for material for his humor, he showed complete lack of concern for current protests against the ill treatment of Indians.[37] After a chapter in *Roughing It* devoted considerable space to a portrayal of Indians as "treacherous, filthy and repulsive" beggars and insisted that the only people who could pity the Indians were those who observed them at a distance, concluding sentences which call for Christian sympathy and compassion for "those poor naked creatures" seem even more perfunctory addenda than the concluding paragraph of the *Roughing It* chapter on Chinese.

Although the public excitement over the Chinese question undoubtedly stimulated Twain's own memories of Chinese whom he had observed in Virginia City and San Francisco, several factors other than opposition to race prejudice contributed to his writings about Chinese in *The Galaxy* as well as in *Roughing It*.

Mark Twain's shift from a somewhat xenophobic attitude toward Chinese[38] was largely due to three influences. The first has already been noted: Mark Twain's transition from a journalistic group of writers in Virginia City to a literary group in San Francisco. The second influence was Anson Burlingame, whom Mark Twain regarded with "adoration" after Burlingame in Honolulu praised Twain's writing and helped him with the famous story about survivors of the *Hornet*. This

---

[36] *Contributions to* The Galaxy, xvi–xvii.   [37] *Ibid.*
[38] See Foner, *Mark Twain: Social Critic*, 186.

personal loyalty to Burlingame largely explains Mark Twain's vigorous support of the Burlingame Treaty in 1868.[39] But the most important influence on Mark Twain's writing about Chinese in "Goldsmith's Friend Abroad Again" and in *Roughing It* was the current popularity of Bret Harte.

Mark Twain's biographers frequently use the word "meretricious" in allusions to Harte's renown at this time, and Harte himself would have defended their critical judgment of the popularity he owed "The Heathen Chinee." Yet Mark Twain, the showman, loved the kind of fame and fortune lavished on Bret Harte in 1870 and 1871. Miserable in Buffalo, worried about the health of his wife and at times nearly maddened by the crying of his sickly first-born child, anxious to turn out another book quickly to collect a record-making profit, pressured to lecture and write on subjects of current interest, Mark Twain could hardly fail to be aware of the Chinese problem not only as a topic of the times but also as a strong factor in Bret Harte's mounting reputation. Bret Harte had also defended the Digger Indians, whom he had observed in Uniontown, but it was the fluke of "The Heathen Chinee" that catapulted his fame.

Mark Twain had enthusiastically undertaken the editorship of *The Galaxy's* "Memoranda," believing it an "exceedingly easy" berth at a liberal salary.[40] Acutely conscious of the prestige and independence of publishing in such a journal,[41] he wrote Mrs. Fairbanks that he would rather write for a magazine for two dollars a page than for a newspaper at ten dollars a page: "One takes more pains, the 'truck' looks nicer in print, & one has a pleasanter audience. It is the difference between lecturing in the 'States' & doing the same thing in delectable Nevada."[42] But Mark Twain had a hard time writing his contributions, and more than once furnished scant and uninspired copy instead of the ten pages a month agreed upon for the two thousand dollars a year he was paid.[43] At least one of Mark Twain's contributions to *The Galaxy* was rejected. Not rejected was a joke about an alleged rumor that Louis Agassiz was suffering from "softening of the brain." Referring to a report in the

[39] *Ibid.*, 184–87.   [40] Webster, *Mark Twain: Business Man*, 112.
[41] *Contributions to* The Galaxy, xii.   [42] *Mark Twain to Mrs. Fairbanks*, 132.
[43] Although Mark Twain told Elisha Bliss and Mrs. Fairbanks that he was offered $2,400, he told Mrs. Clemens that he would be paid $2,000. Apparently $2,000 was the sum paid. Mott, *American Magazines*, III, 364.

Journal of Science that the world-famous zoologist and Harvard professor had in one year discovered ten thousand different varieties of fly, Mark Twain's graphic description of the "stately old philosopher" fiercely grabbing and snatching at flies, finally capturing a horsefly with his inverted hat, and "instantly sitting down on it to make the capture a dead moral certainty" anticipates Twain's more celebrated irreverences of New England idols at the Whittier Birthday Dinner.[44]

In August, *The Galaxy* published Mark Twain's picture to appease readers who might feel cheated by diminishing offerings from Twain's pen. From June, 1870, until March, 1871, all Galaxy covers were headed by the announcement "MARK TWAIN, the Great Humorist, writes for Galaxy every month." Mark Twain came to hate the sight of this announcement, not only because he found it dreary to be a "monthly humorist in a cheerless time," but also because he found it extremely galling to rank below Bret Harte in critical esteem and popular attention.

The modern student of American literature has difficulty understanding that Mark Twain could feel his reputation insecure beside Bret Harte's. But as Guy A. Cardwell has pointed out, "Twain's actual achievement was grotesquely underestimated" as late as 1881.[45] It is true that E. L. Godkin's *Nation*, which Mark Twain had reported remarkably "satisfied" with Bret Harte's work in the *Overland*, had also commended some of Mark's "very good things" in "Memoranda." But the praise was hardly the sort to warm the heart of Mark Twain. For the author considered American humorists a queer breed ("a kind of personages whom no other society has produced, and who certainly could in no other society attain celebrity"). When he named the "professionals" (Artemus Ward, Josh Billings, Mark Twain, and Petroleum V. Nasby) the anonymous critic observed that this was "about as odd a profession, by the bye, as has ever been seen." And he noted that although Mark Twain himself had sometimes been "rather vulgar and low," Mark had told some "extraordinarily good stories" and given "not very refined, perhaps, but on the whole harmless amusement to a large number of people."[46] Perhaps what rankled most with Mark Twain at this time was the *Nation's* description of

[44] *Contributions to* The Galaxy, 119.   [45] *Twins of Genius*, 3.
[46] *Contributions to* The Galaxy, xv.

The Galaxy itself as a magazine "born of a divine discontent with the *Atlantic Monthly*."[47]

On January 27, 1871, Mark had written Elisha Bliss that his own popularity was "booming."[48] But Aldrich's Bret Harte Issue of *Every Saturday*, Harte's heralded progress across the continent, his enthusiastic welcome in Cambridge, and finally his signing the ten-thousand-dollar contract with James R. Osgood, publisher of the *Atlantic*, made it seem to Twain that his own boom was comparatively inaudible. To make matters worse, Mark Twain became involved not only in accusing others of "plagiarism" but also in defending himself against the charge.[49] Even his lectures in 1871 brought critical protests that his humor lacked originality and that he was unduly derogatory about Artemus Ward, whose jokes he was appropriating. Mark Twain's lectures now deplored Ward's "coarseness" and implied that the "illiterate showman of the badly-spelled sketches was only the alter ego of Ward himself."[50] In April, Mark Twain gloomily wrote Mrs. Fairbanks that although he was "pegging away" at *Roughing It*, he had little hopes for its success because "The papers have found at last the courage to pull me down off my pedestal & cast slurs at me—& that is simply a popular author's death rattle. Though he wrote an inspired book after that, it would not save him."[51]

DeLancey Ferguson has noted that the success of Bret Harte's stories about California probably prompted Elisha Bliss to propose in July, 1870, that Mark Twain write a book about his own experiences in the West.[52] Although finally *Roughing It* devoted more space to the cross-country journey and experiences in Nevada, when the work was in progress, Mark Twain referred to it as his "California book."[53] In addition to its chapter about Chinese, *Roughing It* includes several reminders of Bret Harte. Instead of the *Overland's* snarling grizzly, which Mark Twain believed Harte transformed into a symbol of the California wilderness opposed to technological invasion, the coyote became Mark Twain's symbol of the vast wilderness of the plains which gave

[47] Mott, *American Magazines*, III, 36.   [48] MTP.

[49] *Mark Twain to Mrs. Fairbanks*, 147–49.

[50] Paul Fatout, *Mark Twain on the Lecture Circuit*, 152–53.

[51] *Mark Twain to Mrs. Fairbanks*, 153.

[52] *Man and Legend*, 155.   [53] *MTL*, I, 185.

the narrator a sense of freedom on those "overland mornings."[54] Chapters LVI and LVII, dealing with the climate and the population in California, resemble Harte's earlier essays in the *Californian* and the *Golden Era*, for at least one of which ("Boonder"), marginalia for *The Luck of Roaring Camp, and Other Sketches* record Mark Twain's admiration. Furthermore, Mark Twain's expository account of the youth and vigor of the Caucasian males in California together with their excitement at the appearance of a woman or child reflects essentially the same point of view as Harte's fictional portrayal of the Argonauts, which California historians sometimes label "perverse romanticism."

More significantly, "Buck Fanshaw's Funeral" includes so many reminders of the currently popular "Tennessee's Partner" that the possibility of a link between the two narratives can hardly be ignored. The most obvious resemblance occurs in the common theme of the devotion of one man to the friend who has died, and here, characteristically, Bret Harte emphasized the pathetic and Mark Twain the ludicrous. But although the style of *Roughing It* generally underscores the differences in the personalities and practices of Mark Twain and Bret Harte, some passages in "Buck Fanshaw's Funeral" sound enough like Bret Harte to have been written by Harte himself. For example, in diction, point of view, and sentence rhythm, the following passage sounds like Harte: "I cannot say which class we buried with more éclat in our 'flush times,' the distinguished public benefactor or the distinguished rough—possibly the two chief grades or grand divisions of society honored their illustrious dead about equally." Henry Nash Smith, who quotes this passage in *Mark Twain, The Development of a Writer*, believes that the conclusion of "Buck Fanshaw's Funeral" shows Mark Twain "now fully identified with the point of view of an upper class that considers itself to be custodian of the official values" and, somewhat contradictorily, an indication that Mark Twain was thinking of his own burlesque of the story of Joseph omitted from *The Innocents Abroad*.[55]

The concluding paragraph of "Buck Fanshaw's Funeral," which reports Scotty Briggs telling "the beautiful story of Joseph and his brethren" to a Sunday-school class and ends with the sentence "I leave it to the reader to fancy what it was like, as it fell, riddled with slang, from

[54] See Henry Nash Smith, *Mark Twain: The Development of a Writer*, 54–56.
[55] *Ibid.*, 63.

the lips of that grave, earnest teacher, and was listened to by his little learners with a consuming interest that showed that they were as unconscious as he was that any violence was being done to the sacred proprieties!" has always seemed to me another obvious echo of Bret Harte. It is a perfect example of the "heart of gold formula" associated with Harte's best-known works, but I have never been sure whether Mark Twain was imitating or mocking the sentimental endings which are, perhaps, the weakest parts of Bret Harte's stories. My belief that "Buck Fanshaw's Funeral" had in Mark Twain's mind some associations with Harte is strengthened by Twain's later intention to use Scotty Briggs in the collaboration with Bret Harte on *Ah Sin*.

Mark Twain had been much taken with Bliss's suggestion that he write a book about the West, particularly since Bliss offered him what at that time was considered an "unprecedented royalty."[56] On July 15, 1870, he began work on the book that would later be given the title *Roughing It*. On that date Sam Clemens wrote his brother Orion that he had signed a contract to have another six-hundred page book ready for his publisher by January 1, that he proposed to "do up Nevada and California, beginning with the trip across the country in a stage," "but that he remembered next to *nothing* about the matter" and thus needed Orion's help with "scenes, names, incidents, or adventures of the coach trip." He explained the urgency of his appeal by the necessity of meeting the deadline in order to receive "the biggest copyright . . . ever paid on a subscription book in this country." Orion responded with a "detailed memorandum" which Mark Twain found very useful, but the proposed book was not ready by the following January.[57]

Writing for *The Galaxy* proved increasingly difficult for Mark Twain. *The Galaxy* for March, 1871, regretfully announced that illness in the Clemens family prevented Mark Twain from furnishing any "Memoranda" that month but promised that the "department so sadly interrupted, will be continued as usual next month."[58] However, on March 4, exactly one month after the publication of Mark Twain's protest about "Three Aces" and Aldrich's "apology" in *Every Saturday*, Sam Clemens wrote Orion his decision "day before yesterday" to get out of *The Galaxy* because he wanted to work on "The California

[56] Ferguson, *Man and Legend*, 155.   [57] *MTL*, I, 174–75.
[58] *The Galaxy*, Vol. XI (Mar., 1871), above "Contents."

book" which was giving him considerable trouble.[59] Two days later Bret Harte signed *his* record-breaking contract. On March 9, 10, and 11, Mark Twain published in the Buffalo *Express* a denial that he planned to withdraw from that paper. "I am a permanency here," he wrote. "I am prospering well enough to please my friends and distress my enemies, and consequently am in a state of tranquil satisfaction." As he had requested Aldrich to correct his misstatement about "Three Aces," Mark Twain now asked journals publishing reports of his withdrawal to correct *their* statements.[60] Yet in less than a month he had sold his interest in the Buffalo *Express* at a loss of $10,000.[61] In the same month Mark Twain's "Valedictory" contribution to "Memoranda" appeared in *The Galaxy*.

Although Mark Twain was now disparagingly referring to his *Galaxy* publishers as "those shuffling gentlemen,"[62] his withdrawals from *The Galaxy* and from the Buffalo *Express* were largely motivated by his passionate determination to get ahead of Bret Harte.

Five days after Bret Harte signed the contract with James R. Osgood and Company, Mark Twain, on March 11, 1871, wrote Orion that he loathed the sight of his "hated nom de plume" in *The Galaxy*, and that he had decided to "keep shady and quiet" for a while.[63] This long, exasperated letter protested an announcement in the *American Publisher*, which Orion edited, that Mark Twain would be a regular contributor. "I have suffered damnation itself in the trammels of periodical writing, and I will not appear *once* a month, nor once in *three* months in the *Publisher*, nor any other periodical," wrote Mark Twain. He felt that he had already cheapened himself by a "year's periodical dancing before the public." All night he had stayed awake "aggravating himself with the thought of seeing the detested name of Mark Twain in print again every month. Mark vowed that after Harte quieted down, he would get ahead and stay there until he published "two books already contracted for and just one more besides, which latter shall make a ripping sensation or I have overestimated the possibilities of my subject." Six paragraphs later in the same letter, Twain repeated: "The

[59] *MTL*, I, 185–86.   [60] MTP.
[61] Ferguson, *Man and Legend*, 157.   [62] *Contributions to* The Galaxy, xiv.
[63] The late Dixon Wecter quotes part of this letter on page 152 of *Mark Twain to Mrs. Fairbanks*. Another part is quoted by Frederick Anderson in his introduction to *"Ah Sin," A Dramatic Work by Mark Twain and Bret Harte*.

man who says the least about me in any paper for three months to come will do me the greatest favor. I tell you I mean to *go slow*. I will 'top' Bret Harte again or bust. But I can't do it by dangling eternally in the public view."[64] To this letter Mark added a long and equally vehement postscript that after a two-day cooling-off period, he felt the same way, only more so.

By the middle of May, Mark Twain was feeling much better. From Elmira he wrote Elisha Bliss acknowledging a substantial check for the "old 'Innocents' " which "holds out handsomely." (As a matter of fact, *The Innocents Abroad* paid Mark Twain $1,200 to $1,500 a month, which, of course, in a year's time brought considerably more than the $10,000 guaranteed Harte by the contract with Osgood.[65]) Expecting his next book to pay even better, Mark Twain announced that he was now thoroughly interested in his work on *Roughing It*, "a thing I have not experienced for months."[66] He had acquired another valuable assistant. Joe Goodman was with him at Quarry Farm, wrote by his side every day, and proved so useful that Mark Twain offered him a salary. Mark felt that his former editor in chief on the *Enterprise* was just the man for "accurate drudgery" and "some little other writing."[67] Mr. Goodman declined the salary but prolonged his visit to Twain in order to help him. On December 6, 1871, Mark Twain copyrighted *Roughing It*.[68]

The year, which had begun with a princely progress east of the man whose writing had focused attention on the West as a literary gold mine, ended with the publication of Mark Twain's challenge to the triumph of Bret Harte.

[64] Typescript in MTP. [65] MTP. Letter file, July–Dec., 1870.
[66] *MTL*, I, 187.

[67] *Ibid*. See also Webster, *Mark Twain: Business Man*, 118–19. This proposition to Goodman, with Twain's appraisal of his former editor, parallels a proposal which Mark Twain made to Bret Harte after the collaboration on *Ah Sin*.

[68] *Mark Twain to Mrs. Fairbanks*, 160n.

6

THE KEELER LUNCHEON

Harte's bright wit . . . consisted solely of sneers and sarcasm.

Mark Twain in Eruption

WHEN, IN 1871, Bret Harte arrived in the East, where Mark Twain had lived for more than three years, Harte, his wife, and two small sons were promptly entertained by Mr. and Mrs. William Dean Howells in Cambridge. In 1903, Howells would report not only his gratification at the warm friendliness of the celebrity but also Howells' misgivings when both Mr. and Mrs. Harte expressed a preference for Nature in New England to Nature in California, and Howells' trials and tribulations as host to a mercurial guest.[1] But immediately after the visit in 1871, intimate family letters of both Mr. and Mrs. Howells reflect some exhaustion after an exciting time but no misgivings. Howells wrote his father that he and Mrs. Howells had met "no young people so congenial" and that the visit was "one of the pleasantest that we've ever had made us."[2] Unlike the Howells-Clemens relationship, the Howells-Harte friendship seems immediately to have achieved a first-name basis, with Mrs. Howells casually referring to "Bret" as well as to "Will." Harte's voice and laughter reminded Howells of his own brother Joe, whom he wanted Harte to meet. In fact, the Howellses and the Hartes had discovered so much in common that they talked of a vacation together at the seashore.

The visit had come about through a "pleasant correspondence" between the assistant editor of the *Atlantic* and the editor of the *Overland* before Harte left San Francisco. As Howells said later, "only by chance," could Harte "be caught in earnest about anything or any-

[1] Howells, "Editor's Easy Chair," *Harper's Magazine*, Vol. CVIII (Dec., 1903), 154.

[2] *Life in Letters of William Dean Howells*, 159.

body,"[3] and a typical Bret Harte letter to Howells, dated November 5, 1870, included a mocking allusion to the "breezy freshness" which Eastern critics were "fond of finding in the *Overland*" and, apparently in response to something Howells had written earlier, a mocking question about whether Howells really pursued his pleasures "grimly" with the intention of gaining food for later thought. But the mockery was followed by an indication that Harte was reading Howells' writings with real perception and appreciation, and the letter ended with an apostrophe to Howells: "O most excellent writer of excellent English."[4] Well pleased, Howells responded by inviting Harte to visit him at his home when Harte came east. On learning that Mrs. Harte and the children would be with Bret Harte in Boston early in 1871, Howells extended his invitation to the whole family.[5]

Mrs. Howells immediately began planning a party—her first in Cambridge, though the Howells family had lived there for five years. Thus Mrs. Howells became one of many hostesses who, throughout Harte's long career at home and abroad, considered Bret Harte a great prize as a dinner guest.[6] Of Mrs. Howells' party for Bret Harte, Howells reported to his father that it was "generally allowed to be one of the most brilliant ever given in Cambridge." And after her house guests had departed for New York, Mrs. Howells wrote her sister-in-law a glowing account of her triumph. "The visit went off splendidly," she said, "but *the party!* How shall I do justice to it?" Sarah Sedgwick had been thrilled to meet the author of "The Outcasts of Poker Flat." Another friend got up from a sickbed to attend the party.[7] And citizens of Cambridge not included in the guest list found many reasons to pass back and forth in front of the Howells' home, where they hoped to catch a glimpse of the famous man from California. For as Mrs. Howells said, "There had been a perfect furore over Bret Harte's writings among nice people here, and he was received with open arms."

The Howells' party was only the beginning of the festivities in Cambridge and Boston. So many requested the pleasure of Harte's company that invitations "from every quarter" had to be declined. At one dinner party, Louis Agassiz put his arm in Harte's and confidently drew

---

[3] Howells, "Editor's Easy Chair," *loc. cit.*, 156.   [4] *Life in Letters*, 158.
[5] *Ibid.*, 160.   [6] For example, see Pemberton, *The Life of Bret Harte*, 222.
[7] *Life in Letters*, 160–61.

the young author aside to discuss "their mutual scientific interest in the last meeting of the geological 'Society upon the Stanislow,'" an allusion to another of the verse monologues of Truthful James.[8] To Harte's amusement, the learned Professor Agassiz even quoted Harte's satiric verses, including the thesis:

> *. . . it is not decent for a scientific gent*
> *To say another is an ass,—at least to all intent;*
> *Nor should the individual who happens to be meant*
> *Reply by heaving rocks at him, to any great extent.*[9]

Writing about his dinners with Harte at Longfellow's, Agassiz' and Fields's, Howells told his father that "it seemed a little absurd for a host to be following his guest about in this way," but Harte had insisted and Howells had enjoyed the experience. Other New Englanders who extended warm and friendly welcomes to Harte at this time included Richard Henry Dana, Julia Ward Howe, Oliver Wendell Holmes, and John Greenleaf Whittier. (Harte was particularly drawn to the abolitionist poet by the strong affection each held for Thomas Starr King.[10]) About Bret Harte's welcome in the East, Bernard De Voto commented bitterly that New England houses "incapable of opening to Mark Twain" received as late as 1875 this "schoolteacher and the son of schoolteachers," whose "sympathy embedded in sweet tales, greatly comforted the nice people."[11]

Although by 1903, Howells had lost much of his enthusiasm for his early friend, his description of the appearance and manner of Bret Harte at the time of the memorable visit affords an interesting comparison with the description in Mark Twain's autobiographical dictations. "He was then, as always, a child of extreme fashion as to his clothes and the cut of his beard," wrote Howells, but his "jovial physiognomy . . . with its straight nose, and fascinating forward thrust of the under lip, its fine eyes, and good forehead, then thickly crowned

[8] Howells, "Editor's Easy Chair," *loc. cit.*, 155. See also William Dean Howells, *Literary Friends and Acquaintances*, 272.

[9] "The Society Upon the Stanislaus," *Writings*, XII, 133.

[10] See manuscript 12471 in the Henry E. Huntington Library, San Marino, California.

[11] *Mark Twain's America*, 191–92.

with . . . black hair" was as winning as his remarkably beautiful voice. As for Harte's reaction to the homage of Cambridge, Howells in 1903 commented somewhat obliquely that "If he took the honors easily that were paid him he took them modestly, and never by word or look invited them or implied he expected them."[12] In 1871, Howells had stated flatly and directly: "Harte is quite unspoiled by his great popularity—which he values at its true worth—and is a thoroughly charming good-hearted fellow."[13]

It was after Harte's visit in Cambridge that Howells was promoted to the position of editor in chief of *The Atlantic Monthly*.

In the same year Mark Twain as well as Bret Harte occasionally joined William Dean Howells and Thomas Bailey Aldrich in Boston for prolonged luncheons, described by Albert Bigelow Paine as periods of "anecdote, reminiscence, and mirth."[14] On November 12, 1871, Mark Twain directed Elisha Bliss to send complimentary copies of *The Innocents Abroad* to the editor of the *Atlantic* and the editor of *Every Saturday*. Mark Twain volunteered the information that he frequently dined with these editors. He asked his publisher also to send a complimentary copy to Ralph Keeler, an eager young man who had been host at a luncheon where there occurred an incident often mentioned in comments on the relationship between Mark Twain and Bret Harte.[15]

Ralph Keeler (identified by Van Wyck Brooks as a prototype for Fulkerson in *A Hazard of New Fortunes*[16]) had contributed to *Every Saturday* and had published a little-known book entitled *Vagabond Adventures*, recording some of his own colorful history. Born in Ohio, he had run away from home to become a clog dancer in a Negro minstrel show but had become instead a cabin boy and bootblack on a steamboat. He had run away from a Mississippi showboat called *The Floating Palace* to study at a Jesuit college in Missouri, only to escape from college to Europe and from Europe to Boston by the roundabout way of California, where he had been a reporter for the *Alta California*.[17]

---

[12] "Editor's Easy Chair," *loc. cit.*, 155.   [13] *Life in Letters*, 159.
[14] *MTL*, I, 192.   [15] Letter to Elisha Bliss, Nov. 12, 1871, MTP. *MTH*, I, 7.
[16] *Howells: His Life and World*, 193.
[17] Howells, *Life in Letters*, I, 137; *Dictionary of American Biography*, X, 279–80.

His life in California was the basis of his claim to friendship with Twain and Harte.

In 1871, Keeler was a proofreader on the *Atlantic* staff. He sometimes accompanied Mark Twain on lecture tours in the Boston area, and at these times the young man's eagerness and naïveté afforded Twain considerable amusement.[18] In all the flurry about Harte and the famous contract in the *Atlantic* offices, Keeler remembered that Harte had published an article of his in the *Overland* in 1869. With pleasure the young proofreader now found that his California editor, far from being changed by recent acclaim, was the same friendly, cordial human being he had known in San Francisco. Consequently Keeler decided to give at the famed Ober's in Boston a luncheon at which Harte would be the guest of honor. Other guests at the Keeler luncheon included not only Aldrich, editor of *Every Saturday;* and Howells, editor of *The Atlantic Monthly;* but also James T. Fields, retired publisher of the *Atlantic.* As Howells remembered it, the Keeler luncheon marked the introduction of Mark Twain to the group.[19]

Because some years later Keeler mysteriously disappeared one dark night from the deck of a steamer bound for Cuba, where he was headed to report an "insurrection," the young man was eventually somewhat romanticized by his famous luncheon guests. In a poem entitled "Lost at Sea," Aldrich commemorated his death, and both Howells and Twain included him in their memoirs. They all liked him, but in 1871 they were apt to make good-natured fun of him—as they did at the Keeler luncheon.

Although the adventurous host had spent more than he could afford, the occasion turned into one of those affairs where everything goes wrong. The beefsteak came in with the flattened soufflé, and Aldrich insisted on calling the mushrooms "shoepegs." As the luncheon progressed, the guests—those dignified arbiters of Eastern literary journals —became increasingly convivial and hilarious. Howells reported that it was "in every way what a Boston literary lunch ought not to have been in the popular ideal."[20] But the shock came in the midst of a "cursing can-of-peaches story" by James T. Fields, when Bret Harte

[18] *Mark Twain's Autobiography*, edited by Albert Bigelow Paine, I, 160–64.
[19] Howells, "Editor's Easy Chair," *loc. cit.*, 156. [20] *My Mark Twain*, 7.

allegedly put his hand on the sealskin-clad shoulder of Mark Twain, the newcomer, and sputtered out, "This is the dream of his life."[21]

Everyone agrees that Harte's words were inept and in poor taste. George R. Stewart finds the remark "one of the few jarring notes in Harte's visit to Boston."[22]

We know about Bret Harte's barb at the Keeler luncheon only from Howells' reports written thirty years after the incident. And Howells' reactions show considerable ambivalence. In *My Mark Twain* (1910), Howells reported that Twain's immediate response to Harte's words was "a glance from under Clemen's feathery eyebrows" which betrayed his "enjoyment of the fun."[23] After all, there were "joint mockeries" which occasionally concentrated on their host, "who took it gladly." Nevertheless, in 1902, at the news of Harte's death, the scene which flashed before Howells' eyes was the Keeler luncheon, Harte's hand on Twain's shoulder, and Harte's jeering words.[24] In 1903, Howells began his *Harper's* account of the incident by remarking that although Harte was a tease, his teasing was "of the quality of a caress, so much kindness went with it."[25] But if, during the years, Howells had maintained some affection for Harte, he had developed much more affection for Twain. At the time of Mark's death in 1910, Howells was a "desolate" old man mourning for a marvelous friend whom suddenly Death had "set apart from all other men in a strange majesty."[26] And for Howells at that time, the dominant impression of the earlier incident was that the discourse of the Keeler luncheon—"so little improving, but so full of good fellowship"—had been interrupted by Bret Harte's "fleering dramatization of Clemens's mental attitude towards a Symposium of Boston illuminates."[27]

In the memory it is possible for a little bruise to spread and blacken. At "convivial" luncheons, words are apt to escape from restraint, and in the ensuing years Howells would make allowances for statements by Mark Twain which had been far more unrestrained than Bret Harte's

[21] Howells, *Life in Letters*, I, 157. As far as I have been able to discover, this letter to Aldrich dated May 7, 1902, was Howells' first written mention of the incident.

[22] *BHAE*, 194.   [23] Pages 6–7.

[24] Howells, *Life in Letters*, 157.

[25] Howells, "Editor's Easy Chair," *loc. cit.*, 156.

[26] Clara Clemens, *My Father*, 291.   [27] *My Mark Twain*, 6.

on this occasion. Furthermore, in public lectures earlier in the year, Mark Twain himself had been considerably more patronizing of his old friend Artemus Ward, whose humor Mark compared unfavorably with Harte's.[28] Bret's words at the Keeler luncheon stuck in Howells' mind mainly because Howells recognized an element of painful truth in their implications about Mark Twain's attitude toward the "Boston illuminates."

According to Bernard De Voto, "Harte could not withhold a sneer at Mark's advancement."[29] But at that time, Mark Twain had not advanced far among New Englanders. The editors of the Twain-Howells letters believe that Howells remembered the Keeler luncheon "vividly" but doubt the reliability of his memory when he reported: "Clemens seemed not to hit the favor of our community of scribes and scholars as Bret Harte had done, when he came from California and swept them before him, disrupting their dinners and delaying their lunches with impunity, but it is certain he did not, and I had better say so."[30] It has been suggested that Mark Twain's invitation to speak at a dinner given in January, 1875, by H. O. Houghton and Company for "a few of the contributors" to the *Atlantic* "tends to refute" this recollection of Howells, but the Houghton dinner at which Mark Twain was one of twenty-eight guests was held eight years after Mark Twain came East."[31] Most Mark Twain biographers, including Albert Bigelow Paine, have agreed that at those dinners in and around Boston in the early 1870's, Harte was lionized whereas Mark Twain, if present, "sat below the salt."

However that may be, it seems clear that at these social gatherings with Eastern literati, Bret Harte was far less impressed by the company he kept than was Mark Twain. In 1866, when Anson Burlingame in Honolulu had commented on Mark Twain's genius, he had advised the writer that what he needed was "refinement of association." "Seek companionship among men of superior intellect and character," he said. "Refine yourself and your work. Never affiliate with inferiors; always climb."[32] Mark Twain did not really need that advice. Just as in San Francisco seven years before the Keeler luncheon, Mark had been proud

---

[28] Fatout, *Mark Twain on the Lecture Circuit*, 153.
[29] *Mark Twain's America*, 163.   [30] *My Mark Twain*, 47.   [31] MTH, I, 53.
[32] See Paine, *Biography*, 287, 731.

of his affiliation with the *Californian* because it circulated "among the highest class of the community" and was the "best weekly literary paper in the United States," he now considered New England's Brahmins the highest class in the community and the *Atlantic* the best literary monthly in the United States. In 1871, Mark wrote his sister-in-law Mollie Clemens that making friends in Yankeeland was "a slow, slow business," but when friends *were* made there, they were friends worth having. He believed no section in America "half so good to live in as splendid old New England," no city "so lovely and lovable as Boston, almost in sight of which" it was then Mollie's "high privilege to live."[33]

Not until November, 1874, was Mark Twain's work accepted for publication in *The Atlantic Monthly*. Then, after a careful appraisal, the editors concluded that they were very generous in paying Mark Twain sixty dollars for "A True Story" in recognition of the literary value of its three pages.[34] Although this sum amounted to only two and one-half cents a word and Mark Twain could command double that sum, "no acceptance, then or later, ever made [Twain] happier, or seemed more richly rewarded" than this first acceptance of his work by the *Atlantic*. "And thus," observed Paine, "Mark Twain entered into the school of the elect."[35] According to Howells, Mark Twain submitted so readily to revisions of his contributions that his proof sheets came back a veritable "mush of concession."[36]

Moreover, for his wife's sake if not for his own, Clemens was apparently willing to submit to social as well as literary revisions. Mrs. James T. Fields, the wife of the publisher, was a woman of discernment who recorded in her diary impressions of the two young married couples— the Clemenses and the Hartes—in their early days in the East. She saw Harte as "a dramatic, lovable creature, with his blue silk pocket-handkerchief and red dressing slippers, and his quick feelings," entirely too casual about time and money. Mrs. Harte seemed to her "not handsome

---

[33] Webster, *Mark Twain: Business Man*, 118.

[34] See Edward Weeks and Emily Flint, editors, *Jubilee*; see *also MTH*, I, 25–26.

[35] *Biography*, 514. In 1875, Mark Twain wrote Stoddard that he was writing a series of articles for the *Atlantic* at $20 a page, which was more than they paid anybody else. He was not satisfied with the price but he put up with it without complaint because, he said, "the awful respectability of the magazine makes up." *MTL*, I, 248.

[36] *My Mark Twain*, 19.

but with good honest sense," "appreciative," of her husband but in this period of Harte's triumph "not certainly at her best." Mrs. Clemens she described as "so white and delicate and tender"—and so self-controlled, and Mr. Clemens as idolizing his wife but often bringing the blood to her face by his "bad behavior," which was apt to be due to forgetfulness and to be followed by abject remorse. "It cannot be altogether easy to have care of such a man" wrote Mrs. Fields, yet it seemed to her that Mark Twain "spent the larger part of his life on his knees making apologies. . . . His wife had told him to see how well we behaved (poor we) and he knew he had everything to learn."[37]

In 1866, Bret Harte had informed Massachusetts readers of the Springfield *Republican* that in California, where, after all, visiting celebrities were by no means rare, there was little obsequiousness. Men and women pass for what they are worth from a California standard, he had said, and he had insisted that California sentiment ran "rather to satire and skepticism than to tuft-hunting and toad-eating."[38]

In Cambridge and Boston five years later, Bret Harte had acted—sometimes regrettably—by this pattern. Bret Harte was never overawed by Eastern literary men, even by Emerson, with whom Harte sturdily maintained his own intellectual self-reliance.[39] Few besides Longfellow (whom Harte venerated[40]) escaped what Howells described as Harte's "corrosive touch of subtle irreverence." But New Englanders also recognized that Bret Harte "did not apparently care to hear himself praised but could very accurately and perfectly" discern excellence in others. Because of this perceptiveness and discrimination, even James Russell Lowell had, for a time at least, a friendly feeling toward Bret Harte.[41] Ironically, most of the Brahmins seemed to enjoy Harte's irreverences, whereas Howells described as a "hideous mistake" Mark Twain's most famous attempt at familiarity with New England's immortals.

[37] "Bret Harte and Mark Twain in the 'Seventies,' Passages from the Diaries of Mrs. James T. Fields," edited by M. A. DeWolfe Howe, *The Atlantic Monthly*, Vol. CXXX (Sept., 1922), 342–48.

[38] *San Francisco in 1866*, 71.

[39] *BHAE*, 202–203.

[40] Mrs. Fields's account of Harte's walk with Longfellow contradicts Mark Twain's assertion that Harte was incapable of strong and sincere feeling. "Bret Harte and Mark Twain in the 'Seventies,' " *loc. cit.*, 344.

[41] Howells, "Editor's Easy Chair," *loc. cit.*, 155.

This context explains but does not excuse the ineptness of Harte's words about Mark Twain at Keeler's luncheon. But more important and certainly more representative of Harte's real sentiment is his tribute to Mark Twain in a lecture on "American Humor" delivered in Farwell Hall, Chicago, on December 10, 1874, and again in Association Hall, New York, on January 26, 1875. At that time Bret Harte repeated his critical judgment expressed earlier in California, a judgment to which he would adhere consistently for the rest of his life: "Mark Twain stands alone as the most original humorist that America has yet produced."

Harte added: "He alone is inimitable."[42] By this time, Bret Harte knew how painful to Mark Twain had been Aldrich's belief that Twain had feebly imitated the best-known example of Harte's humor. And Harte's words were intended not to probe but to heal a wound.

[42] "American Humor," *The Lectures of Bret Harte,* edited by Charles Meeker Kozlay, 26–27.

7

THE BEGINNING OF ANOTHER FRIENDSHIP AND THE END OF A CONTRACT

I have been lately pretty well abused from unexpected sources.

BRET HARTE to MARK TWAIN, December, 1872

WHEN MARK TWAIN directed his publisher, Elisha Bliss, to send complimentary copies of *The Innocents Abroad* to William Dean Howells, "editor, 'Atlantic,' " and Thomas Bailey Aldrich, "editor, 'Every Saturday,' " he specified that the copies should be sent in care of James R. Osgood and Company.[1] Although Mark Twain told Bliss that he had dined with Howells and Aldrich more than once, Twain recognized that in November, 1871, both Howells and Aldrich were acquaintances rather than personal friends.

As early as December, 1869 (one month before Harte's review in the *Overland*), Howells had reviewed *The Innocents Abroad* in the *Atlantic*. When Mark Twain called at the office of James T. Fields to thank the publisher for the favorable review, Fields had introduced him to the reviewer, who was readily forgiven his consistent misspelling of the new author's name as "Clements." Mark Twain had long been wanting to meet Howells and to cultivate an association with the *Atlantic*, for he was acutely conscious of the "influential position" of an *Atlantic* editor.[2] But the acquaintance with Howells, begun in 1869, was slow in developing. Not until five years later did Mark Twain achieve the coveted status of a contributor to the *Atlantic*.[3]

"A True Story," Mark Twain's first writing published by this revered New England journal, had for its subject the sufferings of a slave mother as reported by a white narrator who in post-slavery days

[1] *MTH*, 7–8.
[2] *Ibid.*, I, 5, 109n. Characteristically, the facetiousness clothed essential truth.
[3] *Ibid.*, I, 7, 9.

74

employed the Negro woman as a cook. In Mark Twain's prose sketch, the Union Army plays a liberating role akin to that symbolized in Bret Harte's poem "Banks and the Slave Girl," published in the *Golden Era* on October 26, 1862. But "A True Story" is closer kin to Howells' "The Pilot's Story," an early poem which had gained for this other Westerner a place among the elect. Published in the *Atlantic* in September, 1860, "The Pilot's Story" had for its subject the sufferings of a slave mother as reported by a Mississippi River boat pilot. To Howells' embarrassment, newspapers sometimes republished his rather fervidly romantic verses in prose form.[4] As the title indicates, Mark Twain's "A True Story" (which appeared in the *Atlantic* for November, 1874) is more realistic than the verse narratives of either of his literary mentors, Harte or Howells.

Coincidentally, just as Mark Twain's friendship with Thomas Bailey Aldrich had begun with correspondence about Bret Harte, Twain's first direct communication with Howells of which there is a record also involved Harte. This communication was a telegram sent on January 7, 1872, to W. D. Howells at the *Atlantic* office asking Howells to relay to Bret Harte, Mark Twain's telegram about the plight of a "sick & needy poet," W. A. Kendall. Twain asked Harte to head a petition to a steamship company for Kendall's free passage back to California and directed Harte to sign the names of Clemens, Howells, "and the other boys" to the petition. There is no clue as to whether Howells had been asked if he wanted his name signed, but Twain's wire indicated that he himself would send the poet fifty dollars. Mark Twain was then in Wooster, Ohio, on a lecture tour on which he said he "squandered no end of money," including seventy-five dollars to hire a locomotive so that he would not have to get up at two o'clock in the morning to catch a train.[5] That the *Atlantic* was Harte's publisher and Howells was known as Harte's friend and host may explain why Mark Twain chose so indirect a way of communicating with Harte.

Twain's first two letters to Howells show the man from Hannibal, Missouri, busily cultivating his acquaintance with the two New Eng-

[4] Gordon S. Haight, "Realism Defined: William Dean Howells," in *Literary History of the United States*, edited by Robert E. Spiller *et al.*, II, 887.

[5] *LL*, 172. See also Fatout, *Mark Twain on the Lecture Circuit*, 170; *MTH*, I, 9.

land editors. One letter, dated June 15, 1872, thanked Howells for a complimentary copy of one of Howells' own books, informed Howells that *Roughing It* had been "bought & paid for" by thirty thousand people, and sent "love" to Howells and "the other Atlantics & Every Saturdays."[6] Twain's second letter to Howells expressed Mark's pleasure in Howells' complimentary review of *Roughing It* in the latest issue of the *Atlantic* and included the famous comment that Mark Twain felt like a mother relieved to learn that her baby had turned out to be white when she feared it would be mulatto.[7] This letter was also written in June, 1872.

Before this time, Mark Twain and Bret Harte had resumed cordial relations approaching their old intimacy in California. On April 1, 1872, perhaps aware that Mrs. Clemens thought a humorist something "perfectly awful,"[8] Bret Harte jokingly proposed that a marriage be arranged between his son Franky and Twain's new daughter Susy, provided the father of the girl would furnish adequate dowry and earn his living by some means other than writing humor. The letter shows Harte in a mood of affectionate gaiety indulging in a bit of April foolery:

217 East 49th St.
April 1st '72

My dear Clemens,

Thank you for your remembrance, and accept the hearty congratulations of this household. I was, I confess, slightly surprised; Mrs. Harte by some occult feminine instinct was not. These women assume a superiority at such times which is simply disgusting.

I am glad its a girl. If she behaves herself she shall marry my Franky, provided her father does the right thing in the way of dowry and relinquishes humor as a profession. My Franky has early exhibited those talents calculated to render a woman happy, and as a circus rider, car conductor, Negro minstrel or butcher's boy would attain professional eminence.

What I want to say, however, is that we send all kinds of good wishes to you and yours, and let loose a shower of blessings on the cradle of the little stranger. My wife, I think accepts it as a good omen for herself, and in her present not very robust state she needs that com-

[6] Howells' book is identified in *MTH* as probably *Their Wedding Journey*. *MTH*, I, 10.

[7] *Ibid.*, I, 11.   [8] *Mark Twain to Mrs. Fairbanks*, 63.

fort. I hope before another six weeks passes you can return these congratulations four-fold—no! thats too many!—I mean in kind.

Mrs. Harte sends her sympathetic love to your wife and I am always

Yours

BRET HARTE[9]

On June 13, 1872, Mrs. Warner of Nook Farm wrote her husband
George (brother of Charles Dudley Warner) that Mark Twain had
just dropped by on his way from the carriage shed to tell her that he
was going to the station at a quarter of five for Bret Harte, who was
coming for a visit. "I hope I shall get a sight of him," Mrs. Warner
said. She and Twain both wished that George could be present.[10] Apparently the Twain family and the citizens of Hartford, like the citizens of Cambridge, looked upon Bret Harte's visit as something of an
occasion.

Two days later Twain wrote his third letter to Howells. He was
obviously in great good humor, he showed growing self-assurance, and
he made several references to Bret Harte. In the gay, facetious spirit
later to characterize his bombardment of Aldrich with twenty of his
own photographs in separate packages, Mark now inquired of Howells
how he could get a copy of Howells' portrait published in *Hearth and
Home*. Twain said he wanted this portrait to hang in his parlor beside
the portraits of Oliver Wendell Holmes and "Bret Harte's as published in Every Saturday." "If I had yours to put alongside of them,
I believe the combination would bring more souls to earnest reflection
and ultimate conviction of their lost condition than any other kind of
warning would."[11] Twain wrote that he was sending his own portrait
to Howells. Bret Harte, he said, had just visited the Twain's home in
Hartford. Harte had insisted that "his family would not be without
[Howells'] portrait for any consideration." Bret Harte had said that
"his children get up in the night and yell for it." Mark Twain added
a postscript: "62,000 copies of 'Roughing It' sold and delivered in 4
months."

During this summer Mark Twain worked on the book later to
become famous as *The Adventures of Tom Sawyer*. At the time of

---

[9] Hitherto unpublished letter, MTP.
[10] Quotation from Mrs. Warner's letter of June 13, 1872. See Index File, MTP.
[11] Paine, *Biography*, 537–38; *MTH*, I, 11–12, 63.

his letter to Howells, Mark Twain knew, no doubt, that Bret Harte's enviable "Atlantic Monthly contract" had not been renewed.

When Bret Harte signed the contract with James R. Osgood and Company, ten thousand dollars seemed a very large sum. Harte did not face the fact that twelve was a large number of stories and poems for him to produce in a year. And while, as a newly discovered celebrity, he was dined and copiously wined and enjoyed as the best of company, where were the time and seclusion he needed for writing? Not at home. Not abroad. During that first year Bret Harte lived gaily, so that Howells would remember him as "a part of our youth that was glad and knew it."[12] But by the end of the year Harte had contributed to the *Atlantic* only seven compositions.[13]

Although he had missed the end-of-year deadline, Harte continued to furnish material to make up the deficiency. That he honestly believed he had done so is indicated by a letter written to James R. Osgood from Morristown on December 12, 1873. Surprised to learn from Osgood that the publisher believed his account still short of the promised number, Harte listed the equivalent of seven short stories and seven poems, making a total not of twelve, as promised, but of fourteen works submitted. Since his contract was with the publishing firm rather than the *Atlantic* magazine, and since the contract specified publication of Harte's poems and sketches in Osgood's "periodicals," Harte included on his list two contributions to *Every Saturday*. With Osgood's consent, one long story which Osgood had published as a book was counted the equivalent of two stories in the *Atlantic*. In addition, Harte had offered Osgood "Handsome Is As Handsome Does," a parody of Charles Reade's novel *Put Yourself in His Place*. Wayne Burns, author of *Charles Reade, A Study in Victorian Authorship*, considers Harte's parody "brilliant."[14] But in the 1870's, because of his own business relations with Charles Reade, Osgood decided not to publish one author's satire of the work of another author in the same publishing "stable." It seemed to Bret Harte that, though tardily, he had sent his publisher even more than he had promised; nevertheless, when

[12] *Life in Letters*, II, 156.

[13] *BHAE*, 207. Howells was mistaken in saying that Harte contributed only one story and two or three poems. See Howells, "Editor's Easy Chair," *loc. cit.*, 158.

[14] See pages 276–78.

he learned that Osgood was dissatisfied, he offered to furnish another sketch or poem without charge.[15]

Like many another author publishing with Osgood's firm, Bret Harte more than once urged Osgood to furnish him with a statement of his account.[16] Far from being arrogant about his own position in relation to the contract, Harte now asked Osgood to parallel Harte's own list with a list showing the publisher's reckoning of what Harte had submitted and what he still owed.[17] But Osgood, with all his enterprises and all his geniality and generosity to his authors, was hardly more systematic as a businessman than was Harte himself. Whether Osgood furnished the statement requested by Harte I do not know, but the records show that James Osgood and Bret Harte remained friends.

Critics who concede that Harte submitted the number of works agreed upon nevertheless maintain that he did not live up to the spirit of the contract because the quality of his work was inferior. A writer seldom exercises complete control of the level of his own work. After the initial surprise and delight evoked by Harte's earliest stories of California and the succeeding furor over "Plain Language from Truthful James," Harte's next writing was almost inevitably anti-climactic. Generally rated the best of the lot submitted to the *Atlantic* in fulfillment of the contract is "How Santa Claus Came to Simpson's Bar," selected to represent Harte in the *Atlantic's Jubilee*. This story represents Harte at his most sentimental. More interesting to readers of the twentieth century, I believe, would be "The Princess Bob and Her Friends." In a Kafkaesque combination of realistic details and ironic allegory, this portrayal of an Indian girl on the frontier of 1860 condemns the mistreatment of Indians not only by the frontiersmen but also by uniformed soldiers engaged in a great civil war to test the durability of a nation conceived in liberty and dedicated to the proposition that all men are equal. Also published in the *Atlantic* during the year of Harte's alleged default was Harte's poem "Concepcion de Arguello," which Josiah Royce believed the best thing Harte ever wrote.[18] Not all of Harte's work appearing in the *Atlantic* during that disastrous year was as inferior to his earlier work as it is reputed to be.

---

[15] *BHL*, 14.   [16] Weber, *James Ripley Osgood*, 137–38.   [17] *BHL*, 13–14.
[18] *California, from the Conquest in 1846 to the Second Vigilance Committee in San Francisco: A Study of American Character*, 15.

Of Harte's *Atlantic* stories during this period, two which include a a character named Henry York provide insights into the Mark Twain–Bret Harte relationship. York was one of the owners of the "Amity Claim" in that early story, "The Iliad of Sandy Bar," about two close friends who quarreled bitterly over a trivial matter. Like the Christopher Newman of Henry James's *The American,* published seven years later, Henry York of "The Iliad" made a fortune in California and then traveled in Europe, where he acquired considerable polish. Through Harte's stories in which York is a character runs an autobiographical thread leading finally to the Mark Twain–Bret Harte play *Ah Sin,* in which York was the hero.

These stories reflect Bret Harte's own disillusionment and doubt at the very time he was riding the crest of the wave of his popularity. The first story Harte submitted to the *Atlantic* after he came east was entitled "The Poet of Sierra Flat." This story begins with an account of doggerel whose "absolute vileness" and "gratuitous imbecility of thought" brought a popular reception much like the actual reception of "The Heathen Chinee." Significant are Harte's comments that this popularity was due to "ennui begotten of stagnant business and growing civilization" and that "some ambiguities of expression gave rise to many new readings, notes and commentaries, which I regret to state, were more often marked by ingenuity than delicacy of thought or expression."[19] In this story York appears briefly in support of law and order.

More important in relation to the Twain-Harte play *Ah Sin* is Harte's next story in which York appeared as a character. Entitled "A Monte Flat Pastoral," it tells of a failure's retreat into a dream world. In this story, written when it was generally believed that Harte himself had "struck it rich," York indulges in reflections surprising in a man who had recently made in "one week's clean-up . . . the modest sum of fifty thousand dollars": "Although it was clear moonlight the familiar prospect never to him seemed so dreary. The dead waste of the broad Wingdam highway never seemed so monotonous . . . so like the old man in its suggestion of going somewhere and never getting there."[20]

Another title for "A Monte Flat Pastoral" is "How Old Man Plunket Went Home." York and Plunkett would reappear with the

[19] *Writings,* II, 42–43.   [20] *Ibid.,* II, 237, 241.

Heathen Chinee in *Ah Sin*, but under the influence of Mark Twain, their personalities would suffer radical changes. Following "A Monte Flat Pastoral," York appeared again in Harte's play *Two Men of Sandy Bar*. Then, after becoming the hero of the play on which Harte and Twain collaborated, York never appeared again in any of Harte's stories.

In the month of June, following the birth of Jessamy, Harte's first daughter (whose arrival was anticipated in the April 1 letter to Twain), Bret Harte wrote Howells a letter in which he enclosed a poem for the *Atlantic*, and mentioned works he hoped to write, but explained that for the past two months the new baby had occupied his "attention as author to the exclusion of all else."[21] Like Twain, Harte found writing in a house with a crying baby difficult. And the houses in which the Harte family lived were apt to be crowded and to afford little opportunity for the seclusion which Harte needed for his work.

The following suggestion was written on July 25, 1872, from Morristown, New Jersey, where Harte's elder sister, Mrs. Eliza Knaufft, kept a family hotel:

> MY DEAR CLEMENS:
> Could not you and I find some quite rural retreat this summer where we could establish ourselves (after your Elmira or Buffalo fashion) in some empty farm house a mile or two from our families, and do our work with precious intervals, of smoking, coming home to [?] at abt. 3 P.M.? Think of it.[22]

The Hartford Directory for 1872 records "Samuel L. Clemens" and also "Mark Twain, author." Furthermore, it lists "F. Bret Harte, poet, author," as a boarder at the home of Mr. Clemens.[23] This is odd, since during his first two years in the East, Harte and his family made the New York or Morristown homes of Mrs. Knaufft their headquarters, and I have come across no Bret Harte letters with a Hartford heading.[24]

That Mrs. Harte was unable to find a place she liked well enough

---

[21] *BHL*, 70–71. The year is not given but the month and the work contemplated suggests that the letter was written in 1872 rather than in 1875.

[22] Hitherto unpublished letter, MTP.

[23] See Rodman Gilder Notes, MTP. I am particularly indebted to Mr. Frederick Anderson for calling this to my attention.

[24] *BHAE*, 204.

to settle permanently became a source of great anxiety to Bret Harte. Many letters to his wife written while Harte was away lecturing urge upon her the advisability of establishing a home. In one such letter Harte wrote:

> Oh, Nan, I weary of boarding or living in a house with others. If we can find some quiet home of our own, this winter, in some country place, near New York, even if Morristown is out of the question, I think we will not regret it. So I wish to hear [*sic*] you telegraph me of your success [in finding a place]. Even if you have to pay one hundred and twenty-five dollars per month, I think it would be better. We must have a good *comfortable* home—for the boys' sake if not for our own.[25]

Harte told his wife that if he could establish her in a house in a cheerful neighborhood, he would come home to it with "intense satisfaction." At one time Harte's aging mother and his stepfather, Colonel Andrew Williams, lived with the Hartes in a house rented in Morristown. Bret Harte's mother died in 1875, the year of the birth of his second daughter, Ethel.

As Harte's wheel of fortune turned downward, he was called upon to pay the price of his notoriety. In California many who had admired him and sincerely rejoiced in the good fortune which came to him in 1871 felt hurt that he did not write them after he left San Francisco. Harte *did* write a rather curt business letter or two to John Carmany, who had succeeded Anton Roman as publisher of the *Overland,* and who had been unwilling to agree to the terms on which Harte had conditioned his remaining as editor.[26] Also, Harte wrote to Mrs. Josephine Clifford of the *Overland* staff, and as long as she lived, Mrs. Clifford staunchly combated criticism of Harte.[27] But other California acquaintances complained that when they themselves went east and chanced upon him on the sidewalks of New York, Harte seemed not at all glad to see them. Contradicting this was Noah Brooks's report that Harte welcomed him when he came to New York and seemed the same friendly person he had known in California. Nevertheless, although Bret Harte never equaled the bitterness of Ambrose Bierce,

[25] *BHL,* 35–36.
[26] See *ibid.,* 7–8. Later letters to Carmany can be found in the *Overland Monthly* Letters, Bancroft.
[27] See "A Letter from a Friend," *loc. cit.,* 222–25.

who asserted that San Francisco was the "paradise of ignorance, anarchy, and general yellowness,"[28] Harte had not forgotten California's real-estate promoters who wanted to suppress his stories on grounds that their portrayal of California discouraged the kinds of immigrants whom these businessmen wanted to attract to the state. And Harte remembered other Californians who had tried to prevent his appointment to the faculty of the University in Berkeley because of his mockery of journalistic attempts to minimize earthquakes.[29] Bret Harte's proposal that he and Noah Brooks found a "Society of Escaped Californians" betrayed a rankling hostility toward the place and people whom Harte's fiction had taught many readers to love.[30] This disparagement of California, which had troubled Howells on Harte's arrival in Cambridge, infuriated Californians. Consequently, the good will of Harte's former associates on the *Overland* was outweighed by the animosity of some Californians who felt neglected and other Californians who were envious of Harte's meteoric rise to international fame. After news of Harte's disappointments and failures reached the West Coast, vindictive writers took full advantage of the vulnerability of the former leader of San Francisco's literary group.

Particularly savage before and after Harte's fall was W. A. Kendall, the "sick & needy poet" for whom, at Mark Twain's request, Bret had once headed a petition for free passage to California from New York. In the wire to Howells about Kendall's plight, Twain had commented, "I do not know him but I know he is a good fellow and has hard luck." According to Franklin Walker, however, Kendall habitually railed against those who succeeded, and Bret Harte was merely his chief target.[31] In the San Francisco *Chronicle*, Kendall described Harte as "a loose and not infrequent borrower of large sums and a cool ignorer of the gracious loaners."[32] Specifically, Kendall charged that Harte had swindled contributors to the *Overland*. Walker says that Kendall's "long-suffering friends" finally concluded that "his genius was not great enough to compensate for his eroticism and improvidence."[33]

The following letter, written the day after Christmas of a generally

[28] Paul Fatout, *Ambrose Bierce, the Devil's Lexicographer*, 248.

[29] Merwin, *The Life of Bret Harte*, 216.

[30] *BHAE*, 200.   [31] *Literary Frontier*, 353.   [32] *BHAE*, 221.

[33] *Literary Frontier*, 226–27. In 1876, Kendall committed suicide in San Francisco.

discouraging year, shows Harte's reaction to Kendall's criticisms in 1872:

December 26th/72

MY DEAR CLEMENS:

I have been lately pretty well abused from unexpected sources but I think the enclosed caps the climax. Do you remember the man to whom you gave $50; for whom I raised $60 and procured by begging a first class passage to San Francisco and to whom I sent anonymously $25, when I was rather poor myself? Well—this is the reptile! And worse than all, this is the second or third time that he has thus requited me.

Now what in the name of all that is diabolically mean, am I to do? I dont mind his slander: that I can refute—but how am I to make this dog know that he is a dog and not a man?

You wrote me from London that you had heard that Osgood had taken £ 50 from Hotten and given him the copyright of my new book. I believe Osgood did it for the best, but as I had no idea of condoning that pirate Hotten's offenses for £ 50, I repudiated it at once. I told Osgood not to send him advanced sheets of my new story, and to say that Mr Harte annulled the contract. He did so—and I see by the Spectator that Hotten has quietly reproduced all the book except that story, without ever paying the £ 50, and further has had the advantage of his previous announcement that he was "authorized by Mr. Harte etc." Further, the book contains somebody else's story foisted upon me. But that'll do today. I will see you I hope on the 3rd. I saw your brother-in-law at Elmira the other day.

Yours

HARTE[34]

The John Camden Hotten mentioned by Harte is, of course, the English publisher whom Twain had attacked in the *Spectator* as John Camden "Hottentot" when the unscrupulous man had suggested that "Carl Byng" was another pen name for Sam Clemens. In 1872, Hotten had pirated Mark Twain's *The Innocents Abroad*, with an admiring preface by Artemus Ward's agent and biographer, Edward P. Hingston. Twain had been pleased at first, but changed his mind and then characteristically forgot he had once held a very different opinion.[35] Twain's deliberate and public cut of Hingston in London apparently had nothing to do with Hingston's rather shabby treatment of Artemus

[34] Hitherto unpublished letters, MTP.   [35] Paine, *Biography*, 464.

Ward, for which Harte had censured him in the *Overland*. As Harte's December, 1872, letter to Twain indicates, Hotten had lost no time in bringing out a pirated edition of *The Complete Works of Bret Harte in Prose and Poetry*, which had realized considerable profit for Hotten but none for Harte.

If Harte's work had deteriorated, his reputation continued for a while under its own early momentum. In Britain as well as in America, Harte was still praised and pirated. That the publisher James R. Osgood was far from writing off Harte completely as a bad bargain is indicated by Osgood's proposal on March 27, 1873, to issue a "complete" American edition of Harte's collected writings. To this proposal Harte readily agreed: "If you think a 'complete' edition would pay you here, by all means get it up."[36]

Osgood was having his own financial troubles. In 1873 he sold the *Atlantic* and *Every Saturday* to Hurd and Houghton and H. O. Houghton and Company.[37] Although Aldrich and Howells may have had forebodings of disaster, news of the transfer came as a complete surprise to Harte, who had recently requested from Osgood a statement of his account.[38] That Harte continued to try to satisfy Osgood about the fulfillment of the earlier contract is further indicated by the following letter:

> Morristown N. J.
> April 15th 74

My dear Osgood,

I enclose herewith the poem; I have so extended and altered it—wh. accounts for my delay—that it is really a new poem; a vast improvement on the one I intended to send you, and is worth to me about $400. That at least is what I should ask for it, were I to offer it for sale. I do not think I have done anything as good for the length; I am quite certain I have never done anything as elaborate. Read it any how. I think you will like it apart from your business interest in it, and give it to Clark to read to Mrs. Clark.

It is yours, my dear Osgood, if you will so accept it, as my voluntary acknowledgment of your conscientious fulfillment of your part of our late contract, and as an effort on my part to adjust the little differences which exist between us in regard to my performance, and a recognition of and atonement for my delay in execution. It will make

---

[36] *BHL*, 22.   [37] Weber, *James Ripley Osgood*, 144.   [38] *BHL*, 13–14.

according to the statement I furnished you, fifteen articles given to you between the date of our first contract and today, and covered and compensated by the $10,000 paid me during the twelvemonth of our contract.

If you dont like it—or this, please enclose the poem at once to 713 Broadway. I want the poem in any event to go into print soon.

Yours always, my dear Osgood,
BRET HARTE.[39]

By sending a poem rather than a story, Harte was offering Osgood a genre which critics of that day, including Howells,[40] considered the medium of Harte's best work. Nevertheless, assertions that Harte, through irresponsibility, failed to live up to his contract continued to be made. In time, Mark Twain added his testimony that "Harte's indifference concerning contracts and engagements was phenomenal."[41]

---

[39] Published by permission of the Yale University Library, where it is deposited. It should be remembered that Osgood was the publisher of several of Harte's books as well as of sketches and poems submitted in fulfillment of the contract. At the same time Carl J. Weber criticizes Harte for writing this letter, he quotes Harte's words about Osgood's "conscientious fulfillment" of Osgood's share of the contract as an admirable contrast to E. C. Stedman's remarks about Osgood to Bayard Taylor. See Weber, *James Ripley Osgood*, 146–47.

[40] "Editor's Easy Chair," *loc. cit.*

[41] *MTE*, 280.

8

"THOSE NECESSARIES OF LIFE"

For as you know I write slowly and with exceeding labor.

BRET HARTE to MARK TWAIN, 1874

IN THE EAST as well as the West, Bret Harte demonstrated all too convincingly how to lose friends and alienate people. Stories of his misdeeds sprang up like dragon's teeth—some of them real, some hallucinations. Many tall tales portrayed Harte as a gay dog living it up in the world of fashion. Stories focused on his extravagancies, his debts, his efforts to evade bill collectors, and—what sometimes seemed worst of all in the eyes of nineteenth-century men of property—his impenitent gaiety about his own sins. Many who heard and told the stories, however, thoroughly enjoyed Harte's humor about his own predicament. Among the latter was John Hay, who recalled that he had once complained to Harte about his own lack of funds. " 'Your own fault,' said the wise Argonaut. 'Why did you fool away your money paying your debts?' "[1] Few who heard such stories suspected that Harte's gaiety was a veneer for desperation.

But why was Harte, whose individual stories and poems still sold phenomenally well, in financial straits?

The chief reason seems to have been that even though Harte had demonstrated in San Francisco and would demonstrate again his ability to handle with meticulous care governmental funds for which he was responsible, when it came to his own finances, he had no "money sense." For that matter, neither had Mark Twain.

Another reason for Harte's financial straits was that, like Twain, Harte had expensive tastes. But unlike Twain, Harte could not afford to indulge them. Also unlike Twain, if he overindulged—as Twain did

---

[1] William Roscoe Thayer, *The Life and Letters of John Hay*, II, 402.

when the sands of his own financial fortunes began shifting—Harte's wife had no fortune to tide the family over. Harte liked to dress well, and at least once, tailors had to sue to collect money he owed them.[2] Also, Harte had an expensive family. Reportedly he and his wife frequented fashionable places, including Newport, and lived at fashionable hotels, although his letters afford little evidence of this taste on his part. Moreover, the famous Harte, known as a gay and witty companion, was continually sought by famous and wealthy men whose incomes, though less publicized than Harte's, were much more solid. This, of course, increased his tendency to live beyond his means.

As a way out of his difficulties, Bret Harte turned to lecturing, and like Mark Twain, he lectured on tours arranged by Redpath.[3] A man named Kirby was also Harte's agent at one time.[4] These lecture tours took Harte north to Canada, south as far as Georgia, and west as far as Kansas and Nebraska.

Since Harte and his family had lived beyond their means from the beginning of their sojourn in the East, Harte was sometimes harried by his creditors even when he was on lecture tours. His most successful lecture—at Tremont Temple in Boston—was delivered with a bailiff in the wings.[5] On more distant travels Harte anxiously telegraphed money to his family: $200 if he was lucky; more often, $150 or even $50; once he ruefully apologized that he was unable to send anything at all. When there was money, he sent most of it to his wife, reminding her, however, that sums must be apportioned among his creditors. After a letter from Macon, Georgia, filled with his sympathy for Southerners in the throes of Reconstruction, Harte assured Mrs. Harte that he had not forgotten his task of reconstructing himself: "I enclosed a draft for one hundred dollars as an evidence that I remembered I was still in debt, and had a heap of practical work to do yet before I rode ahead redressing political grievances."[6]

From Berkeley Springs, Virginia, he wrote that he had met Southern colonels who made his "poor Colonel Starbottle an utter failure." "If I could dress Robson, and get him to speak as I heard the real Virginia Colonel Starbottle speak yesterday, I could make him famous."[7] In

---

[2] *BHAE*, 214.
[3] See *BHL*, 132, and *BHAE*, 219. With Redpath, Harte disagreed about a contract.
[4] *BHL*, 20–21. [5] *BHAE*, 210–11. [6] *BHL*, 43. [7] *Ibid.*, 24.

Harte's letters, this is the first inkling of his lifelong illusion that he would one day write a play so popular that its financial return would free him from the drudgery of hack writing and the torture of lecturing.

Although at times Bret Harte arrived in a town barely in time to dress himself in a Pullman car compartment into which he had brought his trunk from the baggage car, newspaper reporters picked up the old clichés about his being a "handsome fop." "They may be right—I dare say they are—in asserting that I am no orator, have no special faculty for speaking—no fire, dramatic earnestness, or expression, but when they intimate that I am running on my good looks—save the mark! I confess I get hopelessly furious," he wrote his wife. "You will be amused to hear that my gold 'studs' have again become 'diamonds,' my worn-out shirts 'faultless linen,' my haggard face that of a 'Spanish-looking exquisite,' my habitual quiet and 'used-up' way, 'gentle and elegant languor.' " "I certainly never expected to be criticized for being what I *am not*, a handsome fop."[8]

Once when he made an unexpected $100 on a lecture, he sent it to Mrs. Harte and insisted: "It is yours, for yourself, Nan, to buy 'minxes' with, if you want."[9] A few days later, in Omaha, he could not resist buying from an Indian trader bearskins for rugs for himself and his little daughter Jessamy, and two mink skins for his wife. These last, which he described as "remarkably beautiful," he sent by express to 45 Fifth Avenue.[10] Bret Harte could not afford to buy mink even in that fashion. For the most part, he adhered to a rigorous schedule in an attempt to pay off his debts.[11]

On the lecture platform Bret Harte was always less successful than Mark Twain. The Brahmins had shown a decided preference for the insouciant new writer who had a keen wit and could turn a polished phrase, but the usual audience, familiar with Harte's fiction and expecting someone who would dress and talk like Kentuck, Colonel Starbottle, or Yuba Bill, felt cheated. Instead, on the platform appeared a slender, diffident, low-voiced, meticulously dressed man, whose approach to his subject, "The Argonauts of '49, California's Golden Age," was detached, historical, critical. His whimsical humor was at times

---

[8] *Ibid.*, 26.   [9] *Ibid.*, 27–28.   [10] *Ibid.*, 30.

[11] Apparently his older sister Eliza had helped him carefully budget his expenditures before he started on the tour. See *ibid.*, 28.

subtly allusive. His interpretation of California history was impression-istic but perceptive. Shrewdly Harte pointed to the significant contribu-tions of Padre Junipero Serra and the westward migration of the Mor-mons led by Brigham Young.[12] Harte's attitude toward the Mormons was in marked contrast with that expressed in *Roughing It,* where Mark Twain voiced popular prejudice. That Harte's more successful lectures were in the cities of Boston, Washington, and New York was not mere chance. On tour, Harte was particularly pleased with his reception in Ithaca, the home of Cornell University, whose students, he told his wife, had the culture but not the conceit of Harvard.[13] (Harte's delivery of the Phi Beta Kappa poem at a Harvard commencement had been an embarrassing failure, but the fault was not Harvard's.[14]) At one stop on his lecture tour Harte noted sympathetically that the people seemed "preternaturally serious and depressed, as if they had come from my lecture instead of going to it."[15] He concluded this letter to his wife: "Take care of the children, teach them to avoid becoming lecturers, caution Totty [Jessamy] against marrying a poet, and believe me, Nan, dismally your Frank."

In contrast, Mark Twain—still kept at arm's length by many of the critics—was embraced by the people. Like Bret Harte, Mark Twain had a small, slender figure, but with his cherished drawl, his shock of reddish hair, and his suits looking a bit rumpled in spite of Livy's care, Mark could be fitted into the West popularized by Harte's fiction and Twain's own *Roughing It.* Twain's subjects were apt to be autobio-graphical, his approach intensely personal. In dialect he told about Hank Monk and Horace Greeley, Jim Smiley and his jumping frog, "His Grandfather's Old Ram." But Mark Twain's best yarns were about Mark Twain, and on the lecture platform it was the personality of the man rather than the power of his words that projected. Mark's humor was deadpan but not difficult. His effects, carefully calculated, relied heavily on the dramatic pause. Mark's speeches make not very good reading today, but with Mark giving them, they made excellent listening in the 1870's.

Mark Twain's popularity was by no means limited to American small towns. In fact, he preferred city audiences and had one of his best

[12] *Writings,* II, ix–xxxv.
[13] *BHL,* 34.

[14] *BHAE,* 201–202.
[15] *BHL,* 32.

receptions in New York.[16] In August, 1872, Mark Twain sailed for England, where his books and lectures were so well received that his nephew Samuel Webster would believe Mark's genius was discovered by the English.[17] In 1873, Mark Twain made a second trip to England, lectured in London, and found himself so popular that his rooms at the Langham Hotel were "like a court." In America it was rumored that Harte, too, would soon leave for London, but Harte denied newspaper reports of the rumor. "I have too much unfinished work to complete here," he told Osgood. "I think I will 'keep' to another year with my English friends."[18]

Notwithstanding his success, Mark Twain—like Bret Harte—professed intense dislike of lecturing. His reasons, however, were different. Mark disliked the physical discomforts and inconveniences of travel on his lecture tours. To minimize them as much as possible, he spent money freely on the best hotels, the best foods, the most luxurious means of transportation available.[19] Harte suffered from the same inconveniences, but he could not afford to hire a private locomotive to avoid getting up at two o'clock in the morning, and he was romantic enough to dramatize near disasters. Once when the engine of his train broke down on a Kansas prairie, he hired a saddle horse, strapped his lecture and a blanket on his back, and in the best tradition of Bret Harte fiction, raced the fifteen miles to Atchison in order to be on time for a lecture.[20] Mark Twain reacted with disgust to the small towns on his lecture circuits and to the small-town people who exacted too much of his time. "All towns are alike," he once said. "All have the same stupid trivialities to show, & all demand an impossible interest at the suffering stranger's hands."[21] Bret Harte, on the contrary, was intensely interested in the people and places he visited, and to his wife wrote affectionate and charming accounts of his experiences. Nevertheless, on these tours Harte suffered from loneliness and exhaustion and—most of all—from shyness of the groups of people staring at him from the shadows of partly filled auditoriums. Bret Harte appealed to audiences; Mark Twain mastered them. And Mark Twain's ability to control, to

[16] Neider, *Autobiography*, 181–82.

[17] Webster, *Mark Twain: Business Man*, 127.

[18] *BHL*, 22–23.

[19] Fatout, *Mark Twain on the Lecture Circuit*, 122.

[20] *BHL*, 27.

[21] Fatout, *Mark Twain on the Lecture Circuit*, 122.

force laughter even at a story that was not funny, gave Mark a sense of power and achievement denied Harte.[22]

During these years Mark Twain was not among the highest paid lecturers, and his lavish expenditures cut into his profits.[23] As Paul Fatout demonstrates in his detailed account of *Mark Twain on the Lecture Circuit,* Mark continued to lecture mainly because the lure of the platform was irresistible. But liking it or not liking it, both Mark Twain and Bret Harte lectured intermittently for years. And both men saw as their reasons for lecturing debts, described by Mark Twain as "those necessaries of life."[24]

Mark Twain's interest in the Buffalo *Express,* which he sold at a loss of $10,000, had been bought for $25,000 on a loan secured by Jervis Langdon. When Samuel Langhorne Clemens married Olivia Langdon, he and his bride—with an amazing assortment of relatives and friends—traveled in a "palace car" from Elmira to Buffalo, where Mr. Langdon had provided the couple with a luxuriously furnished home staffed with a cook, a housemaid, and a coachman. When her father died in 1871, Mrs. Clemens inherited a comfortable fortune of at least a quarter-million dollars.[25] And although Mark Twain was sensitive about having married a wealthy woman and he insisted on his own independence, he had no worries about his wife and children being in want if his own earnings failed. But they did not fail. From the very beginning, Mark Twain's books sold very well indeed. Their popularity continued and increased. Twain worked hard at his lecturing, not to keep the wolf from the door but to live in a manner to which he was determined to become accustomed.

The luxury in which Mark Twain lived after his marriage to Olivia Langdon contrasted dramatically with the increasingly straitened circumstances of Harte. The Clemens family moved to Hartford in 1872. In 1874, Mr. and Mrs. Clemens completed an astonishing new home there. The five acres of land on which the house stood were worth $31,000, and the house itself cost $70,000. Within three years at least $21,000 worth of furniture was installed.[26] Walter Blair estimates that

---

[22] Neider, *Autobiography,* 146–47. See also Paine, *Biography,* 1290; Howells, *My Mark Twain,* 54–55.

[23] Fatout, *Mark Twain on the Lecture Circuit,* 150.

[24] *LL,* 172.   [25] *Ibid.,* 63, 142.   [26] Andrews, *Nook Farm,* 72.

the cost of the Clemens' house in a depression year was $122,000, probably the equivalent of $350,000 to $400,00 today.[27] A show place of the community, the house and grounds were viewed with mixed reactions. Everyone agreed that the Clemens' place was expensive, but more than one questioned its taste. At this time Mark Twain cherished unwavering faith in those "pecuniary canons of taste" later defined by Thorstein Veblen. When Mrs. Isabella Hooker accused Mr. Clemens of not caring for a pretty lamp shade if it was inexpensive, Mark Twain explained that "he had no knowledge or taste himself & so when an established house said a thing was good & charged a good price for it he felt sure it was worthy of Livy & that was all he cared for."[28]

In 1874, Mark Twain sent photographs of the house and his children to Howells, who replied that he and Mrs. Howells thought the Clemens' house and babies "the prettiest in the world." When, after repeated invitations, Howells finally brought his wife for her first visit in March, 1875, Mrs. Howells politely complimented Mrs. Clemens on the house, and Howells wrote his father that the Clemenses were generous hosts "with inextinguishable money and a palace of a house." But Howells confided to his father that he liked his own less pretentious house better.[29] After Mark Twain's death, Howells would whimsically write that the Clemens' house was of the "English violet order of architecture."[30] The comments of Mrs. Hooker and Howells are noteworthy in relation to Mark Twain's later assertion that the provocation for his most explosive words to Harte was Harte's facetious criticism of the Clemens' house and its furnishings.[31]

In the year the Clemens family moved into the "handsomest mansion in Hartford," Bret Harte still had the reputation of commanding top pay for his writing. Apparently written in answer to Mark Twain's inquiry about comparative prices paid in the open market for literary goods produced by the two writers, the following letter underscores the causes of Harte's financial difficulties and reflects Harte's awareness

---

[27] *Mark Twain & Huck Finn*, 18.   [28] Andrews, *Nook Farm*, 86.
[29] *MTH*, I, 43, 70f.   [30] *My Mark Twain*, 7.
[31] *MTE*, 278. Not at the time of the visit but years later, Howells said that Harte made fun of the caterer's silver epergne used at Mrs. Howells' famous party. Mark Twain had read this recollection ("Editor's Easy Chair," *loc. cit.*) of Howells' before he recorded his own accusation about Harte's criticism of the furnishings of the Clemens' house.

that his friend and former literary protégé was at this time getting along much better than he.

MORRISTOWN, N. J.
August 8th/74

MY DEAR CLEMENS,

The *Times* paid me $600 for the "Rose of Tuolumne" which occupied a page and a column of the Sunday edition and $500 for "John Oakhurst." These were my own figures,—I might have asked and got more I dare say—particularly for Oakhurst which I estimated as occupying less space but which really was longer than my first story. I only asked what I would have received from any first class magazine for the same material. My dealings—which only consisted in my naming my price and handing the Ms (unread) in response to an invitation from Jennings—were with Jones, the Publisher.

I think *you* ought to get more, as you are much more valuable to a newspaper than I am. I certainly shall say so, if they condescend to consult me. Of one thing you may be certain, I shall keep up the market price—I can afford, less than you, even, to lower it, for as you know I write slowly and with exceeding labor. More than that I think that you and I owe it a duty to our profession to keep up its equity at least in this way—and to this crowd of traders this way is the most telling. And still more—you and I have raised the compensation of other literary men about 50 per cent, by simply demanding and getting these prices.

Of course the other fellows dont see this. A day or two after it was reported in the papers that I received $400 for a poem in the *Atlantic* a poet cut me dead in the street and afterwards wrote a savage *critique* in wh. he endeavored to show how much a line I asked and that it wasn't worth the money. Yet I happen to know that he asked and received $50 more for his own stuff—in consequence of what he was pleased to term my "insolence"—for his publisher told me so with the added remark that I "was ruining his trade." Another publisher told me that you and I had "spoiled" the market—"men that were content with $2.50 a page now asked $5.00" because you and I asked $50.

You know as well as I that a man couldn't get $50 a page if he turned them out every day—and that even at those extravagant prices I make barely a decent living by my work in the magazines. Please God, with my novel—if I ever get it done—I'll be able to pay my debts and lay something by. And yet there are people who hearing that I get $500 per story of 8 pp. imagine I'm rolling in wealth, and rush to me for a donation of $100 to assist struggling genius. H.H.

Of course all this is confidential. You will continue to inform people that I habitually turn out my $50 page per day and that it is my usual custom to eat from gold plate with a butler in a white cravat before me. That you have always deplored my extravagant prices, and that only personal friendship kept you from doing my work at one third the price in the interests of literature.

Raymond tells me you have dramatized your last book and that its good. I never thought of you in that way. I dare say you will get before the spotlight before I do—but the stage is large and there is audience for us both. Wherefore go on, my dear boy, and conquer. No one will applaud louder than myself—among the claque.

I'm sorry to hear of the exceeding insecurity in the supply of maternal nourishment for your latest born. I've been through all that—and have walked Bellevue Hospital at night through the female nurses looking for the biped cow, with a telegram from my wife in my pocket that my poor little girls life hung upon that chance. I never before analyzed the sensations I used to experience on beholding the female breast; I am satisfied now that what I thought was frivolity and weakness was simply the premonition of the father.

Heaven send your little one a good cow—who doesn't make too much of her importance to your well being. Give my regards and Mrs. Hartes quickest sympathies to your wife. My own home is, and has been all summer but little better than a hospital. Mrs. Harte has been very sick, my mother and stepfather both old, are very infirm, and the doctor's horse stops of his own accord at our gate. For myself I'm very blue and dyspeptic—but for all that, dear Clemens,

Always yours
BRET HARTE.[32]

The dramatization of Mark Twain's latest book was, of course, *The Gilded Age*, in which John Raymond starred as Colonel Sellers. Harte's use of the word "claque" is an allusion to a passage in *Roughing It* wherein Mark Twain reported with questionable accuracy his totally unnecessary precautions to insure applause for his famous San Francisco lecture on the Sandwich Islands.[33]

The novel on which Harte was working was *Gabriel Conroy*. Harte

---

[32] Hitherto unpublished letter, MTP.
[33] Fatout, *Mark Twain on the Lecture Circuit*, 38–39.

evidently resented the contrast not between Clemens' way of life and his own but between the gay, profligate life which popular imagination attributed to Harte himself and the actual circumstances in which he now lived. Particularly noteworthy in the light of Mark Twain's later allegations that Harte wrote with haste and carelessness is Bret Harte's reminder: "for as you know I write slowly and with exceeding labor."

Like Bret Harte, Samuel Clemens had four children. The eldest, Langdon, died when he was a baby. The Clemens' daughters were named Susy, Clara, and Jean. In 1874 the Clemens' "latest born" was Clara. Until Mrs. Jane Clemens died in 1890, she was cared for in Keokuk by Mollie, Samuel's sister-in-law, and by Orion, whose idealism and improvidence exasperated the increasingly successful younger brother. But Mark, of course, contributed to the family's support, and when she died, his mother willed her money not to Orion but to Samuel because, Mark Twain said, it had come from him.[34] As years passed, more and more numerous were the eminent visitors entertained in the spacious Hartford mansion.

In this period of increasing prosperity, Mark Twain received from relatives, would-be relatives, strangers, and old acquaintances many requests for aid. To some letters asking help, Mark responded generously; to others, acidly. He wrote a particularly long and angry reply to one woman writer who had sent him a begging letter. The trouble with her, he said, was that she was suffering from false pride and was living beyond her means.[35] These irritating qualities Mark Twain would later attribute to Bret Harte, who also asked his help.

Yet Bret Harte was still a celebrity. Until very near the end of his stay on the Atlantic seaboard, Harte continued to be an occasional and apparently a welcome guest in the Clemens' house. Twain lent him various sums of money, eventually—according to Twain's not always reliable memory—totaling $3,000.

The Christmas season of 1875 found Harte (perhaps already in debt to his friend Twain) asking a favor. He reminded Twain of a time when their roles had been reversed. But like Mr. Micawber, Harte believed that his fortune still lurked around the corner.

[34] Neider, *Autobiography*, 221.   [35] Letter in MTP.

45 FIFTH AVENUE
December 24th/75

MY DEAR CLEMENS,

Do you remember that some years ago when Bliss wanted a book from me for his House, you told him you would use your influence provided he did the decent and honorable thing to you in some contested point of business? Well you remember I wrote a letter to him saying "that on the representation of my friend Mr. Clemens etc., I would accept to" I remind you of this only that I want to ask a similar favor at your hands—I want you to use your influence with him for *me*.

I have asked Bliss to advance me a further $1000 on my copyright of "Gabriel Conroy." He has already advanced between $3 & $4000, but by reason of his contract with Scribner & Co, has received $3000 of it back, so that his actual risk is only about $1500—if as much. Indeed, if his representations to me of the sale of his books are correct, he runs no risk whatever.

Bliss thinks he can't do it. I think he *can*. I want you to think he can. I need the money 1st, because my play at the Union Square Theatre may not see the footlights this season on account of Rose Michel. 2nd because I dont want to sacrifice my dramatization of "Gabriel Conroy" for the "money down" that I need this minute. Raymond, who has written to me for it, will I believe make me as fair an offer as he did you if I can wait.

So I ask you, in the common interest of our trade to help me—and to do the best you can to persuade our common enemy—the publisher to make this advance. You know Bliss better than I do—you are, I think one of his stockholders. You will of course satisfy yourself that the company runs no risk in an advance—but you, as a brother author, will appreciate my anxiety to get the best I can for my work—and why I may perhaps have to wait for it. At all events I know you will do your best for me, and I am, very confidently,

Always yours
BRET HARTE[36]

Harte's play at the Union Square Theatre was *Two Men of Sandy Bar*. Since the dramatization rights to *Gabriel Conroy* later became an issue between Bret Harte and Mark Twain, Harte's expression of unwillingness to sacrifice these rights for cash in hand in this time of need

[36] Hitherto unpublished letter, MTP.

should be kept in mind. Also noteworthy is his reminder that Twain had benefited by securing for Bliss publication rights for Harte's novel. If the benefit had not occurred, Harte would hardly have mentioned it when he and Twain were on good terms and Harte was asking a favor. Harte referred to it again in a bitter letter to Twain after their collaboration on *Ah Sin*. That letter, referred to but, I think, not accurately described by Bernard De Voto, will appear in a later chapter of this book.

The following letter also concerns the dramatization of *Gabriel Conroy*:

45 FIFTH AVENUE
Jan 2d/76

MY DEAR CLEMENS,

Raymond would not agree to my terms—so that our negotiations were at an end before I got your letter, and the question of his ability to play "Gabriel Conroy" was not mooted. I think you are right in the main in what you say,—certainly I should not have been shrewd enough to deliberate whether the running of two plays on alternate nights by the same actor would reduce our income.

So that I still am open to an offer and wait for the coming actor who can personate Gabriel Conroy. I thought I had found him in John McCullough, who seemed to me to look the part,—who had a simple, natural strength and suggestion of pathos in his physical aspect, but he, although never doubtful of his ability to do Hamlet or King Lear, does not think he can play Gabriel Conroy.

I have been such a tremendous fool in disposing of my first play as I did—that I feel wary. To think that Stuart Robson has it in his pocket while he is quietly drawing a good salary from his manager for not playing it, and that its appearance at all depends entirely upon a manager and an actor who can afford to do without it—is exasperating.

Try and make Bliss do something for me. You can if you choose make him think it is the proper and in the end the profitable thing— certainly it is no risk to him.

Yours always.
B.H.[37]

In the same year Bret Harte had occasion to act as intermediary be-

[37] Hitherto unpublished letter, MTP.

Mark Twain as a young man, from a photograph by Gurney

Bret Harte in 1871, from a woodcut
in *Every Saturday* (January 14, 1871)

tween Mark Twain and a German publisher. On August 21, 1876, Baron Tauchnitz wrote to Bret Harte from Leipzig:

My dear Sir,

I hope my last lines of March 29 reached you safely and also the payment.

Being desirous to include also the name of your friend Mr. Samuel Clemens (Mark Twain) in my series, I take the liberty, not knowing his address, to ask you whether you would have the great kindness, to communicate my wish to Mr. Clemens. I think I might begin with his last book "Tom Sawyer," which would just fill one of my volumes.

I hope these lines may find you quite well. Pardon me the liberty I have taken.

Believe me always

Yours faithfully
Tauchnitz[38]

Bret Harte acted promptly. The following letter was written on September 3 from 713 Broadway, New York:

My dear Clemens,

I have received the enclosed note to-day. The Baron is a good fellow. Considering the fact that we have no copyright on the Continent, and that he could steal but *wont*, and that his editions are the perfection of letter press, and that to be on his list is a kind of guarantee to the English reading people there I'd advise you to accept his offer. He will send you from £50 to £100 according to the size of the book— as a gratuity. Of course as his books are contraband in England, it doesn't interfere with your rights *there*.

You have, of course, read all the critics have said about my play. It seems to me a little like the three parts of a charade with the answers left out, but it's pretty and picturesque, and Robson is satisfied. If you come to town, let me send you tickets.

I cannot understand why Bliss delays my book. He promised to bring it out on the 1st of Sept. but I have heard nothing of it, and it seems to be dead. You are a stockholder in the Concern. Shore him up.

Yours ever
Bret Harte[39]

---

[38] Letter in MTP.

[39] Hitherto unpublished letter, MTP. See also Edgar H. Hemminghaus, *Mark Twain in Germany*, 9.

This correspondence was the beginning of a long association between Twain and Tauchnitz with which Twain later expressed great satisfaction. It may be remembered that Mark Twain had also complained of the American Publishing Company's failure to issue *his* book at the time promised. In 1869, Mark Twain accused Elisha Bliss of postponing the publication of *The Innocents Abroad* in order to give precedence to books by other authors.

9

GABRIEL CONROY, TOM SAWYER, AND
TWO MEN OF SANDY BAR

... he has wronged me in a private way: that is *my* business, not *yours;*
but he was *my* partner, no one shall abuse him before me.

Sandy Morton in Two Men of Sandy Bar

Although Mark Twain and Bret Harte had re-established a
friendly relationship and maintained it at times on warmly affectionate
terms, the basis of the association was unstable and shifting. Since 1871,
Twain's reputation as a writer and lecturer had been growing and giving signs of greater durability than Harte's. Yet not all observers could
read the signs. Notwithstanding the fact that Mark Twain, alone or in
collaboration, had produced before 1876 three substantial books, and
Harte, in contrast, had produced only short stories, sketches, and sentimental or satiric verses, Eastern critics continued to consider Harte as
a writer more seriously than they considered Twain.[1] Moreover, in
the market place, Harte still had the reputation of selling phenomenally
well, and to the day of his death, his name was one to "conjure with."
Consequently, when publishers secured something from his pen, they
trumpeted their triumphs in advertisements.[2]

With the publication and sales of *The Innocents Abroad,* Elisha
Bliss had converted Mark Twain to the advantages of the subscription plan over all other methods of publication and distribution of
books. Mark frequently urged the subscription method upon his friends,
including William Dean Howells, Thomas Bailey Aldrich, Charles
Dudley Warner, Joel Chandler Harris, and even Harriet Beecher

[1] For a more recent appraisal of New England's view of Mark Twain, see Albert
E. Stone, Jr., *The Innocent Eye: Childhood in Mark Twain's Imagination,* 34.
[2] Noah Brooks, "Bret Harte: A Biographical and Critical Sketch," *Overland
Monthly,* Vol. XL (Sept., 1902), 206.

Stowe.[3] Although several were tempted to put aside their scruples against this method which many considered not quite respectable, the subscription plan was never so profitable for other writers as it was for Mark Twain. Nevertheless, through Mark's persuasion, Bret Harte agreed to write for Mark Twain's publisher a novel to be sold by subscription. As Mark Twain said, Bliss "recognized that a contract for a full-grown novel from Bret Harte was a valuable prize."[4]

When Harte settled down to fulfill his part of this new contract, he found writing the promised novel the hardest work he had ever attempted. The following letter to Elisha Bliss gives some insight to his problem:

713 BROADWAY
N. YORK July 21st [1874?]

MY DEAR BLISS,

Here are, in all, 49 pp.—counting those that I have already sent you wh. you have not acknowledged.

One chapter more—thank Heaven—will complete the "Prologue." The mere labor of writing it is nothing. But as I have to dispose of my characters so as to use them advantageously in the remaining "Book,"—it is the hardest work I have done.

I have written about 350 pp. to make this beggarly 49 that I finally send. My only hope is that the Prologue done and the story fairly launched I shall get on faster. Otherwise it wont pay.

Meanwhile how am I to live? I've been a month at 50 pp.

Perhaps you can answer me that. At all events let me hear from you. I hope to send you the last chapter complete,—tomorrow.

Yours,
B.H.[5]

Prodded by Twain, who was prodded by Harte, Bliss reluctantly sent Harte money. Even in 1907, Twain jeered at the "telescopic vision" of Bliss in scrutinizing small sums of "a couple of hundred dollars" advanced to Harte.[6] Like Harte, Twain was convinced that Bliss was running no risk. He was so sure of this that he made himself "personally

---

[3] Andrews, *Nook Farm*, 122. See also the letter from Elmira, Aug. 10 (1881?), to Joel Chandler Harris from Mark Twain, MTP.

[4] *MTE*, 280.

[5] This letter is published for the first time, courtesy of the William Andrews Clark Memorial Library in Los Angeles, where it is deposited.

[6] *MTE*, 280.

responsible" for these advances, which finally snowballed to a sizable sum. At Mark Twain's suggestion, Bliss sent Twain a chapter of Harte's novel as security, writing on the back that it was charged to Twain, so that Harte's indebtedness to him would be clear.[7]

For a year Harte drudged away at writing the novel, and *Gabriel Conroy*, begun in June, 1874, was finally finished, and the last page turned over to Bliss. Then *Scribner's* agreed to pay the American Publishing Company $6,000 for serial rights, a sum that set another money-making record in American fiction.[8] Mark Twain participated in the negotiations among Elisha Bliss, Scribner's, and Harte.

On July 5, 1875, Mark Twain wrote William Dean Howells a detailed account of Harte's enviable contract:

> Bret Harte has sold his novel (same size as mine, I should say) to Scribner's Monthly for $6,500 (publication to begin in September, I think,) & he gets a royalty of $7\frac{1}{2}$ per cent from Bliss in book form afterwards. He gets a royalty of ten per cent on it in England (issued in serial numbers) & the same royalty on it in book form afterward, & is to receive an advance payment of five hundred pounds the day the first No. of the serial appears.[9]

Characteristic of Mark Twain's references to money was his addition of $500 to the figure of Harte's contract with Scribner's. Apparently as news of Harte's good fortune spread, more mythical thousands were added, for in answer to a clipping and a letter from Osgood in May, Harte had written:

> The "more thousands" is good! I don't know how true it is. Six thousand was the exact sum to be paid to Bliss, he afterwards accounting—to me—and the entire receipts of the English sale of the serial for myself solely. This is *entre nous;* indeed, I supposed that the fact of the sale was not to be made public at all, until I saw that paragraph.[10]

For a much longer time than Bret Harte worked on *Gabriel Conroy*, Mark Twain had been working on a novel of his own. In 1873 he had collaborated with Charles Dudley Warner on *The Gilded Age*. Mark had at first welcomed Warner as a collaborator, but before long

[7] Letter from F. E. Bliss to Sam Clemens, Jan. 26, 1877, MTP. See De Voto, *Mark Twain's America*, 163, for support of Harte's belief that Twain was a member of the publishing firm.

[8] *BHAE*, 226f.   [9] *MTH*, I, 93.   [10] *BHL*, 51.

he found the association irksome and eventually became convinced that the only character of the book worth preserving was his own creation, Colonel Sellers.[11] During these years when he was engaged in other enterprises, Mark had worked now and then on his partly autobiographical story about boyhood. This was the first novel he completed alone.

Among the growing number of staunch and determined admirers of the work of Mark Twain at this period was H. O. Houghton of the Riverside Press in Cambridge, Massachusetts. On February 6, 1875, Houghton wrote a confidential letter to Twain explaining his plans to publish a series of novels by "foremost American novelists" in order to give more recognition to American fiction. He asked Twain to contribute the first novel in the series, and when Twain declined, Houghton was very reluctant to take his answer as final.[12]

In mid-June of the same year, when Mark Twain's work on his new book neared completion, Howells read the manuscript and responded with enthusiasm, but suggested some revisions. *The Adventures of Tom Sawyer* was completed on July 5, 1875, and copyrighted by title page sixteen days later. In January, 1876, Howells read the manuscript again and, as Bret Harte had done with the manuscript for *The Innocents Abroad*, made detailed suggestions for revisions. Remarking gratefully that Howells' pencil marks, "scattered all along," "swept away all labor," Mark Twain followed Howells' directions without even bothering to reread the manuscript, although he reminded Howells that he himself had "thoroughly & painstakingly" revised the manuscript before inflicting it upon him.

For all his success and prosperity, Mark Twain was still comparing his achievements with Bret Harte's. Although when the books were published, *Gabriel Conroy* was much longer than *Tom Sawyer*, earlier Mark Twain had estimated *Tom Sawyer's* final length as between 900 and 1,000 pages, and his letter to Howells guessed that Harte's novel would be about the same size as his. In this letter of July 5, 1875, Twain told Howells that he would "dearly like" to see *Tom Sawyer* published in the *Atlantic*, but he doubted that it would pay the publishers or the author to issue it that way. "If I could do as well [as Harte in

[11] See correspondence with Warner about dramatization of *The Gilded Age*, MTP.
[12] MTP.

the Scribner's contract] it might possibly pay me, but I seriously doubt it—though it is likely I could do better in England than Bret, who is not widely known there."[13] Mark Twain added: "You see I take a vile mercenary view of things, but my household expenses are something almost ghastly." In the following week Twain had an idea of a way to increase the income which he could expect from *Tom Sawyer*. He suggested that Howells dramatize the novel and "take for remuneration half the first $6,000 which I receive for its representation on the stage." Perhaps it is another coincidence that $6,000 was the sum which Scribner's had agreed to pay for Harte's novel.

The Adventures of Tom Sawyer was turned over to Elisha Bliss to be issued by subscription. True to form, Bliss failed to have the book ready on time, but its appearance was further delayed by Mark Twain himself, who decided that Bliss was not promoting it sufficiently before publication. Mark Twain was firmly convinced that such prepublication promotion was necessary for the financial success of a book, for as he said, "a subscription harvest is *before* publication, not *after* when people have discovered how bad one's book is."[14] Furthermore, observing that his last book, *Sketches New and Old*, was not selling very well, Mark Twain reasoned that this was the wrong time of year to bring out books of any kind. Consequently, without telling even Howells, who was thus placed in the position of reviewing the book in the *Atlantic* an embarrassingly long time before its publication, Mark Twain instructed Bliss to delay publishing *Tom Sawyer* until autumn, then promote the book for the holiday trade. (It may be remembered that in the letter of November 26, 1870, about Harte's soaring reputation and the cause of the first estrangement between Mark Twain and Bret Harte, Mark Twain had told Charles Webb that Twain had wanted Harte to review *The Innocents Abroad* "early for the Overland & help the sale out there." Mark had been incensed at Bliss's delay in publishing *The Innocents Abroad* until Bliss persuaded him that the delay had increased sales.) On April 25, 1876, Mark Twain inserted in the Hartford *Courant* a partly true announcement that *Tom Sawyer* was

---

[13] *Ibid.*, I, 87–88, 92, 121–22. For evidence that Bret Harte was more widely known in England than Mark Twain believed, see Edward S. Lauterbach, "Forty Years of Fun: The History of Victorian Humor Magazines," an unpublished dissertation at the University of Illinois.

[14] *MTH*, I, 132. See also 95, 112, 117, 129.

ready earlier but its publication was postponed to secure the English copyright, and that it was the English edition which was "unavoidably delayed."[15] Twain also told Howells: "I shall print items occasionally still further delaying Tom, till I ease him down to autumn without shock to the waiting world." The English edition was ready on June 10, 1876.[16]

Bret Harte was no match for so shrewd a schemer as Mark Twain. Earlier, Osgood had been anxious to bring out a book of reprints of Harte's sketches, but Harte had scrupulously insisted that this should be done only after Bliss was consulted. Although both Osgood and Harte believed that Harte's book of sketches would help advertise *Gabriel Conroy*, they deferred to Bliss's judgment and the Osgood book was held back four months or more to give precedence to the novel. As for the promotion of *Gabriel Conroy*, Harte wrote Bliss in April, 1876: "I don't care what you send to your agents, and am willing to trust to your judgment of what will sell."[17]

Gabriel Conroy ran serially in *Scribner's Magazine* from November, 1875, through August, 1876. In advance of this serial publication, Frederick Warne and Company of London published in May, 1876, a three-volume edition to maintain copyright. Clemens may have "shored up" Bliss as Harte requested, for on September 20, 1876, the American Publishing Company deposited *Gabriel Conroy* for copyright in the United States, and the book went on sale near the end of the year.[18]

As a result of Mark Twain's insistence that Bliss delay the appearance of *Tom Sawyer* for more industrious and extensive promotion, the American editions of Harte's novel and Twain's novel were offered for sale to the public within a short time of each other. *The Adventures of Tom Sawyer* was published not only by the American Publishing Company but also by Tauchnitz of Leipzig and by Chatto and Windus of London. Pirated Canadian editions of the English *Tom Sawyer* were offered for sale in the United States. The American Publishing Company's edition, copyrighted by title page on July 21, 1875, was offered for sale in December, 1876.

Whether or not Mark Twain recognized it, by the intrinsic merit of

[15] *Ibid.*, I, 132.
[16] Jacob Blanck, compiler, *Bibliography of American Literature*, II, 187–88.
[17] BHL, 50.   [18] Blanck, *American Literature*, III, 426.

this book he had kept the vow he had made to Orion on March 11, 1871. For though Twain continued to be underestimated by literary critics, after *Tom Sawyer* there should have been little doubt that Mark Twain had "topped" Bret Harte or that he would stay ahead.

Mark Twain's view of the comparative reputations of Bret Harte and himself at this period is revealed in his allusions to Harte in relation to a plan Mark proposed for "Blindfold Novelettes," in which twelve writers would give their versions of one plot including a murder and a marriage. On May 1, 1876, Mark suggested that Howells insert in the *Atlantic* a statement which would keep people from imagining that because Mark Twain's name was attached to the project, the whole affair could be considered merely a joke. Conscious of the drawing power of Harte's name, he proposed that Howells' announcement indicate that the first story would be "Mr. Harte's Version of it." Six months later, his attention focused on the imminent collaboration with Harte, Twain promised to ask Warner and Harte if they would write Blindfold Novelettes. The next day he again wrote Howells promising to ask Harte to be one of "a good & godly gang" to fill in the skeleton plot which he now thought Aldrich might be asked to contrive. Among the "towering names" to entice the reader, Harte now followed Holmes and Howells but preceded Henry James.[19]

It was in 1876 that Anna Dickinson became convinced that Mark Twain was jealous of Bret Harte. Long before Miss Dickinson met Harte, she had been a friend of the Langdon family in Elmira, and after the marriage of Sam and Livy, Anna Dickinson had visited the Clemenses as well as the Langdons. Laura Hawkins and Ruth Bolton in *The Gilded Age* are both believed to have owed certain traits to Anna Dickinson.[20] Mark respected Anna's ability to command top prices as a lecturer,[21] but there was a sense of rivalry between the two of them, and when Miss Dickinson attempted to become a dramatic actress, Howells and Twain, for all their pity at her "aesthetic suicide," found some satisfaction in being able to say, "I told you so."[22] Because of Mark Twain's generous response to her request for letters of introduction in

[19] *MTH*, I, 88, 133, 135, 158, 160.

[20] Young, "Anna Dickinson, Mark Twain, and Bret Harte," *loc. cit.*, 42–43.

[21] Neider, *Autobiography*, 161, 175. See also Fatout, *Mark Twain on the Lecture Circuit*, 129, 146, 162.

[22] *MTH*, I, 156–57. See also Howells, *My Mark Twain*, 57.

England, Anna Dickinson in 1874 called him "a friend worth having."[23] But when, in 1876, a Bret Harte book received a "brutal" anonymous review in a newspaper, Miss Dickinson was convinced by the personal tone of the attack that jealousy was the motive, and she strongly suspected that Mark Twain was the author.[24]

The book so savagely reviewed has not been identified, but if Miss Dickinson's suspicion was justified, it is interesting to note that in 1876 a book by Bret Harte entitled *Wan Lee, the Pagan, and Other Sketches* was published by G. Routledge and Sons, Limited, of London. Perhaps the most appealing of all Harte's stories about children, "Wan Lee, the Pagan" had originally been published in *Scribner's Magazine* in September, 1874. Wan Lee was a mischievous Chinese boy who was stoned to death on the streets of San Francisco in 1869. His pranks might be considered Oriental prototypes of Tom Sawyer's. European reviewers sometimes compared "Wan Lee, the Pagan," with Mark Twain's "Disgraceful Persecution of a Boy."[25]

Gabriel Conroy may not have been the subject of the brutal review resented by Miss Dickinson, but any twentieth-century literary critic would damn it. In fact, in 1910, in a book entitled *Leading American Novelists*, John Erskine included a chapter on Bret Harte not because of Harte's one full-length novel but because the panorama of incidents in Harte's stories about California seemed to Erskine to give Harte the effect of a novelist. Yet the consistency of characterization and the unity of effect which Erskine admired in the mass of Harte's stories are precisely what *Gabriel Conroy* lacks.[26] In its vast cyclorama of California life, *Gabriel Conroy* includes enough material for several novels.

Bret Harte himself always held a special affection for this novel which he sacrificed much time, labor, and money to create. And, in truth, the work includes admirable elements. Its social commentary is shrewd and comprehensive. Among its memorable scenes, the most vivid is Harte's marvelous picture of snow in the high Sierras, which opens the prologue. James Joyce may have had this description in

[23] Letter from Anna Dickinson to Mark Twain, June or July 17, 1874, MTP.

[24] Young, "Anna Dickinson, Mark Twain, and Bret Harte," *loc. cit*, 45–46.

[25] Hemminghaus, *Mark Twain in Germany*, 35n.

[26] John Erskine, *Leading American Novelists*, 368.

mind when he created the strange, snow-haunted scenes in "The Dead" and called the central character of that famous story Gabriel Conroy.

That James Joyce should have been familiar with Harte's novel is not surprising in view of *Gabriel Conroy's* reception outside the United States. It was published by Tauchnitz, by Belford Brothers (Toronto), and in 1880 and 1890 by Chatto and Windus. It was translated into several European languages, including Swedish. In Germany, where it enjoyed immense popularity, Udo Brachvogel, distinguished translator of Longfellow, Poe, Whittier, and Hawthorne, selected *Gabriel Conroy* for his "most ambitious" translation in prose.[27] Thus the popularity of the novel abroad together with Harte's particular affection for the work increased the author's bitter disappointment when Elisha Bliss informed him that by the subscription methods of the American Publishing Company, *Gabriel Conroy* had failed to sell in the United States.

Notwithstanding this failure, Mark Twain continued to profess admiration for Bret Harte's ability as a writer. He admired extravagantly some of Harte's worst creations. Among these was "Thankful Blossom," a sentimental romance written in December, 1876, when Harte—beset by "failure, debt, worry, and ill-health"—showed symptoms of deterioration as a man and as a writer. Nevertheless, Twain always maintained that "Thankful Blossom" belonged "at the very top of Harte's literature,"[28] and Twain liked to recall that Harte worked all night with a plentiful supply of Twain's whisky to complete this historical narrative, which Mark himself insisted on reading to the Saturday Morning Club meeting in his library the following day. This club had been organized by Twain for teen-age girls of Asylum Hill, who met regularly in his home for social and cultural improvement.[29] Twain himself was an honorary member. Papers read before the club were prepared by men and women of literary and intellectual prominence, and that Bret Harte had been invited to appear before them was another indication of his continued though now precarious prestige.[30]

Another Bret Harte creation mistakenly admired by Mark Twain was one Hop Sing, a Chinese character in Harte's play entitled *Two Men of Sandy Bar*. Various reasons have been given for the failure of

[27] Heminghaus, *Mark Twain in Germany*, 12–13. [28] *MTE*, 275–77.
[29] Andrews, *Nook Farm*, 104. [30] Paine, *Biography*, 588.

Two Men of Sandy Bar. Arthur Hobson Quinn's *History of American Drama* blames the star system in vogue on the American stage of 1876 and offers the additional explanation that Harte's characters—Colonel Starbottle, John Oakhurst, Sandy Morton—had been so vividly brought to life in Harte's fiction that playgoers objected to their being tampered with even by their own creator.[31] Harte himself was convinced that the cause of the play's failure was his attempt to fuse "two stories."[32] Judge Joseph Daly—brother, biographer, and ghost writer for the more famous Augustin—insisted that the "amiable author" of *Two Men of Sandy Bar* was unduly apologetic and that the play had been killed by the "unnatural enunciation (not only not Western, but not anything known to civilization)" of the actor Stuart Robson, who played Colonel Starbottle and for whom the play had been written.[33]

Whatever may have been the causes of failure—and there were several—in *Two Men of Sandy Bar,* Harte unquestionably attempted to do too many things. First, he tried to salvage something from "Kentuck," a play about the West on which—as we shall see later—Harte and Dion Boucicault had attempted to collaborate in 1874. Second, Harte was not—as he said—trying to fuse two stories: he was trying to graft onto the plot of "Mr. Thompson's Prodigal" elements in two stories: "The Idyl of Red Gulch" and "The Iliad of Sandy Bar." And the hodgepodge melodrama included not only Colonel Starbottle, whose buffoonery was his main excuse for being; Hop Sing, as irrelevant as the nameless Chinaman of "The Iliad" who had refused to tell why York and his partner Scott had quarreled; but York himself, who had even less excuse than Hop Sing. For since Scott had died in "The Iliad," the two men of Sandy Bar were now Oakhurst and Sandy Morton, who had once been close friends but had become bitterly estranged before the play opened.

The dialogue of Harte's play includes this speech by the derelict Sandy Morton:

There is one man . . . knows me better than any man who lives.

[31] Arthur Hobson Quinn, *A History of the American Drama from the Civil War the Present Day,* I, 113–14.

[32] Bradford A. Booth, "Unpublished Letters of Bret Harte," *American Literature,* Vol. XVI (May, 1944), 140–41.

[33] Daly, *Augustin Daly,* 170–76, 234.

He has done me wrong,—a great wrong . . .—but I will forgive him. I will do more,—I will ask his forgiveness . . .—God help him and forgive him as I do! . . . he has wronged me in a private way: that is *my* business, not *yours* . . . but he was *my* partner, no one shall abuse him before me.[34]

With all their sentimentality, these words define the code of "partners" in Harte's fiction. It was a code in which Bret Harte, perhaps naïvely, believed.

In *Two Men of Sandy Bar*, the two men who had quarreled became reconciled even to becoming brothers by adoption. Henry J. York of "The Iliad" had deteriorated into Harry York, reformed spendthrift of Poker Flat. As the slightly intoxicated "produce merchant of San Francisco," however, he was still a man of "honest sincerity," ready to turn over his bank balance to help a friend. The play concluded with Colonel Starbottle's offer to make himself "personally responsible" for all the play's faults.

But unlike Colonel Sellers, Colonel Starbottle could not guarantee the success of a play. In that era of the theaters of Augustin Daly, poorer plays throve. But with the zealous co-operation of contemporary critics in New York, *Two Men of Sandy Bar* was damned to a very short life. In October, 1876, Howells told Clemens that he thought Harte had reacted "crazily" to the criticism of his play, but that Harte had been "shamefully decried and abused." "Of course no man knows till he's tried how absurdly he'll act, but I wish Harte had not been tried," wrote Howells.[35] In the same month Charles Dudley Warner in Nook Farm wrote Charley Webb in Switzerland about Bret's "row with the critics" over his play. Warner agreed that the actors were largely responsible for the play's failure, yet justifiably he found the play itself "pretty lame." However, Warner told Webb that he thought Harte intended to do better before long.[36]

Bret Harte wrote Mark Twain that he recognized weaknesses in the play, but he thought the production not so bad as critics reported, and he offered to send Mark tickets.[37] Mark accepted, attended the play in New York, and was hugely entertained. Mark Twain agreed that the critics had been unduly severe. (Later he would insist that the play

[34] *Writings*, XII, 378.
[35] *MTH*, I, 162.
[36] Letter of Oct. 27, 1876, MTP.
[37] Letter of Sept. 3, 1876, MTP.

would have succeeded if anyone else had written it.)[38] In 1876, Twain was particularly impatient with Harte for selling all rights to the play to Robson, for Mark was convinced that *Two Men of Sandy Bar* could be doctored until it was entirely successful and that then it would "clear a great sum every year."[39] Mark seems to have had an idea that he was just the doctor and promoter which Harte's play, in its "crude state," needed.

Between 1872 and 1876, Mark Twain had topped Bret Harte. But he was not yet prepared to trim and train and school him patiently.

[38] *MTE*, 275.
[39] *MTH*, I, 152.

10

COLLABORATION ON *AH SIN*

The play is done. We are plotting out another one.

MARK TWAIN to WILLIAM DEAN HOWELLS, February 22, 1877

THAT HOP SING of *Two Men of Sandy Bar* drew much much applause from the audience and was considered the one bright spot in an otherwise dismal failure has generally been attributed to the skillful acting of Charles Thomas Parsloe. This actor had already made something of a name for himself on the American stage. In 1868 he had played Sam Weller in Augustin Daly's adaptation of *Pickwick Papers*.[1] In 1876, in the comparatively minor role of Hop Sing, he had stolen the show from Stuart Robson, the star. The New York *Tribune* praised Parsloe's "skillful and comic" portrayal, and Mark Twain considered Parsloe's Hop Sing a "perfectly delightful Chinaman."

But Hop Sing's success was also due to the notoriety of "The Heathen Chinee." And like the verses referred to in "The Poet of Sierra Flat," "Plain Language from Truthful James" suffered from many misinterpretations. As Dickens, accused of race prejudice in his characterization of Fagin, had created Mr. Riah in *Our Mutual Friend*, Bret Harte, dismayed by misinterpretations and misapplications of "Plain Language from Truthful James," had in 1874 created another Hop Sing, an intelligent, sophisticated, and admired gentleman who attributed deficiencies in a little Chinese boy's education to the fact that he had, perhaps, been negligently permitted to associate too much with American children. "Wan Lee, the Pagan," the sketch in which this Hop Sing appeared, denounced the stereotype stage Chinaman whose mirror image of a race increased race prejudice. The same sketch included Harte's most forthright denunciation of those who "began to think

[1] Marvin Felheim, *The Theater of Augustin Daly*, 96.

that the passage in the Constitution which guaranteed civil and religious liberty to every citizen or foreigner was a mistake."[2]

Although the comic Hop Sing of *Two Men of Sandy Bar* was very different from the Hop Sing of "Wan Lee, the Pagan," he was also different from the Ah Sin of "Plain Language from Truthful James." There was nothing subtle about him and he did not cheat, although his persistent attempts to collect pay for his laundering afforded Parsloe opportunities for humorous pantomime. Furthermore, like Harte's verses about "The Latest Chinese Outrage" (a scathing attack on political and economic discrimination against Chinese), *Two Men of Sandy Bar* left no doubt that the white men owed Hop Sing money.

Moreover, in *Two Men of Sandy Bar*, allusions to various forms of racial discrimination are characteristic of Harte. The race prejudice of the Southern Colonel Starbottle is, as usual, ridiculed. The Mexican's hatred of Anglo-Americans is motivated by physical injury and the insult of being called "Greaser," a term which, like "Jap" and "Nigger," Mark continued to use,[3] although in "Goldsmith's Friend Abroad Again" he seemed aware of the pejorative quality of the term and grouped "Greasers" with other foreign elements badly treated in a San Francisco jail. A popular misconception which Harte's fiction frequently attacks is that members of dark-skinned races are innately treacherous. In *Two Men of Sandy Bar* the most treacherous person is a white man, a fact emphasized at the same time Harte satirized the slang use of the term "white man" as the ultimate compliment.

Mark Twain, who resembled Colonel Starbottle in several ways, never completely outgrew some of these race prejudices which Bret Harte regularly attacked. In *Letters from the Earth*, a compilation of Mark Twain's writings arranged and edited by Bernard De Voto in 1939 but withheld from publication until 1962, Mark Twain satirized man's concept of heaven because "it contains ... every imaginable thing that is repulsive to man, and not a single thing he likes." One of these "repulsive" things is desegregation with its acceptance of belief in the brotherhood of man. According to Mark Twain's Satan:

[2] *Writings*, II, 278. My article "Plain Language from Bret Harte," *Nineteenth-Century Fiction*, Vol. XI (Mar., 1957), 241–60, discusses more fully Harte's writings about Chinese.

[3] For example, see *MTE*, 283. Mark Twain does not capitalize "greaser."

Portrait of Bret Harte in 1885 by John R. Pettie
of the Royal Academy of London

Courtesy of M. Knoedler and Company, New York

Mark Twain, in a 1906 portrait by Samuel J. Woolf

*Courtesy of the Mark Twain Memorial
Commission, Hartford, Connecticut*

The inventor of their heaven empties into it all the nations of the earth, and in one common jumble. All are on an equality absolute, no one of them ranking another; they have to be "brothers"; they have to mix together, pray together, harp together, hosannah together—whites, niggers, Jews, everybody—there's no distinction. Here in the earth all nations hate each other, and every one of them hates the Jew. Yet every pious person adores that heaven and wants to get into it. He really does. And when he is in a holy rapture he thinks that if he were only there he would take all the populace to his heart, and hug, and hug, and hug![4]

In 1876, Bret Harte—needing desperately to bolster his failing fortunes—conceived the idea of writing for Parsloe a play centering on a Chinese character. Aware of Mark Twain's admiration for the Hop Sing of *Two Men of Sandy Bar*, Harte invited Twain to collaborate on the new play. Twain accepted with alacrity.

Recently Mark had found writing in Hartford difficult.[5] Possibly he hoped that Harte (who with all his faults could generally be counted on for gay wit and good company) would provide a stimulus as Joe Goodman had done in rescuing Mark and *Roughing It* from the Buffalo doldrums and as Charles Dudley Warner had done in Hartford when he and Mark had written *The Gilded Age*. In 1874, Mark had urged Howells to "invent a play," which Twain believed would bring in thirty dollars a night in New York and twenty dollars a night on the road. This, he remembered, was what Daly had offered to pay Harte in 1871, with an advance of one or two thousand dollars immediately on delivery of the manuscript.[6] For some time Augustin Daly had also been trying to persuade Mark Twain to furnish him with a play. This Twain had attempted several times without success.[7] In August he wrote Howells that he had "racked himself baldheaded" trying to construct a play but could not do it. Howells' own satisfaction at completing a comedy both pleased and exasperated Mark, for, he asked Howells, "What have you done that God should be so good to you?"[8] Twain persisted in his own attempts, for he remembered with pleasure the financial success of the dramatized *Gilded Age*. In addition to these reasons for accepting Harte's proposal, Twain had never forgotten the fame and fortune brought Harte by "The Heathen Chinee."

[4] Pages 12f., 46. [5] *Mark Twain to Mrs. Fairbanks*, 198.
[6] *MTH*, I, 33. [7] *MTL*, I, 287n. [8] *MTH*, I, 144–45.

On October 11, 1876, Mark happily wrote a confidential letter to William Dean Howells reporting Bret's invitation to collaborate on a play and "divide the swag." Twain said he would put in Scotty Briggs ("See Buck Fanshaw's Funeral, in 'Roughing It,'" he reminded Howells), Harte would "put in a Chinaman (a wonderfully funny creature, as Bret presents him—for 5 minutes—in his Sandy Bar play)." This Chinaman, Mark Twain said, would be "*the* character of the play, and both of us will work on him and develop him."[9] The play would be called *Ah Sin* and thus would exploit enough reputations to be a sure-fire financial success, or so it must have seemed to the two collaborators who went to work in the billiard room at the top of the Clemens' house in Hartford.

From the beginning, Howells was skeptical of the success of the collaboration.[10] He reminded Twain of Harte's reaction to the criticism of *Two Men of Sandy Bar*. There were additional reasons for doubt. Although both Mark Twain and Bret Harte had had earlier contacts with the New York stage, neither was well equipped to write a successful drama. Yet, notwithstanding the failure of *Two Men of Sandy Bar* and the success of *The Gilded Age,* Harte's qualifications were more promising than Twain's.

In the first place, as Arthur Hobson Quinn noted, Harte's "great contribution to modern literature, the portrayal of moral contrasts in human beings from an objective, unmoral point of view, is in itself essentially dramatic."[11] Furthermore, although the American drama was long overlooked as an element in the main stream of American literature, the drama showed many of the same trends and reflected the same influences as those observed in fiction and poetry. And one of the strongest influences of that time was Bret Harte. That Harte influenced the fiction of the period is widely recognized. That Harte also influenced the setting and themes of the current plays was virtually unknown until Marvin Felheim's study of *The Theater of Augustin Daly* in 1956.[12] Augustin Daly's *Horizon*, opening March 21, 1871, in the Olympic Theatre in New York, was not only one of the earliest and most important of American dramas of the frontier; it was also "the first of a series of plays which owe their inspiration to Bret Harte." Professor Felheim believes that Harte and Daly actually anticipated

[9] *Ibid.*, I, 157. [10] *Ibid.*, I, 162. [11] I, 113–14. [12] Pages 68–69, 298–99.

the great literary interest in the frontier so sharply and potently focused by Frederick Jackson Turner's essay on "The Significance of the Frontier in American History" in 1893.[13] Moreover, *Horizon* reflected Harte's realistic portrayal of Indians together with his social commentary on forces contributing to the deterioration of Indians after their lands were pre-empted by frontiersmen. Daly's *Horizon* also included the earliest of many stage versions of "The Heathen Chinee."

Even though Harte's influence on the American theater was apparent, by 1876 Harte had demonstrated that if, as Quinn and other critics have believed, Harte's talent was essentially dramatic, he had considerable difficulty in transmuting dramatic talent into successful drama.[14] For when Harte had tried to dramatize his legend of the West, he soon recognized his own limitations and called on his friend, the famous Irish playwright Dion Boucicault, for aid.

Collaboration proved unsatisfactory. Boucicault found Harte "dilatory and erratic" about working hours, "anxious to get work done" but inclined to "scurry over the ground more rapidly than is consistent with safety." Boucicault's most serious objection was to Harte's irritatingly indefinite financial arrangements with Daly about pay for the collaborators. For Boucicault was aware of the prestige value to Daly of the combined names of Harte and Boucicault. And for this value, Boucicault felt that Daly should pay considerably more than the one hundred dollars a night which Harte had agreed to. At one time it was decided that Boucicault would provide the dramatic structure, ask Daly to approve it, and then turn the play over to Harte, who would write most of the dialogue. But finally Boucicault wrote Daly to pay him one thousand dollars for his doctoring up of the play but not to associate his name with the production. "Let the play be Harte's alone," he said. "He can take as much or as little of my plans as he likes—And you will pay me for helping him over the stile."

Boucicault made a "cast *raisoné*" of the play on which he and Harte had worked. Its title was "Kentuck," a name which both Boucicault and Daly liked because it seemed "good familiar Brethartish."[15] Kentuck, of course, is a character in "The Luck of Roaring Camp." Notwithstanding their difficulties in collaboration, Boucicault and Harte

---

[13] *Ibid.*, 70.   [14] Pemberton, *Bret Harte, A Treatise and a Tribute*, 246–47.
[15] Daly, *Augustin Daly*, 170ff.

remained lifelong friends, and one of Harte's weaknesses as a drama-tist was his continued faith in Boucicault as a great master of the "gram-mar of the theater."

But *Two Men of Sandy Bar*, Bret Harte's final version of his first play about the West, bore little resemblance to "Kentuck." Reportedly the author sold this play to the actor Stuart Robson for three thousand dollars, with the promise of an additional twenty dollars a night to the limit of another three thousand dollars.[16] But if Mark Twain con-verted Harte to his own belief that Harte had sold the rights to this play for much too low a price, Robson as well as Harte felt cheated. At one time there were rumors that Robson and Harte had quarreled, but after an encouraging reception of the play in Washington, Robson wrote Harte the following letter:

> THE ARLINGTON, WASHINGTON
> October 6, 1876
>
> MY DEAR BRET,—You will be glad to hear that we are doing an excellent business, and that John T. Ford predicts even greater success in Baltimore. The papers are enthusiastic in praise of the play, and alto-gether I am well satisfied. Will you credit me with the fact that I have never lost faith in my venture? . . . The Washington papers have certainly treated us well, which, after the many misrepresentations made of the play, is most gratifying.—Believe me, your friend truly,
>
> STUART ROBSON[17]

After its brief run in New York and a more successful showing in Wash-ington, *Two Men of Sandy Bar* went on tour and later was translated into German by Herman Herschel of Hamburg.[18]

Although Mark Twain's association with the American theater seemed more successful than Harte's, it was, in fact, more limited.

Characteristically, Mark Twain's assertions about his interest in writ-ing and procuring plays are contradictory. Among reminiscences of Bret Harte in *Mark Twain in Eruption* is Twain's declaration that his re-porting for the old *Morning Call* of the nightly performances in all six of San Francisco's theaters resulted in a revulsion against the theater so severe that for forty years he had been unable to look at even the

---

[16] *BHAE*, 230.   [17] Pemberton, *The Life of Bret Harte*, 259–60.
[18] Quinn, *American Drama*, II, 109–10. See also unpublished letter, May 12, 1879, to Herman Herschel, Hamburg, William Andrews Clark Memorial Library.

outside of a theater building without "a spasm of the dry gripes." As for the inside, he said, he knew next to nothing about it, and in all the intervening years, he had seldom had a sight of it or even "a desire in that regard which couldn't have been overcome by argument."[19] The truth is that Mark Twain's interest in the stage was prolonged and persistent. For Twain as well as for Harte, Howells, and Henry James, writing a successful play was a "never suppressed desire." Not many years before his *Eruptions* about Harte, Mark Twain declared that to write a drama is "the greatest of all arts" and "requires the highest talents possible and the rarest gifts."[20] He tried more than once to write a play—with and without a collaborator. But as Howells, who tried to collaborate with him on a play, recognized, Mark Twain's dramatic gifts were those of the actor.[21] That Mark Twain knew "next to nothing" about the business of writing and producing a play was probably true.[22]

Before collaborating with Bret Harte in 1876, Mark Twain had served an apprenticeship as a playwright, but his experiences hardly qualified him as a journeyman or master. Back in 1867 he had planned but never completed a dramatization of "The Quaker City Holy Land Excursion."[23] In 1873 a play entitled *Roughing It* had appeared on the New York stage, but this burlesque of Western life was not a dramatization of Mark Twain's novel; it was Augustin Daly's adaptation of a popular Parisian revue on which "some of the experiences of Mr. Mark Twain" had been "superimposed." The dramatization of *The Gilded Age* was a tremendous success. For one week's performance in Philadelphia, Mark Twain cleared $1,616.16.[24] This play enjoyed a phenomenally long run and, according to Twain, brought him a profit of $70,000.00.[25] But the extent to which Mark Twain could claim credit for the success of this play is open to question.

To begin with, Charles Dudley Warner had written half the novel, though not the part which brought to life the memorable Colonel Mulberry Sellers. Mark Twain's irritability at working with Warner (resulting in "prejudices and dislikes" which he mistakenly believed he

[19] *MTE*, 255.   [20] Felheim, *The Theater of Augustin Daly*, 289–99.
[21] *My Mark Twain*, 23, 51–52.   [22] Webster, *Mark Twain: Business Man*, 235.
[23] Felheim, *The Theater of Augustin Daly*, 299.   [24] *MTH*, I, 159.
[25] Felheim, *The Theater of Augustin Daly*, 300.

had outgrown by September, 1876)[26] was increased when a hostile reviewer expressed the belief that Mark Twain was coasting on his reputation and letting somebody else do his writing for him.[27] Then in April, 1874, Gilbert S. Densmore, a reporter for the *Golden Era*, had dramatized the Twain-Warner novel for a California theater. This same Densmore had once helped himself to Bret Harte's "M'liss." Without the author's consent, and without bothering to make clear that his version was not Harte's own work, Densmore had written an elongated narrative of sixty-two chapters and given it the name of Harte's popular story. The outraged Bret had called the action a "forgery" and a "swindle on the public."[28] But when Twain learned from a review in the San Francisco *Chronicle* that Densmore's dramatization of *The Gilded Age* was a success, he (1) wrote a letter to the *Chronicle*, (2) requested from Warner what amounted to a relinquishment of any share in the financial success of a play centering on Colonel Sellers, and (3) for a "handsome sum" (four hundred dollars) bought Densmore's dramatization.[29]

Charles Dudley Warner generously yielded his rights to the dramatization entitled *The Gilded Age* just as Howells would later relinquish "gratis" all rights to an attempted sequel on which he collaborated with Twain.[30] In 1874, however, Warner felt a little hurt at being squeezed out and there was a rumor that relations between Warner and Twain were strained, but the two remained apparent friends and Mrs. Clemens' regard for Warner never wavered.[31] After a trial run in the provinces, *The Gilded Age*, now owned exclusively by Mark Twain, opened at the Park Theatre in New York on September 16, 1874. The star was John T. Raymond, who had already successfully played the leading role in Densmore's dramatization in San Francisco.

In answer to current gossip about Twain's use of the Densmore version, Raymond on November 3 published in the New York *Sun* a letter saying that although the Densmore play was an excellent one, the production in New York "was entirely the work of Mr. Samuel L.

---

[26] *MTH*, I, 150–51; II, 686–87. See also notes of Miss Lyon, Nov. 19, 1933, on a copy of the agreement between Clemens, Warner, and the American Publishing Company, MTP.

[27] Neider, *Autobiography*, 274.   [28] *BHL*, 23.

[29] See letter of May 5, 1874, to Charles Dudley Warner, MTP. *MTH*, II, 862.

[30] *My Mark Twain*, 26.   [31] *MTH*, I, 151.

Clemens."[32] It has been suggested that Raymond's motive was a belief that the play would attract smaller audiences if part of the work was attributed to Densmore.[33] Bret Harte's letter of August 8, 1874 ("Raymond tells me you have dramatized your last book and that its good"), expressed some surprise at Mark Twain in the role of playwright but indicated that Harte did not question Twain's authorship.[34] Nevertheless, Howells believed that the dramatization made famous by Raymond was substantially not Mark's script. "To me, at least," Howells said, "Clemens never pretended that he had the least hand in it."[35] In a letter to the editor of the Hartford *Post*, Mark Twain insisted that he had entirely rewritten the play three times. But apparently this letter was never mailed. Six or seven months later he wrote Howells that when the opportunity offered, he intended to "pile that play onto the thief Densmore's shoulders!"[36]

The controversy about how much of the play *The Gilded Age* was written by Mark Twain has never been settled. Probably Densmore himself came closest to the truth when he wrote that the character of Sellers was Mark's and the "arrangement of incidents" became Mark's "by purchase."[37] At any rate, William Winter, dean of New York drama critics in 1874, judged that the play possessed "practically no merit whatever except as a vehicle for the actor."[38] And DeLancey Ferguson agreed that the play owed its success to Raymond's "stage sense."[39]

On the play's opening night in New York, Mark Twain made an astonishing curtain speech in which he directly criticized to the audience the star's portrayal of the central role. After *The Gilded Age* had made a long and profitable run, Twain made another curtain speech in which he referred to "these actors of mine, this play of mine, this success of ours," and stated that he had no desire to "criticise or abuse"

---

[32] Raymond's letter can be found in William Winter's *The Life of David Belasco*, I, 66–67.

[33] *MTH*, I, 84. [34] See Chapter VIII in this volume.

[35] *My Mark Twain*, 22.

[36] *MTH*, I, 83. For the editor's interpretation of what Mark Twain meant by these words, see page 84. It sounds to me as if he meant to claim the play if it was good and disclaim it if it was bad. This is about what he did in his curtain speeches. See also *ibid.*, II, 862.

[37] *Ibid.*, II, 862. [38] *The Life of David Belasco*, 67.

[39] *Man and Legend*, 174.

either the actors or the play. But privately he continued to insist that Raymond was "a pygmy of pygmies" and that "in the hands of a great actor," the "piteous turnip-eating scene . . . would have dimmed any manly spectator's eyes."[40] Nevertheless, when he and Howells attempted a sequel, it was this comic aspect of Colonel Sellers which they exaggerated to what seemed to Raymond the "brink of lunacy."[41] In 1875, Howells praised Raymond's acting, but after Mark wrote that Raymond was taking too much credit for the characterization of Colonel Sellers, Howells said he had inserted a barb in his criticism.[42]

Regardless of who wrote the play or who deserved the credit for its success, Mark Twain exulted in the profit which the dramatization of *The Gilded Age* brought him. When the play went on tour, he hired an agent to follow the company, count the gate receipts, and see to it that the author's share was duly paid. The agent was to report every day by postcard the amount of Twain's half of the intake, and when these cards arrived at the Hartford house at dinnertime, Mark read aloud the figures and pranced around the table waving the cards in triumph. When Bret Harte invited Mark Twain to collaborate on a play about Ah Sin—a character even better known than Colonel Sellers —Twain was hoping to repeat the financial success of *The Gilded Age.*

With these not very encouraging backgrounds of experience in collaborating and in writing plays, Mark and Bret began their work together. Twain wrote Howells that he and Harte would each form a plot and then they would select the best of the two plots and combine them. (This scheme Howells would consider "as nearly nothing as chaos could be" when Twain later proposed it to him.)[43] At the beginning of the collaboration with Harte, Twain worked eight or nine hours a day for six days, and this, he said, "nearly killed" him.[44] He asked Howells to arrange secretly for the printing of a title page which could be used in application for copyright.

Later Mark gave Albert Bigelow Paine a different account of the way he and Harte worked. "Well," he said, "Bret came down to Hart-

---

[40] Paine, *Mark Twain's Autobiography*, I, 89–90; Neider, *Autobiography*, 19.

[41] Felheim, *The Theater of Augustin Daly*, 300. Professor Felheim quotes the late Dixon Wecter.

[42] *MTH*, I, 80–83.   [43] *My Mark Twain*, 22–23.   [44] *MTH*, I, 157.

ford and we talked it over and then Bret wrote it while I played billiards, but of course I had to go over it to get the dialect right. Bret
never did know anything about dialect." "Hardly a fair statement of
the case," comments Mr. Paine, asserting that both men worked and
worked hard.[45]

Mark Twain's 1907 account of the way he and Harte collaborated
begins like the dealing of cards in a poker game when stakes are high:
"I named my characters and described them; Harte did the same by
his. Then he began to sketch the scenario, act by act, and scene by scene.
He worked rapidly and seemed to be troubled by no hesitations or inde-
cisions."[46] Mark Twain was remarkably consistent in his statements
that Harte wrote rapidly and easily, though other acquaintances and
Harte himself are equally consistent in statements to the contrary. On
the whole, however, Mark Twain's words here are generous.

After the preliminary sketch of *Ah Sin*, the "filling in" began. Mark
told his biographer:

> Harte set down the dialogue swiftly and I had nothing to do except
> when one of my characters was to say something; then Harte told me
> the nature of the remark that was required. I furnished the language
> and he jotted it down. After this fashion we worked two or three or four
> hours every day for a couple of weeks, and produced a comedy that
> was good and would act. His part of it was the best part.

As the two friends worked many hours together on *Ah Sin*, in their
minds and hovering over their tensions were memories of old ties, old
rivalries, and, perhaps, old wounds. But in the beginning, both seem
to have worked together without discord. In November, Mark Twain
took time off for a visit to the Howellses. There he talked so enthusiastically about the work in progress that he convinced Mrs. Howells
that the play would be "tremendously funny" and made the doubting
Howells like what he heard about it.[47] By December the first drafts
of *Ah Sin* had been completed, and the collaboration entered concluding
stages of revisions and arrangements for production. Harte's funds were
lower than ever, and to bring in an immediate sum to tide him over
and provide for his family until profits from the play should begin

---

[45] Paine, *Biography*, 587.   [46] *MTE*, 277.   [47] *MTH*, I, 165.

coming in, he frenziedly completed "Thankful Blossom," the story which Mark Twain read with admiration to the Saturday Morning Club meeting in the Clemens' library the next day.

On December 16, 1876, Bret Harte wrote the following business and personal letter to Mark Twain. The letter was headed 45 Fifth Avenue, New York—the home of Mrs. Knaufft.

MY DEAR MARK,

I got a short note from Parsloe yesterday, making an appointment to meet me at Dutton's at 10:30 to-day. I was there, waited an hour, but *he* didn't come. At about 3 P.M. he called on me here, where after some desultory talk I read him those portions of the 1st & 2d acts that indicated his *role,* and he expressed himself satisfied with it, and competent to take it in hand. As nearly as I could judge he was pleased.

Of the contract, its nature, what would be his share of the profits, and generally what *we* should expect from him *I said nothing.* In fact I was only too glad to leave all that business with you. He talked,—a little prematurely I thought—and with a certain egotism that I had noticed before—about his having made the fortunes already of certain people to whom he had been subordinate, and of his intention now of trying to make his own. He intimated that he was hereafter "going to look out for himself." To all of which I said nothing, and shall deliver him into your hands without committing you to even a single suggestion. He is to go with me to Hartford on such day as I may name early next week, and twelve hours before, I shall give you notice by telegraph of our coming. You can, if you like, meet us at the Station, and we can go to your lawyer's at once.

You will be surprised, I dare say, that with all my anxiety to push our play into print I am still halting and fussing over the manuscript. I've been revising the 1st and 2d acts—writing myself *up* and you down, that is trying to make myself more easily intelligible, and you not quite so *prononcé.* I find that Mrs. H's opinion of the real Plunketts jumps with your wife's, and I think we'll have to modify Miss P. at least. I think that Mrs. H. and Mrs. C. represent fairly our feminine auditors, and as we are not constructing women "after our own image" or as we have seen them, I suppose we will have to defer to their ideas of what a woman ought to be.

I hope, dear old boy, that you are better in health, and that Nature has let up generally on your bowels. For myself, I was quite knocked up by my last day's work, and when I got back to N.Y. was for a day or two unable to do anything, and "the Ba" might have put her finger on me as an illustration of "shop head" and "ledder heard."

Remember me kindly to your wife, Mrs. Langdon and Miss Hess. Tell Mrs. Clemens that she must forgive me for my heterodoxy—that until she does I shall wear sackcloth (fashionably cut,) and that I would put ashes on my head but that Nature has anticipated me, and that I feel her gentle protests to my awful opinions all the more remorsefully that I am away; say to Miss Hess she is n't from Boston, and that I always agreed with her about the natural infamy of Man; tell Mrs. Langdon I forgive her for liking you so much, and her general disposition to weakly defer to your horrible egotism and stubbornness; and then kiss Susie for me and implore "the Ba" on your bended knees, to add me to the Holy Family.

Always, dear old fellow,
Yours
B. H.[48]

The author of "The Luck of Roaring Camp," "Wan Lee, the Pagan," and "The Queen of the Pirate Isle" always harbored a particular affection for children. "The Ba" was Mark's pet name for Clara, his second daughter. In September, Mark had written Mrs. Fairbanks that the little girl, then two years old, had "added many graces, & 2 or 3 new words."[49] Mark Twain had started out systematically to record the sayings of "the Ba" and her elder sister Susy, and both Mark and Livy sometimes reported what the children said in their prayers.[50] One prayer was regularly elongated to include each member of the Clemens' household—which Twain called the "Holy Family."[51] Mrs. Langdon was Mark's mother-in-law and Miss Hess was Fanny C. Hesse, Clemens' secretary, who left his employ the following year but worked for him again in later years.[52]

In relation to *Ah Sin,* several elements in this letter are particularly noteworthy:

The first paragraph provides a preface to the friction between Charles T. Parsloe, the actor to play the title role of *Ah Sin,* and the author who created the character to be portrayed. The underlining of the word

[48] Hitherto unpublishhd letter, MTP.
[49] *Mark Twain to Mrs. Fairbanks,* 202.
[50] *MTH,* I, 143.   [51] Paine, *Biography,* 583.
[52] *MTH,* II, 626. Mark Twain also spelled the name Hess. See *ibid.,* I, 164.

role suggests that Harte resented in Parsloe the same kind of presumptuousness of which Mark complained to Howells about Raymond.[53] Parsloe seems to have begun the association with a chip on his shoulder and an aggressive consciousness of his own success in *Two Men of Sandy Bar*. At this time, Harte reacted to egotism with considerable forbearance. In bringing Parsloe to Hartford to discuss matters with Mark Twain, Bret Harte became an instrument to the formation of an alliance between Twain and Parsloe from which Harte would eventually find himself rather spitefully excluded.

A second point worth noting is that Bret Harte apparently had as much faith in Mark Twain's business acumen as he had doubts of his own.

Third, the letter indicates that at this stage of the collaboration, far from being desultory and erratic about revisions, Harte—who had, perhaps, learned his lesson with Boucicault—was taking pains to the point of fussiness over the manuscript. This was a practice on which Pemberton would later comment when he and Harte successfully collaborated on another play.

Next in this Bret Harte letter enters the problem of the Plunketts, which plagued the two authors from the beginning to the end of *Ah Sin*. The name is strangely intrusive. On the staff of the Virginia City *Enterprise* there had been a real Plunkett, mentioned in Mark Twain's *Autobiography* in relation to the famous duel.[54] In Bret Harte's "M'liss," written before Twain and Harte had become acquainted, there appears a judge of that name. Moreover, it will be remembered that Harte's early story of failure and disillusionment, "A Monte Flat Pastoral," was subtitled "How Old Man Plunkett Went Home."

Ah Sin is not included in the collected writings of either Bret Harte or Mark Twain, but in 1961 the Book Club of California published an "amanuensis copy" of one text of the play. In this text Bill Plunkett was a comic character, the "champion liar of Calaveras." He was the friend of York, a mining engineer, whom the miners considered a snob because he wore gloves and a "stove pipe hat," and when the whisky bottle was passed around, he refused to drink with the miners. In the characters of Plunkett and York, it is not difficult to recognize caricatures of Mark Twain and Bret Harte.

[53] *Ibid.*, I, 81.   [54] Neider, *Autobiography*, 113.

The setting of *Ah Sin* is in the Stanislaus region not far from Columbia and Fiddletown. The mining camp of the play is called Deadwood, although the actual Deadwood (the famous mining center where Joaquin Miller reputedly wrote his first poem) is near Scott's Bar in northern California. The names of Scotty Briggs of "Buck Fanshaw's Funeral" and of Scott, York's partner who died in "The Iliad of Sandy Bar," may have been suggested to Mark Twain and Bret Harte by John W. Scott, who discovered gold in the Klamath area in 1850. In the mining center of *Ah Sin*, men prospected for gold and women prospected for husbands.

The plot of *Ah Sin* was complicated by means of the old trick of assumed names and mistaken identity. The "real Plunketts," of whom Mrs. Harte and Mrs. Clemens disapproved, were two females: Mrs. Plunkett (on whose malapropisms the script heavily relied for comedy) and her "wilful and practical daughter," whom York sent for when Bill Plunkett disappeared. Since Mark Twain referred to the Plunketts as "My old Plunkett family,"[55] he evidently substituted them for his originally planned contribution: Scotty Briggs, who disappeared from the collaboration more completely than Bill Plunkett disappeared in the play. Harte's attempt to persuade Mark Twain to defer to the feminine perceptions and critical judgment of Mrs. Harte and Mrs. Clemens is worth remembering in relation to later, more detached criticisms of the Plunketts.

The concluding paragraphs of Harte's letter of December 16, 1876, show him very close to the Clemens family and thinking of them all with affectionate concern. The propitiatory tone suggests some disagreement with the family, and any questioning of Livy's judgment by Harte may well have seemed sacrilege to Mark, even if he himself was not inclined to act upon her judgment in the matter of the Plunketts. But in view of Clemens' later charges that Harte had insulted Mrs. Clemens, Harte's respectful attitude toward her in this letter is of particular interest.

The contract which Harte was only too glad to leave to Mark was promptly devised. Among the Mark Twain Papers in Berkeley is a copy of this contract signed first in Hartford by Samuel L. Clemens on December 30, 1876, and then in New York by Brett Harte and Chas

[55] *MTH*, I, 192.

Thos Parsloe on January 5, 1877. In contrast with financial arrangements between Harte and Daly for "Kentuck"—arrangements so vague and indefinite that Boucicault had protested to Daly—this contract is extremely detailed and specific. Notwithstanding Mark's expressed aversion for such legal jargon,[56] the *Ah Sin* contract is filled with "party of the first part," "party of the second part," "the said parties of the first and second part," "the said Parsloe," and "the said Clemens and the said Harte." Its complicated machinations would have delighted Tom Sawyer. But whether the phrasing was Mark Twain's or his lawyer's, the contract clearly conveyed to Parsloe the exclusive right to perform or cause to be performed the play *Ah Sin* "throughout the whole world" and during his whole lifetime on certain conditions.

These provisions were essentially as follows:

1. Clemens, Harte, and Parsloe were to share equally in the gross profits of the performances after deducting expenses of printing, posting, and the usual salary or percentage to an agency for contracts with managers.

2. Parsloe was prohibited from employing additional actors or advance agents unless two of the three parties approved.

3. Clemens and Harte should decide whether they wished an agent to travel with Parsloe, with the right to examine contracts made by Parsloe and statements of profits made to him by managers, or whether Parsloe himself should make these reports of profits due Clemens and Harte. If an agent was employed, he should be paid by Clemens and Harte. Weekly reports of the agent or Parsloe were to be made to "said Clemens or any person designated by him."

4. Legal steps to prevent infringement of dramatic rights could be instigated by any two of the parties, but costs must be paid by all three.

5. For the duration of the contract, Parsloe should not perform in any play other than *Ah Sin* unless the weekly net profits of the three should fall to an average of $350 a week "during the whole period of six consecutive months." If Parsloe broke the agreement, he must pay Clemens and Harte $25,000, "not as a penalty but as damages sustained by said Clemens and Harte."

6. Clemens agreed to advance Parsloe $1,000 for payment of expenses in staging the play. Parsloe and Harte would repay Clemens two-

[56] Neider, *Autobiography*, 205.

thirds of this sum from profits of the play. If there were no such profits, Parsloe would not be required to pay, but Harte would still be bound for one-third of the sum.

7. If Clemens and Harte disapproved his additions, Parsloe must pay them $25 for each time he ad libbed.

In this contract, Samuel L. Clemens and Brett Harte were clearly parties of the first part and Charles T. Parsloe was the party of the second part.

On February 22, 1877, Mark Twain wrote Howells a letter rejoicing in the election of Hayes, suggesting as commissioner of Indian affairs a man who knew Indians "yet" had some humanity in him (Twain insisted that knowledge of Indians and humanitarianism seldom existed in the same person), urging Howells and his wife to come for a visit, and announcing of the collaboration with Harte on *Ah Sin*: "The play is done. We are plotting out another one."[57]

[57] *MTH,* I, 172–73.

11

DISSENSION

No, Mark, I do not think it advisable for us to write another play together.

BRET HARTE to MARK TWAIN, March 1, 1877

JUST WHEN MARK TWAIN'S INTENSE HOSTILITY to Bret Harte began is uncertain. Thirty years later Mark Twain believed that resentment had seethed in his mind for some time before the explosive scene reported in *Mark Twain in Eruption*. According to this report, for a fortnight Harte had made himself "liberally entertaining" with "smart and bright sarcasms leveled at everything on the place." Although he was always sensitive about criticisms of his house and furnishings, Mark Twain said he had "endured" Harte's sarcasms for Mrs. Clemens' sake until the "last day." Then came what Twain called "the last feather," which seemed to him a "slight and vague and veiled satirical remark with Mrs. Clemens for a target." Harte denied that even by implication he intended any criticism of Mrs. Clemens, and Twain admitted that if he himself had been in a friendly mood, he would have accepted Harte's denial. But he was not, and he was too angry to give Harte's "reasonings a fair hearing." Instead, Mark Twain's long-smoldering indignation flamed into bitter words, and in his rages, Mark Twain was an accomplished flame thrower.

As he remembered it on February 4, 1907, Mark Twain in 1877 had said "in substance" this:

Harte, your wife is all that is fine and lovable and lovely, and I exhaust praise when I say she is Mrs. Clemens's peer—but in all ways you are a shabby husband to her, and you often speak sarcastically, not to say sneeringly, of her, just as you are constantly doing in the case of other women; but your privilege ends there; you must spare Mrs. Clemens. It does not become you to sneer at all; you are not charged

anything here for the bed you sleep in, yet you have been very smartly
and wittily sarcastic about it, whereas you ought to have been more
reserved in that matter, remembering that you have not owned a bed of
your own for ten years; you have made sarcastic remarks about the
furniture of the bedroom and about the table ware and about the servants and about the carriage and the sleigh and the coachman's livery
—in fact about every detail of the house and half of its occupants; you
have spoken of all these matters contemptuously, in your unwholesome
desire to be witty, but this does not become you; you are barred from
these criticisms by your situation and circumstances; you have a talent
and a reputation which would enable you to support your family most
respectably and independently if you were not a born bummer and
tramp; you are a loafer and an idler, and you go clothed in rags, with
not a whole shred on you except your inflamed red tie, and *it* isn't paid
for; nine-tenths of your income is borrowed money—money which, in
fact, is stolen, since you never intended to repay any of it; you sponge
upon your hard-working widowed sister for bread and shelter in the
mechanics' boarding-house which she keeps; latterly you have not ventured to show your face in her neighborhood because of the creditors
who are on watch for you. Where have you lived? Nobody knows.
Your own people do not know. But *I* know. You have lived in the
Jersey woods and marshes, and have supported yourself as do the other
tramps; you have confessed it without a blush; you sneer at everything
in this house, but you ought to be more tender, remembering that
everything in it was honestly come by and has been paid for.[1]

These words were weighted with accretions of thirty years of bitterness. Evidence in letters makes several points questionable.

The first questionable element is Mark Twain's assertion that his
words were spoken on the last day of collaboration on *Ah Sin*. As we
have seen, as late as February 22, 1877, Twain had happily written
Howells that he and Harte had finished *Ah Sin* and were beginning
to collaborate on another play.[2] If Harte's "veiled" satirical remark
which Mark believed was aimed at Mrs. Clemens was the "heterodoxy"
for which Harte asked Mrs. Clemens' forgiveness in December, 1876,
Mark Twain and Bret Harte had continued their collaboration for two
months after this disagreement.

In the second place, Twain's statement about Harte's sneering atti-

---

[1] *MTE*, 278–79; Neider, *Autobiography*, 298–99.   [2] *MTH*, I, 172.

tude toward women in general and Mrs. Harte and Mrs. Clemens in particular is questionable not only on the grounds of Harte's respectful deference to the literary judgment of Mrs. Harte and Mrs. Clemens in relation to the Plunkett characters in *Ah Sin* but also on the conclusively contradictory grounds of hundreds of letters which Bret Harte wrote over a period of thirty-two years to his wife. Many of these letters have been included in *The Letters of Bret Harte,* edited by his grandson Geoffrey Bret Harte and published by Houghton Mifflin in 1926. Many additional letters to his wife remain unpublished, largely because they so monotonously concern sums of money which he sent her regularly.

The cause of Twain's outburst against Harte is more uncertain than the time of it.

Difficulties in the collaboration on *Ah Sin* have been tentatively attributed to Bret Harte's physical ailments and anxieties, yet Mark Twain apparently was not very well, either.[3] The year 1876 had been for Twain one of many irritations. Because he was "idle," he had written long letters to Howells.[4] He was irritated with Mollie Clemens, his sister-in-law, because she and Orion (like Harte's sister) were operating a boardinghouse. He wrote an unpleasant letter to his old friend Will Bowen, for whom he prescribed a dose of salts for reminiscing about the "happy days of yore."[5] After Howells recommended to Mark Twain the *Atlantic's* "Contributor's Club" as a place where he could "spit his spite" at somebody, Twain selected Anna Dickinson as the object of his criticism in an anonymous paragraph in the first "Contributor's Club," appearing in the *Atlantic* in January, 1877.[6] Mark Twain may have been irritated even with *Huckleberry Finn* to such a degree that he made a "ferocious" steamboat smash the raft and thus end for three years the journey of Huck and Jim down the Mississippi River. Thus Bret Harte was not the only individual to make Mark Twain angry on a "majestic scale." Walter Blair wisely observes of Twain's irritations at this time: "When a man could get fumingly angry at so many things it is impossible to identify any one cause for a specific outburst."[7]

---

[3] See Harte's letter of December 16, 1876, in Chapter VIII of this volume.

[4] *MTH,* I, 154. [5] Blair, *Mark Twain & Huck Finn,* 150.

[6] *MTH,* I, 156–57. [7] Blair, *Mark Twain & Huck Finn,* 151.

Although Mark Twain's resentment of Harte had a deeper source, superficially Mark's words reflect the irritation of the man of property—particularly the nineteenth-century man of property—with the spendthrift.[8] Mark Twain's assertion that "Harte offered me his note, but I was not keeping a museum and I didn't take it" parallels his assertion that his brother Orion's notes were also worthless.[9] That Harte, at the time of the collaboration on *Ah Sin*, was poor and in debt and that he owed money to Twain is not questioned. Taking time from writing stories (which continued to sell) to work on *Two Men of Sandy Bar*, *Gabriel Conroy*, and *Ah Sin* further increased his debts. Later Bret Harte would remember the winter of 1877 as the darkest period of his life.[10] Mark Twain's report of his own outburst reflects his apparent belief that Harte's poverty itself deprived him of the right to criticize his betters. "I cannot get away from the feeling that business failure means disgrace," Mrs. Clemens would write her sister, Mrs. Theodore Crane, in 1894.[11] Mark Twain felt the same way until he himself went bankrupt. Then he said it was nothing to be ashamed of.[12] Mark Twain could be a little like the Widow Douglas, who objected to the uncleanness of Huck's smoking a pipe but saw no harm in dipping snuff because "she done it herself."

If Mark Twain accurately reported what he said to Bret Harte when the two were attempting to work together at Hartford, Twain's report also indicates that Harte tried to reason with him but got nowhere. That Harte should react in this way is consistent with the testimony of Harte's daughter that in times of disagreement, her father was generally ready to listen to statements of his opponent's position in the controversy.[13] But if Mark Twain said all that he thought he had said and was not merely reporting a good many things that he wished he had said, it is difficult to believe that even Bret Harte would have asked him for another loan, and it seems even more incredible that Mark Twain should have suggested to Bret Harte that the two write another play together. Yet evidently Harte *did* try to borrow more money from Twain and was refused on the grounds of Twain's "pov-

[8] See Thayer, *John Hay*, II, 7.

[9] *MTE*, 279–80. See also Neider, *Autobiography*, 221.

[10] *BHL*, 308.   [11] Brooks, *The Ordeal of Mark Twain*, 144.   [12] *LL*, 299.

[13] Interview with Miss Ethel Bret Harte in Ojai, California, November, 1957.

erty." And evidently Mark Twain *did* propose another collaboration and was refused by Bret Harte.

Frequently alluded to but never before published is the following letter which Bret Harte wrote to "Mr. Saml L. Clemens" on March 1, 1877.[14] This letter fairly definitely sets the time of the open break between Mark Twain and Bret Harte as occurring within the eight-day period following Twain's letter to Howells on February 22. Harte's letter suggests that shortly after Mark wrote Howells that he and Harte were beginning a new play, Bret left Hartford for New York, where he received from Mark a letter which made him extremely angry. Evidently, for Harte, the "last feather" was not what Mark Twain said but what he wrote:

> 713 BROADWAY, N. Y.
> Mar. 1, 77

MY DEAR CLEMENS,

As I've been writing for my bread-and-butter for the last few days, and as your letter called for no answer except I should receive one from Ford, which I should have forwarded promptly, and as nothing has come from Ford, I have taken my own time to talk with you. Had I written the day after receiving your letter, I hardly think we would have had any further correspondence or business together. As it is I'm not anxious to write this. But there are a few things I must say to you.

First. As to the American Publishing Co.

If Mr. Bliss was a business man he would have sent *me* a statement of my a/c *when it was due*, and given me an opportunity of examining it—of knowing what he was doing and what he had done about my property, and what profit I was to expect from it. He would have exhibited his charge for "interest on advances"—a charge so preposterous and outrageous that if he will look at his contract he will see that it is so, and if he comes in contact with my lawyer he will know it is so.

Second—As to his sales of my book and the amount of copyright: *No publisher of any of my works, at any day, or time has done as badly as he has.* It is no answer to this to repeat your formula "that the book was delayed by me, that my reputation has suffered by it, that I had lost my popularity &c. &c &c." The only test is what other publishers are doing now, and since then, and at the time of Bliss' publication, with my *other* books. Mr. Osgood offered Robson $250 *advance* (without *interest*, of course) on the sale of the much abused play of "Sandy Bar"—

[14] See Bernard De Voto's note, *MTE*, 281.

which he would offer to the trade at 65¢. Inside of a month, Osgood had credited me on account of "Thankful Blossom"—a book published originally in a daily newspaper and sold by Osgood for 60¢—with one half the amount of copyright that Bliss shows for his sales in 5 mos of a book that a magazine paid $6000 for, and which he sells for $3.50. In brief, Osgood has sold more copies of "Thankful Blossom" in a month, than Bliss has sold of "Gabriel Conroy" in five months,—and on looking over my copyright accounts, I find I have never in my literary experience sold less than four or five thousand copies in the first three months of publication. Either Bliss must confess that he runs his concerns solely in *your* interest, and that he uses the names of other authors to keep that fact from the public, or else he is a fool. No sane business man would advance $6000 dollars on a book, of which in 5 mos he sold only 2000 copies, unless he had some other reason for it. I dont think his friendship for me goes as far as that. Possibly he may have carelessly made up his accounts. Ticknor of J. R. Osgood & Co, to whom I stated the case, tells me that from his experience of the dealings of the regular trade with subscription houses, that Bliss has probably already disposed of at least 2000 copies to the trade *alone*. Even Bliss' advances of $6000 cannot cover the loss I shall have from respectable publishers by publishing with *him*. Now, this is somewhere wrong, Mark, and as my friend you should have looked into Bliss's books and Bliss's methods, quite as much with a desire of seeing justice done your friend, as with the desire of seeing what chance you had of recovering any possible advance of $500 on our mutual work, if it failed.

As Harte's words indicate, there is a break in the letter here, and the rest is written on separate pages.

I have written this on a seperate [*sic*] page that you might show the preceding ones to Bliss. I only add one other fact *(to yourself solely)* which *you* may have forgotten. I had forgotten it, until looking for my contract with Bliss I found a letter from you of the same date. You requested me to tell Bliss that his contract with me was of *your* making and out of your influence with me as a friend, and you afterwards admitted to me that a disputed question of one or two thousand dollars was settled in your favor by *virtue of that contract so made.* I am willing to admit that your loan of $750 wipes out that obligation, nor should I have referred to it, but for the tenor of your letter the other day, which struck me as being inconsistent with the facts.

Now, as to "Ah Sin"! First:

Parsloe called here and showed me your letter. I dont object to San Francisco as the place of debut, except that from my own knowledge they prefer something with an Eastern endorsement, and I really can't see how our main idea of bringing out the play in a small town so that we might be able to superintend rehearsals, is furthered by this. *Secondly.*

If there is any one thing that we are sure about, regarding our play—anything that we do *know*, by actual experience, by general report, by universal criticism, by the consent and acknowledgment of the public—it is that Parsloe is a perfect Chinaman! Now to spend five or six hundred dollars to send him to San Francisco to *study Chinese character* is simply preposterous—so preposterous, that even the honest fellow himself saw it. Without waiting for my opinion, he told me he would n't do it. And in saying this to you I think I have overlooked your implied insult—an insult I admit I felt keenly when he shewed me your letter—of your offering this actor, in a mere whim and idiotic impulse—the very sum you refused to advance your collaborature [*sic*] who called that actor into life, who had given already four or five weeks of his time to you, and whom you refused on the plea of *poverty!*

No, Mark, I do not think it advisable for us to write another play together. Your offer of "$25 per week and board"—is flattering I admit—but I think that if I accepted it, even *you* would despise me for it. I can make about $100 per week for a few weeks here at my desk—my only idea of asking you for an advance was to save me from the importunity of my creditors, and give me that quiet, which as a nervous man yourself, you ought to know is essential to composition. I had not the slightest idea of your speculating out of my poverty, but as a shrewd man, a careful man, a provident man, I think you will admit that in my circumstances the writing of plays with you is not profitable.

Allowing even that I came to you on a salary of $25 per week, as I could not, after your letter, break bread or eat salt with you—don't you see as an economic man, as a shrewd man, that my *board* at the cheapest hotel would cost me at least $7.50 per week and that I should have only $17.50 to support my wife and 4 children. I know it can be done cheaper than that, but I think I'll struggle on here on $100 per week—and not write any more plays with you.

As to the play, already written,—except a protest against your marring it any more by alterations until it is rehearsed, and a special, and I think not improper request that you will try to allow me some understanding of the characters I have created, you can do with it, according to your business shrewdness and sagacity, as you may deem best for both of us—subject to my endorsement.

I think I object to San Francisco.

I have no answer from Ford. I shall telegraph him again tomorrow.

Yours very respectfully
BRET HARTE

Mr. Saml L. Clemens
Hartford

P.S. I have kept a copy of this letter.[15]

Scrawled with pencil on the back of the last page are these words in Mark Twain's handwriting: "I have read two pages of this ineffable idiotcy [*sic*]—it is all I can stand of it."[16]

If Mark Twain stopped reading this letter at the end of the second page, he stopped very soon after Harte began discussing Bliss's sales of *Gabriel Conroy*, with Harte's assertion that no other publisher had at any time sold so few of his books.

Bret Harte was by no means the only author to distrust Elisha Bliss. Howells believed it characteristic of Bliss to do 50 per cent of what he said he would do.[17] Six months before Harte's angry letter to Twain, Charles Dudley Warner had cautioned Charles H. Webb against relying on Bliss as a publisher.[18] In 1876, Mark Twain himself made so many public criticisms of Bliss's management of the American Publishing Company, that Bliss protested.[19] Four years later Mark Twain contemplated two lawsuits against the American Publishing Company, which he again accused of swindling *him*.[20]

Bret Harte's accusations become more understandable if paralleled with "Mark Twain's Quarrels with Elisha Bliss" as interpreted by Hamlin Hill in *American Literature* for January, 1962. In 1869, Mark

[15] Hitherto unpublished letter, MTP. If Bret Harte kept a copy of this letter, his copy is lost. For preservation of the letter, I am indebted to Mark Twain and the Mark Twain Estate. For permission to publish it, I am indebted to the Bret Harte Family, particularly to Mr. Lawrence K. Bret Harte.

[16] For permission to quote these words, I am indebted to the Mark Twain Estate.

[17] *MTH*, II, 700.

[18] Letter from Charles Warner in Nook Farm, Oct. 27, 1876, to Charles H. Webb, MTP.

[19] Andrews, *Nook Farm*, 123.

[20] See letter to Osgood, Dec. 31, 1881, MTP.

Twain had threatened to hold Bliss and the American Publishing Company "legally responsible" if the sales of *The Innocents Abroad* fell short of what he had been led to expect them to be. However, according to Hill, Twain's quarrels with Bliss about *The Innocents Abroad* and *Roughing It* were "mild compared to the tempest over Bliss's publication of *Tom Sawyer.*"

In the middle of the summer of 1876, Mark Twain concluded that the real reason for Bliss's original tardiness in publishing *Tom Sawyer* was that he was publishing too many books by other authors. Among these books by other authors, of course, was *Gabriel Conroy*, which Mark Twain had persuaded Bret Harte to give to Bliss. We have already observed that when Bret Harte—in his letter introducing Tauchnitz to Mark Twain—wondered why Bliss failed to issue *Gabriel Conroy* at the scheduled time, Bliss had for months been under considerable pressure from Mark Twain to promote *Tom Sawyer* but hold off publication to a period more advantageous to sales. On June 24, Mark Twain wrote Bliss: "I shall be mighty sorry to see Tom Sawyer issue when any other book of the firm is being canvassed or within six months of *being* canvassed." In July, Mark Twain again wrote Bliss recalling Bliss's earlier explanation that a subscription publisher could not successfully canvass a number of books simultaneously. "Therefore," wrote Mark Twain, "I am solicitous about Tom Sawyer—more so than I would be about another book, because this is an experiment. I want it to run by itself, if possible and pushed like everything."[21]

Because sales of *Tom Sawyer* were disappointing by Mark Twain's standards, he broke with Bliss for a time and, unknown to Bliss, planned to turn over his next book to Elisha's son, who intended to establish a subscription firm of his own. On April 1, 1879, however, Elisha Bliss, angling for another book from Mark Twain's pen, promised: "This Co . . . exists to publish books for you in the future."[22] The words sound very much like Bret Harte's. And if the statement was not true of the company in the past, it indicated the ultimate effect of Mark Twain's pressures in 1876.

Hamlin Hill concluded that Mark Twain's assertions about Elisha Bliss in *Mark Twain in Eruption* were "surprisingly accurate." Bret Harte's grievances against Bliss had at least equal validity. It is true

[21] Page 450.   [22] *Ibid.*, 452n.

that, aside from its artistic weaknesses, Harte's novel with its ironic portrayal of the complexities of California's social, industrial, and economic life was the wrong kind of book to sell by subscription, whereas Mark Twain's nostalgic portrayal of small-town boyhood had much more appeal for the usual subscription buyers as well as for more sophisticated readers like Howells. Nevertheless, Bret Harte had reason to believe that Bliss had exerted himself much more in promoting *Tom Sawyer* than in promoting the sales of *Gabriel Conroy* which Bliss and Mark Twain had led Harte to expect. Moreover, Harte's belief that Bliss was deliberately or inadvertently misrepresenting the actual sales of *Gabriel Conroy* resembled Twain's insistence that Bliss defrauded him on *Roughing It*, a judgment which Hill defends by comparing the sales of another Mark Twain book, *A Tramp Abroad*. Furthermore, Harte's complaint that Bliss sent him no accounting was not only reasonable in itself but based specifically on the original agreement,[23] and the fact that Bliss informed Twain rather than Harte of the financial status of Harte's novel gave Harte additional grounds for believing that Mark Twain had some kind of proprietary interest in the American Publishing Company. At one time Harte seems to have consulted a lawyer named Walker about the possibility of forcing the company to furnish him with a statement.[24] This issue was to appear again in the wrangle over dramatization rights of *Gabriel Conroy* which Mark Twain eventually claimed because of advances made to Harte during the publication of the novel.

Harte has been considered an ingrate for writing this letter of March 1, 1877, because at the time he owed Twain money. Harte seems to have reasoned that his debt to Twain for advances on the novel was conditioned on a deficit in the sales of *Gabriel Conroy*, and since he received no statement of the amount or nature of the deficit, he was not convinced that he owed Twain money for advances from the publisher for which Twain had made himself "personally responsible." However this may be, there is considerable discrepancy between the $750 which Bret Harte said he owed in 1877 and the $1,500 which Mark Twain in 1907 remembered as the sum of Harte's debt to him. I do not know on what Mark Twain based his estimate or how, after the quarrel, Harte's debt to Mark Twain increased to $3,000. But we

[23] See letter to Osgood, *BHL*, 51.   [24] *BHL*, 247.

have already noted that when Mark Twain talked in terms of money, he was apt to grow expansive. Harte, though a poor manager of his own business affairs, was generally precise in mentioning sums. In the March 1 letter to Twain, Harte would hardly have understated the amount of Twain's loan to him.

Authors and publishers are traditional foes, and in the financial failure of *Gabriel Conroy*, both Bret Harte and Elisha Bliss felt cheated. As late as 1881 the American Publishing Company listed among its "assets" a debt of Bret Harte for $2,000. (Needless to say, Twain objected to the listing of Harte's debt as an asset.)[25] In 1907, Mark Twain dictated that when Elisha Bliss realized that *Gabriel Conroy* was a "white elephant" and as a subscription book was valueless, he sold the serial rights to "one of the magazines" for the "trifling sum" of $3,600, which Twain identified as the exact amount advanced to Harte in royalties.[26] Thus, even though Mark Twain's figures are wrong (he had originally told Howells that the enviable Scribner's contract brought $6,500, which was also wrong), his final statement on this subject indicates that the American Publishing Company through *Gabriel Conroy* suffered no apparent deficit for which Mark Twain had had to assume responsibility.

Another conclusion is obvious. If Mark Twain and the American Publishing Company had lost money on *Gabriel Conroy*, time spent on the novel and *Ah Sin* had left Harte destitute. And what seems to have stung Bret Harte most was that after urging the impoverished Harte to spend more time with him collaborating on a second play, Mark Twain had offered Parsloe the same sum which he had refused to lend his old friend and literary adviser Harte on the plea of his own "poverty." Mark Twain was currently involved in numerous speculations. This was the spring that Senator John P. Jones sent him a check for $23,000 to cover Twain's loss in an investment made on the Senator's recommendation.[27] Mark Twain apparently cashed the check with a sense that justice was done, but felt no inclination to emulate the Senator's action by covering Harte's loss in an investment made on Twain's own recommendation.

That Bret Harte at this period was averaging $100 a week was

[25] See letter to Osgood from Clemens on "Sunday," 1881, MTP.
[26] *MTE*, 281.   [27] Neider, *Autobiography*, 230–32.

probably an exaggeration. His sentence about giving Mark Twain several weeks of his time was apparently a reference to the new play which Mark mentioned in his February 22 letter to Howells. Harte's opening statement about writing for his "bread-and-butter for the last few days" suggests the possibility that Harte had stopped work on the play to write stories for money which he desperately needed. But hard up as Harte undoubtedly was, Mark Twain's suggestion that Bret Harte work for him on a salary of $25 a week was insulting. A little more than twelve years before, Bret Harte, an editor, had offered Mark Twain a job in San Francisco, and though the job paid only $50 a month, Twain was glad to get it because he believed the *Californian* "the best weekly literary paper in the United States." Since that time, Harte had been considered the highest-paid writer in this country.

More noteworthy in Harte's March 1 letter to Twain are references to *Ah Sin*. Parsloe and Twain were already allied against Harte, and—whether he liked it or not—Bret had become the "party of the second part." A few days after Harte wrote this letter to Twain, he met Parsloe on Broadway and inquired somewhat anxiously for news about the rehearsals of *Ah Sin*. Whereupon Parsloe answered that if there was anything Harte "ought" to know, Parsloe would tell him. Reporting the incident to Twain, Parsloe gloated that Harte's face had turned red and then Harte had walked away.[28] The letter in which Parsloe recounted this incident asked Mark Twain's advice about street posters for the play.

But most significant of all are indications in Harte's letter that Twain was making changes in the manuscript and that Twain and Harte had come to direct disagreement about the portrayal of the Chinese character Ah Sin.

On April 2, Bret Harte in Washington, D.C., wrote another letter to Mark Twain. The salutation was extremely formal:

MY DEAR MR. CLEMENS,

Mr. J. I. Ford, who has theatres in Washington, Baltimore and Philadelphia came up to Balt. day before yesterday, by appointment, to speak to me about our play.

I learn from him, *first,:* That he has made an offer to Parsloe for the first week in Washington and the second in Baltimore, (the engage-

[28] Letter from Parsloe to Clemens, Mar. 9, 1877, MTP.

ment to commence in the early part of May), on the following terms: Ten per cent of the weekly expenses of the Theatre—i. e. Two thousand dollars, and 50 per *centum* on all gross receipts over the $2000. This gives a surety of $200 for each of these two weeks, and if he plays to a good business—(i. e. $6000 per week;) of course we come in for $2,000, per week.

2nd. By this arrangement we have an opportunity of attending rehearsals a week before, and the promise that, if on rehearsal, we desire to let the engagement go by—(to write up partly—) it shall not be at *our* expense.

My reasons are for favoring this:

1st. We shall know by May 1st *whether we have or have not* a play;

2nd. We shall learn at the same time, whether *we have or have not an actor in the titular part.*

3rd The $200 will at least pay our expenses here to find out that important fact.

4th If we fail—it is a local failure and will not hurt our other work as much as a metropolitan *fiasco.*

5th. That I dont see we can do anything else.

6th That I dont see that Parsloe is offering anything better.

When I dont see that Parsloe has either declined or accepted Ford's offer it seems to me that we ought to do something about it. I want to realize on my work as soon as possible, and I dont think that either you or I can afford to have an actor walking around the streets of N.Y. with an unacceptable play of *ours,* in his pocket.

Please let me know by telegraph to 7 1 3 B'way if you accept Ford's offer. Then I can hunt up Parsloe, and make him give me a reason why he doesn't say yes or no, and make him say yes—if you agree with me.

Yours t.
Bret Harte

Mr S. L. Clemens[29]

Bret Harte's emphasis of the word *ours* should be kept in mind.

[29] Hitherto unpublished letter, MTP.

12

THE SHORT UNHAPPY LIFE OF A PLAY

> The Chinaman is going to become a very frequent spectacle all over America, by and by, and a difficult political problem, too. Therefore it seems well enough to let the public study him a little on the stage beforehand.
>
> MARK TWAIN—Curtain Speech on the
> First Night of *Ah Sin* in New York

FORD'S OFFER WAS ACCEPTED. From the stage of Ford's Theatre in Baltimore at eleven o'clock in the morning of April 27, 1877, Mark Twain happily wrote Howells that Mark was "needed every moment during these daily rehearsals." Nevertheless, he was stealing a second to wish that Howells could observe with him the astonishing phenomena of the theater, for even as he wrote, one group of people engaged in furious and chaotic combat—shouting, shooting, apparently dying in agony only to be tossed into the Stanislaus River—while another group sat near by, calmly discussing the cost of living in Baltimore.[1] Notwithstanding this naïveté, Mark Twain, the "divine amateur," was directing the professional actors. Moreover, disregarding Harte's objections, Mark Twain busily worked over the play in Baltimore and made plans to superintend rehearsals in Washington, D.C., where the drama would be "hurled at the public."[2]

Ah Sin opened at the National Theatre in Washington on the night of May 7, 1877. Parsloe was unusually nervous and wrote Twain that the presence of Harte was an added annoyance.[3]

Mark had fully expected to be present, but an attack of bronchitis kept him from the Washington *première*.[4] However, he wired Parsloe that he had prepared two speeches—one to be given if the play was a

[1] *MTH*, I, 175.   [2] *Mark Twain to Mrs. Fairbanks*, 204.
[3] Letter to Mark Twain, May 11, 1877, MTP.
[4] *Mark Twain to Mrs. Fairbanks*, 204.

143

failure, and the other to be given if the play was a success. He suggested that Parsloe give the audience a chance to vote which it should be. When the actors were called before the curtain to take their bows, Parsloe read Mark Twain's telegram and the audience enthusiastically voted the play a success.[5] Bret Harte sent backstage his congratulations to the actors and then left the theatre believing the play a hit.[6]

With some reservations, the theater manager was of the same opinion. The following day Ford wrote Twain that he had sat through *Ah Sin* from beginning to end and was "fully satisfied" with the performance. The crowded house, the applause of the audience, and the cash receipts—which had come to almost five hundred dollars—were all satisfactory. On the whole the play seemed to him well acted, the female Plunketts being particularly well portrayed, but the performance of Parsloe left something to be desired. Twain was needed, he said, to bolster Parsloe and to make some improvements in the play itself. Ford told Twain that he had urged President Rutherford B. Hayes to attend that night.[7] *Ah Sin* was expected to remain in Washington for the rest of the week and then travel under the direction of Ford, who would take it to New York during the summer season.

At least one drama critic wrote of the Washington performance that *Ah Sin* showed "the distinctive handiwork of both authors."[8] Years later Mark Twain would report that "when the piece was staged" the critics "praised my share of the work with quite a suspicious prodigality of approval, and gave Harte's share all the vitriol they had in stock." Like some other statements by Mark Twain, this one was not altogether accurate. Strangely he prefaced it with the assertion that Harte's part of the play was the best part, "but that did not disturb the critics." Yet the early reviews of *Ah Sin* in Washington were so encouraging that on May 9, William Dean Howells wrote to Mark Twain: "I'm very glad to see by the papers that your play started off well." Already Howells seems to have assumed that *Ah Sin* was Mark's play and Mark's responsibility. He added sympathetically: "You must have had an awful time working over it in Baltimore."[9]

[5] Paine, *Biography*, 589.   [6] *BHAE*, 235.

[7] Letter from Ford to Clemens, May 8, 1877, MTP.

[8] "Special Despatch to the *World*" from Washington, May 7, 1877, clipping in MTP.

[9] *MTH*, I, 177.

If, in 1877, Twain believed that Harte's part of the play was best, that belief did not prevent his making additional revisions after the Washington *première*. Harte did not like the changes. Both Parsloe and Twain found Harte irritatingly unco-operative about revisions.[10] But Mark's brain was teeming with ideas. Later in May he dashed off to Bermuda with the Reverend Joseph Twichell, and in June and July he dashed off a melodrama of his own entitled *Captain Simon Wheeler, the Amateur Detective*.[11] Perhaps after Harte turned down Twain's suggestion that the two work together on another play, Mark set out to prove that he could write one by himself. He proved that he couldn't. Twain insisted that he had the time of his life writing it,[12] but if this farce illustrates Mark's current ideas of what a play ought to be, Harte's objections to Twain's revisions of *Ah Sin* are understandable. *Simon Wheeler, the Amateur Detective* was even worse than *Ah Sin*.[13] In time, Mark Twain himself recognized that it was "dreadfully witless & flat."[14]

Some idea of the nature of Mark Twain's revisions of *Ah Sin* can be gained from an incident which Judge Joseph Daly recounts in the biography of his brother Augustin. But the incident needs to be placed in the context of Bret Harte's California.

A popular bit of local color in Bret Harte's stories and poems about the West was his account of the Chinaman's skill as an imitator, especially when a Chinese character solemnly and serenely imitated the white man's vices. This is, of course, the central irony of Harte's famous verses about the sins of Ah Sin as reported by Truthful James. The same trait was heavily relied upon as a source of humor in the play's characterization of Ah Sin. Although Harte regularly emphasized the cleanliness of the Chinese, he cited as an exception John Chinaman's manner of sprinkling clothes to prepare them for ironing. According to this tale, whose authenticity Californians still vouch for, John Chinaman would "fill his mouth with perfectly pure water from a glass beside him, and then, by one dexterous movement of his lips in a prolonged expiration, squirt the water in an almost invisible misty shower

---

[10] Letter from Parsloe to Twain, May 11, 1877, MTP.

[11] *MTL*, I, 294. See *LL*, 197–201, for evidence of Mark Twain's zest for melodrama at this time.

[12] *MTH*, I, 187.   [13] *Mark Twain to Mrs. Fairbanks*, 206n.

[14] *MTH*, I, 246.

on the article before him."[15] Harte's story was that white employers, after the first shock, admired and even commended the Chinaman for his dexterity. Then Harte related an old California joke that one day when a lady in San Francisco had complimented her Chinese cook on the deft way he had spread white sauce on certain dishes, John China-man had referred to the clothes-sprinkling technique and smilingly informed her that his method with the white sauce was "allee same." Apparently stage business called for the dramatization of this anecdote at the end of one act of *Ah Sin*.

Mark Twain believed that the scene would have been a great success in San Francisco but that it would not be properly understood in the East. Consequently, he went home, thought the matter over, and devised new stage business which he considered important enough to telegraph Parsloe. The following telegram Judge Daly published:

> Instead of blowing water, seize your brazier and blow a cloud of ashes. The men after sprawling and butting into each other will have their eyes full of ashes and in their blind fury will proceed to snatch each other by the throat—a natural thing for such ruffians to do; whereupon you smiling down upon them a moment, may sweetly say "Me gottee gagement me no can waitee" or words to that effect and be sliding out as the curtain strikes the floor. Please try this tonight and telegraph the result.[16]

In this telegram to the actor, Mark Twain was apparently more concerned with revising Parsloe's stage business than with revising the script. In the published version of *Ah Sin* the words "Me got 'gage-ment. Me go." occur on page 31 in the middle of Act II. There is no indication of Ah Sin's spewing either water or ashes, but at the end of Act II, on page 46, Ah Sin jumps on a table and "shrieking and gib-bering Chinese," he seizes a flatiron and turns the miners into a "picture of consternation."

The problem of what happened to the script of *Ah Sin* after December, 1876, when Bret Harte wrote Mark Twain that he was mulling over the first two acts, trying to strengthen his own contributions and modify Twain's, is an interesting one. We know that both before and after the Washington opening, Mark Twain made many revisions of

[15] "Bohemian Days in San Francisco," *Writings*, XVIII, 151.
[16] *Augustin Daly*, 236.

which Bret Harte disapproved, but the nature of these revisions cannot be positively determined because no complete text in the handwritings of Mark Twain and/or Bret Harte is now known. For years the existence of the *Ah Sin* manuscript has been a mystery tantalizing bibliophiles and literary historians. Albert Bigelow Paine guessed that it might lie in "some managerial vault," and someday be "dragged to light."[17] When the library of Augustin Daly was auctioned after his death, what was judged to be a promptbook of *Ah Sin* was found. This manuscript is now in the Clifton Waller Barrett Collection of "Bret Hartes" in the Alderman Library of the University of Virginia.[18] The manuscript, "the only complete text known to exist," is not in the handwriting of either Mark Twain or Bret Harte, but with it are fifteen pages of apparent revisions, most of them in pencil in the handwriting of Mark Twain. Since these pages agree almost word for word with the same passages in the prompt copy, and since this copy was in the possession of Augustin Daly, it seems likely that this text is a copy of the play as it was presented in New York after Mark's revisions in Baltimore. This is the text of *Ah Sin* which was published by the Book Club of California, and Frederick Anderson's "Text Note" reports "several pages of revised and discarded dialogue in the handwriting of Harte and Twain in the Mark Twain Papers at the University of California Library in Berkeley." The published text includes a facsimile of one of these pages. It shows that Mark Twain changed a speech of one character, Judge Tempest, from "I know not what to say" (as Harte had written it) to the more colloquial, "Well, I don't know of anything further to say." It also shows, in Mark Twain's handwriting, a stage direction for Ah Sin to steal the judge's handkerchief while the judge is speaking.[19] These two emendations probably represent Twain's main objectives in revision: (1) to make Harte's rather stilted dialogue more realistic, and (2) to elaborate the "comic business" of the Chinese character, Ah Sin.

Although finally it is Twain's work rather than Harte's which dominates the play as a whole, it is possible to recognize in the published version elements appearing in earlier writings of both Bret Harte and Mark Twain. For example, the plot apparently began as

---

[17] Paine, *Biography*, 590.
[18] Letter from Clifton Waller Barrett, Dec. 18, 1958.   [19] *Ah Sin*, xviii.

a vague adaptation of Harte's story "A Monte Flat Pastoral: or How Old Man Plunkett Went Home." As in Harte's story, Plunkett is a liar. Living in Calaveras County, California, he has not been home to see his wife and daughter in the "States" for years. In Harte's story, Plunkett's lies are motivated. Plunkett is a pathetic old failure escaping into a world of fantasy from a real world which he finds unbearable. In the play *Ah Sin,* however, there is no pathos. Plunkett is not so old, and he lies for the love of lying. Even when he is believed dead, his lying ghost haunts the play. One New York critic recognized that this "champion liar of Calaveras," this "Baron Munchausen of American literature," showed the master hand of Mark Twain.[20] So did the female Plunketts. In Harte's story, the ideal mother and daughter existed only in the mind of the lonely old derelict, and reality fell far short of the ideal. In the play, the vulgar mother and daughter find counterparts in the purportedly refined wife and daughter of a San Francisco judge. It is probable that York and the three Tempests began as Bret Harte characters. If they remained Harte's characters, they are the most crude and banal people Harte's mind ever conceived.

In the play, as in Harte's story, York falls in love with a girl in a photograph whom he mistakes for the daughter of his friend Plunkett. (This incident was probably suggested to Harte by Clemens' own experience of falling in love with the girl in a miniature which he saw in Charles Langdon's stateroom on the *Quaker City.*) *Ah Sin* includes allusions to an episode in which the hero saved the heroine from what seemed certain death in a buggy behind a runaway horse. Three weeks after the play opened in New York, the aunt of the little Clemens girls narrowly escaped death in a similar manner near Quarry Farm. The fact that the actress at one time pretends to be her own aunt suggests a possible link between the episodes, but if this is true, the published version of *Ah Sin* includes very late revisions by Mark Twain. Mark had refused to allow Howells to publish in the *Atlantic*'s "Contributor's Club" Mark's account of the rescue near Quarry Farm, and it was Paine's belief that Twain had never permitted the incident to be used in any form.[21] In stating his objections to Howells' publication of the story, Mark Twain commented that "delicacy—a sad, sad, false deli-

---

[20] Review of *Ah Sin* in the New York *World,* clipping in MTP.
[21] *MTL,* I, 304–307, 309.

cacy" deprives literature of its two most valuable sources: "family circle narrative and obscene stories."[22] In *Ah Sin,* Mark Twain managed to include the latter in a bit of dialogue between miners who discuss the sinking of a shaft into "Mary Ann" before making it altogether clear that "Mary Ann" is a mine endearingly personified. The phallic images evoked by the dialogue resemble those of the candle and the candlestick in Twain's *Letters from the Earth.*[23] That this dialogue in *Ah Sin* was contributed by Mark Twain is evidenced by the fact that the words in the promptbook are almost identical with words in Mark Twain's handwriting on the loose pages with the book found in Augustin Daly's library.

Certain themes in the play might have been introduced by either Bret Harte or Mark Twain. These include satire of a jury swayed by irrelevant appeals to passion and prejudice and then adjourned to safeguard the jurymen's bets on a dogfight which erupted in the midst of the trial. The description of the "American jury" as "a synonym for ignorance and savage stupidity" reminds us of a similar indictment in *Roughing It,* and the "yellow pup" charged with unfair "leg holts" in the dogfight is a legitimate descendant of the famous Andrew Jackson of "The Jumping Frog of Calaveras County." Like "The Heathen Chinee," *Ah Sin* includes card-playing scenes. Though Ah Sin at one time stacks the cards, the playing is restricted to Caucasians and the plays show that the author has more firsthand knowledge of card games than Mark Twain was ready to grant Bret Harte. In Act IV, when the play reaches a climax with the proposed lynching of an innocent man, Judge Tempest condemns the vigilance committee and the erratic procedures of the kangaroo court. But as for social commentary in the play, the New York critic who paid tribute to the "Baron Munchausen of American literature" also wrote:

> The moral purpose of the piece—if it can be imagined that Mark Twain would write a play with any moral purpose—is to show not only that all men are liars but that women in San Franciscan society are no better. Falsehood is the venial sin exposed and made not lovable but highly amusing.[24]

[22] *MTH,* I, 203.   [23] Page 40.
[24] This review of *Ah Sin* in the New York *World* gives a fairly comprehensive synopsis of the play.

The critic might have written much the same thing about the title role of Ah Sin. It may be remembered that Twain told Howells that "This Chinaman" was to be "*the* character of the play" and that both Bret Harte and Mark Twain would "work on him & develop him." Later Harte and Twain had disagreed vehemently about the portrayal of this role. In the published version of the play, Ah Sin is ubiquitous and functions as both a marplot and a *deus ex machina*. He is befriended by both York and Plunkett, he serves them both, and the play ends with all characters shouting "Hurrah for AH SIN." Some of the humorous incidents to which Ah Sin contributes are typical of Harte's stories about Chinese. There are the familiar jokes about the Chinese queue and the Chinaman's ability to make an incredible number of articles disappear up his voluminous sleeves, although in the play a carpetbag becomes the chief receptacle. The funniest scene shows a San Francisco lady giving patronizing instructions to Ah Sin on how to set a table. She tells him to watch her and do exactly as she does. Nervously she drops a dish. Whereupon Ah Sin, following her example, conscientiously throws to the floor every dish remaining on the table. The incident is typical of Harte's stories about Chinese in that the humor is at the expense of the Caucasian.

But finally, the Ah Sin of the Mark Twain–Bret Harte play is the peculiar "Heathen Chinee." Unlike Chinese servants in most of Harte's stories written before and after this play, he is inept and unreliable. He is a thief and a liar who wants to marry an Irish girl and go back to China. At one time he takes a gorgeous costume from his carpetbag and goes into a song-and-dance routine which allegedly he learned hanging around theaters in San Francisco. He "jabbers a lot of Chinese" recorded as "ti kelly kee chow."[25] In short, he comes close to the stereotype which Harte specifically rejected in "Wan Lee, the Pagan," when he prefaced his description of a Chinese character with these words:

> Before I describe him I want the average reader to discharge from his mind any idea of a Chinaman that he may have gathered from the pantomime. He did not wear beautifully scalloped drawers fringed with little bells—I never met a Chinaman who did; he did not habitually carry his forefinger extended before him at right angles with his body, nor did I ever hear him utter the mysterious sentence, "Ching a ring a

[25] *Ah Sin*, 88.

ring chaw," nor dance under any provocation. He was, on the whole, a rather grave, decorous, handsome gentleman.[26]

In the play, one character calls the Chinaman a "moral cancer," an "unsolvable political problem." Although these words are spoken by the villain, almost every character in the play at some time speaks scornfully of Ah Sin. Much of the humor is at his expense. His frequent beatings and cuffings are supposed to be comic, and crude jokes about Ah Sin *because* he is Chinese are clumsy antecedents of jokes on the Negroes Jim and Nat in the "Evasion" chapters in *Huckleberry Finn.* Mrs. Tempest's assertion that when Ah Sin shakes his head, "it makes me nervous to hear his dried faculties rattle" is a distant relative of Huck's report that "The nigger kind of smiled around gradusly over his face, like when you heave a brickbat in a mud-puddle."

The New York opening of *Ah Sin* was scheduled for Tuesday, July 31, 1877, in Daly's Fifth Avenue Theatre. Playbills announced that Mr. Parsloe would appear in his "Great and Original Creation of The Heathen Chinee." In giving the names of the authors, the playbill emphasized that the drama had been "produced under the immediate supervision of Mark Twain."

The cast of leading characters included the names of actors and actresses known and liked in England and America at that time:

SHIRLEY TEMPEST, A San Francisco Belle and Heiress of adventurous spirit	*Miss Dora Goldthwaite*
MRS. TEMPEST, The Fashionable and Fastidious Mother of the above young lady	*Miss Mary Wells*
MRS. PLUNKETT, The too apparent cause of Mr. Plunkett's absence from home	*Mrs. G. H. Gilbert*
CAROLINE ANASTASIA PLUNKETT	*Miss Edith Blande (From the Gaiety and Criterion Theatres of London)*
HENRY YORK	*Mr. Henry Crisp*
BRODERICK, A Knave through circumstances over which he *ought* to have control	*Mr. Edmund Collier*
BILL PLUNKETT	*Mr. P. A. Anderson*

Act I was in Plunkett's cabin on the Stanislaus River. Act II took

[26] *Writings*, II, 264.

place in Ah Sin's laundry. Act III was in York's cottage. Act IV was set first on a roadside and then in Judge Lynch's court.

Word got about that on opening night in New York, Mark Twain would give one of his famous curtain speeches. "I want to *be with you* opening night" and "hear your speech," wrote Mrs. Clemens somewhat anxiously from Hartford.[27] Her concern was understandable. Perhaps she remembered her husband's curtain speech on the opening night of *The Gilded Age* three years earlier when he had criticized the acting of the play's star, John T. Raymond. In April, Mark had written her that Harte and Raymond had not been absent from his thoughts and his hate for months. And since that time, Mark Twain's hatred had not cooled. In such a state of mind, as his wife knew, Twain was hardly noted for his restraint. He did not share the belief of Sandy Morton that though a quarrel between two "partners" might be bitter, it was a private matter to be kept to themselves. And already Mark had been expressing himself freely. Two days before *Ah Sin* was scheduled to open, Mrs. Clemens urged Mark not to say such "harsh things" about Bret Harte. Like Desdemona, Olivia Clemens assured Mark that it was her love for her husband which made her plead for his former friend. Since Harte was so miserable and she and Mark were so "desperately happy" and living such comfortable lives, she said, Mark could "easily afford to be magnanimous."[28] But when Mark hated, magnanimity was not his way.

Ah Sin opened in New York to a full house including many distinguished men. According to Joseph Daly, "Sothern, Boucicault and Brougham and all the literary lights in town" were in the house. As on the opening night in Washington, the audience was responsive and at the end of the third act, both authors were called for.[29] Bret Harte was absent in Washington. Consequently, only Mark Twain answered the audience's request.

In contrast to his curtain speech on opening night of *The Gilded Age* in which Raymond had starred, Mark Twain's curtain speech for *Ah Sin* criticized the play but praised the actor, about whom he and Bret Harte had disagreed. The play *Ah Sin*, Twain said, was "a work of great labor and research, also of genius and invention—and plagiar-

---

[27] *LL*, 203.   [28] *Ibid.*, 194, 203.
[29] Review in New York *World*. See also Daly, *Augustin Daly*, 234.

ism." To be sure the audience did not miss the irony of the first two terms, he pointed out illustrations of its "lack of invention" and spoke particularly of its "didacticism." But the real shock of Mark's speech comes in his statement of what the play taught. Wearing a dazzling white linen suit[30] (long before the white suit became a familiar aspect of his showmanship) Mark Twain stood before that New York audience and said:

> Whoever sees Mr. Parsloe in this piece sees as good and as natural and consistent a Chinaman as he could see in San Francisco. I think his portrayal of the character reaches perfection. The whole purpose of the piece is to afford an opportunity for the illustration of this character. The Chinaman is going to become a very frequent spectacle all over America, by and by, and a difficult political problem, too. Therefore it seems well enough to let the public study him a little on the stage beforehand. The actors, the management, and the authors have done their best to begin this course of public instruction effectively this evening.[31]

If these words were intended as sarcasm, they were, as Mark Twain once wrote of an article by the Reverend T. DeWitt Talmadge, "certainly the opaquest sarcasm that ever got into print."[32] Wrote the drama critic of the New York *World*: "Ah Sin is a contemptible thief and an imperturbable liar." The New York *Times* found him a "typical Chinaman." Many people liked Mark's speech better than the play. And Twain's words praising Parsloe's interpretation of the role are argumentative in tone, as if Mark had overruled an adversary but still felt the need to defend his position.

Immediately after the first-night performance, Mark Twain sent word to Livy that the play had succeeded.[33] On August 3 he jubilantly wrote Howells: " 'Ah Sin' went a-booming at the Fifth Avenue. The reception of Col. Sellers was calm compared to it." Twain was convinced that if only Harte's name had been "suppressed," the play would have been received as favorably by critics as by the theater audience, and he regretted that he had not thought to suggest that Harte's

[30] Daly, *Augustine Daly*, 234; Paine, *Biography*, 590.
[31] DeLancey Ferguson, "Mark Twain's Lost Curtain Speeches," *South Atlantic Quarterly*, Vol. XLII (July, 1943), 269.
[32] Buffalo *Express* (Monday, May 9, 1870).
[33] See letter from Olivia Clemens to Mollie Clemens, from Quarry Farm, July 29, 1877, MTP.

name be dropped. He admitted that "My old Plunkett family" seemed coarse and vulgar on the stage but attributed this to the "outrageously and inexcusably coarse way" in which the roles were acted. As for Ah Sin, he told Howells: "The Chinaman is killingly funny. I don't know when I have enjoyed anything as much as I did him. The people say there isn't enough of him in the piece. That's a triumph—there'll never be any *more* of him in it."[34]

Like the first reviews after the Washington *première* of *Ah Sin*, reviews in New York papers following the first-night performance there showed critics agreeing that *Ah Sin* had elements of popular success, the kind "most admired by managers." With an undertone of cynicism they reported that the authors "wanted to write an amusing play and they have succeeded."[35] But as time and the play wore on, adverse criticism became more audible and direct. Twain rationalized unfavorable reviews by quoting John Brougham (famous actor, playwright, and theater manager), who, Mark said, had advised him to list elements in the play which drama critics found objectionable and he would have proof that the play contained "all the requirements of success and a long life." Mark Twain agreed with this principle. For as he said:

> Nearly every time the audience roared I knew it was over something that would be condemned in the morning (justly too) but must be left in—for low comedies are written for the drawing-room, the kitchen & the stable, & if you cut out the kitchen & the stable the drawing-room can't support the play by itself.[36]

Evidently Mark Twain believed that success in the theater came from giving the public what it wanted. Was that the explanation of Mark Twain's curtain speech warning against the Chinese immigrant, whom he had so valiantly defended in "Goldsmith's Friend Abroad Again"? For in 1877 (marked by Kearnyism in California), the popular outcry against the "yellow peril" was louder, the truth of Truthful James was forgotten, and Harte's ironic line "We are ruined by Chinese cheap labor" had become the battle cry of bigots.[37]

[34] *MTH*, I, 191, 193.

[35] For excerpts from clippings of reviews in Mark Twain's scrapbook for 1869–78, see *MTH*, I, 194n.

[36] *MTH*, I, 193.

[37] In Washington, Californians were exerting considerable pressure on Congressmen for additional anti-Chinese legislation, including a modification of the Burlingame

It seemed to Mark Twain that there was as much money in the house for *Ah Sin* the first two nights as in the "first ten of Sellers." Perhaps the one cheering aspect of the remaining history of *Ah Sin* is that Mark Twain's faith in Brougham's formula for popular success proved unfounded.

As initial interest in the play flagged, Mark Twain sought manfully to promote *Ah Sin*. In the same letter in which he discounted the value of dramatic criticism, Twain proposed to Howells a plan whereby he hoped to propitiate the critics. He said that by a blunder "which nobody was seriously to blame for," he had been quoted as saying that New York critics were unjust, stupid, and dishonest. In the letter to Howells he enclosed a paragraph insisting that he not only had never said such a thing but had never even thought it. On the contrary, the enclosed paragraph asserted that the criticism of *Ah Sin* had been just. In fact, Mark said, "the criticisms of the great New York dailies are always just, intelligent, and square and honest." Mark's idea was that Howells could publish in the *Atlantic* the enclosed paragraph introduced by some such words as: "In a letter to Mr. Howells of the Atlantic Monthly, Mark Twain describes the reception of the new comedy 'Ah Sin,' and then goes on to say . . . ." Here Howells would quote Twain's praise of the New York dailies. Livy advised against the plan and Mark said Howells should not "think of it" if it were "in the least disagreeable." But Mark himself saw no reason why Howells should object. For, Mark naïvely explained, he had tried a similar explanation and praise on a critic of the New York *World* and "the consequence was a noble notice of the play."[38]

Mark continued to work on *Ah Sin*, trying to doctor it up as he had apparently believed he could have doctored *Two Men of Sandy Bar*. Included in Howells' *My Mark Twain* but evidently deleted by Paine from his publication of the letter to Howells cited in the preceding paragraph are these additional words:

I . . . have left hardly a foot-print of Harte in it anywhere. But it is full of incurable defects: to-wit, Harte's deliberate thefts & plagiarisms,

Treaty. See Hubert Howe Bancroft, *History of California*, VII, 344–45. The republication of "Wan Lee, the Pagan" at this time suggests that Harte's opposition to the anti-Chinese movement had not wavered.

[38] *MTH*, I, 192.

& my own unconscious ones. I don't believe Harte ever had an idea that he came by honestly. He is the most abandoned thief that defiles the earth.[39]

Twain's own account of the way he and Harte worked in writing the play makes any "deliberate thefts and plagiarisms" seem extremely unlikely, if not impossible, in the first drafts. Moreover, if in later revisions of *Ah Sin*, Twain "left hardly a foot-print of Harte," it is difficult to see how, finally, *Ah Sin* could have been filled with Harte's "incurable defects." Clearly Mark's mind was not the sort to be disturbed by the hobgoblin of consistency. The drama critic of the New York *Herald* commented that all the materials of the play were old, with the one exception of the character of the Heathen Chinee.

During this period, Bret Harte spent much time in Washington desperately looking for a job. However, as possible evidence that he had not completely abandoned the play after the Washington opening, George R. Stewart cites a playbill in the Columbia University Dramatic Museum announcing that Bret Harte would speak at one of its performances.[40] Harte complained that passes to *Ah Sin* which he had issued to personal friends were rejected at the door of the theater.[41] At one time Harte wrote Augustin Daly what Judge Daly called a "reasonable remonstrance." He had been unable to secure any account of the play from Twain or his representative. The agent and lawyer in Hartford who was supposed to furnish such accounts had told Harte that he knew nothing about the play after it left Washington. Now Harte appealed to Augustin Daly:

> I don't want any accounts from you or Parsloe, only a simple expression of your opinion as to whether the play was or was not successful, and as one of its authors, this does not seem to me to be an inconsistent request or calculated to wound anybody's—say Parsloe's—sensitive nature. It is the mere courtesy of business.
> Send me a line.[42]

Parsloe and Twain ignored Harte as much as possible. Both wanted to buy Harte out, to cut loose from him in any way they could. Yet, notwithstanding Twain's promoting and doctoring, *Ah Sin* was show-

[39] *Ibid.* [40] *BHAE*, 358n.
[41] Letter from Maze Edwards to Mark Twain, Aug. 31, 1877, MTP.
[42] Daly, *Augustin Daly*, 237.

ing more and more signs of imminent mortality. One week Parsloe would tell Twain that business was poor and Daly took all the receipts. Again he would write that *Ah Sin* was doing better than any other play in New York during the hot weather. By August 6, Twain was calling *Ah Sin* "that dreadful play."[43] Now he believed that his "fatal blunder" had been in putting the play aside before it was finished, waiting too long to make necessary revisions.[44] Although he wrote Mrs. Fairbanks that *Ah Sin* continued to fill the theater during hot weather, the truth seems to be that box-office receipts dwindled week by week for five weeks, with "considerable loss to Daly."[45] And as the popular support faded away, the chorus of criticism swelled. John T. Raymond was saying that *Ah Sin* was the worst play he ever saw, but Parsloe archly wrote Twain that he thought Raymond was prejudiced and felt sure Twain would agree with him.[46] With grieved surprise, Parsloe told Twain that the New York *Sun* "pitches into you and I and leans a little toward Mr. Bret Harte." Parsloe's communications to Twain became increasingly shrill and querulous in tone. He complained that the management of the Fifth Avenue Theatre failed to show proper respect to everyone connected with *Ah Sin,* including Mark Twain, and suggested that Twain see for himself in the Sunday *Herald* how Fiske and Daly were manipulating things for their own benefit. But then, Parsloe had known all along that "Disgustin D" would "do something dirty before I left."[47]

By August 25 services of an agent named Maze Edwards were secured for forty dollars a week. In accordance with the original contract signed by Clemens, Harte, and Parsloe, Edwards would be expected to go on the road with the play and render accounts to the authors. The contract with Edwards makes no mention of Harte. Yet the agent wrote Twain on August 31 that Harte had asked for an accounting, which Edwards had given him and would "if you say so,—continue to give him."[48] Apparently Fiske and Daly had told Harte that Twain intended to make another curtain speech and had suggested that Harte speak the same night. But Harte had declined. Edwards denied that

[43] *Mark Twain to Mrs. Fairbanks,* 205.   [44] *MTL,* I, 301.

[45] *Mark Twain to Mrs. Fairbanks,* 206. Felheim, *The Theater of Augustin Daly,* 297.

[46] Aug. 5, 1877, MTP.   [47] Aug. 20, 1877, MTP.   [48] MTP.

he had refused to honor a pass which Bret Harte had issued but declared he was glad Harte realized at last that as far as arrangements for the play were concerned, Harte was a *"nobody."*

Ah Sin on the road proved even more disappointing than *Ah Sin* in New York. An ambitious itinerary planned to include St. Louis, Troy, Detroit, Pittsburgh, Cincinnati, Louisville, Buffalo, Albany, and Brooklyn was abbreviated. On October 2, Maze Edwards advised Mark Twain that business showed there was something wrong with the play itself, that it must be rewritten, and that the vulgarities of the Plunkett women must be somehow removed. Although Edwards tactfully reassured Mark that no one was better able to rewrite the play than Mark Twain himself, Edwards said that Parsloe knew someone else he could get to do the rewriting.[49] Less than a week later, in Syracuse, New York, the agent informed Twain that even though Edwards and Parsloe had been doing all they could for the play, receipts were so low that the question now was whether to give up immediately or go on until the end of the season. He believed that they should go on "at all costs," but this would be possible only if Twain would advance four hundred dollars.[50]

On October 15, 1877, Mark Twain admitted to William Dean Howells that *Ah Sin* was "a most abject & incurable failure" which would leave the stage permanently within a week. "I'm sorry for poor Parsloe," wrote Twain, "but nobody else concerned."[51] Finally, affairs of *Ah Sin* were turned over to Charles E. Perkins, attorney and counsellor at law, of 14 State Street, Hartford, Connecticut. Perkins asked Clemens for a check for $46.45 as Clemens' half of the salary and expenses owed Edwards to date. Perkins assured Clemens that the amount was Edwards' due.[52]

Thus the famous collaboration on *Ah Sin* ended—"not with a bang but a whimper." As far as is known, Bret Harte and Mark Twain never met again.

[49] MTP.   [50] Letter from Vanderbilt House in Syracuse, Oct. 7, 1877, MTP.
[51] *MTH*, I, 206.   [52] Letter in MTP.

13

THE PRINCE, THE PAUPER, AND THREE TRAMPS

Ah! impostors, were they? Are you?

The "INNOCENT MINER" to MARK TWAIN

EVEN THOUGH BRET HARTE AND MARK TWAIN were out of sight of each other, their relationship had not ended. Both lived for many more years, during which the intensity of Twain's feeling about Harte and the vehemence of his invective did not diminish. During those years the popularity of Mark's writings grew, and notwithstanding what seemed to him financial catastrophe, he became increasingly and deservedly more successful as a writer. Furthermore, since he was an unusually colorful figure and an accomplished showman, his words, his deeds, and the details of his family life were highly publicized. Although there were frequent rumors about Bret Harte, not many people knew the facts about him during his lifetime, and today even fewer are aware that Bret Harte lived and wrote for almost thirty years after the break with Mark Twain. Readers of *Mark Twain in Eruption* may sometimes wonder what Bret Harte was doing during those years and how he reacted to the rumors and to Mark Twain's words.

Begun in 1877,[1] the year of *Ah Sin*, Twain's *The Prince and the Pauper* includes a scene in which Tom Canty, on his way to be crowned King of England, rejects his mother with these words: "I do not know you, woman!" And Mark Twain comments: "The words smote upon the king's soul as the strokes of a funeral bell smite upon the soul of a surviving friend when they remind him of secret treacheries suffered at his hands by him that is gone."[2] Whether or not Mark Twain had

[1] Andrews, *Nook Farm*, 190–91. In the spring of 1877, Mark Twain wrote in his notebook the title *The Prince and the Pauper*. Blair, *Mark Twain & Huck Finn*, 186. Harte's accusing letter to Twain was dated March 1, 1877.

[2] Mark Twain, *The Prince and the Pauper*, 243.

become a prince with a sense of guilt, Bret Harte in the winter of 1877 was nearly a pauper.

"That *awful, terrible last winter!*" Harte would call it and insist that he could never under any circumstances suffer again what he then endured.[3] Early in 1877 the *North American Review* had published a severe critical attack on Harte's writings. Devoting his creative energies to *Two Men of Sandy Bar, Gabriel Conroy,* and *Ah Sin,* Harte had not worked seriously at short-story writing for three years. After the failure of Ah Sin, when he turned again to this resource which once had seemed inexhaustible, he feared that the spring had dried up. Unable to produce short stories, Harte began turning out thin sketches which Charles A. Dana, largely for friendship's sake, bought for the New York *Sun* for one hundred dollars apiece. Whatever Harte's work brought, the larger share went to his wife. But at best, Harte could expect nine hundred dollars a year from these sketches, and this income was far from adequate to support himself, his wife, and four children.[4] Certainly it offered little hope of paying off his debts.

From New York and Washington, where he was desperately trying to keep his head above the swirling waters, Harte's letters to his wife bear with incremental repetition the dreary monthly burden: "I enclose fifty dollars." He enclosed fifty dollars. He enclosed fifty dollars for his wife and fifty dollars for his sister, asking that the money be stretched as far as possible.[5] He wrote that he knew very well the money was inadequate, but it would keep them from being "absolutely penniless."[6] Once when affairs looked a little brighter, he enclosed fifty dollars for his wife and promised another fifty the following day so that she could go to a hotel with a month's board in advance in her pocket. However, he asked her not to go to the Catskills, where she would be too far away for him to join her.[7] Again, he sent ten dollars for his boys. It was, he said, all he had.[8] Sometimes Mrs. Harte did not know where he was, and apparently she urged him to give up all hopes of success in Washington and return to her. When in one ten-

---

[3] *BHL,* 115.   [4] *BHAE,* 238.   [5] *BHL,* 58.

[6] Unpublished letter to Mrs. Harte, Sept. 11, 1877, in William Andrews Clark Memorial Library.

[7] *BHL,* 57.

[8] Unpublished letter to Mrs. Harte, July 8, 1877, in William Andrews Clark Memorial Library.

day period Bret wrote his wife twice and telegraphed twice without receiving a reply, his anxieties for his family multiplied. He reminded her: "I don't . . . know where *you* are or *where I am returning to.*" He sent her fifty dollars in his sister's care. But when his wife *did* write, he called her his "good, patient Nan" and thanked her for her "kind letter." "God bless you, Nan . . . I trust you altogether and I know only the want of money cramps you." He wanted to join her: "If I could do anything by being *there*, more than I am doing here, I would come. *But I must come with money.*"[9] In desperation, he underlined the words.

Mrs. Harte read newspaper gossip about her husband and, of course, suffered from it. As much as possible, Bret Harte tried to save her from knowledge of the extreme precariousness of his position. "You have so hard a time of it there that I cannot bear to have you worried if there is the least hope of a change in my affairs as they look, day by day . . ." he wrote. To add to his worries, Harte's health began to fail. Dickering for an editorship that faded away, grinding out sketches for Dana in order to earn a desperately needed one hundred dollars, anxiously trying to recapture the lost art which had brought him fame, Harte found himself hard up for time as well as for money. Again he was guilty of breaking engagements. But now the cause was necessity rather than irresponsibility, and the practice of not keeping an appointment seemed to him a "shameful" thing. Observing sadly that he feared it had lost him friends, Bret Harte characteristically added: "It was my own fault, and I cannot blame people for not knowing everything."[10]

He continued to work. Osgood agreed to publish his "Story of a Mine," a long narrative which, like *The Gilded Age*, includes accounts of brutality, political chicanery, and shabby political deals in Washington, D.C. "Some of it has been written in the sorest trouble I have ever had," Harte told his wife. When he contributed to *Godey's Lady's Book*, Bret joked to Osgood: "Let the 'Atlantic' tremble!" But he was far from feeling so gay as he sounded. The false front of gaiety which Harte maintained during his most miserable times concealed real suffering.

Bret Harte was right in believing that he had forfeited much good

[9] *BHL*, 58 ff.   [10] *Ibid.*, 60.

will, but he was not destitute of friends. Now, rallying to his aid, some of them set about trying to procure for him a government post. After interviews with President Rutherford B. Hayes, Secretary of the Interior Carl Schurz, and Frederick William Seward (assistant to Secretary of State William M. Evarts), Harte's hopes revived. His ego swelled with reports of a petition to Congress, signed by "Democrats and Republicans, Northern and Southern men" alike—"an almost spontaneous movement in which they all have joined," to urge that he be given a diplomatic or consular appointment.[11]

In reporting to his wife another incident which afforded more solid grounds for satisfaction, Bret's regard for himself wheeled back to a sanely humorous perspective. Learning that enemies were trying to turn Evarts against him by arguing that Harte's extravagancies and debts made him unfit for any financial trust, Harte remembered that John Jay Knox, comptroller of the currency, had been a government inspector of the San Francisco branch of the United States Mint when Harte was employed there. On being informed of the writer's present difficulties, Knox wrote a vigorous testimonial that Harte had held a most responsible position in San Francisco, that in the absence of the appointed official, Harte had been virtually superintendent of the mint, and that he had been in the confidence of one of the best businessmen in California. (Presumably, the businessman was Robert B. Swain.) As a result of Knox's testimony, Harte's account to his wife continued, "in one blow, all the stories of my extravagance, debts, etc., so far as they affected my having a responsible position under Government, were demolished! More than that, Knox's praise of me absolutely clothed me with virtues of integrity, fitness, etc., I didn't know I possessed."[12]

Although Bret Harte did not name the enemies trying to prevent his appointment, Mark Twain was actively among them. Twain even went so far as to write President Hayes attacking Harte as a person unfit for government trust.[13] The President, in some perplexity, consulted William Dean Howells. Guardedly and without Twain's knowledge, Howells recommended that Harte be given a chance at the job.[14]

Not long thereafter, Bret Harte was offered the post of first secretary of the American legation in St. Petersburg, a post which he de-

---

[11] *Ibid.*, 67.

[13] *MTH*, I, 235.

[12] *Ibid.*, 67–68.

[14] *Life in Letters*, I, 251.

clined because he feared the government salary would not be sufficient to enable him to maintain the standard of living expected of an American diplomat in the Russian city. Finally, with considerable relief, he accepted an appointment as commercial agent of the United States at Crefeld, near Düsseldorf, Germany. The assured salary was only two thousand dollars a year, but there was possibility of advancement and a promise of leisure to go on with his writing. About the time of his appointment, Harte told his wife that he was down to his last twenty dollars.[15]

In 1877, Mark Twain's feelings for Bret Harte fused into hate. In that year the publishers of the *Atlantic Monthly* decided to celebrate simultaneously the twentieth anniversary of the founding of that journal and the seventieth birthday of the revered John Greenleaf Whittier. The guest list for the occasion included the most illustrious names among the *Atlantic*'s contributors.[16] But the name of Bret Harte, the writer who six years earlier had been the most publicized of all *Atlantic* contributors, was conspicuously missing.

In contrast with Bret Harte, who at the time of the Whittier dinner was as close to being completely down and out as he would ever go, Mark Twain was thriving as a valued member of the prosperous Nook Farm community in Hartford. Moreover, he was known as a friend of William Dean Howells and a welcomed contributor to the *Atlantic*. Now when Mark Twain dined with the Brahmins of Boston, he no longer sat near the foot of the table. "Jubilantly"[17] he accepted his invitation to the Whittier Birthday Dinner, and carefully he set about preparing a speech which he promised for the occasion. The speech would demonstrate that Mark Twain was no longer an "outsider," that at last he could claim the social prestige, the ease and familiarity with the elect, to which his growing literary fame entitled him.[18]

The occasion at the Hotel Brunswick in Boston on December 17, 1877, was very different from the Keeler luncheon which Bret Harte had tactlessly described as the "dream of Mark's life." At the head table—beside Mr. Whittier, the honor guest, and Mr. Houghton and

---

[15] *BHL*, 65–67. [16] Paine, *Biography*, Appendix O, 1647.

[17] Howells, *My Mark Twain*, 59.

[18] Henry Nash Smith, "That Hideous Mistake of Poor Clemens's!" *Harvard Library Bulletin*, Vol. IX (Spring, 1955), 168.

Mr. Howells, representing the *Atlantic*—sat New England's literary idols: Mr. Longfellow, Mr. Emerson, and Dr. Holmes. Compared with these three, the "illuminates" of the Keeler luncheon at Ober's were demigods. At the Whittier dinner there were fifty-two guests. Mr. Clemens sat beside Mr. Osgood a little more than halfway down the right-hand side of the inverted U of the banquet table.[19]

When Mark Twain was called on to speak, he was introduced by William Dean Howells. Mark's carefully prepared speech was a story about three tramps, "three dead-beats," who visited a California mining camp and imposed themselves upon an "innocent" California miner. The three dead beats were literary kinsmen of the two rascals who later boarded the raft of Huck and Jim on the broad Mississippi. But these earlier impostors called themselves Ralph Waldo Emerson, Henry Wadsworth Longfellow, and Oliver Wendell Holmes.

Mark Twain had hardly begun his speech when it became clear to everyone, including Mark, that his humor was misplaced. But with "demoniacal possession," he continued to the end, while his listeners sat in a state of shock at his blasphemy of the gods, and Howells, who had introduced Mark Twain as a joke-maker who "never left you hanging your head for having enjoyed his joke," hung his head and stared at his plate. When Howells glanced up, he saw Twain "standing solitary amid his appalled and appalling listeners, with his joke dead on his hands."[20] This is the version of William Dean Howells.

Henry Nash Smith, after examining newspaper reports and other contemporary allusions to the Whittier Birthday Dinner, concluded that the immediate reaction to Mark Twain's speech was not so bad as Howells believed.[21] Certainly to the modern reader, the dismay of Twain and Howells seems all out of proportion to the significance of the incident. But after the speech, Charles Dudley Warner and Howells suffered with Twain in a gloom-filled hotel room. "Well, Mark, *you're* a funny fellow," said Warner.[22] The Reverend Joseph Twichell could not think of anything to say or even bear the thought of facing Livy and Mark. Twain sent letters of apology to Longfellow, Holmes, and

[19] See Paine, *Biography*, diagram facing page 1646.

[20] Howells, *Life in Letters*, I, 242–43. See also Blair, *Mark Twain & Huck Finn*, 156.

[21] "That Hideous Mistake of Poor Clemens's!" *loc. cit.*, 148–49.

[22] Howells, *My Mark Twain*, 61.

Emerson (who was more than a little puzzled by the whole episode.) To Howells, Twain wrote a letter suggesting that a manuscript already accepted for publication in the *Atlantic* be returned. Assuring Mark Twain that his writing would help and not hurt the *Atlantic* for many a year, Howells did not return the manuscript; nevertheless, even though it was already in type, he postponed publishing it until a later issue.

Mark Twain continued to brood over the affair. "My sense of disgrace does not abate," he wrote Howells. "It grows. I see that it is going to add itself to my list of permanencies—a list of humiliations that extends back to when I was seven years old, and which keep on persecuting me regardless of my repentancies."[23]

Perhaps the most interesting aspects of a study of Mark Twain are those "curious confusions of memory and imagination" which, as Albert Bigelow Paine said, resulted more than once in "a complete reversal of the facts."[24] This same faculty resulted in some of Mark's greatest fiction, and it appears fascinatingly in many things he said.

Among the "list of permanencies" which rankled in Mark Twain's memory was the Keeler luncheon. The authorized edition of Mark Twain's *Autobiography* (1924) includes a passage "written about 1898," recording Mark Twain's rather sentimentally patronizing memories of Ralph Keeler. Keeler, as Mark Twain remembered in 1898, was "the modestest young fellow that ever was," who from his "lowly obscurity" looked "humbly up" to distinguished men. "When he got a smile and nod from Mr. Emerson and Mr. Whittier and Holmes and Lowell and Longfellow," Mark Twain said, "his happiness was the prettiest thing in the world to see."[25] By that time, not only had Mark Twain transferred to Keeler the attitude toward Boston's Brahmins which Bret Harte had allegedly ridiculed in Mark Twain, but Twain's halting enumeration of the famous names, Longfellow and Holmes and Emerson, like the emergence of associative links from the unconscious to the conscious mind, evokes the memory of the famous Whittier Birthday Dinner.

Farther back in Mark Twain's humiliations was the "Three Aces" which Aldrich had called an unsuccessful attempt to imitate Bret Harte.

---

[23] *MTH*, I, 212ff.   [24] Paine, *Biography*, 676.
[25] Paine, *Mark Twain's Autobiography*, I, 154.

After the fiasco of the Whittier Birthday Dinner, Mark Twain would have been enraged by any new suggestion that he had again echoed Bret Harte. Yet the familiarity of Mark's speech had a good deal in common with the gay irreverences which New Englanders had found so amusing in Bret Harte when he was widely entertained in Cambridge in 1871. Furthermore, Mark's words at the Whittier Birthday Dinner included clearer and more numerous reminders of Harte than had Carl Byng's "Three Aces."

Mark began by saying that the occasion was "peculiarly meet" for digging up reminiscences of literary folk; consequently, he would reminisce. The time was thirteen years before (1864), when Mark had moved from Nevada to California. The place was the southern mines of California (now known as the "Bret Harte country"). In the 1870's, whatever their disillusionments with the man, in the minds of these contributors to the *Atlantic*, this country was Bret Harte's literary domain. *Roughing It* had staked out Mark Twain's claim in Nevada, a fact indicated by one hostile reviewer's description of Mark's speech as "high flavored Nevada delirium tremens."[26] In the Whittier Birthday Dinner speech, Mark was once again moving into Bret's territory.

The action of Mark Twain's yarn began when Mark, on a tramp through the mines, knocked at dusk on the door of a lonely cabin in the foothills of the Sierras. (If Mark Twain had arrived in this way at the cabin of Jim Gillis on Jackass Hill, so had Bret Harte, earlier.) The central character was an "innocent miner," Mark's version of the "Honest Miner," a Western cliché appearing in Harte's "M'Liss." The personality of Mark Twain's miner suggests not only Jim Gillis but also the Truthful James of Harte's "Plain Language from Truthful James" and "The Society upon the Stanislaus," admired and quoted by the great Agassiz. When the "innocent miner" took over the narrative, in a deadpan manner like that of Truthful James he told Mark of three other "littery" men who had come knocking at his door earlier. They were dead beats. Mark would later say that he went to live with the Gillises at a time when, because of Orion's bad judgment, Mark was low in funds. In the opinion of the Gillis brothers as well as of Mark Twain, Bret Harte was a dead beat.

Jim Gillis had once (in a manner which Mark Twain associated with

<hr>

[26] Smith, *Mark Twain: The Development of a Writer*, 103.

Bret Harte) tossed a dollar to a couple of "musical tramps."[27] The tramps in Mark Twain's speech were not particularly musical but they recited poetry. They also cheated in a game of euchre, and the denouement following the production of too many "right bowers" was chaotically similar to the conclusion of the card games in "Plain Language from Truthful James" and in Act I of *Ah Sin,* which had completed its dreary run not long before.

When the "I" of Mark Twain's speech told the "innocent miner" that the three tramps calling themselves Emerson, Longfellow, and Holmes were impostors, the miner said to Mark Twain: "Ah, impostors, were they? Are *you?*"[28] But by this time the silence at the dining table was so loud that the question went almost unheard.

Actually, the incongruities which constitute the humor of Mark Twain's speech are funnier and far milder violations of conventional standards of decorum than the incongruities of Bret Harte's early parody of Poe's "Ulalume" entitled "The Willows" (published in the *Californian* in 1862). But if the New Englanders knew of Harte's burlesque verses about a dead beat who seduced a girl named Mary in the private room of a saloon from which he was evicted because he could not pay his bill, Poe was not a New England god. And if the Whittier Birthday Dinner speech was, as Henry Nash Smith has suggested, an act of unconscious aggression,[29] it seems less likely that Mark Twain (whose reactions were almost always intensely personal) was attacking abstract literary values than that he was betraying repressed hostility to these New England Brahmins who had once so warmly welcomed Bret Harte to Cambridge and so humiliatingly rejected Mark Twain. Twain may have been "obscurely aware of his own guilt," but his sense of guilt was mixed with the frustration of his attempt to show himself and the world that he had kept his six-year-old vow to top Bret Harte, that he had supplanted Bret Harte with the "Atlantics," and that he could beat Bret Harte at his own game.

There is a possibility that after the Whittier Birthday Dinner, Mark made a gesture of reconcilation with Harte and was rebuffed.

[27] *MTE,* 282–84; Neider, *Autobiography,* 300.

[28] Paine, *Biography,* 1647. The idea of an impostor, of course, was basic to the structure of *The Prince and the Pauper,* a work in progress at this time. In that narrative Tom Canty was the impostor who was finally recognized.

[29] *Mark Twain: The Development of a Writer,* 97–100.

One of the many stories about Bret Harte's nonpayment of debts has as many versions as a ballad. The story concerns a rich friend who admired Harte's work and made to Harte many small loans which finally mounted to a substantial sum. On one anniversary, the friend returned Harte's notes all canceled and tied in a bundle. Harte responded to this generous gesture with angry words of insulted dignity and a prompt return of the bundle of notes. About returning the money, however, he said nothing. On these basic details, all versions agree.

Bernard De Voto, citing Thomas Wentworth Higginson's account of a story Twain told him when the two men were crossing the Atlantic on their way to Europe, believed that the notes were returned on Harte's birthday, that "B. wrote one of the most brutal letters" Mark Twain had ever seen, and that Mark himself may well have been the man who returned the notes and received "this characteristic treatment."[30] As Mark Twain told the story, the sum owed totaled $3,000 (the amount Twain said Harte owed him). According to Mark Twain, the friend's return of the notes to Harte was prompted by "warm and kind and brotherly feeling," and Harte's indignant reply "permanently annulled the existing friendship."[31] If the beneficent friend *was* Mark Twain, the story suggests that some vestiges of friendship between Mark Twain and Bret Harte had survived *Ah Sin*. However, the most interesting and illuminating aspect of Mark Twain's version is the specific date he gave: "the 24th of December, '77."

If Mark Twain's date is correct, the return of the notes occurred within a week after Mark's humiliation at the Whittier Birthday Dinner. During this period, Mark Twain felt increasingly penitent and friendless. He suffered not only from his own mortification and the disapproval of his wife and closest friends but also from scathing criticisms in several newspapers. The "most rancorous criticism" had come from the Springfield *Republican,* the journal in which Bret Harte had published his early praise of Mark Twain.[32] Its editor, Samuel Bowles, had written for the Whittier dinner a venerating letter which by contrast increased the shock of Mark's speech because it was read just before Mark Twain was introduced.[33] And Bowles had continued

[30] *Mark Twain's America,* 163. [31] *MTE,* 273.
[32] Smith, *Mark Twain: The Development of a Writer,* 103.
[33] See Blair, *Mark Twain & Huck Finn,* 156.

to be a loyal admirer of Bret Harte. On December 23, the day preceding the date Mark Twain gave for the return of Harte's notes, Mark had written Howells a self-accusing letter emphasizing his growing sense of disgrace and his conviction that the Whittier Birthday Dinner speech had damaged his reputation throughout the country. On December 24, the date Mark Twain gave for the return of Harte's notes, the Springfield *Republican* published another severe criticism of Mark Twain's speech, which it declared had "excited more attention than any other feature of the feast," because the speech was like a "fly in amber . . . neither rich nor rare," and caused people to wonder "how the devil it got there."[34]

If Bernard De Voto's guess is correct, Mark Twain's thoughts may have turned to the man who had once been his intimate friend but whose reputation Twain himself had repeatedly attacked during the closing year. In the Clemens household in Hartford, Christmas was traditionally observed, and it is conceivable that on this particular Christmas, Mark Twain may have been unusually receptive to the Christmas message of "Peace on Earth, good will to all men." Mrs. Clemens was always on the side of magnanimity and had urged Mark Twain to be generous to Harte.

But that Bret Harte in this most miserable winter of his life would have had difficulty in recognizing the gesture as an act of brotherly love or even an attempt to propitiate the gods is certain. Eighteen hundred and seventy-seven was the year of *Ah Sin,* the year in which Mark Twain wrote his wife that Harte had not been absent from his hate for months, the year Parsloe and Twain had made caustically clear to Harte that he had no right even to inquire about the play he originated, the year Mark Twain had written the President of the United States that Harte was unworthy of trust in a government appointment. After this barrage of animosity over a period of months, the return of the notes, underlining Harte's poverty and Mark Twain's affluence, could have seemed to Harte only an added insult, the kind of "Parthian shot" mentioned too often in Harte's fiction.

According to another version of the story of the notes returned to Harte, the wealthy friend was "a banker and broker, with an ambition to be considered a patron of the arts and literature." The time was

[34] Smith, *Mark Twain: The Development of a Writer,* 103.

New Year's Eve, and the cancelled IOU's were intended to give Harte a "fresh start for the year." Indignant at being made the object of charity, Harte reportedly exclaimed, "Damn his impudence!" When Noah Brooks, the teller of this version of the tale, asked Harte what he was going to do about it, Harte answered: "Going to do about it? . . . Going! I have made a new note for the full amount of these and have sent it to him with an intimation that I never allow pecuniary matters to trespass on the sacred domain of friendship."[35]

The words might have been spoken by Colonel Starbottle, whose pomposity Harte ridiculed. Nevertheless, paralleled with Twain's entry in the calendar of Pudd'nhead Wilson ("The holy passion of Friendship . . . will last throughout a whole lifetime if not asked to lend money"), the speech attributed to Harte affords another illustration of a basic difference in these two men's attitudes toward money. For it was Harte's romantic illusion that money was relatively unimportant between friends. "To be a man's 'partner,' " Harte said, "signified something more than a common pecuniary or business interest; it was to be his friend through good or ill report, in adversity or fortune."[36] Harte had attributed the same feeling to Mark Twain, but the past year could hardly have failed to convince Bret Harte of his mistake.

Albert Bigelow Paine suggests that Mark Twain's chagrin over the Whittier Birthday Dinner may have influenced his resolve to spend the next two years in Europe.[37]

Regularly referred to as a happy sequel to the Whittier Birthday Dinner is the *Atlantic* breakfast in honor of Oliver Wendell Holmes to which Mark was invited soon after his return to the United States. After some hesitation and the persuasion of Charles Dudley Warner, Mark accepted the invitation on condition that he be permitted to speak early in the program.[38] He volunteered to let Howells read his speech ahead of time and strike out anything he wished. Again it was Howells who introduced Twain to assembled guests, but this time Howells said only: "We will now listen to a few words of truth and soberness from Mark Twain." Mark began by referring to the guest of honor as the first great literary man he ever "stole" anything from. Explaining in

[35] Merwin, *The Life of Bret Harte*, 236–37.   [36] *Writings*, II, xxiv.
[37] *MTL*, I, 319.   [38] *MTH*, I, 281–82n.

some detail how by chance he had used the same dedication for *The Innocents Abroad* that Dr. Holmes had used for his *Songs of Many Keys*, Mark said that when this slip was called to his attention, he had written an apology to Dr. Holmes, who had graciously replied that it was all right and that no harm had been done. Dr. Holmes added that he believed we all "unconsciously worked over ideas gathered in reading and hearing, imagining they were original with ourselves."[39]

With this position at this time, Mark Twain was in wholehearted agreement. Eventually Mark Twain's memory confused the Holmes breakfast with the Whittier Birthday Dinner.[40]

[39] Paine, *Biography*, 659–60.
[40] Smith, *Mark Twain: The Development of a Writer*, 111.

14

"THE BEST OF ALL EVIDENCE"

He was an incorrigible borrower of money; he borrowed from all his friends; if he ever repaid a loan the incident failed to pass into history.

MARK TWAIN about BRET HARTE, 1907[1]

WHEN IN MAY, 1878, Bret Harte accepted the appointment as commercial agent of the United States at Crefeld, Mark Twain, having left Hartford in March, was already in Germany. On May 26 he wrote Howells that the family was "divinely located" in Heidelberg, that he was enjoying the view, and that for the first time in months, he felt inclined to work. On June 2, Howells answered with a letter informing Twain that during the summer he might be joined by their "whole fraternity," including James R. Osgood, George Waring (an engineering friend and *Atlantic* contributor), Thomas Bailey Aldrich, and John Hay. Howells said he knew Twain would be glad to see Hay and Osgood. With careful casualness, Howells added: "Harte, you know, has got a consular appointment somewhere in Germany."[2] Howells did not mention his own responsibility for the appointment.

From the Schloss Hotel in Heidelberg, Mark Twain wrote a long letter in reply. Dated June 27, the letter began as follows:

MY DEAR HOWELLS:

What do the newspapers say about Harte's appointment? Billiardly-speaking, the President (through persuasion of Evarts, I judge) scored 400 points on each, when he appointed Lowell & Taylor[3]—but when he appointed Harte he simply pocketed his own ball.—Now just take a

[1] *MTE*, 272.   [2] *MTH*, I, 231, 233.

[3] Bayard Taylor, who had been appointed minister to Germany. That Taylor was not cordial or helpful when Bret Harte arrived in Germany may be at least partly explained by the fact that he had crossed the Atlantic on the same boat with Mark Twain. *MTH*, I, 227.

realizing sense of what this fellow is, when one names things by their plain dictionary names—to wit: Harte is a liar, a thief, a swindler, a snob, a sot, a sponge, a coward, a Jeremy Diddler, he is brim full of treachery, & he conceals his Jewish birth as carefully as if he considered it a disgrace. How do I know? By the best of all evidence, personal observation. With one exception: I don't know him, myself, to be a thief, but John Carmany, publisher of the Overland Monthly, charges him with stealing money delivered to him to be paid to contributors, & the defrauded contributors back Mr. Carmany. I think Charley Stoddard said Harte had never ventured to deny this in print, though W. A. Kendall, who published the charge in the San Francisco Chronicle, not only invited him to deny it, but dared him to do it. O, the loveliness of putting Harte into the public service, after removing Geo. H. Butler from it for lack of character! If he had only been made a home official, I think I could stand it; but to send this nasty creature to puke upon the American name in a foreign land is too much.

I don't deny that I feel personally snubbed; for it seems only fair that after the letter I wrote last summer the President should not have silently ignored my testimony, but should have given me a chance to prove what I had said against Harte. I think I could have piled up facts enough to show that Harte was fitted for the highest office in the gift of the city of New York.

Now there's one thing that *shan't* happen. Harte shan't swindle the Germans if I can help it. Tell me what German town he is to filthify with his presence; then I will write the authorities there that he is a persistent borrower who never pays. They need not believe it unless they choose—that is their affair, not mine.[4]

If, as Mark Twain said, Bret Harte tried to conceal his Jewish blood, he was not very successful, for William Dean Howells believed that one reason James Russell Lowell developed a dislike of Harte was that Harte was a Jew.[5] If Bret Harte seldom referred to his Jewish ancestry, his reticence is understandable in terms other than race prejudice.

Bret Harte's paternal grandfather was Bernard Hart, a wealthy Jew who for twenty-two years was secretary to the New York Stock Exchange Board. He was also an active member of the first synagogue established in New York.[6] In 1799, Bernard Hart married Catharine Brett, of a well-known New York Dutch family, lived with her less

---

[4] *MTH*, I, 235–36.   [5] "Editor's Easy Chair," *loc. cit.*, 155.
[6] Merwin, *The Life of Bret Harte*, 5f.

than a year, became the father of a son named Henry (who eventually became the father of the writer Bret Harte[7]) and then left his Gentile wife and son, although he provided somewhat meagerly for their support. Five years later Bernard Hart married an orthodox Jewess named Zipporah Seixas, who bore him several children, one of whom was also named Henry Hart. Although there was considerable family resemblance, and the son of Catharine Brett told his sons about their Jewish grandfather, not until after Bret Harte's death did the descendants of Zipporah Seixas learn that their grandfather had once taken unto himself a Gentile wife. Now if Bret Harte's grandfather did not want to claim his descendants with Gentile blood, Bret Harte and members of his family were hardly the kind of people to go about insisting on the relationship.

According to Howells, the reason Lowell kept Mark Twain at a distance was that Lowell believed Twain also was Jewish.[8] And as for the suspicion that Harte considered being Jewish a disgrace, Mark Twain had probably forgotten a complaint in one of his own notebooks that a Jew who traveled on the same boat with him from San Francisco to Nicaragua in 1866 was too familiar and acted as if he thought the other passengers on the boat regarded the Jew as a white man.[9]

Mark Twain's "evidence" that Harte was a "thief" should also be examined in context.

It happens that in relation to Carmany's charges, we have from Harte a personal letter to this former business associate. After he reached the East, Harte received from Carmany several letters, one of which included an inquiry about manuscripts. On April 11, 1871, Harte replied that all manuscripts which he had received had either been returned to the authors or left in an *Overland* office. He explained that his delay in answering Carmany's inquiry had been due to "a month's siege of scarlet fever in the family," and he thanked Carmany for sending him the latest issue of the *Overland,* which he commended as an "admirable number."[10] The tone was cordial. If Carmany believed Harte had defrauded contributors to the *Overland,* that belief had not prevented his trying very hard to keep Harte as editor when

[7] The *e* was added to the name by Bret Harte's father to differentiate his own name from that of another Henry Hart campaigning in an election year. *BHAE,* 17.

[8] *My Mark Twain,* 46.   [9] # 6 (1886), 20, 24 f., 27, 45.

[10] Unpublished letter in the William Andrews Clark Memorial Library.

Harte came East.[11] In 1875, convinced that with the author of "The Luck of Roaring Camp" had gone the "glory of the Overland," Carmany tried to persuade Harte to return to San Francisco and resume his editorship.[12] From Cohasset, where with high hopes he was writing *Two Men of Sandy Bar* for Stuart Robson, Harte rejected Carmany's offer with a rather rancorous reminder that he and Carmany had failed to agree to terms in 1870 and—as it turned out—an inaccurate assertion that in the East, Harte could earn without drudgery three times as much "security, honor, and respect" as he could count on in California as the head of the *Overland*. That Harte's pride had been deeply wounded is obvious in the conclusion of this letter:

> ... If we could come to terms—I do not see how I could make the Overland's "sanctum" the literary Mecca of the West, after the Prophet had been so decidedly renounced by his disciples. I think that even a California community would see the ridiculousness of my returning to a magazine that had, under the thin disguise of literary criticism, abused me at the *expense of its own literary record*. And even if this stultification should not be inconsistent with California's ideas—I should lose, as I would deserve, the honorable respect of many thousand readers East who were more shocked than even myself at that spectacle of shameless ingratitude and blundering malice!
>
> Permit me to thank you again for your offer. I believe you are very honest and manly in it. Nothing but a very positive preference for myself, and a kind disposition to confess a mistake—which, however, I think you yourself will see is *irretrievable*—would have prompted your pleasant offer.[13]

The charge that Harte borrowed large sums and then ignored those to whom he owed money had been widely publicized in W. A. Kendall's attack on Bret Harte in the San Francisco *Chronicle* of December 15, 1872.[14] It may be remembered that long after Mark Twain knew of the charges of both Kendall and Carmany, he had welcomed Bret Harte to his home and had been eager to associate with Harte in a business venture in which, he said, the two would "divide the swag." Stung by the ingratitude of Kendall ("the sick & needy poet"), Harte

---

[11] *BHAE*, 184. [12] Cummins, *The Story of the Files*, 145.
[13] This hitherto unpublished letter is among the *Overland Monthly*, 1865–1875, letters in Bancroft.
[14] *BHAE*, 221, 357.

had written Twain in December, 1872: "I dont mind his slander; that I can refute." When Harte was near the peak of his fame, he underestimated the potential damage of slanderous words. In time he recognized their power but became convinced of the futility of replying.

An examination of the many stories about Harte's debts leads to at least one conclusion: although Harte contracted too many debts, most of the stories about them were based on hearsay. Even Mark Twain, while calling Harte a "swindler," said, "I don't know him, myself, to be a thief." William Dean Howells, answering President Hayes's inquiry about appointing Harte to Crefeld, did not ignore these stories but wrote: "Personally I have great affection for the man, and personally I know nothing to his disadvantage. . . . He is notorious for borrowing and was notorious for drinking. *This is report*. He never borrowed of *me*, nor drank more than I, (in my presence) and yesterday I saw his doctor who says his habits are good, now; and I have heard the same thing from others."[15]

The *Mark Twain–Howells Letters* published in 1960 show a break of three months following Twain's letter to Howells about Harte, and Twain's next letter to Howells inquired if Twain had in any way offended Howells.[16]

When the editor of the *Atlantic Monthly* wrote President Hayes that he knew nothing to Bret Harte's disadvantage, he was being somewhat contradictory, for he also reported that he had once seen Harte arrested for debt. This, of course, was not a matter of hearsay. Howells' memoir after Harte's death gave a more detailed account of Harte's experience with the bailiff. On the night of Harte's successful lecture at Tremont Temple in Boston (December, 1872), an officer of the law had appeared at a dinner where Harte was guest of honor before the lecture, had accompanied Harte to the building already filled with people eager to hear the celebrity speak, and had waited in the wings while Harte was on the platform. When the much-embarrassed Howells tactfully observed, "Well, Harte, this is the old literary tradition: this is the Fleet business over again," Harte allegedly smote his thigh, and crowed out, "Yes, the Fleet!" In 1903,

---

[15] Italics are Howells'. *Life in Letters*, I, 251. According to George R. Stewart, the most reliable evidence points to the conclusion that Harte was, in fact, a moderate drinker. *BHAE*, 221, 357.

[16] *MTH*, I, 239.

Howells reported the anecdote not to show that Harte was irresponsible about money but to demonstrate that Harte could enjoy a joke at his own expense.[17] As we have seen, Harte's letters make it very doubtful that Harte found this experience as amusing as Howells thought he did.

That Bret Harte never intended to repay what he borrowed has been emphatically denied by those in positions to know what they were talking about. One of these witnesses was Noah Brooks, who as editor of the *Alta California* and assistant editor of the *Overland Monthly* held positions which enabled him to know both Mark Twain and Bret Harte very well. If there were any truth to the charges of Kendall and Carmany, Noah Brooks would have been able to verify them. But according to Brooks:

> It would be grossly unjust to say that Harte was a species of Harold Skimpole, deliberately making debts that he did not intend to pay. He sincerely intended and expected to meet every financial obligation that he contracted. But he was utterly destitute of what is sometimes called the money sense. He could not drive a bargain, and he was an easy mark for any man who could.[18]

When Henry Childs Merwin was at work on his biography of Bret Harte (published in 1911), he received an unsolicited letter from Mrs. Charles Watrous, whose husband handled Harte's business affairs for many years and who had accompanied her husband on at least one visit to Harte during his years of service for the State Department.[19] Included in the letter was the following testimony:

> . . . After going abroad, Mr. Harte from time to time—whenever able to do so—sent through the business house of my husband and son money in payment of bills he was yet owing,—and this when three thousand miles removed from the pressure of payment,—which too many would have left unpaid. Life was often hard for him, yet he met it uncompainingly, unflinchingly and bravely.[20]

The same letter described Harte as "a kindly, sweet soul, one without gall, bitterness or envy."

---

[17] "Editor's Easy Chair," *loc. cit.*, 157.
[18] Merwin, *The Life of Bret Harte*, 214.   [19] *BHL*, 232, 234.
[20] Merwin, *The Life of Bret Harte*, 214.

Also pertinent is the following passage in a letter which Joaquin Miller wrote T. Edgar Pemberton after Harte's death:

> It was published up and down (in California) for years that he left a lot of bills unpaid. When I returned to settle down here in the early eighties I found these stories furiously revived. I denied them. Then it was published that he had left a lot of unpaid bills in New York also. I wrote to John Hay, then editing *The Tribune.* He assured me that he did not owe one dollar in New York: that he was a man of singularly strict sense of honour in money matters; that he had once offered to assist him when ill in Washington, but that Bret Harte had seemed so hurt at the idea that he was sorry he had tried to help him. . . . Yes, our gifted Secretary of State knew Bret Harte a heap better than any one else, and, as you can see, loved him and trusted him entirely.[21]

In 1878 when Mark Twain wanted to warn the Germans that the recently appointed representative of the United States government would not pay his debts, Twain could not foresee that he himself would one day be "hauled from a sick-bed" and brought before a New York court by the holder of a claim of $4,500 which Twain then found it difficult to pay.[22] The same letter which abusively protested Harte's appointment to Crefeld "privately" gave Howells the good news that Mark and Livy were no longer "feeling poor." After a little figuring the day before, the two had concluded that, thanks to interests from the coal company established by Livy's father as well as to income from their own investments, there was more than enough money for the Clemens family to live in Hartford on a "generous scale." But now that they were "fixed at last," Mark felt sure that the "communists & the asinine government" would "go to work and smash it all."[23] He also expressed distrust of Canadians, all of whom he suspected were "born pirates." Mark Twain's prosperity had not made him less suspicious or less in need to "spit his spite."

The Harte canker festering within Mark Twain was aggravated by literary as well as by financial and political fortunes. Just before leaving America for Europe, Mark had believed that as a result of the

[21] *The Life of Bret Harte,* 149–50.
[22] See the New York *Recorder* for July 15, 1895. The writer concluded that this treatment of Mark Twain "looked a good deal like persecution." MTP.
[23] *MTH,* I, 236–37.

Whittier Birthday Dinner speech, he had been plummeted from New England's Parnassian heights to an abyss of obscurity. Notwithstanding Howells' assurances to the contrary, Mark had doubted that he would ever again be a welcome contributor to the *Atlantic*. But now, in 1878, he told Howells he had no "printable stuff" to offer to the *Atlantic* at the moment but there would be some before long. Mark Twain was particularly anxious to know the reactions of American writers to Harte's appointment. "Have you heard any literary men express an opinion about the appointment?" he asked Howells. "Who were they —& what said they?"

On the night before Mark Twain wrote this letter, Mrs. Clemens had been startled to discover in his notebook, passages about a proposed work in which Captain Wakeman would visit "various heavens." At one gate a barkeeper was received with such salvos and swarming angels that he thought he was "*the* lion of Heaven," but almost immediately he was dropped into "solid obscurity." According to Mark Twain, the worst part of all was the barkeeper's penance. For thirty weeks, "day and night he must carry a torch & shout himself hoarse to do honor to some poor scrub whom he wishes had gone to hell."[24]

This may be the earliest appearance of the theme of a protagonist cast down from his high estate which Bernard De Voto traced as it developed from a dream sequence and reappeared obsessively in a large part of the Mark Twain Papers, particularly in unfinished manuscripts of 1898 and 1899 and "most clearly" in the determinism of "What Is Man?" privately published in 1904. In "Symbols of Despair," the concluding chapter of *Mark Twain at Work*, De Voto observed that sometimes the fallen man is virtuous, an innocent betrayed, but at other times the "victim of catastrophe . . . is guilty and knows he is guilty, and a large part of the story is his effort to appease and justify himself."[25]

[24] *Ibid.*, I, 236.
[25] *Mark Twain at Work*, 115–20.

15

THE COMMERCIAL AGENT AND A
ROYAL ACADEMY DINNER

... I consider that no higher compliment has been paid American humor than that the type of American drawn by your greatest English humorist has been supplanted by types drawn by Lowell, Artemus Ward, and Mark Twain.

BRET HARTE, 1880

SIX WEEKS AFTER ACCEPTING the appointment as United States commercial agent in Crefeld, Germany, Bret Harte bade his family what he believed was a temporary farewell and embarked for Europe. There was not enough money for his wife and four children to travel with him. Besides, he felt too insecure in his new political appointment to risk a family exodus which might end with all six of them being stranded in some unknown country in Europe. As it was, he had to borrow from his friend and publisher Charles A. Dana enough money to tide them over until his own earnings from the State Department would be available. He assured himself that his wife and children would be safe in America near his sister, and that as soon as he was established abroad and reasonably certain of being able to make them comfortable, they would join him. When Bret Harte's ship moved from Hoboken pier on that sultry day of June 28, 1878, Harte had no idea that he was leaving America never to return.[1]

The crossing, which he had hoped would raise his spirits and better his health, proved disappointing. James Osgood was "jolly" and Colonel Waring was "kind," but Harte, though generally a good sailer, was sick in soul and body and secretly envying those other passengers who were "down in their berths, dreadfully seasick, and soon over it."[2] He busied himself with daily reckonings of the ship's course to send to "Wodie," his eldest son, and he managed to jot down notes which

[1] *BHAE*, 249. [2] *BHL*, 76.

he hoped to use in fiction later on. As soon as he landed at Plymouth, on July 8, 1878, Harte telegraphed his wife.

Bret Harte liked his first glimpse of the English countryside, but London seemed coldly indifferent to his presence. From a quiet little hotel recommended by Osgood, Harte wrote his wife that he had only one strong feeling in "great, solid, earthly, powerful, and practical London. I am *awfully* lonely!"[3] He remembered Joaquin Miller's "ridiculous advice" (that to succeed in London a poet must dress flamboyantly and tickle the fancy of Duchesses[4]), admitted that the advice might be sound, but declared that he would rather "go away unnoticed than follow it." Harte *did* go away unnoticed, but he resolved to return after taking over his duties in Crefeld. After what seemed to him the "sluggish nightmare" of London and a "confused sort of hysterical experience" of three days in Paris, where he learned from his wife's nieces, Dora and Gertrude Griswold, that French and English papers had "copied all the ugly things" that were said about him in America, Bret Harte spent a sleepless night on the train and "with a very small stock of assurance," arrived in Crefeld on July 17, 1878.

There he found rain. Disconsolately he wrote his wife that he had delivered his letters to his predecessor and expected to take possession of the consulate the next day. "It's been uphill work ever since I left New York, but I shall try to see it through, please God! I don't allow myself to think over it all, or I should go crazy." He mailed this letter in the afternoon. In the evening he wrote Nan another letter, hoping to "take a little of the blues out of the first."[5] But day after day it rained in Crefeld, and Bret Harte hated it. He was tired. He had a sore throat. The German food did not agree with him. He disliked German music, German militarism, and the fat German people. He noted that though Germans seemed to eat and drink a great deal, they seldom got drunk. Nevertheless, "The Gentle Bacchus has somehow put his seal on them. Miserable dyspeptic that I am, God help me from ever becoming one of these fat-witted rosy satyrs."[6]

But German children, like children everywhere, appealed to Bret Harte, and to his own children in America he wrote charming letters about things he saw which he thought would interest them, such as

[3] *Ibid.*, 75, 78.
[5] *BHL*, 79, 81.
[4] Marberry, *Splendid Poseur*, 86.
[6] *Ibid.*, 85.

three children about the age of his little daughter Ethel, holding hands and singing a song to a stork perched on a near-by chimney. Harte enclosed the German words of the song together with his own rhymed translation in English and suggested that his son Frank learn the song and teach it to his sister. Although he tried to make letters to his wife equally entertaining, they throbbed with loneliness and disillusionment. On the day of his arrival, he wrote her that he would not send for her until he saw clearly that he could stay himself. He foresaw the possibility of his own disappointment and could not bear the thought of watching her suffer in the same way. If worst came to worst, he resolved to stick it out for a year and save enough to return home and try to rebuild his life there.

Not long after his arrival, Harte learned with distress that his appointment had deprived the consul at Barmen, "one of the oldest and most efficient consuls in the service," of a dependency. The manner in which the Crefeld consulate had been taken away from Mr. Edgar Stanton disturbed Bret Harte not only because it seemed to the new consul that the older man, who had generously befriended him, had been treated like a child, but also because what happened to Stanton increased Harte's own sense of insecurity. He reminded Mrs. Harte that they must both keep in mind a horrid possibility: "I am likely at any moment, with or without cause, or why or wherefore, to be *removed*."[7] He was also haunted by the fear of becoming ill.

Through the aid of Stanton, Harte secured the services of R. F. Schneider, an interpreter who would act as vice-consul at least until Harte learned more about the language and his own duties at the consulate. Harte and his vice-consul got along well together, and the lonely American became a welcome visitor in the Schneider home. German translations of Harte's works continued to be exceedingly popular, and even though the first of a series of articles giving his too frank impressions of Germany for the *Berliner Tageblatt* brought some cooling of German enthusiasm for Bret Harte, he was soon making friends and enjoying considerable German hospitality.[8]

Soon after arriving in Crefeld, Bret Harte had received letters from English friends who regretted having missed him on his midsummer stop in London. One of these letters came from the historian James

[7] *Ibid.*, 80, 83.   [8] *BHAE*, 263.

Anthony Froude, who now invited Harte for a visit to his country home in Devonshire. Affairs in Crefeld had prevented Harte's rejoining Osgood in Paris and returning with him to England, as the two had planned in London. But Harte accepted Froude's invitation for the latter part of August, and even though Harte was ill at the time of his visit, he was very grateful for Froude's sponsorship and hospitality. On a second trip to England Harte met many people who accepted him graciously and became his good friends. Among these were Lord Houghton, whom he had known earlier in America, and Colonel William Frederick Webb, a retired officer of the English Army, who with his wife resided at Newstead Abbey, the home of Lord Byron. The Webbs were extremely cordial, insisted that the American poet consider Newstead Abbey his "English home," and sent word to Mrs. Harte that she and the children must visit there as soon as they came to England.[9] At the Webb's, Harte met the Duchess of St. Albans, who found him the shyest man she had ever known, and one of the most appealing.[10] She invited him to visit her and her family at Bestwood, a pleasure which Harte deferred, but the two became friends. At different times she gave Bret Harte pictures of herself, her son, and her husband, and these pictures Bret sent back to his wife and two little girls in America.

His new English friends promptly exerted their influence to secure lecture invitations for Harte in England. But Bret Harte did not, like Mark Twain on his first taste of English hospitality in 1872, conclude that he would "rather live in England than America."[11] On the contrary, in a letter to Frankie about his visit to Newstead Abbey, Harte recalled the bloody histories of some noble titles and estates and objected that in England "property is everything. Men are an afterthought" and "a weary tramp walking the highroad may not rest himself in the hedge for fear of frightening the partridges out of it into somebody else's domain." Cynically he pointed out to his wife the commercial value to himself of the titles of his new acquaintances, and when recognizing that an invitation to lecture was issued him only because he was the friend of a Duke, he described the English as a "na-

[9] *BHL*, 77, 91, 96.
[10] Letter to George R. Stewart from Geoffrey Bret Harte included in correspondence relating to *BHAE* in the University of California Library, Berkeley.
[11] *LL*, 177.

tion of snobs."[12] Yet if, like Mrs. Clemens (who at times was made uncomfortable by English snobbery[13]), Bret Harte was less enthusiastic about the English than was Mark Twain, the natural friendliness and hospitality of Froude, Houghton, the Webbs, and the St. Albans family weakened Harte's cynicism and warmed his heart.

In much better spirits, the Commercial Agent returned to Crefeld and settled down to his routine job, which he seems to have handled with considerable efficiency.[14] He continued to study the German language and achieved some success, though like Mark Twain, he still had trouble with German verbs. Nevertheless, he had developed enough German vocabulary to assume more of the duties of his office. To the State Department in Washington, he wrote unusually readable reports even about the Crefeld rain. Though he now lived in Düsseldorf, where he had more friends, he could commute to Crefeld in less than an hour by train, and sometimes he kept the Crefeld office open after hours.[15] On his doctor's orders, he went to Switzerland for a month in the summer; occasionally he left Crefeld and Düsseldorf to arrange lectures in England and Germany. Nevertheless, he did not use up all the time allowed him for leaves of absence. At least once, he rejected an invitation to the St. Albans' in order to stay in Crefeld and work. He was careful not to take money from his office fees until more than enough to pay office expenses had accumulated.[16] At the end of the year, business had increased one-third, and he asked and was granted an additional allowance of $250 a year for clerical aid.[17]

Fairly systematically, Harte set about trying to straighten out some of the tangles in his own finances. Underscoring every word, he wrote: *"I will not make a single debt."*[18] He sent to America money to reduce old debts, and by the end of the first year in Crefeld had succeeded in paying off at least one in full. This was his debt to Charles A. Dana, the friend and publisher who had not forsaken him in those darkest of days in Washington, and who had showed continued faith in him by lending him money to begin his new venture abroad.

Harte's letters from Crefeld show constant concern for his family. Enclosures averaged about $150 a month, and early in 1879 he ar-

[12] *BHL*, 99, 107.
[13] Howells, *My Mark Twain*, 12–13.
[14] *BHL*, 133.
[15] *BHAE*, 261–62.
[16] *BHL*, 105, 111.
[17] *BHAE*, 261.
[18] *BHL*, 106.

ranged with Schroeder and Company to guarantee his wife this amount, although he assured her that he hoped to supplement it with his writing so that she could be "pretty sure of calculating upon two hundred dollars each month."[19] His letters to his wife were addressed to her at the home of his sister, 45 Fifth Avenue, or to an address in West Washington Place, New York, or during summers to the Sea Cliff Hotel at Sea Cliff, Long Island. At Christmas time he took pleasure in sending not only personally selected gifts for each member of the family but additional sums of $50 or $100 which he specified should be used exclusively for gifts for her and the children. On December 7, 1878, he wrote Mrs. Harte: "God keep you from beginning the year in debt or even anxious about money." Contrary to the assertions of Mark Twain, Bret Harte did not leave all the responsibility to God.

In March, at the end of his first year in Crefeld, Harte wrote his wife that he felt he had made a good record there. "By good luck, I fear, more than by my management, the consular business will exceed this year any previous year, and I can hand over to the Government quite a handsome sum."[20] He was not sending for the family to join him, he told her, because he was thinking of asking the State Department to change his location. Germany, he felt, was not a good place for his health, for his writing, or for his pocketbook. At this time he seems to have been clearly aware that he needed more money for four objectives: to support himself, to support his family, to pay his debts, and to pay passage of five persons to Europe. But more than that, he kept in mind that he needed money enough to get them all back to America if his political appointment came to an end.

Harte soon discovered that most American officials with positions comparable to his own had independent incomes on which they relied to supplement their salaries. Since he had no such income, he must turn to writing and lecturing for the needed supplement. Consequently, even though Harte had long believed that the only way to improve the quality of his fiction was to give himself a period of rest, or, as Mark Twain put it, to let the tank fill up again, now—whether he felt like it or not—Harte worked on stories. And these stories sold, the money being generally sent directly from the publisher to Mrs. Harte. But Bret had few illusions about their quality or reception. "I grind out the

[19] *Ibid.*, 117, 138.   [20] *Ibid.*, 111, 134.

old tunes on the old organ and gather up the coppers," he said, "but I never know whether my audience behind the window blinds are wishing me to 'move on' or not."[21]

Hoping to get a thousand dollars or so "ahead," he resolved again to "go through the agony and misery of the lecture work." On December 2, 1878, he lectured to about four hundred English people at Wiesbaden and received very complimentary notices in the German papers.[22] In January, 1879, Harte returned to England to fill the first of a series of lecture engagements which would take him to Hull, Nottingham, the Crystal Palace at Sydenham, Manchester, and Brighton. He also accepted invitations to lecture at Oxford, Cambridge, and Norwich.[23]

Financially the lectures were a "miserable failure."[24] Harte's shyness and diffidence were against him, his voice at times being so low that people in the back of the room protested they could not hear.[25] However, English newspapers gave him good reviews, some of which Mark Twain cut out and pasted in his scrapbook. The first item in Mark's scrapbook for 1878–79 is a clipping from the London *Daily News* reporting a Bret Harte lecture. The reviewer described Harte's vein of humor as "much more English and less thoroughly Yankee" than that of his contemporaries, more "humane . . . than the amazing paradoxes of Mark Twain." Bret Harte, the reviewer said, was a "disciple but not an imitator" of Dickens. Mark Twain was a joker, a user of tricks, whose *The Innocents Abroad* demonstrated how the peculiarly American fun always failed. The reviewer believed that American humor never approached the masterpieces of Thackery and Dickens because it lacked reverence and sympathy.[26]

Thus, although in England as in America, Harte's lectures were received with far less popular enthusiasm than were Mark Twain's, they increased his prestige. On July 4, 1879, *Vanity Fair* published a caricature of Bret Harte by the famous cartoonist, Leslie Ward, who signed himself "Spy." In contrast with Joaquin Miller's pose of a crude, wild westerner, Spy's caricature of Harte suggests a foppish man about town. Harte had difficulty seeing himself as the cartoonist saw him, but he

---

[21] *Ibid.,* 154. [22] *Ibid.,* 111, 115. [23] *BHAE,* 265.
[24] *BHL,* 132. [25] *BHAE,* 256–57.
[26] See the London *Daily News* (Jan. 29), 2, MTP.

hoped that the publicity would increase attendance at his lectures. As a matter of fact, the caricature even more than the reviews indicated that Bret Harte had become something of a personage in England.

A newspaper review of Harte's lecture in Wiesbaden described Bret Harte in 1878 as having a "slim, elegant figure" in spite of his "probably fifty years." Bret Harte, telling his wife about the German review, commented: " *'Funfzig* looks even older than our 'fifty.' It's of no use, you see, for me to try to appear young, Nan—but really, I've got *very old* lately. I feel it in many ways. . . . I've only one idea now—to get enough money to *rest*."[27] At the time of this review, Bret Harte was forty-two years old.

By the end of 1879, Harte faced the fact that he could never be well in Germany, a conclusion confirmed by his doctors. In Crefeld he complained of colds, headaches, toothaches, failing eyesight, dizziness, rheumatism, insomnia, and sore throat. Not all his ailments were psychosomatic, and his concern for his health was more than the egocentricity of the hypochondriac. He had a deadly fear that illness would prevent him from lecturing, prevent him from writing, prevent him from keeping his job, and thus lead to utter destitution for himself and his family. Therefore he spurred himself on to the agony and misery of lecturing; this agony and misery increased his bad health; and then he tried to "get well and strong enough" to go back to the agony and misery. With customary outward gaiety, Harte took considerable punishment.

His wife urged him to try stimulants. On her advice he tried German wines, which he had written her were good and cheap, but they simply made him sick. His German doctor prescribed Bordeaux, but that didn't work either. The truth was that "almost every form of wine or alcohol" now disagreed with him, and his stomach turned against food as well as drink.[28]

Before he left the United States, Bret Harte had learned his lesson that rumors, with or without foundation, can do considerable harm. As an employee of the State Department, he seems to have tried to avoid even the appearance of evil. He was aware of the risk he was running in absenting himself from Crefeld to lecture or to follow his

[27] *BHL*, 115, 121.   [28] *Ibid.*, 104.

187

doctor's prescriptions of a change of climate. But he was not prepared for a rumor which reached him about this time via his fifteen-year-old son Frank.

Frank's letter, written in April, 1880, referred to some recent "trouble" his father had had in Germany. Puzzled by the reference and concerned by the anxiety this must have caused his wife, Harte gave her a detailed account of a recent incident which he now believed closed. Some weeks earlier while he was confined to his room with a sore throat, Harte had received from an English friend in Düsseldorf a clipping from a German newspaper stating that the Consul was sick of Germany and planning to resign. Commenting that it was "well known" the "genial poet" was "beset with ungovernable passion for 'fire-water' ('feuerwasser—brandy') brought on by his early habits in California: that his Government had sent him to Germany hoping to cure him of it . . . but that, alas, it was all in vain," the paragraph reported that "now the 'genial poet' was about to return to San Francisco 'where he could indulge himself freely.' "[29]

Furious, Bret Harte consulted a lawyer in Berlin and demanded a retraction or a suit against the newspaper. To Harte's German friends who had observed him in Crefeld and Düsseldorf day by day, the story was simply absurd. Most indignant was Harte's German physician, who wrote a letter to the newspaper testifying that he had attended Harte regularly and that the rumor was altogether untrue. The German newspaper retracted the story and apologized. Other papers denounced the original paragraph and copied the retraction. At that time and in that place, Bret Harte was vindicated. Yet, sick at heart, he wrote his wife: "I knew—what I didn't dare tell my friends—that paragraph—*that slander came from America!*"[30] The shocked, indignant words are underlined in Harte's letter.

If Bret Harte suspected Mark Twain or knew of Mark Twain's expressed desire to warn Germans against him, Harte did not mention Twain's name. He could hardly have known that almost exactly a year earlier, on April 15, 1879, Mark Twain in Paris had written William Dean Howells another letter filled with invective against Bret Harte, including a charge of drunkenness. After eight pages, beginning with fond and at times jocular references to Mrs. Howells' good taste

[29] *Ibid.*, 139, 176.   [30] *Ibid.*, 177.

and the Howellses' beautiful new home in Belmont, Mark launched into the old, chronically bitter theme:

It was splendid in the President to appoint Mr. White.[31] The more I think of the matter the more I am satisfied that the President never appointed Bret Harte. Evarts simply *crowded* that shameless scoundrel in. You have seen by the papers that Harte has deliberately swindled two German publishing houses, by selling each the *sole* right to print one of his books. Poor Boyesen is here in this expensive city, & has got to *stay* here till his wife is confined in July, & every cent of silver is worth its weight in gold to him; well, two German publishers were going to buy some of his literature, but all of a sudden comes a letter from a famous German author a week or so ago, freighted with disappointment—the publishers have reconsidered the matter, & say in plain terms that they must decline to buy anything of an American author, now, *unless he will give bond to indemnify them in case he has sold the sole right to some other German publisher!* It comes hard on Boyesen. We like Boyesen & his wife, heartily. Poor fellow, there are *12* Orions in his family. That's enough to make anybody warm to him.—

Do you know, I wanted to take that German author's letter & send it to the President & say "When your Excellency found that George Butler was drunk, on his way to his new post, you dismissed him before he got there; here is a new appointee who is also a drunkard, & is a thief besides: is it not a case for dismissal?"—But I couldn't seem to word a formal state paper just right in my mind, & I wouldn't send one that wasn't in every way a proper thing for the head of our country to read—so I've dropped it for the present. I told Bret Harte, just before the Presidential election, that the New York Custom house was the right place for him, & that I thought him an unfit person for our foreign service. I would think so yet, only the Custom house has latterly become too clean a place for such a dirty bird as he is.

Good night, my boy—Yrs Ever

MARK

But Mark had still not got the subject out of his system even for the time being, so the letter continued:

Chatto sent me Harte's new book of Sketches, the other day, ("An

[31] Andrew D. White, founder and first president of Cornell University, had been appointed to fill the vacancy left by Bayard Taylor's death in Germany. See *MTH*, I, 262n.

Heiress of Red Dog," etc). I have read it twice—the first time through tears of rage over the fellow's inborn hypocrisy & snobbishness, his apprentice-art, his artificialities, his mannerisms, his pet phrases, (such as the frequent "I regret to say,")—his laboriously acquired ignorance, & his jejune anxiety to display it. O, my God! He rings in *Strasse* when street would answer every purpose, and *Bahnhof* when it carries no sharper significance to the reader [than depot] than "station" would; he peppers in his seven little French words (you can find them in all his sketches, for he learned them in California 14 years ago,)—he begins his German substantives with "lower case" generally, & sometimes mis-spells them—all this with a dictionary at his very elbow— what an illustration of his slovenly laziness it is! And Jack Hamlin talks like a Bowery gutter-snipe on one page, & like a courtier of Louis XV's time on the very next one. And he has a "nigger" who talks a "dialect" which is utterly original. The struggle after the pathetic is more pathetic than the pathos itself; if he were to write about an Orphan Princess who lost a Peanut he would feel obliged to try to make somebody snuffle over it.

The second time I read the book I saw a most decided brightness on every page of it—& here & there evidences of genius. I saw enough to make me think, "Well, if this slovenly shoemaker-work is able to command the applause of three or four nations, what *mightn't* this ass accomplish if he would do his work honestly & with pains?" If I ever get my tedious book finished, I mean to weed out some of my prejudices & write an article on "Bret Harte as an Artist"—& print it if it will [would] not be unfair to print it without signature.

Tauchnitz called the other day—a mighty nice old gentleman. He paid me 425 francs for the Innocents—I think he paid me about 6 or 700 fr. for Tom Sawyer (it being new); he is going to print Roughing It by & by, & has engaged advanced sheets of my new book. Don't know what he will pay for the two latter—I leave that to him— one can't have the heart to dicker with a publisher who won't steal.

Can't you get up a plot for a "skeleton novelette" & find two or three fellows to join us in writing the stories? Five of us would do. I can't seem to give up that idea.

I knew the President would veto that infamous Chinese bill.[32] I wish I knew whether Belmont was a P.O. or a country seat.

Yrs Ever
MARK.

[32] See *MTH*, I, 263. That it was loyalty to Burlingame rather than defense of Chi-

P.S. If I should think of anything more to say about Harte, I will telegraph.[33]

In this letter Mark Twain directly expresses a continuing ambivalence toward Harte's work. Yet it is not altogether clear whether the effusion was set off by Mark's belief that Harte was responsible for Hjalmar Hjorth Boyesen's[34] rejections or by the fact that Chatto had just sent Mark Twain Bret Harte's recently published book of sketches, *An Heiress of Red Dog and Other Tales.*

Mark Twain was right that the work was inferior. And the weaknesses that he mentioned in this letter were more valid grounds for criticism than were the elements in Harte's writings to which he had objected in an entry in his notebook two weeks earlier. On March 28, 1879, he had recorded an idea for a burlesque scene showing Harte's characters protesting that they had been misrepresented and required to use impossible dialects. But at that time, Mark's chief objection seemed to be that Harte's fiction aroused in the "upper classes" too much sympathy for "whores" and "burglars."[35] Walter Blair cites another notebook entry, August 1, 1879, in which Mark Twain refers to "Harte's saintly wh's and self-sacrificing sons of b's."[36]

As for the charge that Harte sold the same work to two German publishers, I do not know the facts. Perhaps relevant to the German author's letter is Bret Harte's warning to his English agent in 1895 that some German publishers at times made false claims to a contract with an author in order to warn off other publishers and thereby reduce the price by eliminating competition.[37] If the newspaper report was true and if Harte's actions did, in fact, cause German publishers to reject Boyesen's work, it certainly did not cause them to reject Harte's. In the letter to Howells it is apparent that Twain was acutely aware of the continued popularity of Harte's work in England and on the Con-

nese which motivated Mark Twain's reaction to the "infamous Chinese bill" is suggested by his approval in the same year of an article by J. B. Harrison entitled "Certain Dangerous Tendencies in American Life." See *MTH*, I, 241, 244–45n.

[33] *MTH*, I, 260–62. Also published by George Peirce Clark, "Mark Twain on Bret Harte," *Mark Twain Journal* (Spring and Summer, 1958), 12–13.

[34] A professor of German at Cornell who sometimes contributed fiction and criticism to the Atlantic. *MTH*, II, 906.

[35] See Notebook, # 14, 18, MTP.   [36] *Mark Twain & Huck Finn*, 114.

[37] *BHL*, 409. See *MTH*, II, 619–20n., for a charge by Edward H. House that Mark Twain twice sold the dramatization rights of *The Prince and the Pauper.*

tinent. In Germany, Harte's fiction had paved the way for the publication of Twain's own writing, and Harte's work would outsell Twain's to the end of the century.[38]

An interesting indication of the way Mark Twain's mind worked can be observed in the juxtaposition of his statement about wanting to write an anonymous article attacking "Bret Harte as an Artist" with his praise of Tauchnitz, a fairly clear echo of Bret Harte's praise of this German publisher in the 1876 letter recommending Tauchnitz as a publisher of *Tom Sawyer*. Also indicative of unconscious associative processes of Mark Twain's mind are the allusions to Orion and Chinese, two themes which frequently cropped up near Twain's mentions of Harte.

If Mark Twain reacted with ambivalence to the literary quality of Bret Harte's work, he was equally ambivalent toward Harte's ability to command good prices. A letter to Howells immediately preceding the one quoted here was almost as unpleasant about Mark's sister-in-law Mollie Clemens as this one was about Harte. Its enumeration of the exasperating foibles and futilities of Twain's brother included a scornful mention of Orion's naïve belief that if Harte's stories could command from the *Times* $100 a column, Orion could produce work that would bring the same pay.[39]

Although the rumors reported in Mark Twain's letter to Howells suggest that Bret Harte was now without honor in his own country, Harte was increasingly honored in England. He was invited to become a member of the famous Rabelais Club, and one evening, "to everybody's apparent applause and satisfaction but my own," he told his wife, Harte was nominated presiding officer for the next meeting. At this club he met many celebrities, including Thomas Hardy, the artist George du Maurier, and Henry James, whose reputation in England was also growing. One Sunday, Harte spent what seemed to him a "delightful hour" in the home of George Eliot, whose work Bret Harte—unlike Mark Twain—much admired. The admiration was mutual, for the English novelist praised Harte's fiction and invited him

[38] Hemminghaus, *Mark Twain in Germany*, 2. Harold Blodgett, "Heard from the New World," in Spiller *et al.*, editors, *Literary History of the United States*, I, 634.
[39] *MTH*, II, 256–57.

to call again—a rare compliment, for after the death of George Henry Lewes she received few visitors.[40]

In 1879, six months after Spy's caricature for *Vanity Fair* identified Bret Harte as one of the leading "Men of the Day," Mark Twain was invited to make the Fourth of July speech before the Anglo-American Club of Students at Heidelberg, Germany. The invitation was delivered by Frank Harris, who came "prepared to be worshipful," but in his first conversation with this American writer, Harris was so shocked by Mark Twain's violent verbal attack on Bret Harte as a "plagiarist and dead beat" that Harris wrote of Twain: "I never want to see that man again; never again do I want to talk to him." As long as he lived, Frank Harris never completely outgrew this revulsion.[41] Almost thirty years would pass before Spy caricatured Mark Twain for the "Men of the Day" series in a *Vanity Fair Supplement*.[42]

Also in 1879, when Bret Harte was soberly at work on his routine job of approving invoices in Crefeld, he received from the President of the British Royal Academy a formal invitation to reply to the "Toast to Literature" at that year's Royal Academy Dinner in London. Bret Harte was the first American writer to be thus honored. He appreciated the honor but could not bring himself to accept or decline. According to Henry Childs Merwin, "the prospect of speaking at the dinner loomed more and more horrific in his imagination, while the uncertainty in which he left the matter was a source of vexation in London."[43] At the last minute Harte declined and James Anthony Froude had to substitute for him. Surprisingly, the invitation was repeated the following year. Although he felt that the honor properly belonged to James Russell Lowell, then American ambassador to England, Harte—in order to please his wife—finally summoned courage to accept the invitation.[44]

On Saturday evening, May 1, 1880, Bret Harte stood before a "distinguished company" gathered at Burlington House in London. According to reports in the London *Times* and the London *Daily News* for May 3, the group included the Prince of Wales and other members

[40] *BHL*, 163–64.   [41] Fatout, *Mark Twain on the Lecture Circuit*, 199.
[42] Meltzer, *Mark Twain Himself*, 216.
[43] *The Life of Bret Harte*, 260.   [44] *BHL*, 170–71, 178.

of the royal family, the Prime Minister (Mr. William E. Gladstone), the Lord Chief Justice, the Lord Mayor of London, many Members of Parliament, two archbishops, and "others." Among the others were "T. Huxley, A Sullivan, J. A. Froude, A. Trollope, and R. Browning."[45] The President of the Royal Academy introduced Bret Harte. And this is what Sir Frederick Leighton said:

> I have now to ask you to drink to the interest of Science and Literature. . . . In coupling a name with Literature I propose to take a rather unusual course: for I shall call upon a writer who owes us no allegiance save that of friendship to the country in which he is now a guest. [Cheers.] An English writer, nevertheless, for English is the tongue in which he delights the unnumerable host of his readers; English is the tongue in which he has clothed a humor, racy and delicate at once, and has married to it a most subtle pathos—a pathos so deep, so tender, and so penetrating that we rise from his pages half believing that wrong is an untoward accident in the world, and goodness the one abiding, inextinguishable thing. [Cheers.] This company will be glad, I am confident, of the opportunity thus offered to it of welcoming in its midst the great American humorist, Bret Harte. [Loud cheers.]

Harte's speech began with a humorous reference to the problem of literary pirating which plagued authors on both sides of the Atlantic: "I presume I am selected to answer this toast as a native of a country which reads more English books and pays less for them than any other nation. [Laughter.]" He acknowledged the President's introduction as a tribute not to himself but to his country and his fellow countrymen. "I recognize in your kindly greeting the same welcome extended to Hosea Biglow, Hans Breitman, Artemus Ward, and Mark Twain. [Cheers.]" The brief toast concluded with a defense of American humor which seems to be a direct reply to the reviewer in the London *Daily News*, who, while praising Harte's lecture, had disparaged American humor in general and had criticized Mark Twain in particular:

> . . . It has been settled by your reviewers that American literature is American humor, and that this American humor is a kind of laughable impropriety, more or less scantily clothed in words. It has been settled that you are a sober people, and that nobody in America takes life seriously—not even a highwayman—and that our literature is a reflex of

[45] *BHAE*, 266–67, 360.

our life. But I think that a majority of this Academy are kind enough to recognize some principles of Art underlying this characteristic. And I consider that no higher compliment has been paid American humor than that the type of American drawn by your greatest English humorist has been supplanted by types drawn by Lowell, Artemus Ward, and Mark Twain.[46]

The words came from a man who acknowledged Dickens as his master. And the speaker knew something about rhetoric. He knew that the most emphatic position in a sentence is at the end because the last word is apt to remain in the minds of the audience.

Harte's audience at Burlington House was friendly and responsive. "Loud cheers" greeted him when he rose to speak, frequent cheers interrupted his words, and after the dinner was concluded with speeches by the Lord Mayor and the Archbishop of Canterbury, the Prince of Wales asked that Mr. Bret Harte be presented.[47] At the first mention of Mark Twain's name, there were "Cheers." Since Mark Twain made no secret of his antipathy for Bret Harte, it seems reasonable to assume that some of the loud cheers at Harte's concluding tribute to Twain were also cheers for the generosity and critical integrity of Bret Harte.

[46] *The Lectures of Bret Harte,* 31–33.
[47] *BHAE,* 267.

16

THE INTENT OF "THE MODEST CLUB"

... the intent of the Club is, by superior weight, character & influence to impair & eventually destroy the influence of [illegible]—not from any base feeling, but from a belief that this is a thing required in the interest of the public good.

MARK TWAIN to WILLIAM DEAN HOWELLS, 1880

ON MAY 18, 1880, less than three weeks after the Royal Academy Dinner, Mark Twain invited William Dean Howells and his wife to become members of a club, of which at the time Mark Twain was the only member. The "peculiar" name of the new organization would be "The Modest Club," the chief qualification for membership would be modesty, and the official symbol, a single violet. Twain asked Howells to treat as confidential the fact that "the intent of the Club, is by superior weight, character & influence, to impair & eventually destroy the influence of [illegible]—not from any base feeling, but from a belief that this is a thing required in the interest of the public good."[1] Observing that he had long believed there ought to be "an organized gang *of our kind*" (the italics are Mark Twain's), Twain showed particular interest in learning whether Howells thought the club might also include among its members John Hay, who in 1879 had become assistant secretary of state. The editors of the Mark Twain–Howells letters note that the illegible name of the person whose influence should be destroyed was "almost certainly Bret Harte" and that the cancellation which made the name illegible was probably made by Howells.[2]

To Twain's invitation, Howells replied with facetious approval of the "Modest" idea but ironic doubt that anyone other than himself and Twain was modest enough to become a bona fide member. Hay,

[1] *MTH, I*, 308–309.   [2] *Ibid.*, 310n.

196

to whom Howells transmitted Mark's invitation, replied in the same jocular tone that a club which would hold Mark and Howells and himself "and then reach out for H. etc.,—and still keep modest,—staggers and fatigues the faculty of wonder." But Hay offered his house for the first meeting.[3]

That either Howells or Hay had any idea of ganging up against Harte is doubtful.[4] The best reason for doubting this is that in answer to Harte's request for transfer from Crefeld, President Hayes about this time promoted Harte to the consulship in Glasgow, next to the largest city in Great Britain. Almost certainly, Howells could have prevented the appointment, for his close and cordial relationship with President Hayes, his wife's cousin, continued and his letter to Mark Twain about the Modest Club mentioned a "magnificent" six-day visit which he and Mrs. Howells had recently enjoyed in the White House.[5] But Harte owed his new appointment chiefly to John Hay, who—according to Clarence King—"never lost an opportunity to work" for Harte. Harte's first intimation of his promotion came from an item in the London *Times*, but it was a personal note from Hay which brought the first confirmation of the news.[6]

Six months earlier Mark Twain had praised John Hay as a good influence on national politics and had half-jokingly told Howells that Mark himself considered running for an office which "majestic ignorance & incapacity, coupled with purity of heart, could fill." He added: "This naturally reminds me of Bret Harte—but let him pass."[7]

After Mark Twain's Modest Club proposal, Hay's regard for Harte showed no signs of diminution. It would be interesting to know what prompted John Hay some months later to write to Bret Harte:

> I want before my sands run out to say "How?" to you once more, and to assure you of my eternal love and esteem. . . . *I* do not know what Heaven meant by creating so few men like [Clarence King][8]

[3] Thayer, *John Hay*, I, 439. Editors of *MTH* suggest that the "H." may stand for Higginson. *MTH*, I, 311.

[4] Apparently Hay, who had met Mark Twain with Bret Harte in New York in August, 1872, when the two were on good terms, failed to recognize the intensity of Mark Twain's present hostility for his former friend. *LL*, 363.

[5] *MTH*, I, 310. See also 251n. and 276n. for indication of the close relationship of Howells to his wife's cousin, President Hayes.

[6] *BHL*, 170, 173.   [7] *MTH*, I, 274.   [8] *BHL*, 194.

and you. The scarcity of you is an injury not only to us, but to yourselves. There are not enough of you to go round, and the world pulls and hauls at you till you are completely spoiled. . . . Well, good-bye, and good health and good spirits and everything good be yours.[9]

Characteristically, Bret Harte had refused to be impressed by the company he kept at the Royal Academy Dinner. In a grumbling letter to Mrs. Harte he described his speech there as "neat," "not bad and not very good," and the whole affair as "a good deal of trouble for very little result." His reaction to the letter from Hay was very different: he kept it with him always and reread it many times when he was depressed. He had become so accustomed to thinking of himself as banished and defamed in his homeland that words of encouragement and acts of loyalty from Americans moved him deeply. Hay complained of his own vexations of spirit in Washington, and among those vexations were avid seekers of patronage. "They have even asked for Glasgow—never more than once in my presence." Harte realized that it was the loyalty of these few friends which kept him at his post.[10]

Even though he was pleased with his promotion, Harte went to Scotland with forebodings, and he found there even more rain than in Crefeld. With the return of his neuralgia and extreme depression, it seemed to him that his transfer on account of health resolved into a "ghastly farce." As soon as possible, he escaped to Paris briefly, not for Parisian night life but for Parisian sunshine. When, with improved health, he returned to Glasgow, he responded with appreciation to the kind Scottish people who drank his health on his birthday, and to the Scottish scenery—especially at Innellan, a "lovely little watering place on the Clyde," where he lived for a time and commuted daily to his office in Glasgow. When he moved to the city, Harte resided rather drearily in a hotel. And drearily he wrote his wife: "I'll write as soon as I am settled—or anything but a weary wanderer on the face of the earth."[11]

The five years of Harte's consulship in Glasgow were relatively prosperous, yet his position there was far from enviable. He had been appointed by a Republican administration not long before the President's term of office would expire, and he realized that after the election, many new office seekers would be clamoring for his job. Harte

9 Pemberton, *The Life of Bret Harte*, 222.
10 BHL, 170, 178, 194.   11 *Ibid.*, 188.

did not rely on his preface to Frank H. Mason's campaign biography of President James A. Garfield to secure his tenure. In 1881, Hay resigned from the State Department. With Garfield's assassination and the succession of President Chester A. Arthur came new uncertainty for Bret Harte.

Occasionally Harte was visited in Glasgow by acquaintances from England or America: William Black, whom he had met and delighted during an interval of London Bohemianism between Crefeld and Glasgow;[12] Edwin Booth, the actor; Hay; and Clarence King. Charles Watrous also came to Glasgow bringing welcome reports of the appearance and welfare of Mrs. Harte and the children, with whom Watrous kept in touch in America. Lieutenant John A. Tobin, U.S.N., on special assignment in Glasgow, did much to mitigate Harte's sense of exile. Happily Bret reported to his wife that he and Tobin were "fast friends and good Americans."[13] But most of the time, the Consul in Glasgow was terribly lonely.

London was always beckoning. According to James Anthony Froude, Harte's movements, "like those of Royalties and Cabinet Ministers," were reported in newspapers.[14] Robert Browning and Harte exchanged recent publications.[15] Harte dined with Arthur Wing Pinero and Oscar Wilde; Thomas Hardy, after urging Harte to lecture to the Dorchester Lecture Society and visit in the Hardy home, was much annoyed when Harte declined.[16] London hostesses vied for Harte's presence. Even James Russell Lowell, learning by chance that Harte was in the city, urged him to attend Mrs. Lowell's first London dinner party and by his presence make the occasion "yet more historic."[17] But most of all Harte was lured to London by the possibility of meeting old friends from America. In September, 1882, an invitation from James Osgood was irresistible. "Imagine *who* I found at dinner?" Harte wrote his wife. "Clarence King, Howells, Aldrich, Dr. Martin, John Hay, Booth, and Warner—of my dear old friends, and Henry James, Alma-Tadema, Conway, of the ones I knew here. It was a most

---

[12] *BHAE*, 269. [13] *BHL*, 197.

[14] Pemberton, *The Life of Bret Harte*, 224.

[15] "Things That Happened 1881 ... 1888" (hereinafter cited as Bret Harte's Diary) in the handwriting of Madame Van de Velde. Berg Collection, The New York Public Library (hereinafter cited as BC).

[16] *Ibid.*, Oct. 26, 1883. [17] Pemberton, *The Life of Bret Harte*, 22:

wonderful coincidence to find all these men together in London—it would have been most remarkable for New York or Boston. In King and Dr. Martin I went back to the old San Francisco days. In Howells, Hay, and Aldrich to the first days of my arrival in the East."[18] Harte's pleasure in meeting his countrymen was sincere. Like many another middle-aged man at a reunion, Harte was relieved to discover that his friends, like himself, were getting fat.

Both Osgood and Howells wrote Mark Twain about this remarkable dinner, and both wished that Mark could have been there.[19]

Repeatedly Bret Harte and his wife canvassed the advantages and disadvantages of the family's joining him in Glasgow. But there was the uncertainty of his tenure, the old problem of the expense of bringing five people to Europe, setting up housekeeping in a foreign country, and then finding enough money to return to America in the event he should be dispossessed of his consulship. Bret Harte sent his wife the full $3,000 a year which he was paid as consul and relied on his pen to meet his own expenses. Although contacts in London stimulated Harte's ideas and promoted English interest in his work, they also increased his expenditures. The combination of his social, literary, and consular activities resulted in a very demanding schedule for a man whose health was still poor, and since Harte continued to write slowly, it is probable that need for some uninterrupted hours in which to write also influenced his failure to bring his family to Glasgow at this time, for Harte's mind was turning again to playwriting as a means of getting enough money ahead to provide more security for himself and family. But whether any or all of these were the real reasons or merely good reasons for the separation, the decisions which kept an ocean between Bret Harte and his family were not exclusively his own. On September 17, 1883, Harte suggested that his family come to Glasgow instead of his coming to America as his wife wished. Moreover, though Hay advised Harte not to leave his consular post for a trip to America during the new election year, Harte told his wife that he would come anyway if she believed he should.[20] Repeatedly Bret Harte expressed the hope that the family would be reunited on the Continent, in Britain,

[18] *BHL*, 212. [19] *MTH*, I, 413–14.
[20] *BHL*, 235–37. For additional evidence that the negative decision about the family's joining Harte in Europe was at least partly Mrs. Harte's, see pages 185, 250–53.

or in America.[21] But this reunion was something he seemed both to desire and to dread.

Although the family remained separated, there was a constant exchange of letters with detailed accounts of family experiences and many expressions of affection. Sometimes Mrs. Harte was slow in answering Bret's letters, even to acknowledge receipt of funds enclosed. The following brief excerpts fairly represent the tone of Harte's letters to his wife in relation to her handling of the regular remittances. On July 17, 1882, he wrote: "You have not yet acknowledged receipt of my draft from Dana for two hundred and fifty dollars sent June 23d. I enclose you another for the same amount, payable August 1st. I hope you are better. Try to go somewhere this summer where you can have complete change and rest, and do not mind a little extra expense." When he learned that she had gone to the Adirondacks, he was pleased. "Don't come back too *soon*," he told her. "I would rather you would give yourself more freedom in expense than run risks and have discomforts." In September, he wrote: "I hope you have not hurried back from the Adirondacks too soon." But occasionally he expressed the hope that she could save a bit so that if something happened to interrupt the regular remittances of $250 a month, she would not be inconvenienced. Harte's letters to his wife were generally signed with her pet name for him, "Limick." "I keep nothing from you," he once wrote her. "Write me fully and frequently, and above all, select *some permanent address*."[22]

The nearest approach to a home that Bret Harte knew in the last twenty years of his life was the residence of the Van de Veldes. Arthur Van de Velde was chancellor of the Belgian Legation in London, and his wife was the daughter of Count de Launay, Italian ambassador at Berlin. The Van de Veldes had nine children, but they also had a large house and many servants. "It is the most refined, courteous, simple, elegant, and unaffected household that can be imagined," Harte wrote his wife in October, 1882. "They have adopted me into their family— Heaven knows how or why—as simply as if I had known them for years."[23] He thought one reason was that Madame had loved America

[21] That Harte's invitation was made in good faith is indicated by his telling Pemberton that he hoped relatives would come to Glasgow soon so that he could establish a home. See *BHL*, 190. See also *BHAE*, 270.

[22] *Ibid.*, 205–206, 211–13, 242–43.   [23] *BHL*, 215.

ever since she had visited there with her father thirty years earlier when she was a girl.

Harte had met the Van de Veldes in 1878 on one of his first lecture tours in England. The acquaintance developed into friendship in 1881. On February 18, 1881, he recorded in his diary that he dined for the first time at their London home at 15, Upper Hamilton Terrace, N.W.[24] In the autumn, the Van de Veldes became so concerned by his obvious ill health that they took him to their summer home at Bournemouth, and when at the end of the month he was still not very strong, they accompanied him back to Glasgow.[25] In November, Madame persuaded Harte to see her personal physician in London, and before long Harte felt well enough to resume work on a story which he had begun in January. When the story was completed, Madame Van de Velde translated it into French and it was published immediately in *Figaro*.[26] Back in Glasgow, Harte was ill again and unable to work, but the Van de Veldes insisted that he come to them for Christmas, and when he arrived very early in the morning of December 24, he discovered the whole family already up and waiting to receive him. Recording in his diary that it felt like home, Harte unwrapped Christmas gifts with the family.[27] Thereafter, the Van de Veldes made him feel that wherever they were, he was at home and welcome. A room in the Van de Velde house was known as his, and summer or winter, this room always contained some possession of Bret Harte's as a token of his ownership. Later, a front room upstairs was furnished as a library with a large desk and bookshelves. Harte noted with satisfaction that it was a comfortable place to write.[28]

Madame Van de Velde was herself a writer. She was aware of Harte's fame and she had considerable respect for his talent. When he was in the Van de Velde home, she not only saw to it that he had a place and uninterrupted time in which to write; she also encouraged him to improve. She talked over with him his ideas for fiction, made suggestions, criticized stories after they were written. Sometimes she collaborated with him; often she translated his work; later, when there were typewriters, she even typed some of his manuscripts. There can be no doubt

[24] BC. [25] *BHAE*, 278.
[26] Bret Harte's Diary, Nov. 8, 1881, and Jan. 23, 1882, BC.
[27] *Ibid.*, Dec. 24, 1881, BC. [28] *Ibid.*, Nov. 17, 1883, BC.

that Harte's renewed interest in writing and the increased vitality of some of his later stories were due to this gracious woman.

Although Madame's generosity should not be minimized, the association had certain advantages for her. Through Harte she met many interesting and distinguished Americans, including Clarence King and John Hay, who frequently dined in her home when they were in England. Harte also introduced her to publishers for her own work, and her translations of his stories found immediate markets. He entertained her and her husband at the Rabelais and other London literary clubs which had welcomed Bret Harte as a member; occasionally he was her host at Innellan or in Glasgow. On these visits, Madame was generally accompanied by some of her children: Marguerite, Monique, Berthe, or Maurice, her eldest son.[29] Maurice, who wanted to be a diplomat, served an apprenticeship as Harte's secretary in Glasgow.

Bret Harte described Madame as "un-English." Certainly she was not Victorian. She and Harte both disdained those *mores* which caused Nathaniel Hawthorne to decline to meet George Eliot, and Mark Twain and William Dean Howells to scuttle away from dining with Maxim Gorky after newspapers reported that the Russian author's mistress had accompanied him to America.[30] Yet Arthur Van de Velde apparently saw no reason to object to his wife's relationship with Bret Harte; on the contrary, Monsieur offered the American the "kindness and almost brotherly friendship" which made possible Harte's residence in the Van de Velde household.

It was this relationship to which Mark Twain alluded when he referred to Bret Harte's being "kept" by a woman when he was consul in Great Britain.[31]

In London as well as in America there was gossip about Harte's position in the Van de Velde household. Some of the gossip was generated by rival hostesses whose invitations Harte had declined.[32] Both Harte

[29] *Ibid.*, Jan. 31, 1882, BC. The Van de Velde children are mentioned several times in Harte's diary.

[30] Paine, *Biography*, 1282–85. See also Webster, *Mark Twain: Business Man*, 259.

[31] *MTE*, 282. Twain said that Harte was "kept" by two women in Great Britain. Since I consider the allegation essentially false and I can only guess the identity of the second woman whom Mark Twain had in mind, it seems decent not to mention this woman's name.

[32] *BHL*, 216–17. See also Bret Harte's Diary, Nov. 4, 1881, BC.

and the Van de Veldes broke with acquaintances who gossiped unpleasantly about them.[33] Among those who did not take the gossip seriously was Mrs. Harte's niece, Gertrude Griswold. When Miss Griswold came to London, Madame helped her find lodgings, gave a dinner party for her at the Van de Velde home, and conducted her on tours of London. Harte, when in London, was a frequent caller at the Griswold flat. Another friend who apparently paid no attention to the gossip was John Hay. Not only did he himself accept Madame's hospitality, but Mrs. Hay took her children to the Van de Velde home for tea.[34]

During the years of separation, Bret Harte did not forget his own children. He wrote them numerous letters and repeatedly urged them to write to him. He tried to take more than a monetary responsibility for their education. However, when he once criticized the handwriting of eleven-year-old Jessamy, he added a postscript that he was aware his own handwriting disqualified him as a critic, and he ended by apologizing that he had been "signing his name all day—and writing a story all night." Of the four children, the eldest—Griswold—remained aloof and unresponsive to his overtures. If this boy, the mother's favorite, resented the distant man, this father *in absentia*, his resentment is understandable. But the father continued to try to appeal to him. "Make Wodie send me his portrait," Harte wrote his wife. "I am weary of asking for it! As weary as I am of asking him to write to me. I have had *two* letters from him in *five* years." Two months later, after writing a letter to Frank, Harte again appealed to Mrs. Harte: "I wish you would ask Wodie to write to me once in a while. He might in that way suggest something by writing frankly and regularly where and how I could help him. At present I know of his affairs only through your occasional records of his hopes and disappointments."[35]

Harte felt very strongly that his children, especially his daughters, should grow up in America and be educated as Americans. When Griswold, Frank, Jessamy, and Ethel showed interest in becoming respectively a writer, an actor, a painter, and a singer, the father at first did not encourage them. He saw no evidence that they had great talents. Their mother's ambitions to become a famous singer had been frustrated. The career of their cousin, at one time prima donna in the Paris

[33] Bret Harte's Diary, 1882, BC. [34] *Ibid.*, June 28, 1887, and *passim*, BC.
[35] BHL, 230, 266, 272, 367.

Opera, ended unhappily. Bret Harte himself was believed to have great talent, but his life had been an unending struggle. He wanted for his children more security than he or his wife had known. But when the children persisted rather romantically in following their individual interests, Harte did what he could to help them, and when any of them achieved some success, he delighted in the role of proud father.[36] This was particularly true of his feeling for Frank. When the boy showed his determination to become an actor, Bret Harte introduced him to Dion Boucicault, Lawrence Barrett, Edwin Booth, and John McCullough.

Mark Twain's story about Frank Harte and John McCullough, the tragedian, finds flat contradiction in Bret Harte's letters.

According to Mark Twain, a young man came to see McCullough, said he was Bret Harte's son just back from a visit to his father in England, and had with him a letter of introduction and recommendation from his father. McCullough told the boy he was expected and immediately gave him a job. Frank was very appreciative but not surprised, for his father, he said, had told him that he would write McCullough in advance. According to Twain, McCullough had Harte's letter in his pocket but did not read it to Frank because what the letter said "in substance" was this:

> My boy is stage-struck and wants to go to you for help, for he knows that you and I are old friends. To get rid of his importunities, I have been obliged to start him across the water equipped with a letter strongly recommending him to your kindness and protection, and begging you to do the best you can to forward his ambition, for my sake. I was obliged to write the letter, I couldn't get out of it, but the present letter is to warn you beforehand to pay no attention to the other one. My son is stage-struck, but he isn't of any account and will never amount to anything; therefore don't bother yourself with him; it wouldn't pay you for your lost time and sympathy.[37]

Mark Twain's words here can be paralleled with Harte's. On December 15, 1882, Bret Harte wrote Frank about a long talk he had had with Dion Boucicault about Frank's interest in becoming an actor:

> He said he would see you whenever you could call or make an ap-

[36] For example, see *ibid.*, 247–48.
[37] MTE, 289. Also Neider, *Autobiography*, 304–305.

pointment with him, and that he would give you his advice frankly, and, in case he thought you were fit for an immediate engagement, would do all in his power to help you to it. Whether this means that he will be ready to take you *himself* in hand, I cannot say; he is a man immersed in his own business, but as that is dramatic, theatrical, and managerial, your interests may come together. Of one thing you can count surely; I believe he will be frank with you; not to discourage you solely, if you are not all that you think you are, but to show you what you can do in the way of a beginning. This is what McCullough said he would do for you, at my request—and *not*, as your mother writes to me that he said to you—"be rude to you, if necessary, to keep you off the stage." It is scarcely worth while repeating that I never *could* nor *did* say anything of the kind or write anything like it to McCullough. I told him that if it were true that you were physically not up to the active requirements of the stage, he ought to dissuade you from it.[38]

According to Mark Twain, "John McCullough stood by the boy and pushed his fortunes on the stage and was the best father the lad ever had." According to the boy's mother and the boy's descendants, Bret Harte's son owed McCullough the disappointment of "broken promises."[39] But for aid and encouragement in launching his career on the stage, Frank was indebted to Dion Boucicault and Lawrence Barret, to whom he was recommended by his father Bret Harte.[40] Two additional conclusions in relation to Mark's anecdote about McCullough seem self-evident: first, that McCullough said nothing to the boy in disparagement of his father is inaccurate; second, that Frank's experience with McCullough occurred before and not after Frank's visit to his father in Glasgow and London.

This visit took place in 1884. After Harte decided to defer his long-planned trip to America until after the Presidential election, he again suggested that Mrs. Harte and the children visit him during the summer. At first Mrs. Harte declined the invitation, then changed her mind, and finally determined to send the two boys. Although the many changes of plan inconvenienced Harte, who was involved in a new writing project, he gladly paid both fares on the North-German Lloyd

[38] *BHL*, 220. [39] *Ibid.*, 211.
[40] See Geoffrey Bret Harte's comment, in *ibid.*, 368. See also Bret Harte's Diary, Apr. 9, 1883, BC.

steamer scheduled to leave New York on September 17. At the last minute Griswold decided not to come, but Frank arrived safely and was with his father for two months. After this visit, during which Frank was entertained generously by his father and his father's friends (including the Van de Veldes, the Duchess of St. Albans, and James Anthony Froude), Bret wrote the boy's mother expressing some concern about Frank's health but concluding: "He is a most singular mixture of a man and boy; with the thoughtlessness of the one and the independence of the other, and a perfect satisfaction in both."[41]

Another incident of 1884 concerned *Gabriel Conroy,* that old bone of contention between Bret Harte and Mark Twain. There is considerable oversimplification in Bernard De Voto's assertion that "Mark as publisher, personally underwrote advances to Harte and had a quarrel over the stage rights of 'Gabriel Conroy' for his pains."[42]

In January, Bret Harte received from Joaquin Miller and Mrs. Harte warnings that a play entitled *Gabriel Conroy,* purportedly by Bret Harte, had appeared on Broadway.[43] On learning that it was McKee Rankin, an actor, who was using the Harte name as well as material from the Harte novel, Bret telegraphed Charles Watrous to notify Rankin that Harte owned the "*dramatic* copyright" of *Gabriel Conroy.* Watrous replied that the adapter, a Mr. S. S. Andrews, said that the American Publishing Company of Hartford had sold him the dramatic copyright, alleging that the company had advanced Harte one thousand dollars on account of it. Two letters written from the American consulate in Glasgow show Bret Harte very honestly trying to get to the facts of the case.

The first of these letters, dated February 5, 1884, was to Harte's wife, at that time in New York. Enclosing a copy of a letter he had written Watrous, Harte told Mrs. Harte: "I do not honestly *believe* that I ever parted with my dramatic copyright to the Publishing Company in any way—or particularly in the way indicated. But, unfortunately, my memory of that particular advance is somewhat confused. Although I do not doubt that it is as I have related it, I cannot *swear* to it, and I beg you to recall, if you can, all the circumstances of the transaction." Oddly enough, Harte could not remember the name of

[41] *BHL,* 262.   [42] *Mark Twain's America,* 163.
[43] *BHL,* 246. See also Pemberton, *The Life of Bret Harte,* 267–68.

Elisha Bliss. "I remember that Mark Twain used his influence as director in my favour, but I am quite oblivious of there being any other security than the sales of the book itself. If I had been tempted to give my dramatic copyright as security, I certainly should have *told you at the time*." Harte urged his wife to communicate to Mr. Watrous anything she could remember about the transaction.

Though more detailed about the *Gabriel Conroy* business, the second letter, which was to Harte's business manager, shows the same attempt to recall the exact facts. The similarity of Harte's letter to his wife (including parts which I have deleted to save space) and his report to Watrous evidences Harte's lack of subterfuge.

> ... I am amazed. The American Publishing Company of Hartford contracted with me for the publication of my novel of "Gabriel Conroy" in book form, on payment of a royalty—advanced in certain sums on certain dates—upon the sale of the volume, but to the best of my recollection at no time did they ever contract for or pay anything on account of my dramatic copyright. An advance over and above the advance stipulated for in the contract was made by them some time after the book was published, but it was solely on account of royalties to accrue hereafter, and if I mistake not Mr. Clemens, who was then a shareholder or director in the Company, became personally responsible for the amount advanced in event of the royalties not being sufficient to repay it. As the American Publishing Company have never given me an account of sales, but simply contented themselves with saying there was nothing due to me, I am unable to say whether the amount was ever realized.
>
> The dramatic copyright was an afterthought of my own, taken out at my own request during the publication of the story (in reference to offers I had to dramatize the story) for my better security. I asked the President of the Publishing Company to attend to it for me, and he agreed to do so. But neither he nor the American Publishing Company ever preferred any claim to it whatever; in fact, as the only value a dramatization of the novel then had in the eyes of purchasers was because *it was my dramatization*, I cannot conceive what value the dramatic copyright would have been to the American Publishing Company, unless I had contracted to make the play for them, which certainly was not contemplated. If, however, my memory is at fault, and there was at one time a *bona-fide* transfer of the dramatic copyright to the Ameri-

can Publishing Company, they must have some document—if it be only a receipt—to show for it.

If they will exhibit it to you or Judge Dittenhoefer, I will be satisfied; if they cannot and rest upon some *implied* right in the property, I will try to find out what legal remedy I have. Perhaps Judge Dittenhoefer will know.

In no case am I in any way connected with McKee Rankin's present play nor has he any right to use my name as a consenting party.[44]

Judge Abram Josef Dittenhoefer was a distinguished American lawyer who served as legal counsel for the Frohmans and for David Belasco.[45] Among Mark Twain's papers were Bret Harte's letters of December 24, 1875, and January 2, 1876, showing that Harte had told Twain that his experience with *Two Men of Sandy Bar* had taught him to be wary of selling the dramatic rights of his novel.[46] In April, 1886, Bret Harte wrote Mrs. Harte about a proposal made to him to collaborate with other playwrights in dramatizing *Gabriel Conroy* for a London production. In this letter Harte referred to "those villainous Hartford publishing people" who had "sold the right (which they declared belonged to them) for a thousand dollars to some American actor."[47] But Harte did not mention Mark Twain's name.

Just a month before Harte wrote the two letters to his wife and Watrous, Mark Twain had instructed Charles L. Webster, to whom he had transferred full control of his interests connected with the American Publishing Company: "If the book business interferes with the dramatic business, drop the former—for it doesn't pay salt; & I want the latter rushed." Through Webster, Barrett, and Howells, Mark was again angling for an association with the much-maligned Raymond, who had so profitably interpreted the role of Colonel Sellers.[48]

Earlier disappointments had cured neither Harte, Howells, nor Twain of the illusion that alone or with a collaborator, he could create a play that would strike it rich. The hopes of all three prospectors in the field of drama were fixed on popular and therefore financial success

---

[44] *BHL*, 246–59.   [45] Felheim, *The Theater of Augustin Daly*, 56.
[46] See Chapter IX of this volume.
[47] Letter in William Andrews Clark Memorial Library. Item 20 in *Calendar of the Francis Bret Harte Letters*.
[48] Webster, *Mark Twain: Business Man*, 161, 230–31. Howells, *My Mark Twain*, 25–26. See also *MTH*, I, 449, 454n.

rather than on artistic achievement. Yet for Bret Harte, at least, the money that he hoped to make playwriting was not an end in itself but a means of enabling him to give his whole time to writing an American-English novel, which he was "feverish" to work on.[49]

Bret Harte was pleased by the continued popularity of his fiction, but he now recognized that from slowly written short stories which brought little revenue after their initial sale, he could expect only a scanty living. At this time he regarded them as mere potboilers. But not long after his arrival in Glasgow, he attended an amateur theatrical which dramatized one of his own short romances, and it seemed to him that few changes were required in the dialogue of his fiction to make it suitable for the spoken dialogue of the play. Since the familiar Bret Harte yarns were still in great demand, why should he not turn them into plays and reap a richer harvest?

Harte's belief that he had it in him to write a good play was shared not only by Madame Van de Velde but by such professionals as Dion Boucicault, Sir Arthur Sullivan, and the popular English comedian John Laurence Toole, who was eager for a chance to enact the role of a Bret Harte character.[50] At Boucicault's suggestion, Harte tried to dramatize "The Luck of Roaring Camp," and in October, 1882, Howells in Switzerland wrote Mark Twain that John Hay and Clarence King had been to hear Harte read this absurdity in which the Luck had been resurrected, changed to a girl, and with her California guardians of Roaring Camp, transported to Paris.[51] On reading Boucicault's criticisms and directions for revisions of this version, which represented two months' hard work, Bret Harte ruefully concluded: "It seems I can write dialogue like an angel, draw character like a heaven-born genius, but I can't make *situations* and *plots*."[52] Nevertheless, he persevered, but when a later dramatic version of "The Luck" was praised and accepted by Toole, Harte himself decided against its production on the grounds that even if the farce were successful, it would disappoint and distress those who had read and loved the story.

Several other ventures in playwriting, which included collaborations with Madame Van de Velde and with the French novelist Edmond

[49] *BHL*, 204.
[50] *Ibid.*, 201, 206–207, 210, 213; Pemberton, *The Life of Bret Harte*, 275.
[51] *MTH*, I, 416. [52] *BHL*, 213.

"The Heathen Chinee," Spy's caricature of Bret Harte,
was published in *Vanity Fair* (January 4, 1879).
It was number 191 in the "Men of the Day" series.

"Below the Mark," Spy's caricature of Mark Twain, was published as Number 1117 in the "Men of the Day" series in *Vanity Fair Supplement* (1908).

About, failed to bring the success of which Harte dreamed. But Harte's relationships with these and later collaborators seem to have been pleasant. When Dion Boucicault proposed using some of Bret Harte's characters and scenes in his own dramas, Harte's punctilious recognition of the literary property rights of his collaborator, Madame Van de Velde, is apparent in a letter to Frank Harte, who sometimes represented his father in negotiations with producers in New York.[53]

During these years Mark Twain and William Dean Howells also collaborated on a play. This collaboration affords illuminating parallels with the earlier one between Mark Twain and Bret Harte on *Ah Sin*. This time the idea for the collaboration originated with Mark Twain. Like *Ah Sin*, as originally conceived, the play would center on a character already known to the public and associated with an actor who had interpreted the role. For the Twain–Howells play this central character would be Colonel Sellers, and both Twain and Howells would work on him and develop him further as a scientist and a dreamer. The character of Colonel Sellers to be developed in the play had many prototypes, including Orion Clemens and Mark Twain himself, but the dominant one was the Colonel Sellers as portrayed by Raymond, that "devil" who had netted Mark Twain $70,000 for the earlier play.[54] The method of collaboration proposed by Mark Twain also resembled the method Mark said was used for *Ah Sin*. Howells would develop characters and plot, and when he had finished, Twain would take the manuscript, "re-write the Colonel's speeches & make him properly vulgar and extravagant."[55]

Although the collaboration between William Dean Howells and Mark Twain on "Colonel Sellers as a Scientist" began with an enthusiasm equaling if not exceeding the enthusiasm of those first days of collaboration on *Ah Sin*, in time the relations between Twain and Howells also became strained. Eventually Raymond rejected the play because he believed the role of Colonel Sellers had been "exaggerated to

---

[53] *Ibid.*, 296, 355–56. Harte's collaboration with Joseph Hatton on a dramatization of "M'liss" will be considered in a later chapter of this volume.

[54] Howells, *My Mark Twain*, 24; *MTH*, I, 372.

[55] *MTH*, I, 372. See also *The Complete Plays of W. D. Howells* edited by Walter J. Meserve, 206. In the letter quoted here, Mark jokingly tells Howells that he will expect "¾ of the pecuniary result. (How liberal, how lavish, I seem to grow these days!)"

the brink of lunacy," a verdict with which Howells was inclined to agree.[56]

Just as Bret Harte had attempted to revise the first two acts of *Ah Sin* by writing himself "up" and Mark Twain "down," William Dean Howells tried to moderate the role of Mark Twain's Sellers and give more attention to the other characters in the play. At one stage, when Mark was dickering with an actor whom Howells found considerably more objectionable than Raymond, Howells (like Boucicault in the collaboration with Harte on "Kentuck") asked Mark to pay him outright for his services but dissociate his name from the project. "No one knows yet that I've helpt you," wrote Howells. Mark Twain refused, and in at least one "red-hot" letter to Howells tried to shame Howells for his suggestion.[57] But as the editors of the *Mark Twain–Howells Letters* note, Mark's words to Howells were mild in comparison with his words about Bret Harte.

William Dean Howells was now depending somewhat anxiously on his writings to support himself and his family, where there were recurring illnesses, but Mark Twain was forging ahead financially and becoming absorbed in big business. Even though both Howells and Harte still outranked Twain in critics' appraisals of the literary significance of their achievements, Howells knew the value of Mark Twain's genius and had rightly predicted that many of Twain's contemporaries would be known chiefly because of their association with him. At times Howells himself was not altogether happy at standing in the shade of Twain's spreading fame, but Howells was one of the fairest and most generous of friends and he felt himself indebted to Twain for "many generous acts." Yet even Howells became nettled when Twain began sending him communications about the Sellers play through Twain's agent and nephew, Charles L. Webster. Relations between Howells and Twain became tense.

The crisis was ended by Howells' magnanimity. Sometimes within a crucial four-day period Howells offered to read the proofs for Mark Twain's latest book, *The Adventures of Huckleberry Finn*. The offer may have been relayed through Webster. However that may be, Twain

[56] Felheim, *The Theater of Augustin Daly*, 300. See also *MTH*, II, 506, 508, 556–57.

[57] *MTH*, II, 473, 475, 476n.

found Howells' generosity breath-taking and with gratitude accepted the offer. He explained that gout had kept him from writing Howells, but that he was all right again.[58]

Continued negotiations about the production of "Colonel Sellers as a Scientist" were varied, prolonged, and unsuccessful. Under the title of "The American Claimant, or Mulberry Sellers Ten Years Later" the play was finally scheduled for a "trial matinee" to be financed by Howells and Twain at the Lyceum Theatre, but on Howells' advice, the play was withdrawn from Daniel Frohman, and the authors paid a forfeit.[59] When, after some soul-searching, Howells wrote Mark Twain that he acknowledged half the "folly" and consequently would assume half the misery and half the financial loss, Mark replied that Howells was mistaken in assuming half the responsibility. The "folly," Mark said, was *all* Howells'.[60] Although the original agreement was that Howells would take one-third the profit and Twain two-thirds, when the play failed, Howells and Mark Twain each paid $350.[61] In *My Mark Twain*, written soon after his beloved friend's death, Howells professed a fond illusion that the play might have succeeded on Broadway if given a chance.

As a matter of fact, the personally undramatic Howells was an abler and more productive playwright than either Bret Harte or Mark Twain. Although he tried again, Mark Twain never succeeded in writing a play. William Dean Howells wrote or translated thirty-six, collected by Walter J. Meserve and published by New York University Press in 1960. When Howells learned from Edward W. Bok that Twain had sold the serial rights of his novel *The American Claimant* to the *Ladies' Home Journal* for $6,000, Howells wondered a bit what Mark Twain had done about Howells' part of the plot of the play on which it is generally believed that Mark Twain's novel was based, but Twain assured Howells that he had not used the play.[62] Finally, contrary to Bok's expectations, the British and American serial rights to *The American Claimant* were sold to the McClure Syndicate for $12,-

[58] *Ibid.,* I, 391; II, 481–83, 609, 667.

[59] *Ibid.,* II, 559. Ses also Felheim, *The Theater of Augustin Daly,* 300.

[60] *MTH,* II, 559.

[61] Howells, *My Mark Twain,* 26. See also *MTH,* II, 565n., that Howells originally sent Mark Twain a check for $500.

[62] *MTH,* II, 644n., 645; Felheim, *The Theater of Augustin Daly,* 300.

000, a sum double the amount paid by Scribner's to Harte for serial rights to *Gabriel Conroy*.

It was the age of the business tycoon, and for Mark Twain writing was a business. Like Silas Lapham, whom in several ways he resembled, Mark Twain could—and sometimes did—squeeze out partners. These included Charles Dudley Warner and Howells as well as Bret Harte. Added to the history of the collaboration on "Colonel Sellers as a Scientist," the history of *Mark Twain's Library of Humor*, which includes some of Bret Harte's writings, affords another indication that Edward H. House may not have been altogether wrong when he accused Mark Twain of "habitual readiness to avail himself of the labor of others."[63]

The Twain–Howells letters from 1881 to 1888 include many allusions to the project of a library of humor. The idea had originated with George Gebbie, a Philadelphia publisher.[64] Howells agreed to work with Mark Twain in compiling "Gebbie's Cyclopedia" provided Mark would assure him of $5,000, for Howells explained that he could not afford to spend his time on a project which might bring no money. Mark Twain readily agreed to the sum of $5,000 to be paid Howells "whether the book succeeds or fails."[65]

After the agreement Howells worked steadily according to plan, but Mark Twain had too many other irons in the fire. As years dragged on, and the library of humor was still not published, Howells on June 27, 1884, asked Twain to send him an advance of $2,000 for his work, which he felt was substantial enough to justify the request. Mark Twain demurred on grounds that it would inconvenience him because, through his newly organized publishing firm, Charles L. Webster and Company, he was financing his own latest book for which, to his annoyance, he was having to read proof. Howells responded: "If I had written

[63] *MTH*, II, 633n., 644n.

[64] *Ibid.*, 331n. After some unsatisfactory dickering with Gebbie, both Mark Twain and William Dean Howells became suspicious of the "Scotchman" and considered the possibility of "honorably" using Gebbie's idea but publishing with another firm, namely Osgood's. Mark Twain convinced himself that this could be done ethically if *he* did not tell Osgood of Gebbie's plan but Osgood learned of it from another source and then suggested the idea to Mark. See *ibid.*, I, 348–50. Mark's reasoning here resembles that of the "murderers" Bill and Jake Packard on board the *Walter Scott* in *Huckleberry Finn*.

[65] *MTH*, I, 347, 361, 363.

half as good a book as Huck Finn, I shouldn't ask anything better than to read the proofs; even as it is I don't." And so, though he had already read the typescript, Howells read the proofs which Mark Twain sent him.

In October, 1885, because of a contract for exclusive publication of his work by Harper and Brothers, Howells asked that his name not be used on the title page of that humor anthology, which he suggested might better be called "Mark Twain's Library of American Humor." However, he explained that the work was now complete except for an introductory essay, and he again asked Mark Twain to send him $2,000, reminding his friend that with the $500 already advanced, the sum would still equal only half the $5,000 which Mark had agreed to pay.

Again Mark Twain did not send the money. This time he explained that his funds were tied up in the publication of General Ulysses S. Grant's *Memoirs,* and every dollar meant as much to him as to a "famishing tramp." But if Howells really needed the money, Mark would get it for him, even if he had to use violence. Howells, of course, was not the man to insist. If, like Bret Harte in 1877, Howells found Mark's plea of temporary poverty not very convincing, he did not say so. Instead, he wrote Mark Twain in December: "I'm more rejoiced than I can tell you at the gigantic triumph of the Grant book."[66] Mark Twain's publishing firm had sent Grant's widow a phenomenal and highly publicized first check for $200,000.

Publication of the humor anthology had been taken from Gebbie and given to Osgood, but the work finally ended up with Mark Twain's own publishing firm. The total sum which Mark Twain paid Howells for his work on the library of humor was finally $2,600.[67] When Twain told Howells that the withdrawal of his name from the title page would mean pigeonholing the anthology for years, the conscientious Howells felt uncomfortable about taking even this money for work on which Mark himself had realized no profit. Consequently, reminding Mark that the work of compilation had been done almost entirely by himself and Charles H. Clark, managing editor of the Hartford

[66] *Ibid.,* II, 492–94, 498n., 537, 539, 541.
[67] *Ibid.,* II, 584. In this letter Howells enclosed proof for his "Editor's Study" for the May *Harper's* in which he commented that the American public loved Mark Twain's books because of the kindness, good will, shrewdness, and generosity of an American life which they faithfully portrayed.

Courant, Howells now offered to take the work off Mark's hands and find a publisher himself. But Mark Twain realized that this meant the book would go to Harper's and that Harper's would allow Howells' name to be added to the title page, an addition which Twain now decided he did not want.[68] Eventually the work was reorganized by Mark Twain, and in 1888, under the title *Mark Twain's Library of Humor,* published by Charles L. Webster and Company, with no mention of Howells on the title page.[69] Albert Bigelow Paine believed that this *Library of Humor* sold very well.[70]

As finally published, *Mark Twain's Library of Humor* began with "The Notorious Jumping Frog of Calaveras County" and included nineteen other contributions from Mark Twain's pen. It also included the following works by Bret Harte: "Plain Language from Truthful James," "A Jersey Centenarian," "A Sleeping-Car Experience," and "The Society on the Stanislaus." In March, 1882, Twain wrote Howells that he was "at work on Bret Harte" but not enjoying it:

> He is the worst literary shoe-maker, I know. He is as blind as a bat. He never sees anything correctly, except Californian scenery. He is as slovenly as Thackeray, and as dull as Charles Lamb. The things which you and Clark have marked, are plenty good enough in their way, but to my jaundiced eye, they do seem to be lamentably barren of humor. Still I think we want some funereal rot in the book as a foil.[71]

Samuel Charles Webster, who had access to the records of Twain's publishing firm, seems to have had some doubts that in the use of Bret Harte's writings, Mark Twain was above reproach. In January, 1885, when he was considering the transfer of the anthology to his own publishing firm, Mark Twain wrote Charles Webster about a 2 per cent royalty to be offered Osgood for selections in the compilation of humorous writings. "My only objection," wrote Mark Twain, "is, that the publisher may be sued for damages for using copyrighted matter without obtaining consent—in which case Osgood would have to pay 30 percent of such damage; whereas if you publish it I must pay

---

[68] Webster, *Mark Twain: Business Man,* 376.

[69] Howells, *My Mark Twain,* 17–18.

[70] Paine, *Biography,* 857. The editors of *MTH* say that the sale was small in comparison with the sale of Mark Twain's other books. *MTH,* II, 539.

[71] *MTH,* I, 396.

all the damages. Not much danger of such a suit, but of course there is *some*."[72] The son of Charles Webster explains that the question of copyright had come up because Osgood or Houghton, Osgood published most of Bret Harte's books. And Mark Twain's nephew added a wry comment: "Some of the books by Bret Harte from which Mark Twain drew selections still survive, with Mark Twain's caustic comments on the margins."[73]

Samuel Webster also noted that although in 1906, Mark Twain complained that Charles Webster "suppressed the 'Library of Humor' so long and finally issued it so clandestinely that I doubt if anybody in America did find out there was such a book," Mark Twain in 1886 advised Charles Webster about *Mark Twain's Library of Humor*: "I should not approve of advertising it at all except by obscure private circular."[74]

As far as I know, Bret Harte never protested the use of his writings in *Mark Twain's Library of Humor*.

To believe that his business associates had defrauded him was characteristic of Mark Twain. Yet in *Mark Twain, Business Man*, Samuel Charles Webster shows how his father, Charles Webster, was wrecked physically and financially by his association with Mark Twain. "Anyone who had business dealings with Mark Twain led a violent life, anyone who worked for him was entitled to the world's pity . . ." wrote De Voto, reviewing *Mark Twain: Business Man* for the New York *Herald Tribune*.[75] Noting that Mark Twain added Charles L. Webster to the roster of publishers who "by superhuman uninterrupted stupidity had mishandled his books and cost him hundreds of thousands of dollars," Bernard De Voto pointed out that "everyone who ever published Mark Twain and many who did not are on the roster, beginning with the first one, Charles H. Webb and coming right down to Harper & Brothers."

[72] Webster, *Mark Twain: Business Man*, 294–95.
[73] *Ibid.*, 295. The books referred to probably include *Tales of the Argonauts* (Boston, 1876) and *The Twins of Table Mountain* (Boston, 1881), donated in 1963 by Mrs. Samuel C. Webster to the Mark Twain Collection of the University of California Library in Berkeley. For calling this to my attention, I am particularly indebted to Professor Robert E. Burke of the University of Washington.
[74] Webster, *Mark Twain: Business Man*, 350.
[75] "The Other Side of Some Mark Twain Stories," *loc. cit.*, 3.

In the light of widely held derogatory opinions of Bret Harte's business dealings with Mark Twain and others, and the Modest Club's assumption of its "superior weight, character & influence," it seems worth mentioning here that Harte's record in relation to men with whom he had business dealings stands up very well in comparison with Twain's. Osgood and Dana, Harte's oldest publishers, continued on good terms with him. Charles Watrous, Mrs. Watrous, and the son who succeeded his father as Harte's business agent in America remained Harte's friends and staunch defenders during Harte's life and after his death. At one time Watrous suggested that his son and Harte's son go into business together.[76]

Another example of a business associate who became Bret Harte's warm personal friend can be found in A. P. Watt, who in 1885 became Harte's literary agent in London. More than once Harte expressed to Watt appreciation for his services. From the consulate in Glasgow on May 21, 1885, Harte wrote Watt: "It is hardly necessary for me to repeat what I have already told you of my satisfaction with the financial result of your busines arrangements with the publishers, both here and in America." Complimenting Watt for the "great tact, delicacy, and patience" of his transactions, Harte remarked that until authors knew a little more about business and were less likely to find that it interfered with their freedom in writing, they should employ a businessman to represent them "with those other business men, the publishers." He was sure that authors could find no better representative that Mr. Watt. The letter continued: "I am quite convinced that the commission I pay you has been fully returned by the appreciation of the market value of my work through your efforts, to say nothing of the saving of time and trouble to me during the progress of that work." In characteristically affectionate tone the letter concluded: "I am, dear Mr. Watt, Very truly yours, Bret Harte." And on March 6, 1892, Harte wrote a sequel testifying that he was delighted to find after six years that he wished to alter nothing of the earlier praise, which the continued association with Watt had fully justified.[77]

Although Mark Twain's vehement and active hostility to Bret Harte was one of the most consistent attitudes of his life, there were times during the years of Harte's consulship when Twain's animosity showed

[76] *BHL*, 232.   [77] *Ibid.*, 275–76, 365.

some signs of wavering. In a letter to Howells on September 3, 1880, Mark Twain mentioned Bret Harte three times, once without a sneer and the third time with a grudging citation of Harte's literary judgment. A letter from Frank Soulé, whom Mark described as "one of the sweetest and whitest & loveliest spirits that ever wandered into this world by mistake," reminded Twain of the days when he and Harte were two struggling young writers in San Francisco eager for praise from the older man, who now wanted Mark Twain's help in getting his poems published. Mark urged Howells, who planned a trip to the West Coast, to look up Soulé, ask to see the poems, and then offer to tell Osgood or some other publisher what he thought of them. In supporting his own judgment that Soulé had written some good poetry, Twain commented: "I have heard Harte and honester men say so."[78]

Both Mark Twain and Bret Harte were concerned with international copyright, and in February, 1884, Twain suggested to their mutual friend Laurence Hutton (lobbying in Washington for a copyright bill) that Harte would "promise" something if properly approached.[79] In George Washington Cable's famous April Fool's joke on Mark Twain in 1884, Thomas Bailey Aldrich and Dean Sage needled Mark Twain about his detestation of Bret Harte. Aldrich wrote: "I am making a collection of autographs of our distinguished writers, and having read one of your works, *Gabriel Conroy*, I would like to add your name to the list."[80] Dean Sage's request was made for a young girl who admired Mark Twain's poem "The Heathen Chinee."[81] When Mark Twain received what he considered a bona fide letter from a Miss Josephine Beemer inquiring where she could secure "Wan Lee, the Pagan," Mark Twain simply directed Charles Webster to inform Miss Beemer that the author of the story was Bret Harte.[82]

During these years when Harte was lionized in England and when his now stereotyped tales of California continued to interest readers of popular fiction throughout the world, in America it was always open season for snipers at Bret Harte's personal reputation. Frequently scandalmongers concentrated on his absence from Glasgow. In September,

[78] *MTH*, I, 325–27.
[79] Letter addressed from Hartford, Feb. 4, 1884, MTP.
[80] *MTL*, II, 441. [81] Paine, *Biography*, 769.
[82] The date of Miss Beemer's letter was Apr. 28, 1884, MTP.

1883, Mrs. Harte without comment enclosed in one of her letters a clipping from the New York *Tribune*, to which Harte responded: "If a paragraph that seems to be written in *good-will* can contain a wanton fling at you, and an intimation that I do not live in Glasgow and have always been irregular there, what may not be said when the pen is sharpened by envy or malice?"[83]

Although he refused to break off his association with the Van de Veldes, in other respects Harte seems to have tried to avoid criticism. When American newspapers criticized him for becoming "snobbish" or "un-American," he stayed away from social functions in London and Berlin; as a result it was rumored that friends had kept him away by force because his work was suffering. Once when reports of Harte's absence from Glasgow were called to the attention of the State Department, Harte was asked to issue a denial. This he did, and the Department expressed its satisfaction.[84] But perhaps the most damaging attacks were innuendoes and jokes such as allusions to the "Consul of the United States in Glasgow, resident in London."[85] "But isn't it hard!" Harte exclaimed to his wife, who had loyally defended him. "There are no *complaints!* . . . and nothing to complain of at the Consulate. I am always there when wanted."[86]

The record supports Harte's insistence that he was "*rather* a good Consul." His Vice-Consul was an extraordinarily efficient lawyer named William Gibson, with whom—as with his assistant R. F. Schneider in Crefeld—Harte remained on cordial terms long after the business association ended. That his Vice-Consul liked and respected him was a source of great satisfaction to Bret Harte, and he was particularly pleased when the habitually reticent Scot complimented the Consul on handling accounts more scrupulously than his predecessors. Bret wrote his wife that he took no special credit for it, since it was largely a matter of his hating "pecuniary meanness." "I spend all that the Government allows me for office rent and clerk hire on the things themselves and not *on myself*, with the result that my office is better equipped than some of the better-paid Consuls."[87] At times Harte's services to his government went beyond the performance of routine duties. On a visit to the island of Iona, he discovered the graves of nineteen American

[83] *BHL*, 235. [84] *Ibid.*, 235, 237. [85] *BHAE*, 271.
[86] *BHL*, 274. [87] *Ibid.*, 205, 271.

seamen whose ship had been wrecked in 1865 and whose graves had been marked at the expense of the Duke of Argyll. When Harte suggested that the names of the seamen should be placed on a durable memorial there and that the Duke should be thanked for his courtesy, the State Department thanked the Consul and acted upon his suggestion.[88] Again, when an American fisherman rescued by a British ship was stranded without funds, Bret Harte from his own pocket paid for the man's needs in Glasgow and procured passage for him back to America.[89] More than once this American official who could not go home aided other Americans to get there. That the people of Glasgow held Bret Harte in some esteem is indicated by their asking him to sit with other prominent citizens of Glasgow for a painting of the Royal Exchange.[90]

Fifty years before Harte's time, James Fenimore Cooper at Lyons, France, had set a precedent for a "traveling consul." Ill health and the depressing climate of Glasgow, together with the literary stimulation and warm personal welcome which Harte received in England, resulted in too many absences from Glasgow, but there is substantial evidence that while he was away, Bret Harte kept the direction and responsibility of the consulate in his own hands.[91] He was in constant communication with his office, and checked documents carefully. The historian of the consulate specifically recorded: "Although it is said that Consul Bret Harte, while in charge of this consulate, was often absent from his post, the business of the consulate was kept up to date and the records carefully entered and compiled."[92]

During his entire tenure of the consulship, Bret Harte never felt secure, yet the petulant sense of being unappreciated by his government, which sometimes crept into his letters from Crefeld, never appeared in his letters from Glasgow. On February 28, 1882, he wrote his wife that he knew he might at any moment be removed to make a place for somebody else. He acknowledged his indebtedness to John Hay. "On the other hand," he said, "the Department have treated me with what I am sometimes vain enough to think *peculiar consideration*. I have

[88] See Merwin, *The Life of Bret Harte*, 267–68. See also *BHAE*, 273–74.

[89] Merwin, *The Life of Bret Harte*, 268–69.   [90] *BHL*, 198.

[91] See the quotation from a letter by William Black, in Pemberton, *The Life of Bret Harte*, 250.

[92] *BHAE*, 271–73.

never asked for anything nor made a suggestion regarding my official busines or the Service generally that has not been attended to. I have been repeatedlly thanked by the Department."[93] In explaining his hesitancy about returning to America for a visit in 1883, Harte told his wife that it might be superstition, but he had a "strong feeling" about returning to America that ran through all his "longings" and all his "desires to return." "Perhaps it is because *I have been singularly lucky while I have been here in Europe.*"

> My affairs have prospered; I have a market for my wares; I am not dependent upon publishers' whims or caprices; I have had no extraordinary expenses; I have been kept in my official position without any effort on my part and against outside influence. I have for the first time in my life known what it is to be independent. I dread one step—one unconscious act, that may change the luck.[94]

With the shift to a Democratic administration under Grover Cleveland, Bret Harte had a premonition that his consulship would be one of the spoils claimed by the victor. "I sit here and work and calmly wait!" he told his wife. On March 4, 1885, President Cleveland was inaugurated. On March 13, apologizing for an unusual interval between his letters to his wife, Harte explained that he had just finished one short story and was hard at work on a longer one which he had promised the *Illustrated London News* for May:

> I am working thus breathlessly to make the most of advantageous offers that do not occur every day, and to avoid being stranded hopelessly here, in case I shall not be able to keep my office. Philosophical as I may try to be, it is not a pleasant thing to lose three thousand dollars a year, and although I ought to be thankful that I could earn a living by my pen, I doubt if I could do it long, or work well as I do (by "well" I mean with less strain and feverishness), with the consciousness that *your actual sustenance and that of the children* depends upon my hourly labours. I do not know how long my popularity will last with the public, and I must make the most of it now.[95]

On July 18, Bret Harte learned (again from the London *Times*) that a new consul had been appointed for Glasgow. He did not blame

---

[93] *BHL*, 204–205.   [94] *Ibid.*, 237.   [95] *Ibid.*, 268, 271.

the administration or suspect any new machinations against him personally. But he was shocked to read in New York newspapers that the reason given for his removal from the Glasgow consulate was "inattention to duty."[96]

About Harte's removal, of course, there was more gossip. According to one story, while the President with his private secretary Daniel Lamont was fishing in a lake in the Adirondacks, Cleveland chanced upon one of Harte's stories in the New York *Sun* and read the story from beginning to end without putting down the paper. After he finished, he asked Lamont if the author was a consul, and when Lamont said "Yes," Cleveland remarked: "Well, be sure and remind me to have him removed when we get back to Washington."[97]

Mark Twain became one of Cleveland's most ardent admirers. Mark had become so thoroughly disenchanted with President Hayes that in time he would insist that the Republican party had stolen the Presidency from Mr. Tilden to give it to Mr. Hayes.[98] In 1882, Twain had remained with Howells, a staunch Republican. But in 1884 he had disagreed with Howells and had become the only Nook Farm Republican to vote for the Democratic candidate.[99] In an unusually scurrilous campaign, Blaine was accused of doubtful financial dealings and Cleveland of fathering the child of a widow, who was his mistress. Howells did not vote for Cleveland because Howells objected to society's double standard which can ostracize the woman in such extramartial affairs but accept the man without question. With engaging inconsistency, Twain told Howells that to hold such conduct against a bachelor was hypocrisy. Mark Twain participated in the campaign and signed an "Appeal to the Republican Voters of Connecticut" to support Cleveland, yet his humorous public allusions to the sins of both Presidential candidates suggest that he had some reservation about the man he supported.[100] After Cleveland won the election, however, Mark had a conference with the President-elect, and thereafter his admiration for

---

[96] *Ibid.*, 284.

[97] See Noah Brooks, "Bret Harte: A Biographical and Critical Sketch," *loc. cit.*, 205.

[98] Neider, *Autobiography*, 303. For Howells' references to malicious comments about Hayes, see *Life in Letters*, II, 32.

[99] Andrews, *Nook Farm*, 115.

[100] *MTH*, II, 501, 503. Also see pages 509n., 511n.

Cleveland was fervid. Mark Twain once declared that of all the public men of that day, Cleveland stood first in his "reverence." Moreover, he said, "Cleveland *drunk* is a more valuable asset to this country than the whole batch of the rest of our public men *sober.*"[101]

It is safe to conclude that Cleveland's removal of Bret Harte from the Glasgow consulate did not diminish the President in Mark Twain's esteem.

[101] See *LL,* 218, 221.

17

BRET HARTE'S "MODERN INSTANCE"

Bret Harte has deserted his family, and that is the plain English of it.

Mark Twain in Eruption

WITH THE LOSS of the Glasgow consulate, Bret Harte at a not very healthy fifty faced the urgent necessity of deciding (1) how to compensate his family for the loss of a yearly income of $3,000, and (2) whether this could best be done by returning to an America from which it seemed to him he received only complaints and criticism. To solve the first problem he would have liked an editorial position, for he rightly considered that his editorial ability was a capital which he had never fully employed. Some years earlier he had been interested in a proposal for a "Bret Harte Monthly" which he would edit, but with the introduction of an English edition of *Harper's*, the proposal had been withdrawn. Now he had no prospect. He considered the familiar expedient of lecturing, but though he would have forced himself to endure again the old agony, there was the inescapable fact that his lectures never paid very well. He wrote fiction as slowly and laboriously as ever, but the fiction sold. In England the market value was going up; in America it was going down. What to do?

After the published reports of his dismissal from the consulate, there was what seemed to him a long and embarrassing silence from his family and friends in America. But his English friends seemed not to care whether he was a consul or not. The Duke of St. Albans invited him for a visit in Ireland. And the Van de Veldes warmly welcomed him to "his" room in their household and saw to it that he had uninterrupted time to write. And so he went to England to stay until he completed some work which he had started.

Bret Harte had never stopped writing for long. Eighteen eighty-one

225

was the only year in which a new volume of his works failed to appear. Fortunately, he secured the services of A. P. Watt as literary agent in the same year he lost the consulate. Before he began a story Harte generally knew where his work would be published and how much it would bring. This seemed to him to take away half the pains of authorship.[1] Journals publishing Harte's fiction after 1885 include, in America, *Harper's Weekly*, the New York *Sun*, *Scribner's*, *Lippincott's*, and the *Saturday Evening Post*; in England, *Longmans*, *The Illustrated London News*, *Graphic*, *Macmillan's*, *Strand*, *Black and White*, *Idler*, and *English Illustrated Magazine*. To fill Watt's orders, Bret Harte stayed where he was and kept on writing.

In England, Bret Harte continued to be highly regarded as a person and a personage. John R. Pettie, R. A., asked to paint his portrait. The oil painting which this artist exhibited in the Royal Academy in London and later in Berlin shows the former consul with head proudly carried, distinguished profile, carefully groomed hair, and mustache threaded with gray. The erect figure is elegantly clothed in fur coat, an immaculate cuff providing a fastidious white line between the fur sleeve and a smoothly fitting glove.[2] This was Bret Harte as the world saw him. The artist presented the original portrait to Bret Harte and a photogravure to Madame Van de Velde, who hung the original in the dining room and the photogravure in the drawing room of the Van de Velde home at 15, Upper Hamilton Terrace, London, the address which headed most of Harte's letters for the next seven years.

In the same year the association was established with Watt, Harte formed another association, this one with A. S. Boyd, an artist and illustrator whose drawings seemed to Harte to delineate most accurately the California scenes and characters as Harte imagined them and portrayed them in his fiction. Both Boyd and his wife became good friends of the author and welcomed him to their home. Some of Harte's most lighthearted letters during the last years of his life were written to Mrs. Boyd about herself, her husband, and their small son Stuart. Harte's friendships with titled Englishmen (including the Duke of St. Albans, Lord Houghton, and the Marquess of Northhampton) aroused envy as well as wonder in title-conscious Americans, but the English title to which Harte referred with most respect was James Anthony Froude's

[1] *BHL*, 184, 189, 192, 283–86, 310–11.   [2] *BHAE*, 293, 298.

Bret Harte, near the end of his life

Courtesy of Clifton Waller Barrett

A serious Mark Twain, in his famous Oxford gown,
June 26, 1907

title of "Professor of History in the University" at Oxford.[3] After Froude's death, Harte continued his friendship with Froude's daughter, occasionally visiting her at her home near Reading. But Harte's rigid writing schedule forced him to decline many invitations.

Harte tried to spend eight hours at his desk every day, Sundays and holidays, at home or on visits, sick or well. He grew weary of the monotonous work, and in a letter asking his wife and children to write him more often, Harte said, "You cannot possibly hate pen and ink as I do who live in it and by it perpetually."[4] His sons were in their twenties by this time and to a large extent on their own. But Harte continued regular remittances to his wife and daughters, continued plans for their joining him in Europe, continued dreams of a home they might make together. He kept out of debt. But always there was the fear of losing his English popularity and always the painful awareness that with all his hours at the desk, he was barely meeting family expenses month by month and saving nothing for the future. Staying "half as guest" at the Van de Veldes', he spent comparatively little on his own upkeep. His chief luxuries seem to have been good clothes, a box at the theater, and a brougham driven by a man named Lambert.[5]

Harte had permitted A. P. Watt to generate a rumor that the author had a private income and was not dependent on proceeds from his writing. The motivation of this bit of fiction was the belief, held by both Harte and Watt, that if publishers knew the extent to which Harte depended on his writing for a living, they would exploit his need and reduce their prices. Unfortunately, Mrs. Harte seems to have been deceived by newspaper reports into thinking that her husband was making more money and living more luxuriously than his letters indicated, so that she spent more freely than she might otherwise have done, and did not, as he often urged, try to put sums by for a time when their income would be lower.

In 1886, from Bournemouth (where he was probably staying at the Van de Veldes' summer home), Harte replied to one of his wife's letters accusing him of "an expensive predilection" and resenting his cautions to her to be more careful about money:

---

[3] *BHL*, 362–63, 374–75. Froude was appointed Regius professor of modern history in 1892.

[4] *Ibid.*, 354, 492, 495.   [5] *Ibid.*, 367, 394.

I shall only speak of that letter, Nan, as something you have written hurriedly, under a strong misconstruction of the meaning of my few words of caution to you for your own sake and that of the children. . . . I would rather have you generous and uncalculating than selfish and exact, as you well know, and I do not question your bounty or necessary charities,[6] but I only spoke to warn you of the possibility when there was not enough to divide. And now let this talk pass, Nan; there is no one but yourself to whom I should, could, or *would* trust these matters, and whether you like it or not, you must continue to act for yourself and the children and me equally as steward of what I gain in this world. And you must not be angry nor hurt when I venture to hint that the income is *uncertain*.[7]

In the fall of the following year Bret received from Mrs. Harte a cabled demand for a substantial sum of money in addition to his regular remittances. Alarmed by the thought of illness or accident, Harte hastily got together the sum she requested and sent it immediately. For a month he waited for more information about the trouble. His anxiety mounted. At last he received a letter acknowledging the receipt of the money and explaining that it was needed for a trip to the Adirondacks. Harte's reply to this letter makes very explicit Harte's view of his separation from his wife and country:

I am most thankful, dear Nan, I could get it for you, and I do not regret the pleasure it paid for—of which you haven't too much!—but it seemed to me, for people in our circumstances, a rather large *extra* taken in account with the other *extras* I added to the regular draft in view of the summer trip. I thoroughly understand your explanation— but no explanation would have got the money if I hadn't had it or was able to get it—even the sacrifice of your Christmas box, which I hope may not be necessary. I don't want to use it to hang any moral upon, but sometimes when you are naturally impatient of my putting my work—the making of money to support and keep us out of debt, and perhaps provide for an emergency like this—above *everything else*, you will admit I am not far wrong. God knows I should not be an exile here if it were not for fear of the poverty and struggling that I am getting too old to fight against, single-handed, and which would ruin even the

[6] Harte's use of the phrase "necessary charities" suggests Mrs. Makely's definition of the term "lady" as Americans understood it. See William Dean Howells, *A Traveler from Altruria*, 71.

[7] *BHL*, 304–305.

power of work in me. I do not believe I could do the amount of actual labour I perform now if I were, on two thirds of my present income, competing in New York with other writers, at the mercy of publishers who knew of my precarious income and availed themselves of it. The half of my success here—in fact, the whole reason why I am able to keep up my prices—is because my publishers think I am independent, and as a distinguished foreigner I have a peculiar position which my agent makes the most of in dealing with them. These are the selfish considerations that are keeping me here, in spite of estranging years that are ageing *both of us*, apart from each other, and adding an unnatural loneliness to our lives. These are the things that make me ever tremulous and fearful of leaving here, at present, even for a visit home, lest I find my place occupied when I return, and the harvest gleaned by some one else. That is why, when I have promised myself that I should go over to you at some stated time, and my agent has come to me with new work, and the suggestion that I had better not let the offer pass, I have hesitated and yielded at last. All my efforts to get some independence, by means of other work—such as a play, or a position as editor, which would even allow me a leave of absence—have failed. I see nothing ahead of me but my habitual work—as long as opportunity and strength suffice.

I would not go over all this, which I have written to you from time to time since I first thought of returning to America—but it comes back to me—and I dare say it will to you—when I see that the passing years bring no decrease in our expenses or the apparent ability to reduce them. And I would not repeat it if I didn't still live in the hope that, failing to live on less, and put money by for emergencies, I still may be able to save something out of my income, by running no risks and taking every opportunity of increasing it. *I* haven't lost heart yet—if *you* have—I haven't yet given up the hope of being with you all again—and without the precariousness and anxiety that would embitter it for us all.[8]

And thus Bret Harte continued to write fiction, to send his wife money, to discuss the possibility of the family's reunion, and to reside in the Van de Velde household.

The death of Monsieur Van de Velde during an epidemic of influenza in February, 1892, seemed to Bret Harte a "sad breaking up" of the household which had been so hospitable to him. On the day of her husband's death, the death of her father called Madame to the aid of her eldest daughter, who had been nursing the older man in Berlin.

[8] *Ibid*, 322–23. See also *BHAE*, 299.

Bret Harte was left in charge of the London house and, as he said, of "my poor friend's children." But he added, "rather, perhaps I should say they are looking after *me* as their poor parents did."[9] Mrs. Harte's expression of sympathy was quickly acknowledged by a note from Madame in Berlin. For some time Harte continued a member of the Van de Velde household; later he moved to rooms at 74 Lancaster Gate, not far from the Van de Veldes' new residence at 109 Lancaster Gate. The published *Letters of Bret Harte* include none to Mrs. Harte dated between July, 1893, and January, 1895, but that correspondence and remittances continued during those years is evidenced by unpublished letters in the William Andrews Clark Memorial Library in Los Angeles.[10]

With extravagant investments of time and energy, Bret Harte had persisted in attempts to write a successful play. He granted that playwriting thus far had not paid and that it kept him from writing what did pay, but there was always the hope that it *would* pay and give him the respite from fiction-writing which he so sorely needed. However, because Harte believed the narrative episodic and too thin for extension into three acts, T. Edgar Pemberton had difficulty in persuading him to collaborate in a dramatization of Harte's story "The Judgment of Bolinas Plain," and when the resulting comedy entitled *Sue* was produced in New York by Charles Frohman and received good reviews, Harte could not believe in the play's success. Mrs. Harte proudly reported that the play was "lovely," that "every line *told* with the audience," and "every bit of pathos had its effect." Quoting these and other kind words from his wife, Bret wrote his son Frank: "Of course, she is prejudiced! . . . Even if this was not merely her loyal and kind prepossession for my work and was really the feeling of the audience—still it does not make a play a success." He acknowledged the soundness of Mrs. Harte's adverse criticism of the play's end. He gave full credit to Pemberton. And he also reassured Mrs. Harte that he had not sold his rights in it and that he expected to receive a share of its profits as long as it was on the stage.

The favorable critical response to the play was largely due to the acting of Annie Russell, the star. After a run in New York, *Sue* went on

---

[9] *BHL*, 364–65.

[10] For example, see letters to Mrs. Harte dated Sept. 20, 1893; Feb. 22, 1894; Mar. 24, 1894; July 25, 1894; Nov. 24, 1894. See also *BHAE*, 306.

tour in America for two seasons and in 1898 was brought to London, where Harte had a chance to see it. He was delighted with the acting not only of Miss Russell but of other members of the cast. There were reports of full houses, and invitations for the company to tour Australia, South Africa, and Germany. Frohman seemed satisfied, but when the tours ended and there was a final summing up, Harte was faced with the cold fact that *Sue* had contributed very little to the family security or to his own chance for relief from the constant grind of writing. He reacted to this disappointment with rare bitterness.

About the time Bret Harte faced up to the financial disappointment of *Sue*, his wife wrote him that his elder daughter Jessamy was engaged to marry a young man named Henry Milford Steele. Belatedly Bret replied: "I have had no heart to write to you, or to Jessamy regarding her affairs, and even now I can only congratulate her upon finding a husband who can take the place of her father and his precarious fortunes. It is hard to face this fact, which for the last six months I have been trying to avoid."[11]

Jessamy's engagement provided a hook on which Mark Twain hung his account of an incident in the Players Club in New York. Entering the club one evening, Mark Twain found a group comfortably drinking punch and talking, so he drew up a chair. A young man sitting beside him began to speak with great enthusiasm about the Harte family. They were, he said, "cheerfully" and "contentedly" working away to earn their living, Mrs. Harte by teaching music and the two girls by drawing and embroidery. Mark listened to this talk with interest and approval until the praise extended to Bret Harte himself. Mrs. Harte and the girls had told the young man that the husband and father wrote regularly, sent them money every month, but postponed returning because he could not get money ahead for the voyage and at the same time continue to send them the money for their support. At this, Mark could stand it no longer, and "broke out and called the young fellow's hand."

I said, "Oh, that be hanged! There's nothing in it. Bret Harte has deserted his family, and that is the plain English of it. Possibly he writes to them, but I am not weak enough to believe it until I see the letters; possibly he is pining to come home to his deserted family, but no one who knows him will believe that. But there is one thing about which I think

[11] *BHL*, 306, 429–32, 454–56.

231

there can be no possibility of doubt—and that is, that he has never sent them a dollar and has never intended to send them a dollar. Bret Harte is the most contemptible, poor little soulless blatherskate that exists on the planet today.[12]

At this point someone seized Mark's arm and whispered into his ear: "For goodness sake shut up! This young fellow is Steele. He's engaged to one of the daughters."

This makes a good story, and no one will disagree with Mark Twain's preface that "all of us at one time or another blunder stupidly into indiscreet acts and speeches." But the incident in the Players Club is probably one of the things Mark Twain remembered that didn't happen. In 1898, when Jessamy Harte became engaged to young Steele, Mark Twain was in Vienna. He did not return to New York until 1900.[13] As for Mark Twain's assurance that Bret Harte never sent his family a dollar, Harte's grandson reports that during the first fifteen years of his residence abroad, Harte sent Mrs. Harte and his children "over $60,000."[14] The late Geoffrey Bret Harte points out that in those days this represented "quite a considerable sum" and states flatly: "That he let them want for anything is an absurdity."

For transition between his inaccurate account of John McCullough's interview with Frank Harte and his report of his own "blunder" in the Players Club (which concluded his reminiscences about Bret Harte in *Mark Twain in Eruption*), Mark Twain dictated the following paragraph: "I have said more than once in these pages that Harte had no heart and no conscience, and I have also said that he was mean and base. I have not said, perhaps, that he was treacherous, but if I have omitted that remark I wish to add it now."

Mark Twain's autobiographical dictations about Bret Harte include meager outcroppings of truth. Here and there one can discover original fiction. But for the most part, the section about Harte in *Mark Twain in Eruption* is a compendium of gossip about Bret Harte over a period of thirty years.

Although Harte generally paid little heed to rumors from America concerning himself or his family, for he had learned by "sad experience"

---

[12] *MTE*, 291.   [13] Paine, *Biography*, 1059–71, 1110.

[14] See letter dated Sept. 6, 1930, from Geoffrey Bret Harte to George R. Stewart, Rare Books, University of California Library.

that they seldom included anything kindly or truthful, he was surprised to hear, about a month after he anxiously cabled his wife the money for the extra vacation in the Adirondacks, that visiting Americans had gossiped at their hotel and at the United States Legation in London that Harte's family was left in such poverty in America that Mrs. Harte had to borrow money to keep herself and her children from want. But even more surprised was an Englishman who happened to be present when the gossip was repeated, for the Englishman was connected with the London bank and the Bank of British North America through which Harte's substantial monthly drafts to his wife were regularly transmitted. American and English papers carried rumors that Harte was in New York, that he was living luxuriously in England, that he was vacationing in the south of France. Actually, he had not crossed the Channel in more than five years and had seen less of Europe than most American tourists see on the briefest of summer trips. When Albert Rhodes (an American diplomat and writer who had visited Harte at the Van de Veldes' and had recommended Harte's work to French publishers) read in an American newspaper that Harte planned to spend the winter of 1887 in the south of France, Rhodes immediately expressed a wish to introduce Harte to a friend in the same locale. Harte thanked Rhodes for his offer but replied that he hadn't the slightest prospect of going to the south of France and never had had any. "I may have said in somebody's hearing that I should like to go, but if wishes made an accomplished fact, I should, at the present moment, be a millionaire—in America."[15]

In 1888, Harte learned of an article circulated in American papers that he was a ruined spendthrift living in England "on money he had borrowed from his English friends" and that he would probably stay as long as he could borrow from them. The affected regret and commiseration for the decadence of a "once brilliant," "over-praised," but now "played-out" and "broken-down hack" goaded Harte to the point of considering a libel suit, but he concluded that such a suit would give the rumor too much recognition. Nevertheless, Charles A. Dana, on his own initiative, published in the *Sun* of November 8 a denial of the slander. But denials seldom gain as much attention as attacks, and Harte sadly wrote his wife: "Perhaps you have seen the poison, too, as well

[15] *BHL*, 325, 327, 330.

as the antidote."[16] The gossip, of course, was fed by Harte's separation from his family and his relationship with Madame Van de Velde.

Readers on both sides of the Atlantic believed the gossip more readily because of Harte's treatment of sex in fiction which shocked the Mrs. Grundys of the nineteenth century. Bret Harte wrote sympathetically of prostitutes, of married women who were not always faithful to their husbands, and of husbands who sometimes escaped from virtuous but nagging wives. Certain similarities of Harte's heroines to the heroines of Turgenev, Hardy, and Tolstoy have been recognized.[17] In "The Dynamo and the Virgin," Henry Adams observed that Bret Harte was the only writer of fiction for nineteenth-century magazines who, in the manner of the classics, insisted on the power of sex as a motivating force rather than a mere matter of sentiment.[18] But Harte could also observe humorously as well as accurately of "The Argonauts of '49": "There were husbands who had deserted their own wives and in some extreme cases, the wives of others."[19] It was this flippancy about the bonds of matrimony which Victorians could not forgive, and they reasoned that one who wrote so lightly of marriage could not regard his own very seriously.

In the nineteenth century, which regarded its "victory over sex" as its "greatest achievement," said Adams, Eve was a "tender flower." Mark Twain's allegations about Bret Harte's treatment of Mrs. Harte and Harte's relationships with other women should be considered in this context and in the context of Twain's own "deep fear of femaleness," "his intense craving for respectability," and his ultra-Victorian attitude toward sex in literature.[20]

Mark Twain contradicted himself on almost every subject, and many of his contradictions signify nothing more than variations in the impulse of the moment. The inconsistencies of Mark Twain's prudishness on the one hand with his love of pornography on the other can, to a limited extent, be explained by his adherence to the "Victorian belief that smut was all right for men but degrading for women."[21] But in a good many

---

[16] *Ibid.*, 333–34. [17] Merwin, *The Life of Bret Harte*, 76.

[18] *The Education of Henry Adams*, 385.

[19] *The Lectures of Bret Harte*, 7.

[20] Smith, *Mark Twain: The Development of a Writer*, 80; Henry Seidel Canby, *Turn West, Turn East*, 82.

[21] Blair, *Mark Twain & Huck Finn*, 403n.

instances Mark Twain was less concerned with what was right than with what was expedient, and he often found it expedient to support conventions. In the famous conversation with Elinor Glyn, when it seemed to Mark that the two talked with "daring frankness," Mark Twain argued that we are all servants of convention, that we could not subsist without conventions, and therefore, because they furnish us "peace, fairly good government and stability," we must stand by them and conform even when we disapprove of them. When Miss Glyn urged him to publish his brave assertion that like all statutory regulations of sex, conventions interfere with the "higher law of Nature," Mark replied that such a publication was "unthinkable." "I said I had been revealing to her my private sentiments, *not* my public ones; that I, like all the other human beings, expose to the world only my trimmed and perfumed and carefully barbered public opinions and conceal carefully, cautiously, wisely, my private ones."[22]

For these reasons we find considerable confusion in Mark Twain's words and actions reflecting his concept of the nature of woman. We have already noted that during his courtship of Olivia Langdon, he argued that *Gulliver's Travels*, *Don Quixote*, and Shakespeare should be bowdlerized before they were read by virgins. He did not recommend *Gil Blas* to Livy because, he told her, "It would sadly offend your delicacy & I prefer not to have that dulled in you. It is a woman's chief ornament."[23] Mark Twain once asserted that for a woman there is no such thing as the age of consent, that all seduction is rape.[24] Yet in a manuscript whose publication was suppressed until fifty years after his death, he privately recorded the belief that "from youth to middle age all men and all women prize copulation above all other pleasures combined," and in the the enjoyment of this pleasure, women have certain advantages. "The law of God, as quite plainly expressed in woman's construction, is this: There shall be no limit put upon your intercourse with the other sex sexually at any time of life. . . . During twenty-three days in every month (in the absence of pregnancy) from the time a woman is seven years old till she dies of old age, she is ready for action, and *competent*. As competent as the candlestick is to receive the candle. Competent every day, competent every night. Also she *wants* that

[22] Neider, *Autobiography*, 355–56. [23] *LL*, 76, 132.
[24] De Voto, *Mark Twain at Work*, 14–15.

candle—yearns for it, longs for it, hankers after it, as commanded by the law of God in her heart." And in "fair and just compensation" for the fact that "her plant is out of service" three days in the month and during part of her pregnancy, woman has "the high privilege of unlimited adultery all the other days of her life."[25] In other words, as Satan said in *Letters from the Earth*, in matters of sex, "man is a fool; woman a damned fool."

Such sentiments never appear in Mark Twain's travel books or his fiction designed for the general public. In his travel books, as noted by Gladys Bellamy, Mark Twain showed the preoccupation of the moralist with sexual matters.[26] He described Titian's Venus as "the foulest, the vilest, the obscenest picture the world possesses."[27] Yet when he believed financial success of a play required an appeal to the tastes of the "kitchen and stable," Mark Twain could reject that "sad, sad false delicacy" which deprives literature of obscene stories, and he could deliberately add vulgarity for the sake of vulgarity. He could lecture on "The Science of Onanism" to the Stomach Club in Paris, and after he composed "1601: A Fireside Conversation in the Time of Queen Elizabeth" for the delectation of select cronies, he could "roll on the grass" with Joe Twichell, convulsed with laughter at its pornography.[28] And with all this he could remain, as De Voto said, "almost lustfully hypersensitive to sex in print" and actually more squeamish on this subject than either Mrs. Clemens or Howells.[29]

In his attitude toward sex, mental and emotional health, marriage, and family relationships, Bret Harte was much closer to the twentieth century than was Mark Twain. Contrast with Mark Twain's bowdlerizing of world masterpieces for Livy, Bret Harte's indignant refusal to capitulate to the *Overland*'s lady proofreader who tried to prevent the publication of "The Luck of Roaring Camp" because it began with the death of a prostitute in childbirth, and Harte's gratitude for Mrs. Harte's appreciation of the story, an appreciation which gave him courage to demand that it be published unexpurgated in the *Overland*.[30] Bret Harte's manuscripts were never, like Mark Twain's, "a mush of con-

---

[25] *Letters from the Earth*, 40–41.
[26] *Mark Twain as a Literary Artist*, 166.
[27] Fatout, *Mark Twain on the Lecture Circuit*, 198.
[28] Bellamy, *Mark Twain as a Literary Artist*, 311.
[29] De Voto, *Mark Twain at Work*, 15, 85–86. [30] *BHL*, 152–53.

cessions." Because there was less sexual repression with Harte, there was less suppression of his real opinions. He once assured Ralph Waldo Emerson that the gambler and the prostitute had contributed more than churches to the cultural aspects of civilization in the West, a position he supported in fiction describing the bare wooden ugliness of some of the Protestant churches on the frontier.[31] In "A Convert of the Mission" he dramatized the thesis that the Catholic church and the Hispanic way of life recognized emotional, sexual, and aesthetic needs ignored by Anglo-Saxon Calvinists in the barren little settlements of Western pioneers. Harte may have been wrong, but he was not afraid to write what he believed and he made few concessions to expediency.

After critics repeatedly protested that his fiction undermined conventional standards of morality, Bret Harte replied that when "pardoned ticket-of-leave men" and the "repentant Magdalen" supplanted the austere, the virginal, and the righteous in society, he might change his writing practices and submit to the "new Draconian discipline in fiction." But of all the forms in which cant presents itself to suffering humanity, he said, none is so outrageous or illogical as the cant of "Too Much Mercy." And although Harte thought of himself as an artist rather than as a religious man or a moralist, it seemed to him, in all humility, that in writing the fiction to which these critics objected, he was following a precedent set by the "Great Poet" who conceived the parables of the prodigal son and the good Samaritan.[32] Bret Harte's mannerisms of expression have blinded casual critics to the fact that Harte's writings relating to sex fairly consistently adhered to his principles.

Bret Harte's language conformed to nineteenth-century literary conventions more than did Mark Twain's. It lacked that authenticity of colloquial style which was, perhaps, Mark Twain's greatest asset as a writer. Yet Bret Harte had a keenly perceptive though not a profound mind, he spoke in parables, and his creed of more understanding and more mercy for all human beings conflicted with the Puritan bias of many nineteenth-century moralists. Contrary to their belief, Harte's creed was not synonymous with sentimentality. But it did have a good deal in common with the morality of Huckleberry Finn.

Bret Harte enjoyed the friendship of women. Although Twain also liked very well those whom Howells called "the fashionable fair,"

[31] *BHAE*, 203.   [32] *Writings*, I, xviii–xix.

women were apt to be more strongly attracted to Harte than to Twain, and many became Harte's staunchest defenders. Those who liked him, corresponded with him, sometimes aided him, and maintained loyalty to him included Mrs. Jessie Benton Frémont, who had been among the first to recognize his ability as a writer and to further his career in San Francisco; Josephine Clifford McCrackin and Ina Coolbrith, who had known and worked with him on the *Overland Monthly*; Mrs. James T. Fields and Anna Dickinson, who had known him in his first years in the Eastern United States; Mrs. Charles Watrous, who with her husband had visited him in Glasgow; the Duchess of St. Albans, to whom Bret Harte's grandson dedicated the published edition of Harte's letters; Gertrude Griswold, Mrs. Harte's niece; Mrs. A. S. Boyd; Miss Pemberton, the daughter of Harte's most admiring biographer; Mrs. Henniker and Miss Froude, the daughters of his two friends of longest standing in England; and Madame Van de Velde. When Mark Twain dictated that Bret Harte was "kept" by several women "and in the house of one of them he died," the chivalrous defender of Harriet Shelley was slurring many admirable women who were Harte's friends, and he was specifically identifying Madame Van de Velde, who hardly deserved the insult.

It is noteworthy that the women I have named as Harte's friends were almost all nonconformists to the nineteenth-century womanly ideal of "intellectual anonymity."[33] Many of them were the kind of women who caused Henry Adams to declare that "the American woman of the nineteenth century was much better company than the American man."[34] Harte's letters to these women were gay, courteous, polished, but seldom emotional. If the letters which I have been able to examine are representative, Harte did not even address the women by their given names. He treated them as individuals with minds of their own; he showed interest in and respect for their ideas; he enjoyed their letters to him; and sometimes he criticized their manuscripts. For his perceptive consideration, they were apparently grateful. "I could hate the man who could help loving him—or the woman either," wrote Mrs. Fields.[35] When Harte suspected women of setting their caps for him, he was apt to react with guarded amusement, but when London newspapers quoted

[33] Andrews, *Nook Farm*, 89. [34] *The Education of Henry Adams*, 353.
[35] *BHAE*, 230.

one woman as saying she would rather be in the back kitchen with Bret Harte than in the drawing room with the Prince of Wales, Harte was not amused for he knew it would simply create more gossip.[36]

As for intimations that Bret Harte slighted his wife, he seemed in the proverbial position of being damned if you do and damned if you don't. San Francisco friends who knew Harte well maintained that the real reason he failed to appear at the dinner party in Chicago, where he was to be offered the editorship of the *Lakeside Monthly*, was that his wife had not been included in the invitation.[37] Mark Twain's charge that in Cohasset and Newport, Harte had attended dinners where he was the only male guest whose wife had not been invited may be answered by Harte's 1888 reminder to Mrs. Harte that she had always insisted Newport air had a bad effect on her health and that her doctor agreed the climate there made her *"sleepless"* and "intensely nervous."[38] (Oddly enough, in a letter to Mrs. Boyesen, March 3, 1889, Twain accused Howells also of accepting invitations to dinners to which Mrs. Howells had not been invited.[39] Both Twain and Howells were somewhat sensitive on this score, probably because Mrs. Clemens and Mrs. Howells were both semi-invalids and could not keep up the social pace of their exuberant husbands).

Bret Harte's letters to his wife are more self-revealing, more carefully composed, and more interesting than his letters to other correspondents, including his friends among women. The very pains he took to make these letters interesting were in themselves a compliment to his wife, an acknowledgment of her intelligence, and an indication of his sincere respect for her judgment. Harte's letters, published and unpublished, include considerable evidence that he wanted his wife to share his friendships with the Webbs, the Duchess of St. Albans, and the Van de Veldes in his early years in Britain. In 1889, when the Dowager Lady Shrewsbury (whom Harte described as "one of the most popular hostesses in London") visited America, Bret asked his wife and daughter to call on the Englishwoman at her hotel. After a photograph

---

[36] Bret Harte's Diary, June 30, 1888.

[37] See Josephine Clifford McCrackin, "Reminiscences of Bret Harte," *Overland Monthly*, Vol. XL (Sept., 1902), 223–24. See also Charles Murdock's assertion that those who knew the facts of the incident held Harte blameless. *A Backward Glance at Eighty*, 96.

[38] *BHL*, 334.   [39] Unpublished letter, MTP.

of Mrs. Harte was stolen from the Consul's dresser in Glasgow, Harte repeatedly urged his wife to send him others. But she did not. When she complained of changes which time had made in her appearance, he sympathetically reminded her that he, too, was gray-haired and putting on weight. In 1895 he again asked for a photograph: "I send you *my* decrepit, grey-haired, haggard portraits, that you may at least keep some idea of me—but you send me nothing!"[40]

In 1893, Frank Harte achieved what Bret Harte had never been able to do: he established a home in England. From the very beginning, Frank and his father enjoyed a gay and warmly affectionate relationship. Bret Harte was very fond of his daughter-in-law Aline, paid her courtly compliments, and delighted to bring her chocolates, which she liked so well that he sometimes called her the "chocolate girl." The aging man was a frequent and always welcome visitor in his son's home at Weybridge, and when Frank and Aline had two sons—named Richard and Geoffrey—Bret Harte enjoyed buying toys for his grandsons. Although Geoffrey was only seven years old when Bret Harte died, he wrote George Stewart in 1930: "I remember my grandfather very well,—an old man with snow white hair who was extremely fond of my brother Richard and myself. He not only lavished presents upon us at every visit but had a wonderful way of entering our lives with the same comprehension and understanding for children which he shows in his work."[41]

In the year of Jessamy's engagement, Mrs. Bret Harte and Ethel at long last came to live in England. But as in Harte's stories about men in California who talked day after day about how they would return to families in the East as soon as they made their strike, the actual reunion of the Harte family was not the kind of which they had all dreamed. Mrs. Harte and Ethel made their home with Frank. Bret Harte visited them often, and as long as he lived, provided money for their support. But he continued his lodgings in "bachelor" quarters at 74, Lancaster Gate. His grandson believed that it was Mrs. Harte's outbursts of bitterness which made it impossible for Bret Harte and his wife to live under

---

[40] *BHL*, 340, 398.

[41] Letter from Geoffrey Bret Harte to George Stewart, Sept. 6, 1930. Quoted by permission of Mrs. Geoffrey Bret Harte, Professor Stewart, and the Rare Book Department of the University of California Library, Berkeley.

the same roof.[42] Certainly it was impossible for Harte to continue his assembly-line schedule of writing under those conditions, and to keep out of debt and support himself, his wife, and his daughter, he had to keep on writing.

In 1882, when Bret Harte wrote happily to Mrs. Harte about meeting his "dear old friends" Howells and Hay and Aldrich at Osgood's famous London dinner party, Howells had recently completed a novel which was running serially in *Century Magazine*. The title of the novel was *A Modern Instance*, and though Howells and Twain would both insist that they saw themselves in the "false scoundrel" Bartley Hubbard, critics generally agree that the human being who contributed most to Howells' characterization of Bartley Hubbard was Bret Harte, whose initials were borne by both Bartley and Bartley's foil, Ben Halleck. At least one critic recognizes the probable influence of Twain's "bitter condemnations" of Harte on Howells' characterization of Bartley Hubbard.[43] If at the time of Osgood's dinner Harte had read *A Modern Instance*, the scene where Kinney gives to Bartley's baby the gold nuggett which he picked up in "Californy" might well have reminded him of a famous scene in "The Luck of Roaring Camp."[44] But he would have recognized little resemblance between his relation to his own family and Bartley Hubbard's desertion of his wife and child. Harte's responsibility for some of his wife's bitterness and unhappiness over the prolonged separation cannot be ignored. But since unquestionably Harte wrote his family regularly and worked hard to provide them with a comfortable income, that Bret Harte deserted his family seems not to be "the plain English of it."

In seventeenth-century England, John Milton had questioned the morality as well as the necessity of a man and woman living together when the union generated bitterness. In the latter part of the nineteenth century, rebellion against rigid Victorian convention and its complement, hypocrisy, grew increasingly overt. Divorce *did* occur in the days of the old Queen: Harte's diary notes one.[45] Another entry in the diary records Harte's attendance at a play whose cast included "one of Ellen Terry's

[42] *Ibid.*

[43] *MTH*, I, 412–13. See also William M. Gibson's introduction to William Dean Howells' *A Modern Instance*, vi.

[44] Howells, *A Modern Instance*, 250–51.   [45] Entry for June 13, 1884, BC.

husbands." Harte's reaction was simply that the man was a good actor.[46]
Among English and American authors who had marital difficulties,
were divorced, or established unconventional domestic alliances in Victorian England can be listed Charles Dickens, George Eliot, H. G.
Wells, Arnold Bennett, George Gissing, Harold Frederic, and Stephen Crane. Novels, including Hardy's *The Woodlanders*, sometimes
hesitantly advocated a new morality. This morality would find ultimate bold expression in *Lady Chatterley's Lover*. In *A Modern Instance*, William Dean Howells approached the subject of divorce so
cautiously that Robert Louis Stevenson mistakenly believed Howells
was casting aspersions on Mrs. Stevenson. Stevenson responded by
breaking a dinner egagement with Howells and stating flatly that Mrs.
Stevenson had done him the honor to divorce her husband in order
to marry him.[47]

Two years before Howells' novel portraying the effects of marital
friction on the characters of Marcia Gaylord and Bartley Hubbard, a
Bret Harte story included this observation: "It takes the legal matri-
monial contract to properly develop the first class tyrant, male or
female."[48] But Bret Harte did not discuss his marital problems even
with his biographer Pemberton, and Mrs. Harte remained equally
reticent.[49] Nevertheless, if Harte was, in fact, the prototype of Bartley
and Mrs. Harte contributed to the characterization of Marcia, Howells
showed considerable perception when he wrote: "Many a woman who
would be ready to die for her husband makes him wretched because
she won't live for him." And Howells probably came close to the truth
about Harte's feeling toward his wife when Bartley said of his separation from Marcia: "I was sorry for Marcia; it almost broke my heart
to think of the little one; but I knew they were in the hands of friends;
and the more time I had to think it over, the more I was reconciled to
what I had done. That was the only way out, for either of us. We had

<hr/>

[46] Entry for Dec. 1, 1882, BC. [47] Howells, *Life in Letters*, I, 332.

[48] "Jeff Briggs's Love Story," *Writings*, III, 206. For the date of publication in
book form, see Joseph Gaer, editor, *Bret Harte: Bibliography and Biographical Data*,
47, 83.

[49] For possible allusion, however, see Pemberton, *The Life of Bret Harte*, 335–36.
For Mark Twain's assertion that the ass is the "choicest spirit among all the humbler
animals," see "Pudd'nhead Wilson's Calendar" at the beginning of Chapter I of Mark
Twain's novel.

tried it for three years, and we couldn't make it go; we never could have made it go; we were incompatible. Don't you suppose I knew Marcia's good qualities? No one knows them better, or appreciates them more. You might think that I applied for this divorce because I had some one else in view. Not any more in mine at present! But I thought we ought to be free, both of us; and if our marriage had become a chain, that we ought to break it."[50]

But for Francis Brett Harte and Anna Griswold Harte, there was no legal break. Certainly Mrs. Harte could have gained a divorce if she had wished it, but I have found no indication that she ever considered the possibility. As for Bret Harte, far from seeing himself as Bartley Hubbard, who left his wife financially stranded, Harte regarded his separation from his wife as following an American pattern satirized in the separation of the Westgates in *An International Episode*. And with an inconsistency worthy of Mark Twain, Bret Harte objected that Henry James had not regarded that marital situation with appropriate seriousness.[51]

As far as I can tell, Bret Harte maintained real affection for his wife, but with the stubbornness of Bartleby, the Scrivener, he preferred not to live with her. He was no Galahad. Yet Harte was kept in bondage not by any other woman but by the necessity to write fiction that would sell. There Harte's talent found La Belle Dame Sans Merci.

[50] Howells, *A Modern Instance*, 330, 357.
[51] See *BHL*, 159.

18

BRET HARTE AND "THE CRAFT SO HARD TO LEARN"

He hadn't a sincere fiber in him. I think he was incapable of emotion, for I think he had nothing to feel with. I think his heart was merely a pump and had no other function.

MARK TWAIN about BRET HARTE

When it came to literature, all the gay improvidence of life forsook him, and . . . he became a stern, rigorous, exacting self-master, who spared himself nothing to achieve the perfection at which he aimed.

WILLIAM DEAN HOWELLS about BRET HARTE

MOST OF MARK TWAIN'S DAMNATIONS of Bret Harte center on a single trait: lack of sincerity. Specifically, Mark Twain applied this criticism not only to Bret Harte's relations with his family but also to Harte's relations with his work, his country, and his friends.

On New Year's Eve in 1858, Frank Harte, a romantic young man of twenty-two employed as a tutor at a salary of $25 a month in Uniontown, California, wrote in his diary: "The conclusion forced upon me by observation and not by vain enthusiasm that I am fit for nothing else—must impel me to seek distinction and fortune in literature." After this characteristically whimsical beginning, the tone of Harte's entry changed: "Perhaps I may succeed—if not I can at least make the trial. Therefore I consecrate this year or as much as God may grant for my service to honest heartfelt sincere labor and devotion to this occupation—God help me—may I succeed."[1] According to George R. Stewart's definitive biography, *Bret Harte, Argonaut and Exile*, "This consecration of himself he continued steadfastly to fulfill—and to expiate—throughout all his years."

William Dean Howells, perhaps the most discerning literary critic

[1] *BHAE*, 68.

in nineteenth-century America after Edgar Allan Poe, also believed that Bret Harte was a sincere and conscientious craftsman. "He was of the order of literary men like Goldsmith and DeQuincey and Sterne and Steele, in his relations with the outer world," wrote Howells, "but in his relations with the inner world he was one of the most duteous and exemplary citizens. There was nothing of his easy-going hilarity in that world; there he was of a Puritanic severity, and of a conscience that forgave him no pang."[2]

Many other associates as well as Harte's manuscripts bear witness to the truth of Harte's own reminder to his friend Clemens that Harte wrote "slowly and with exceeding labor." Noah Brooks, who had been Harte's assistant editor in San Francisco and who later became one of Horace Greeley's remarkable group of editorial writers on the New York *Tribune*,[3] said that in the course of a long life which had acquainted him with scores of writers, he had never known one "so fastidious and so laborious as Bret Harte."[4] Another biographer who contradicted Mark Twain's appraisal of Bret Harte as a "facile" and "slovenly" writer was T. Edgar Pemberton, who reported that during the many "pleasant hours" of collaboration with Harte on *Sue*, he had ample opportunity to learn that "infinite painstaking" was the "tap-root" of Harte's working methods.[5]

As an editor and critic as well as a writer, Bret Harte seems to have been sincere and to have struggled for precision in himself and in others. Mark Twain's 1867 letter requesting Harte to "be a friend and say nothing about" the "damnable errors of grammar and deadly inconsistencies of spelling" suggests that in the early days in San Francisco, Bret Harte sometimes took Mark Twain to task for carelessness in grammar and spelling as well as in paragraphing. Mark Twain wrote that he had not read the proofs for the Jumping Frog book before it went to press. Of the San Francisco writers benefited by Harte's criticism, one of the most appreciative was Charles Warren Stoddard, who later became professor of literature at the University of Notre Dame. According to Jay Leyda, the search for an ideal state among primitives in the South Seas was transmitted "from Melville through Loti to

[2] *Harper's*, Vol. CVIII (Dec., 1903), 153–54.   [3] Thayer, *John Hay*, I, 334.
[4] Pemberton, *The Life of Bret Harte*, 80.
[5] Pemberton, *Bret Harte, A Treatise and a Tribute*, 243.

Gaugin" and "through Stoddard to Stevenson and Jack London."[6] Stoddard wrote of Harte: "He made me what I am and I owe all to him."[7] Stoddard also testified that Harte was "not afraid to speak his mind" and sometimes proved a severe critic, but he never judged others more severely than he judged himself.[8]

Harte's concern for accuracy of details can be observed in letters to Joseph Hatton about a dramatization of "M'liss" on which the two collaborated in 1890. Determined that stage sets and costumes conform to reality, Harte drew a design for the schoolhouse at Smith's Pocket and described in minute detail the clothes worn by larger and smaller children, by women, by Mexican *vaqueros*, and by miners as he remembered them from his days in California almost forty years earlier. Most interesting in a study of parallels and contrasts between Mark Twain and Bret Harte are Harte's injunctions about the costumes of miners.

As Harte remembered it, the men working the southern mines of California wore white duck trousers and shirts with light-colored bandanna handkerchiefs about their throats, a costume which gave them a picturesque appearance. He specified that one or two of the actor-miners might wear high rubber boots "like fishing boots," but the stage miners must not be made to look crude and rough like field laborers or artisans for Harte insisted that notwithstanding their long hair and mustachios, the real miners were often "refined and educated men with delicate hands, feet, and faces," and except for the stains of red earth on their white clothes, they remained remarkably clean. Vehemently Harte objected to the "usual mistakes" of equipping stage miners with "red flannel shirts and old trousers thrust in their boots," because, he pointed out, the thermometer on the river bars used to mark 100° in the shade."[9]

Perhaps it is not by chance that Bret Harte's words remind us of Mark Twain's description of Scotty Briggs calling on "the pale theological student" to discuss Buck Fanshaw's funeral. Scotty was "a stalwart rough, whose customary suit, when on weighty official business, like committee work, was a fire helmet, flaming red flannel shirt, patent leather belt with spanner and revolver attached, coat hung over arm, and pants stuffed into boot tops."[10] Most of us accept Scotty Briggs as authen-

[6] *The Portable Melville*, xiv.   [7] Pemberton, *The Life of Bret Harte*, 342–43.
[8] Stoddard, *Exits and Entrances*, 248.
[9] *BHL*, 351–53.   [10] *Roughing It*, 242.

tic and reject Harte's picturesque miners and *vaqueros* as false and theatrical. Our acceptance is strengthened by *The Shirley Letters from the California Mines, 1851–1852*, in which Mrs. Clappe repeatedly mentions the red or blue flannel shirts of the miners.[11] Yet Henry Nash Smith has noted that Mark Twain's phrase "stalwart rough" was a cliché and that the hero in red flannel shirt with his trousers tucked into his boots was "a stock character from the contemporary stage."[12]

Bret Harte's miners were drawn from Harte's experience when, as a youth with seven dollars in his pocket and absurd patent leather shoes on his feet, he had made his first trip to the mines two years after his arrival in California from New York. On that expedition he was generously and hospitably received by three miners who turned out to be two college graduates and a bright young farmer. During an evening these miners conversed with Harte about a wide variety of topics including "literature, science, philosophy, everything but business and practical concerns," thereby shattering the young New Yorker's preconceived notions of miners as rough illiterates. In a scene so colorful that it created a lasting image in his mind, he had observed against a background of green foliage a group of miners at work in white suits with knotted "handkerchiefs of coarse blue, green, or yellow bandanna" acrosse their shoulders. In an introduction to his *Tales of the Argonauts*, Harte explained that the white suits were seamen's clothing, condemned by the Navy Department and sold at auction to a local entrepreneur.[13] It is more likely that the white cotton suits he saw were made of manta, for as Harte himself noted in an adjoining paragraph, there were many Mexicans at work in the southern mines. Harte's experience in the mines was limited, and the miners he described in his letter to Hatton may not have been representative. Nevertheless, it is true that many who flocked to California during the Gold Rush were educated men unaccustomed to manual labor. And some Californians argued that because of this there were not enough farmers and skilled workingmen in the state.[14] Moreover, it is reasonable that red flannel

[11] Louise Amelia Knapp Smith Clappe, *The Shirley Letters from the California Mines, 1851–1852*, 38, 40, 120.

[12] Smith, *The Development of a Writer*, 63, 66.   [13] *Writings*, II, xxi–xxii.

[14] See John S. Hittell, *California as a Home for the Emigrant*. Harte had good reason to know this because some Californians bitterly opposed the publication of his fiction on grounds that it would discourage respectable farmers and skilled workmen from moving to California.

shirts and dark woolen trousers would constitute rather uncomfortable apparel in the summer around Hangtown, Angel's Camp, Sonora, or San Andreas, where—as anyone who has driven in August over California's State Highway 49 knows—the thermometer often registers as much as 110°. Bret Harte wanted the play "M'liss" to re-create accurately his image of a particular aspect of a California which he had once observed and which he now remembered as "a land of flowers and blossoms."

Mark Twain had lived among miners and had been a passionate miner himself—as Bret Harte had not. But the difference between Mark Twain's and Bret Harte's portrayals of the places and people of the Far West was not that Twain was an honest craftsman and Harte a careless and dishonest one. Henry Childs Merwin's *The Life of Bret Harte, with Some Account of the California Pioneers* identifies factual sources for even some of the more incredible incidents and characters in Harte's fiction, and Harte himself said that each of his characters was based on at least one real person. But Harte's painting of the California panorama is essentially impressionistic. It is significant that Stephen Crane admired Harte's early sketches and was much influenced—particularly in his use of color—by Harte's work.[15] Also significant is the fact that Harte's first impressions of mines and miners were gained through the eyes of a romantic lad in his teens, whereas Twain was twenty-six and had traveled widely as a journeyman printer and as a river-boat pilot on the broad Mississippi before he crossed the plains to Carson City and went prospecting for gold in Nevada and California.

A scheduled production in London of the Hatton-Harte dramatization of "M'liss" cast with Hatton's daughter in the leading role was postponed for a production of "The Prince and the Pauper,"[16] dramatized by Abby Sage Richardson, whom Mark Twain came in time to detest almost as much as he detested Bret Harte. Although Harte never wrote a successful play about her, M'liss as a character tempted many dramatists.[17] She never attained the life everlasting of Tom Sawyer and

[15] See *Stephen Crane: Letters*, edited by R. W. Stallman and Lillian Gilkes, 159, 209. Crane believed that Mark Twain "overtreats his subject," and Crane commented that "four hundred pages of humour is a little bit too much for me." *Ibid.*, 251.

[16] Pemberton, *The Life of Bret Harte*, 265.

[17] A study of dramatic versions of "M'liss" will be included in a forthcoming biography of Annie Pixley by Professor William L. Phillips of the University of Washington.

Huck Finn, but on the stage M'liss became so famous and beloved as a nineteenth-century heroine that her portrait—like that of her creator—was painted by a member of the Royal Academy in England, and in twentieth-century Hollywood, the role of M'liss could attract as famous a star as Mary Pickford.

Bret Harte was the owner and proprietor of the Bret Harte country of his fiction in much the sense that William Faulkner became master of Yoknapatawpha County in Mississippi, a South which many indignant Southerners find as unrecognizable as many Californians find the California of Bret Harte. It is true, as George R. Stewart pointed out, that Harte's fiction includes such errors in details as turning California poppies red and planting woods in Carquinez, where none grow. Harte was habitually negligent of apostrophes, he split infinitives ruthlessly, and—like Mark Twain—he occasionally misspelled words in letters and manuscripts. Considering the pressures under which he worked, it is surprising that he did not make more such mistakes. Unquestionably, however, he took infinite pains that his fiction should achieve the effect he wished to create. He fought pirated versions of *Gabriel Conroy* and "M'liss" less because they were taking money from his pockets than because they falsified his scenes and characters. So colorful was his image of California and so vivid did he make this image in his fiction that even in the twentieth century those who read Bret Harte more than superficially are apt to find themselves seeing California through his eyes. If what they see is a myth—and Harte *was* a myth maker—the myth includes more essential truth than is generally recognized.

As Henry James indicated in "The Real Thing," genius does not consist of an infinite capacity for taking pains. Bernard De Voto observed that most of Mark Twain's books were "sporadically composed" and that Mark Twain's might be the way of inspiration and genius but it was "not the way of a conscientious literary workman."[18] As examples of Mark Twain's "handsome indifference to minutiae," De Voto cited *Tom Sawyer*'s many inconsistencies and the fact that between the writing of *Tom Sawyer* and *Hucklebery Finn*, Mark forgot the name of Tom's sweetheart and called her Bessie Thatcher instead of bothering to open his own book and find out what her name really was. Gladys Carmen Bellamy clearly demonstrated that Mark Twain's artistry was more

---

[18] See *Mark Twain at Work*, 3, 10, 12.

conscious, more complex, and more conscientious than his earlier critics recognized.[19] Finally, Mark Twain's fiction was more effective than Bret Harte's. But in the kind of negligence of which Mark Twain accused Bret Harte, Twain was not guiltless enough to cast stones.

Evidences of Twain's carelessness with details are multiple in the passages about Harte in *Mark Twain in Eruption*. If Bret Harte forgot the color of California poppies, Mark Twain seems to have confused Yreka, California, with Eureka, a different town across the mountains and a good many miles away. Yreka did not get its name as Mark Twain said it did.[20] Bret Harte did not, as Mark Twain said, arrive in California when he was twenty-three or twenty-four years old; he was between seventeen and eighteen. Harte was not "discovered" by Mr. Swain; his job as secretary to Mr. Swain was given him on the recommendation of Mrs. Jessie Benton Frémont, who—with Thomas Starr King—in a sense did "discover" him. According to Mark Twain, when Bret Harte "died in London, he had been absent from his wife and daughters twenty-six years." When Harte died in Surrey, he had been absent from America twenty-four years. Before his death, he saw his wife and at least one of his daughters many times. Most of these inaccuracies are not very significant. They do suggest that Mark might have been a little more restrained about calling Bret a "slovenly writer."

From 1871, when he left California for the Eastern part of the United States, to his death in 1902, Bret Harte's writing showed more repetition than growth, and as he recognized, he dropped from the main stream of the development of American literature. But the mass "audience behind the window blinds" did not want him to move on. They wanted him to stay outside the windows, and—like children enamored of certain bedtime stories—they wanted him to play the same tunes over and over again. As a writer, Bret Harte needed time. He needed to loaf and invite his soul. But he and his wife and four children needed money. And so Bret Harte continued to turn out his thousand words every day, "Sundays not excepted."

In Mark Twain's oft-quoted letter to Andrew Lang, Mark denied a wish to appeal to the cultivated classes. He said he was out for bigger

[19] Bellamy, *Mark Twain as a Literary Artist, passim.* Specifically, see pages 371–72.
[20] *Historical Map of Siskiyou Co., California,* published by the Siskiyou County Historical Society. I also rely on a conversation with Yreka historian, Mrs. Fred Meamber.

game—the masses. "It is not that little minority who are already saved that are best worth lifting up, I should think, but the mighty mass of the uncultivated who are underneath! . . . they will never know Homer but the passing rhymester of their day leaves them higher than he found them," wrote Mark Twain in defense of *A Connecticut Yankee in King Arthur's Court*, which was under severe attack by English critics partly because of Mark Twain's deviations from the facts of history.[21] In its day, Harte's fiction maintained its popular appeal, and even today it has not altogether lost that appeal. As much as he could in his system of mass production, Bret Harte sought original ideas. And in supplying the market for his goods, Bret Harte managed to say many things he believed about race relations, government, business ethics, psychology, social reform, journalistic practices, the techniques of fiction, and Anglo-American relations. Among the most interesting aspects of a study of Bret Harte are discoveries of the number of lives in the nineteenth century which Harte's life touched and the number of liberal ideas which his popular fiction disseminated.

Many of Harte's stories of his later years dealt with themes introduced in earlier fiction. Several concern problems of the attempted fusion of Hispanic and Anglo-American cultures in California. Appearing in four Spanish-Californian stories is one of Harte's most beloved, amusing, but finally tragic characters: Enriquez Saltello, whose prototype was probably a young friend of the seventeen-year-old Frank Harte who had lived with his mother and stepfather, Colonel Williams, in Oakland. "Maruja" is an allegorical history of California from the days of the mythical Coyote and the Indian mounds to the time when the railroad noisily supplanted the "garden of the world" as a symbol.[22] With age, Harte's thoughts turned more and more to the past, but as he wrote his wife, with his usual "fickleness," he was becoming not more conservative but more "radical," by which he meant more concerned with social reform.[23] Published a year after Henry James's *The Princess Casamassima*, Harte's *novella The Crusade of the Excelsior* reflects the author's interest in reform aspects of the revolutionary doctrines of

[21] Paine, *Biography*, 894–95.

[22] Henry Nash Smith, *Virgin Land: The American West as Symbol and Myth*, 184–85.

[23] *BHL*, 231.

Marx and Bakunin then stirring the world.[24] "A Drift from Redwood Camp" (translated into French by Madame Van de Velde and published in the Parisian journal *Lettres et Arts* before it appeared in English) concerns torture and trade exchanged between Indians and whites on the Western frontier.[25] "Three Vagabonds of Trinidad," appearing in *Punch* in 1900, shows a little Chinese boy and an outcast Indian driven from the settlement by wanton brutalities and finally betrayed by a little "Boston boy" whom they had befriended. Thus Harte's championship of racial minorities continued to the end of his life.

Mark Twain charged that Bret Harte cynically exploited human emotions; in other words, he regarded the "tear of sensibility" as oil which he had been lucky enough to strike.[26] Here again, Mark Twain was throwing stones without remembering that the walls of his own house were made of glass. Mark Twain, "surnamed THE MORAL PHENOMENON," once facetiously suggested to the publishers of the *Californian* that he be made editor of that journal: "You ought to know," he said, "that when I play my hand in the high moral line, I take a trick every time."[27]

If consistency of expression can be taken as a criterion of sincerity, Bret Harte's record stands up well in comparison with Mark Twain's. This has already been noted in the two authors' writings about sex, but it is most easily observed in comparing their writings about racial minorities. Early journalistic essays of Mark Twain and Bret Harte indicate a basic difference in the two men's attitudes toward the familiar and the foreign. The strange and colorful aroused in Harte wonder, in Twain suspicion. This appears not only in the men's writings about Chinese but also in their writings about Indians, Mexicans, and Negroes. William Purviance Fenn questioned Mark Twain's sincerity in the *Galaxy* essays in defense of Chinese.[28] Some Jews protest—with reason—that "Concerning the Jews" is anti-Semitic.[29] In this essay, in which Mark Twain asserted that except for one (the French) he had no race prejudice, he also wrote: "Race prejudice cannot be removed—it is no par-

---

[24] For a fuller discussion of this theme, see my article "The 'Crusade' of a Nineteenth-Century Liberal," *loc. cit.*, 109–20.

[25] *BHL*, 315, 324. Also *BHAE*, 298.   [26] *MTE*, 265.

[27] *Sketches of the Sixties by Bret Harte and Mark Twain*, edited by John Howell, 210–11.

[28] *Ah Sin*, 33f., 45.   [29] Foner, *Mark Twain: Social Critic*, 229–31.

ticular matter."[30] It has been generally believed that Mark Twain outgrew his prejudice against Negroes. Yet because Negroes find *Huckleberry Finn* "racially offensive," Mark Twain's masterpiece was dropped in 1957 from the approved textbook lists for elementary and junior high schools in New York.[31] One who recognizes the absurdity of such censorship can also recognize that the NAACP has some grounds for not enjoying the "mirror image" of a race in Nat, the "nigger" with a good-natured, chuckle-headed face" and "wool . . . all tied up in little bunches with thread . . . to keep witches off." Nat "kind of smiled around gradly over his face, like when you heave a brickbat in a mud-puddle."[32] And twentieth-century Negroes who can plan and execute the March on Washington cannot be expected to find altogether admirable either Jim, the "good Negro" who knew his place, or the funny stories or practical jokes at the expense of characters *because they are Negroes* which constitute a substantial part of the humor in *Huckleberry Finn.* When he wrote *Pudd'nhead Wilson* in the year of the failure of Charles L. Webster and Company, Mark Twain's chief concern was not with exposing the evils of slavery thirty years after Lincoln's Emancipation Proclamation but with exploiting the popularity of Sherlock Holmes and making money.[33]

No one will say that Mark Twain took a moral stand *only* because it was profitable. But more grounds exist for this charge against him than for Twain's charge that Harte's fiction was designed to appeal to human emotions *only* because Harte expected this appeal to make him rich. Although Bret Harte disliked sentimentality, he was temperamentally sentimental. But Henry Childs Merwin was right when he insisted on the "breadth and warmth" of Harte's humanitarian sympathies. "It would be as impossible to imagine Bret Harte taking sides against the oppressed as it would be to imagine him performing his literary work in a slovenly manner."[34]

Yet Harte did not want to preach. As a writer, he was primarily concerned with aesthetics, and he struggled to maintain artistic integrity.

[30] "Concerning the Jews," *The Writings of Mark Twain*, XXII, 273. My thesis is that Mark Twain never lost all his own racial prejudices.

[31] Foner, *Mark Twain: Social Critic*, 214.

[32] *Adventures of Huckleberry Finn*, edited by Henry Nash Smith, 198.

[33] Stone, *The Innocent Eye*, 164, 195. See also *MTL*, II, 590-91.

[34] *The Life of Bret Harte*, 289.

With Chaucer, Harte knew that life is short and the craft is hard to learn. "It is hard to always write in *unity* with one's self!" he said.[35] One Sunday after lunch with Joseph Hatton, Bret Harte lingered over coffee and watched the smoke of his cigar curl upward and drift away to nothingness. He said he would like to write a long poem. "I forget whether he said a great poem, but I think he only said 'a long poem,'" Hatton later recalled. "He meant that he would like to have time to do his very best in an important and sustained effort."[36]

Bret Harte was gratified when, in 1886, John Hay wrote him a charming letter insisting that Harte was just achieving "the full maturity of his powers," and he particularly prized an edition of *Emma* given him by a friend, who wrote inside the cover two quatrains comparing Harte's artistry with that of Jane Austen, whom—unlike Mark Twain—Harte much admired. Nevertheless, the time came when Harte could praise the work of other writers and matter-of-factly refer to "my own drivel."[37] Once he told a friend: "My writing lately has revealed to me hitherto unknown depths of heaviness and stupidity."[38] Reading proofs became for him "the dreariest form of summer and self examination!"[39] And on September 30, 1899, he wrote Mrs. Henniker: "The flowers have gone, and the birds are going—and I and my work remain; I can only hope that I can get *my* leaves off before the trees do theirs."[40]

Mrs. Henniker was the daughter of Bret Harte's old friend Lord Houghton. She wrote fiction which she sent to Bret Harte for criticism, editing, and aid in placing her work for publication.[41] One of her books she dedicated to him. Harte's letters to Mrs. Henniker, written over a period of ten years or more and now among the Clifton Waller Barrett collection of Bret Harte manuscripts and publications in the University of Virginia Library, reveal a good deal about what had happened to the writer and critic during thirty years of drudgery. And what had happened to Bret Harte was certainly not what Mark Twain said had happened to him.

---

[35] *BHL*, 306. [36] Pemberton, *The Life of Bret Harte*, 264.

[37] *Ibid.*, 304; *BHL*, 379.

[38] Unpublished letter to Mrs. Henniker, Feb. 19, 1890, in Barrett Library Bret Hartes (hereinafter cited as BL), the University of Virginia Library.

[39] Unpublished letter to Mrs. Henniker, Feb. 13, 1890, BL.

[40] Unpublished letter, BL.

[41] See unpublished letter to Charles Dudley Warner, Mar. 29, 1892, BL.

To the literary historian, the most interesting parts of these letters are passages in which Harte comments on the works of other writers of that time. These comments show a humility remarkable in a man whose own name had once blazed so brightly on the literary horizon. When he told Mrs. Henniker about "one of the Harpers" showing him a large iron safe containing $60,000 worth of manuscripts, "all paid for and accepted, awaiting their slow turn for publication," he commented that some were by writers whose names "awed" him.[42] By chance he came across Anatole France's *Sylvester Bonnard*, read it, and was "charmed" by it. He particularly liked the lightness with which Monsieur Bonnard's "sound philosophy" was handled, and he found in the book "one of the prettiest studies *I* know of in French fiction. But I don't know as much of it as I ought."[43] Unlike Mark Twain, who showed no hesitation in judging anything—from missionaries to Shakespeare—Bret Harte was diffident about criticizing a writer even in a genre similar to his own. He met Rudyard Kipling at a dinner party and found him not very interesting.[44] Some of Kipling's work he found incoherent—without form. On Mrs. Henniker's recommendation he read *Plain Tales from the Hills*, liked its "freshness of choice of subject, and the apparent truthfulness of character sketching" but was repelled by a certain "smart attitude" of the writer toward his subject. This last comment is particularly interesting since this smartness is an element sometimes criticized in Harte's own fiction. Harte admitted that his criticism of Kipling was "partial and unfair," and he determined to read other works before he judged finally. "Then," Harte added, "I may be no judge at all! However there is always room for anything new and good, whatever the critics may say. I am no critic."[45]

Although Bret Harte was modest and recognized his own limitations, his opinions were his own and he would not pretend that they were different. He has been criticized because of his taste for *The Count of Monte Cristo*, a novel which also appealed to Chekhov.[46] In June, 1890,

[42] Unpublished letter, Jan. 28, 1890, BL.

[43] Unpublished letter to Mrs. Henniker, Oct. 2, 1891. BL.

[44] *BHAE*, 301. See also *BHL*, 386.

[45] Unpublished letter to Mrs. Henniker, headed "Saturday P.M." from 15, Upper Hamilton Terrace, N. W. (no specific date given).

[46] In 1892, Chekhov wrote a condensed but never published version of *The Count of Monte Cristo*. Sounding much like Bret Harte, Chekhov once told a correspondent:

Harte asked Mrs. Henniker to send him "something amusing" to read, for he was getting too old to find any pleasure in being made sad. Mrs. Henniker's stories had a way of ending lugubriously. Harte once complained of her "bill of mortality," with five deaths in "one little volume." His letter about *Scarlet and Grey*, a book including a story on which Mrs. Henniker had collaborated with Thomas Hardy, shows Harte humorously objecting to a sentimental morbidity akin to that caricatured by Mark Twain in Emmeline Grangerford.[47]

Bret Harte agreed to read a poem by Tennyson recommended by Mrs. Henniker but suggested that she would do well to read Emerson. "You have read so much that is smooth and flowing. I'd like you to see something rugged."[48] Nevertheless, Harte's comments on Mrs. Henniker's manuscripts clearly indicate how far Bret Harte was from the new realism of William Dean Howells. His attention was still focused on form, on the means by which a writer secures the effect for which he is working, that effect which Poe considered the first essential of a good story. Bret Harte warned Mrs. Henniker of the danger of reaching a climax too soon and advised her to work up enough interest to permit her to withhold the catastrophe and continue the suspense even to the extent of deceiving the reader a little. Like Henry James, Harte insisted on a distinction between art and life.

In appraising the critical commentaries in Bret Harte's letters to Mrs. Henniker, we must make allowances for the fact that the literary comments were parts of a prolonged, chiefly social correspondence between an older man and the daughter of his contemporary. Most of the letters were hurriedly written, for as in the correspondence with his wife, Harte was always apologizing for appointments postponed because of the pressure of work. Nevertheless, some of the comments illuminate his own personality. "One must be very young to batten on sorrow. . . . Human nature revolts at too much suffering and takes refuge at last in apathy or incredulity."[49]

"Oh, I'm sick of writing one and the same thing!" Oddly enough, he added: "I want to write about devils, terrible, volcanic women, sorcerers, but alas, all they want is stories about Ivan Gavriloviches and their wives." David Magarshack, *Chekhov: A Life*, 261, 278.

[47] Unpublished letter, Sept. 4, 1896, BL.

[48] Unpublished letter, Feb. 13, 1890, BL.

[49] Unpublished letter, Sept. 4, 1896, BL.

And so Bret Harte, whose hair had been white for many years, who was tired and ill and caught in a trap (a cushioned trap of his own design, but a trap nonetheless), asked for light reading, for "escape" literature. For the same reason, after long hours at his desk, he preferred the Royal Thames Yacht Club to the famous literary clubs of London. At the Rabelais, the Beefsteak, and the Kinsmen he was welcomed, but he was expected to talk about what he was writing and what he thought of the latest books. He did not want to talk about himself or other writers. At the yacht club he was permitted to sit and listen. And perhaps because he had no deep interest in yachting, he went back to his writing refreshed.[50] Bret Harte's last reading before he died was Thomas Hardy's *The Woodlanders*, a book in which very little light penetrates the shadows of the trees. For Harte, in particular, it was far from escape literature. Nevertheless, several times he paused in his reading to say, "That is fine—very fine."[51]

Justin McCarthy, who had met Harte earlier in San Francisco and New York, wrote of seeing him again in England at the home of Mrs. Henniker, "a gifted and charming hostess," whose place was "just the house where one who knows his way about London would naturally expect to meet Bret Harte." Occasionally McCarthy saw Harte at other London houses, but he felt privileged to be with him at Mrs. Henniker's, for there one had a chance of finding Bret Harte in a small, congenial company, of talking with him, and of hearing him talk. The Irish historian reported that "no one is made more cordially welcome in literary society, and, indeed, in society of any kind which he chooses to favor with his presence." Harte, he said, was "one of the few Americans who have no especial gift of speech-making, and he is not a great talker—at all events, he certainly makes no effort to shine in conversation, although it is not possible to converse with him for many minutes without discovering, if one did not know it before, that he is conversing with a man of original mind, of keen observation, and of humor as fresh as ever."[52]

It may be true that the old Bret Harte was not the writer and critic the 1870 Harte could have become. His was not the mind which the young Bret Harte might have developed. But Mark Twain was mis-

---

[50] Pemberton, *The Life of Bret Harte*, 334–35.   [51] *BHAE*, 325.
[52] Erskine, *Leading American Novelists*, 348–50.

taken in saying that when Bret Harte "started east in his newborn glory" in 1871, he "had lived all of his life that was to be respectworthy."[53] And the old "Argonaut and Exile" had within him more than one "sincere fiber."

[53] *MTE*, 267.

19

THE "MAN WITHOUT A COUNTRY"
WHO COULD NOT KEEP FRIENDS

... he was a man without a country; no, not man—man is too strong a term; he was an invertebrate without a country. He hadn't any more passion for his country than an oyster for its bed; in fact not so much and I apologize to the oyster.

He couldn't keep a friend permanently.

MARK TWAIN about BRET HARTE

I think our chance for being remembered in the future is the luck we have had in keeping the affections of our friends.

BRET HARTE, December 24, 1901

BRET HARTE SUFFERED from gossip about himself and his family, but the time came when, convinced of the futility of trying to combat such gossip, he would respond with a shrug and quote the motto of the Earls Mareschal of Aberdeen, which he had learned in Scotland: "They say. What say they? Let them say!"[1] But of all the rumors about himself, he found most incredible the report that he did not love his country. "Think of ME *being un-American* when I get into quarrels every day defending my country!" he exclaimed when he was consul in Glasgow.[2] From the beginning of his long years away from home to the end of his life, Bret Harte prided himself on being an American and was quick to take up the cudgels in his country's defense.

Mark Twain's assertion that Bret Harte "hadn't any more passion for his country than an oyster for its bed" provides a strange parallel with Mrs. James T. Fields's report of a conversation with Mark Twain in 1876. "He is so unhappy and discontented with our government that

---

[1] *BHAE*, 292.   [2] BHL, 194.

he says he is not conscious of the least emotion of patriotism in himself," wrote Mrs. Fields. Mark Twain "is overwhelmed with shame and confusion and wishes he were not an American. He thinks seriously of going to England to live, for a while, at least."[3]

To support his assertion that Harte had no feeling for his country, Twain cited Harte's failure to vote in the Presidential election of November, 1876. Mark Twain's criticism may have been justified. But in the context of Twain's own actions and his frequently articulated theories about universal suffrage, the intensity of his censure of Harte's failure to exercise his franchise provides another example of Twainian inconsistency.

At the time Mark Twain condemned Bret Harte for not voting, he called the victory of his own candidate, Hayes, "one of the Republican party's most cold blooded swindles of the American people."[4] During the campaign Mark Twain was somewhat surprised at his own enthusiastic participation, for this was the first Presidential election in which the forty-one-year-old Clemens had taken any great interest.[5] In one phase of the Presidential contest between Grover Cleveland and James G. Blaine, Mark Twain fully intended not to vote, and argued that not voting would be an act of patriotism. At that time he insisted that "if there was any valuable difference between being American and being a monarchist it lay in the theory that the American could decide for himself what is patriotic and what isn't."[6] In his Nevada days when the nation was at war over issues which most Americans recognized as moral as well as political, Mark Twain had exercised the right not to commit himself.

Mark Twain was unwilling to concede to Bret Harte the right to decide for himself what was patriotic because Twain was convinced that in the Hayes-Tilden conflict, Harte's failure to vote was motivated by sheer expediency. According to Twain, Harte was unwilling to commit himself to either side for fear of destroying his chances of a political appointment if the other side won. Another example of Mark Twain's strangely habitual coupling of Bret Harte and Orion Clemens can be found in this attack, for Mark ridiculed Orion for voting on the side of

[3] "Bret Harte and Mark Twain in the 'Seventies,'" *loc. cit.,* 347.
[4] *MTE,* 287.   [5] *MTH,* I, 151.
[6] Paine, *Mark Twain's Autobiography,* II, 17–18.

both Democrats and Republicans so that he would be safe "no matter who won." According to Mark, Orion also was motivated by a desire for political appointment.[7]

The Hayes-Tilden election occurred late in 1876, when Mark Twain and Bret Harte were collaborating on *Ah Sin* in Hartford. That Harte was extremely hard pressed for time as well as money probably explains his failure to return to New York to vote. On October 9 and 10, Harte had been in Washington in relation to the play *Two Men of Sandy Bar*, which he then believed a success.[8] In July, 1877, he was again in Washington, where he signed a contract with Don Piatt to edit a magazine to be called *The Capital*.[9] The efforts of Harte's friends to secure for him a political appointment apparently occurred after the magazine project fell through. Not until May 11, 1878, did Harte write his formal acceptance of the appointment as commercial agent of the United States at Crefeld, Germany.[10] Of course, Harte may have told Twain what Twain said he told him, but it seems very unlikely that Harte came to Hartford to escape voting or that he was seriously considering a political appointment at that time.

Throughout his voluminous writings Bret Harte criticized social injustices, political inequities, and other failures of American people to live up to the principles proclaimed in the Declaration of Independence and the American Constitution. But Bret Harte never questioned the soundness of the principles themselves.

During the year when, according to Mark Twain, Bret Harte failed to vote in a Presidential election, Twain was having a good deal to say against the American principle of universal suffrage, which he called "wicked" and "ungodly." Mrs. James T. Fields noted in her diary that in the summer before Mark Twain had confessed to her his complete loss of faith in our government, he had written an article, "printed without any signature," in which he had proposed as the only solution for the evil of universal suffrage giving every university man ten votes and "every man with common-school-education two votes, and a man of

[7] *MTH*, I, 253.
[8] Unpublished letters to Mrs. Harte, William Andrews Clark Memorial Library. Items 3 and 4 in *Calendar*.
[9] Unpublished letter to Mrs. Harte, William Andrews Clark Memorial Library. Item 6 in *Calendar*.
[10] *BHAE*, 245.

superior power and position a hundred votes, if we choose."[11] Apparently Mrs. Fields alluded to "The Curious Republic of Gondour," which was published anonymously. In fairness to Mark Twain it should be noted that in this essay, even though he argued that "brains and property" should manage the state, he insisted that education ought to control more votes than wealth.[12] In the following year Mark Twain wrote Mollie Fairbanks that he hated "all shades & forms of republican government, now—or rather with an intensified hatred, for I always hated them." He told her that he was trying to develop in young people and coming generations "an honest and saving loathing for universal suffrage."[13]

Mark Twain spoke and wrote many criticisms of monarchs and many loving words about American villagers, so that he is generally believed to have been an ardent democrat. Yet it is a mistake to conclude that his skepticisms of principles and practices of democracy were limited to the 1870's. Twenty years later, in 1897, Mark Twain professed to be "for republics" but wrote William Dean Howells: "I am appalled to notice that wide extension of the suffrage has damaged [England's] manners, & made her Americanly uncourteous on the lower levels."[14] During the years when Twain was expounding his most liberal theories, Howells wisely observed that he and Twain were "theoretical socialists, and practical aristocrats."[15] In his last years, when he was living luxuriously in Stormfield, modeled on an Italian villa, Mark Twain expressed the belief that a monarchy would be established in the United States. According to Albert Bigelow Paine, the possibility aroused in him only a thoughtful indifference.[16]

If Mark Twain sometimes wrote disparagingly of the crowned heads of Europe, he was mightily impressed to be in titled company. He said he was "stricken speechless" when he was applauded and asked to re-

[11] "Bret Harte and Mark Twain in the 'Seventies,'" *loc. cit.*, 347.

[12] Samuel L. Clemens, *The Curious Republic of Gondour*, 3–4, 8.

[13] *Mark Twain to Mrs. Fairbanks*, 208–209.

[14] *MTH*, II, 665. For a Twain attitude toward England approaching Harte's, see Blair, *Mark Twain & Huck Finn*, 188. When Professor Blair concludes that "Clemens left England in 1879 with a lowered opinion of the country," it is noteworthy that 1879 was the year that *Vanity Fair* included Bret Harte among its "Men of the Day" series and the year the President of the Royal Academy first invited Harte to respond to the toast "to Literature" at the Royal Academy Dinner.

[15] *MTH*, II, 628n.   [16] *Biography*, 1466–67.

spond to the toast to "literature" at a Guildhall dinner where new sheriffs and the lord mayor of London were to be installed, for he thought himself the "humblest" in that "great titled assemblage."[17] Although he grew more sophisticated, Mark Twain never really outgrew his awe of titles. "Scoffing democrats as we are, we do dearly love to be noticed by a duke, and when we are noticed by a monarch we have softening of the brain for the rest of our lives," he said.[18] Though intended to be ironic, this passage includes considerable truth about Mark Twain. Remembering his excitement at being invited to the rooms of the German Emperor's sister at the Hotel Metropole, Clara Clemens observed that her father's "inclination toward democratic passions" was "largely cultivated," whereas his "inclination to worship distinction of position" was "largely inborn."[19]

This was not true of Bret Harte. However, Harte, too, had his inconsistencies.

It may be remembered that not long before Mark Twain embarked on the *Quaker City* as correspondent for the *Alta California*, Bret Harte had satirized "Our Foreign Correspondence" for the practice of reporting that the most famed attractions of the Old World were invariably inferior to their counterparts in the New. In *The Innocents Abroad*, Mark Twain portrayed American tourists exhibiting similar chauvinism, which the author satirized so subtly that some American critics, failing completely to recognize Mark Twain's irony, called the book "the American literary declaration of independence from subservience to Europe's superiority."[20] Certainly, when he read and helped Mark Twain edit the manuscript, Bret Harte must have recognized and approved the irony.

After reaching Europe in 1878, however, Bret Harte's attitude made an about face. When his doctor in Crefeld ordered him to Switzerland for his health, Harte became terribly homesick. From the hills overlooking the Lake of Zurich, with "a few of the snow-capped Alps in sight," Bret wrote his son Frank that the steamer on which he trav-

---

[17] *LL*, 179. [18] Meltzer, *Mark Twain Himself*, 214.

[19] *My Father*, 205–206. For other examples of Mark Twain's attitude toward royalty and noble birth, see *MTH*, I, 439; II, 690, 693. And see Paine, *Biography*, 1070–71, 1385–86. See also Twain's comments on the decorum of noblemen's sons in *LL*, 185.

[20] Bellamy, *Mark Twain as a Literary Artist*, 167.

eled, "one of the largest on the Rhine," was "not as *large* nor half as *comfortable* or a quarter as *fast* as the old 'Sewanhaha.' " Of Swiss geography he reported: "I wish I could say that the hills were finer than the Californian Coast Range at Oakland, that the waters of the lake were bluer than Lake George, or that the sky was fairer than an American sky—but it is not." And with what seems to be a complete abeyance of his sense of humor, Bret Harte seriously demonstrated in a letter to his wife that very chauvinism which he and Mark Twain had both burlesqued in 1867: ". . . the Californian mountains and the Coast ranges are vastly superior to these famous Alps—in every respect. As the Rhine is inferior to the Hudson, so is Switzerland to California, and even to the Catskills in New York. The snow peaks visible from my windows are fine, but I have seen finer views from a wayside hotel in California country."[21]

Harte's growing popularity in Great Britain apparently served only to increase his professions of partiality for America. After a visit to Newstead Abbey, where he had been lionized, Harte expressed gratitude for the cordial hospitality of his hosts but told his wife, "for all that, I cannot say that I like England or should like to live there."[22] In Scotland he attributed much of his "mental and physical suffering" to lack of that sunshine which he believed living in California had made essential to his health. Compared with California, he said, his present existence was like living in a dark cellar. He wrote to Jessamy in the Adirondacks of his own longing for American scenery. In 1895, Harte's health was again so poor that he yielded to his doctor's urging and with his friend Colonel Arthur Collins traveled for several weeks in Germany and Switzerland, where he hoped to gain strength. His travels delighted him, and he discovered with surprise that after twelve years in the British Isles, he had suddenly developed a taste for wandering on the Continent. But new scenes recalled the past and the Sierras, now farther away and more inaccessible than ever. "I find my heart going back to the old Sierras, whenever I get above three thousand feet of Swiss altitude," he wrote Mrs. Boyd. And to his wife: "I never knew before how I really loved them, and how they have taken such a hold on my life."[23] Harte's characters and plots grew stale, but not the settings of his fiction. While he was writing even his poorest stories, Bret

[21] *BHL*, 148, 150.   [22] *Ibid.*, 96–97.   [23] *Ibid.*, 193, 229, 408, 412.

Harte, in the world of his imagination, returned day after day and year after year to California.

But during these years, what had happened to the Old Innocent? It may be remembered that in 1872, when he was first lionized in London, Mark had written to Mrs. Clemens: "I would rather live in England than America—which is treason."[24] In 1878 he wrote of the Swiss Alps: "There are mountains and mountains and mountains in this world, but only these take you by the heartstrings." In 1895, when Harte's thoughts were turning back to the Sierras, Twain—following the equator—told Mrs. Clemens that he never wanted to go back to America.[25] Of course, the author of *The Innocents Abroad* had a perfect right to express these sentiments. They may demonstrate that Twain had become less provincial than Harte. But they do not show that Mark Twain loved his country more than did Bret Harte.

Perhaps there is no trait more American than exercising the freedom to criticize America and things American. Even though Harte's fiction is threaded with social criticism of American failure to live up to American ideals, Harte was quick to defend his country and his countrymen against other critics, one of whom was Henry James. Bret Harte admired Henry James's early style and praised the freshness and originality of "Daisy Miller" as well as the vivid accuracy of James's sketches of Newport life in "An International Episode," but he considered James unduly nervous about the unconventionality of Americans abroad.[26] It was the nonconformity of Americans that Harte admired. At a time when "the best of England" seemed to Harte "seriously skeptical of the old and conservative" and "honestly striving toward the new and democratic," Harte found "American flunkeyism" and attempts to ape the English humiliating. Echoing Jean de Crèvecoeur, Harte asserted that 150 years of independence and relative isolation had made Americans into an essentially new and distinct people. And though he honestly admired much in the English character, he believed he was objective in finding Americans superior.

To what he called the " 'Jubilee' craze," Bret Harte reacted with

[24] *LL*, 177. [25] Paine, *Biography*, 637, 1017.
[26] *BHL*, 158–59, 163. Harte believed that, because of overexposure to "extreme Boston culture and European travel," Henry James "looks, acts, and thinks like an Englishman, and writes like an Englishman, I am sorry to say, excellent as his style is." This is probably one reason why Harte overemphasized his own American "flavour."

boredom. He kept away from the "wild, bewildering" celebrations as much as possible and looked forward to the time when "the sawdust and orange peel of the big Jubilee show is swept out of London and people have recovered their senses."[27] It seemed to him that he met "all New York and Boston" on the London streets, and so many Americans looked him up that Harte decided Madame Van de Velde's "quiet, foreign household" began to resemble an American ranch.[28] As always, Madame was a generous hostess and Harte was glad to see old friends, though their visits played havoc with his writing schedule. Harte does not mention seeing Twain, who was in London to write for American newspapers accounts of the Jubilee, which the Clemens family enthusiastically enjoyed.[29]

If Bret Harte objected to the American fervor for British titles, rank, and pageantry, he was even more critical of the privileges enjoyed by English aristocracy, many of whom were his friends. He was particularly indignant that the wealthy and titled could maintain in the midst of densely populated areas vast sporting estates on which partridges and pheasants were bred in order that the proprietors of the estates could come there two weeks out of the year for shooting, which Harte considered "not sport, but wholesale *butchery*."[30] During the period of great social unrest in the 1880's, when the poor were rioting in the streets of London and Henry James was seeing them as "the great army of roughs and thieves," Harte's sympathies were with "these terribly famished creatures," whom the upper classes had "patronized in workhouses, petted in hospitals, and kept at a distance generally with good-humoured tolerance."[31]

Harte's forthright criticisms of English class distinctions were not limited to Harte's family correspondence or dictated in memoirs to be guarded from publication for a hundred years. They were expressed at some length in fiction published in England as well as in America.[32]

[27] *Ibid.*, 277–78. See also pages 208, 272, 317, 331, 343, 444.   [28] *Ibid.*, 318.
[29] Paine, *Biography*, 1043; Clara Clemens, *My Father*, 185. Compare with *BHL*, 443. Harte's point of view was shared by John Hay, when he was ambassador to England.
[30] *BHL*, 320–21.
[31] Lionel Trilling, *The Liberal Imagination*, 74; *BHL*, 302–303.
[32] For example, see the beginning of Chapter V of "A Phyllis of the Sierras," a story ground out rather desperately for the Christmas issue of the *Illustrated London News*. *Writings*, VI, 323–25.

In 1895, when Harte was on a long-deferred visit to Lord Crewe (the brother of Mrs. Henniker), President Cleveland's message about Venezuela resulted in such tension between England and the United States that many believed war was inevitable. Without a moment's hesitation, Harte made it clear to his host that his loyalty was with the United States and if war occurred, he would return to America, even though he was convinced that financially he was far better off in England. "For much as I love my own country," Harte wrote his wife, "it does not love *me* sufficiently to enable me to support myself there by my pen."[33]

Harte did not wish to abuse the hospitality of a country to which he owed much,[34] but with his English associates he was so flagrantly American and made so many comparisons in favor of America that one wonders why his English friends put up with him. According to Madame Van de Velde, it was this very patriotism which endeared him to Englishmen, who were themselves intensely patriotic but soon lost respect for one who cared so little for his own country that he could quickly be won over to their point of view. In an article for the New York *Sun*, Madame wrote that this explained why Bret Harte was "extremely popular in England" and had always been so. Before Harte took up his residence in London, his originality had won him many admirers, she said, but when Englishmen had the opportunity to become acquainted with the man, "they promptly ascertained that no more uncompromising American had ever set foot among them." "Time has not dulled Bret Harte's instinctive affection for the land of his birth, for its institutions, its climate, its natural beauties, and above all, the character and moral attributes of its inhabitants." Madame predicted that eventually Harte could realize his "ardent wish" to return to America, that New York and San Francisco would hail his return, and that the whole nation would welcome its "long absent and distinguished son."

When this mass of silly gossip is sifted the bare and simple truth remains that Bret Harte leads a quiet, simple, dignified, and useful

[33] *BHL*, 418–19.

[34] Madame Van de Velde wrote: "Bret Harte has more than once been asked to lecture in England on English customs and English society, but he has always demurred. He is too grateful for the welcome tendered to him to risk repaying it with the apparent discourtesy of censure; he is too honest and frank to give indiscriminate praise or to lay himself open to the reproach of flattery." See Pemberton, *The Life of Bret Harte*, 225.

existence; that he goes into society less than any other conspicuous American living in London; that he never threw over the humblest of acquaintances for the highest or richest; that he is ever ready to oblige or assist a compatriot; that he faithfully and perseveringly devotes a portion of each day to his profession; and that he often has not known how his health and strength would enable him to meet the many engagements thrust upon him by publishers and editors.[35]

Although Madame Van de Velde came closer to the truth about Bret Harte's feeling for his country than did Mark Twain, her prophecy of his return to the United States was never fulfilled. "I am back again in London, in the fogs and smoke," Harte wrote his wife in October, 1896:

> I am afraid I cannot stand the whole winter here; year after year it seems the more terrible, and the days of semi-darkness harder to bear. Yet everything I get, in the way of criticism, advice, or comment, from America, tells me how utterly *alien* I and my writings have become in my own country—and how I must depend upon appreciations and standing here. When Max Nordau, the celebrated German philosopher and novelist, lately wrote that I was the "Columbus of American fiction" (whatever that means?), and that my countrymen did not appreciate me sufficiently, I thought it might strike some echo in America—but, alas! I have not seen even an allusion to it in my American publishers' *advertisements*!—while here it was copied largely and discussed.[36]

"I am always heartsick for my own country," Harte had written in 1878. Of this malady he was never cured.

In 1895, Bret Harte developed what was thought to be another cold and sore throat, which stubbornly failed to respond to treatment. He continued to write steadily, though sometimes he wrote with a hand so swollen and cramped with arthritis that he could hardly hold a pen. But cramped hand or not, he was trying to write a "long novel." "I don't want to be a cripple quite yet," he said.[37] And he kept on writing.

He was thankful that Watt always had orders for work ahead, but production became increasingly slow and difficult. "Everything lags with age," he noted. "These birthdays as the years go by are no laughing matter." Once when he was visited by Miss Griswold, with her com-

[35] *Ibid.,* 251–56.   [36] *BHL,* 433–34.   [37] *Ibid.,* 197, 423.

panion, a Latin teacher from Baltimore, Harte found the two women enthusiastic about a new kind of "religious 'fad,' " which they said was sweeping America. It was called "Christian Science." "They wonder I have never heard of it! Have you?" Harte asked Mrs. Boyd. "They have books upon it, they expound it to *me*. Our conversation is not flippant nor wildly entertaining."[38] With Miss Griswold he went to the Royal Leamington Spa. Though his doctors recommended them, Harte could not afford the European health resorts and baths haunted by the Clemens family during these years. Much as he enjoyed his travels in Switzerland, Bret Harte could not afford to prolong his stay or take the complete rest and change the doctor ordered.

The lag in his work caused by chronic illness and advancing age resulted in a "financial tightness" more acute than he had known in recent years. By 1899 he found it necessary to work "hard and continuously" to meet his expenses week by week. Because he could not *"really spare the time to go and come—which* would mean nearly *two days,"* Bret Harte had to cancel an Easter holiday he had hoped to spend with Pemberton and to postpone a visit to his wife in Caversham, where she was then living with Frank and Aline. He explained to Mrs. Harte that he was working day and night to finish a story for which he had received a partial advance. "I . . . must plod at my work until it is finished," he told her. "But I expect to be free by the 15th April, and then I will come. I am sorry to disappoint you again—but it is really harder upon me than you."[39]

Californians visiting London during these years naturally expected to meet the man whose stories about California had gained fame for himself as well as for the state. One Californian who inquired about Harte was told that he did not wish to meet Californians and that he would remain for her "a closed book."[40] She could not know that he was also seeing less and less of his English friends or that once he got back to writing after a siege of illness, he dared not stop lest he never get started again.

Bret Harte did not and could not see all those who wanted to meet him in London, but his letters include many affectionate references to

[38] *Ibid.*, 404, 464.   [39] *Ibid.*, 422, 461.
[40] Letter from Mrs. Ella Sterling Mighels to Professor George R. Stewart, Rare Books Department of the University of California Library in Berkeley.

old friends from California and the Atlantic seaboard. Occasionally Americans brought letters of introduction from his sister, Mrs. Wyman, in California. In 1880, Harte had written: "I have been very kindly treated and made much of during my stay in London. But I am more pleased at meeting my old friends of ten years ago, and finding them still loyal and true, than in making any new acquaintances." He continued to feel that way. On July 29, 1900, Bret Harte forsook all other plans in order to share a ten o'clock breakfast in London with "this old countryman of mine whom I have not seen for *thirty years*!" The countryman was Charles H. Clark, that early collaborator with Mark Twain and William Dean Howells on the *Library of Humor*. "I don't think you remember him," Bret wrote his son Frank, "but your mother will. He was Osgood's old partner in the old Osgood-Boston-Howells-Cambridge days. You surely remember Cambridge—and our staying with the Howells! Osgood and I used to treat him as an 'old fogey'—far too old-fashioned and stiff for us—and, lo and behold! here he was at breakfast looking unchanged—with scarcely a grey hair in his head— not a day older in appearance, and poor Osgood dead these five years, and *I* a doddering old Grandfather Whitehead!"[41]

James R. Osgood had been dead *more* than five years. In May, 1892, Bret Harte had attended his funeral.[42] James Anthony Froude died in 1894. Three years later, after a visit to Froude's daughter, Harte sadly wrote Mrs. Harte: "Froude and Lord Houghton were the *two Englishmen* that were equally a part of my American life, and now Froude is dead, and the late Lord Houghton's son is the Earl of Crewe—and even the name is forgotten."

But Bret Harte had little time to spend brooding. He continued to receive and occasionally to accept invitations. Most of the time he spent writing. Once he had told his wife: "I have little else to live for now but to leave a name, and I hope a little something more tangible to you and the children, and I only ask for health and strength to do that." But in May, 1901, he had to write her when she was in Paris with Ethel, who was studying singing under a French master: "My income, far from increasing, is continually becoming more and more uncertain. ... With the ailments I have, I am writing more slowly each year—and I have no *income* but from my pen. You must forgive my repeating this,

[41] *BHL*, 184, 462, 472, 486.   [42] Weber, *James Ripley Osgood*, 262.

but I do not think either you or Ethel or Frank realize it in your plans, or consider how precarious is the living I am making."

That year brought additional sadness in the death of Griswold, Harte's eldest son. At Christmas time, Harte wrote his grieving wife: "God knows it is a sorrowful Christmas—for you—for both of us. Happy only to the one *who has gone*." Sounding less like Mark Twain, Bret Harte added: "I hope you will not forget the living, for all that."[43]

As Harte approached the end of his own life, he became increasingly considerate, affectionate, and appreciative. Although there was not the sycophancy that surrounded Mark Twain's old age, Bret Harte did not lack attention from his family and he did not lack friends.[44]

First among Harte's friends was Madame Van de Velde, to whom he once wrote the following note to accompany a gift:

> MY DEAR FRIEND,—When I beg you to accept the enclosed portfolio I do not for a moment ever expect it to supplant the memory of the old one which is endeared to me by the recollection of the hours you have spent over it in deciphering my exasperating manuscripts and making them intelligible to the printer, or in giving them another chance for immortality by clothing them in the language of your own native land. I am only trying to symbolize in this little gift something of my gratitude to you as amanuensis, translator, critic, and above all— friend.
>
> I am not King of France or I should quote to *my* Prime Minister the words of Louis to Richelieu: "Lord Cardinal, you must take up again the *portfolio* you have laid down. In all my empire there is none worthy to follow you."—Always, dear friend, yours most gratefully,
>
> BRET HARTE[45]

Harte had always been appreciative of small kindnesses: a silk muffler monogrammed by his daughter-in-law, who was concerned about his throat; a box of "incomparable cigars" from his son, whom he chided for extravagance; the hand-embroidered shirt cases of which his wife and daughters seem to have sent him a good many; even the whiffs of feminine perfume which came from the packages in which such gifts were wrapped. Habitually he gave considerable thought to the selection

[43] *BHL*, 306–307, 449, 495, 500.

[44] DeLancey Ferguson, *Mark Twain: Man and Legend*, 310.

[45] Pemberton, *The Life of Bret Harte*, 239–40.

of personal gifts for his family and friends at Christmas time, but in 1901 he was too ill for his usual Christmas shopping. However, he sent each member of his family a little extra money, and he managed to secure for A. P. Watt a matchbox inscribed with words of affection. He hoped that Watt would not object to their sentimentalism. But greatly moved by messages and gifts from those who had thought of him during this season, Harte wrote Mr. Watt: "I think our chance for being remembered in the future is the luck we have had in keeping the affections of our friends."[46]

The words evoke memories of Emerson's aphorism carved on the mantelpiece of the library in the Clemens house at Hartford: "The ornament of a house is the friends who frequent it." Was Harte thinking of that once close friend whose affection he had lost?

One of the most devoted of Harte's English friends was T. Edgar Pemberton. On learning of one author's plans to publish a biography of Bret Harte without Harte's consent, Pemberton set about writing one of his own to forestall the other. For the hastily compiled *Bret Harte, a Treatise and a Tribute*, published in England in 1900, Harte wrote a prefatory note which began with a facetious reference to his biographer's "noble example of sacrifice on the altar of Friendship" and a recognition that in writing the biography, Pemberton was risking "the sneers of my enemies, the pity of my friends, and even the criticism of myself." The note to Pemberton concludes with an awkwardness unusual for Harte:

> What I am trying to say is, that I honestly thank you, even if, in looking over your pages, I shall be conscious . . . that I ought to be already dead to have so much good said of me, for there is still the chance of my trying to live up to your charming ideal of your friend, Bret Harte.[47]

Bret Harte's relationship with his first biographer was on a less businesslike basis than Mark Twain's relationship with Albert Bigelow Paine, who in 1906 began work on the authorized biography of Mark Twain.[48] Pemberton was obviously impressed by Harte's fame and his skill as a writer, and Harte's was the dominant personality, but Harte tried not to impose on Pemberton's friendship. "I don't want to come to you an invalid," he once replied to Pemberton's urgent invitation for

[46] *BHL*, 501. [47] Pemberton, *Bret Harte, A Treatise and a Tribute*, vi.
[48] *MTH*, II, 794.

Harte to visit him. "I sometimes think, in fact, that I ought not to inflict myself on anybody but a callous hotel-keeper, or a regular Gordon Hotel Company, Limited." In May, 1901, when Pemberton was "dangerously ill," Harte stayed with him at his home until Pemberton was better. Expressing admiration for his friend as an *"indomitable worker,* a perfectly cheerful, generous, noble spirit" in the face of an incurable disease from which he had been suffering for years, Bret Harte's letter gave no hint to Mrs. Harte that he himself was even more dangerously ill than Pemberton.[49]

Bret Harte's last letter to his wife was written from 74, Lancaster Gate, W., on January 17, 1902, just before Harte left for the seaside in obedience to his doctor's orders. Harte thanked his wife for a kind and sympathetic note which he had received from her and assured her that he knew she would do all she could for him in his illness if she had the opportunity.

> Had you been in the country this winter with Frank, I should have probably been with you, and you would have had an invalid on your hands! My principal trouble now is a very sluggish *sore throat* (ulcerated) which puzzles the doctor with its slowness of improvement, although he says now it is mending. If the air of Southsea does *not* improve me—or even if it *does*—I still hope to come down to Tunbridge Wells while you are there. With love to all, your affectionate
>
> LIMICK.[50]

The sore throat was cancer, from which he had been suffering for seven years. Some of Bret Harte's gayest and most humorous fiction was written when he was in the greatest pain, and one of his last stories, about Colonel Starbottle, shows some of his old power.

"Pardon this brief line, as my 'foot is in the stirrup,' " Harte wrote Mrs. Boyd in January, 1902. In March he submitted to a throat operation, which was not successful. Even about the operation, Harte could joke, for he wrote Pemberton: "Tell your medical student son that the operation and the instrument were so fascinating that they delighted even the victim." But Pemberton guessed that Harte was aware of the seriousness of his condition.[51] On May 5, while he was writing at his desk in the Van de Velde home, Harte suffered a severe hemorrhage.

[49] *BHL,* 401, 493. [50] *Ibid.,* 502–503.
[51] Pemberton, *The Life of Bret Harte,* 338–39.

He died before the end of the day. By order of Madame Van de Velde, these words from Harte's poem "Reveille" were inscribed on the slab of red granite covering Bret Harte's grave in Frimley Churchyard near Camberley, England:

Death shall reap a braver harvest.

On an adjoining side of the stone were chiseled the words "In faithful remembrance, M. S. Van de Velde," and every year until Madame Van de Velde died, a wreath was placed on the stone.[52]

Although only members of the family, Madame Van de Velde, and a few other friends attended the burial services, Harte's death by no means passed unnoticed. On both sides of the Atlantic, newspapers carried obituaries, and a good many writers were prompted to publish reminiscences. A few raked up the old rumors, some of them stupid and cruel, which had shaped the legend of Bret Harte. But most of the comments were kind. The London correspondent of the New York *Times* reported that far from being a snob, Bret Harte had been "a modest and unassuming gentleman," and the correspondent doubted that Harte had an enemy in London. The *London Literary World* declared that of the many literary men who had died during the year, Harte was the most loved. G. K. Chesterton wrote with admiration of the international quality of Harte's humor, and Watts-Dunton in the *Athenaeum* warmly praised Bret Harte as a man and as a writer. To those who had considered Harte a writer spoiled by prosperity, the greatest surprise came with the publication of Harte's will, documenting the fact that his total property came to less than $2,000.[53] As Bret Harte once warned Mrs. Henniker: "When you sell your books outright for a 'lump sum' only the publisher profits by the 'boom.'"[54]

In America the news of Harte's death evoked in Aldrich and Howells bittersweet memories of a "careless, blithe spirit" who had belonged to their own younger and happier years. "Bret Harte's death brought me the sadness it brought you, and the memories," Aldrich wrote Howells. "Now-a-days when an old friend or companion dies, all the other dear old friends and companions die over again."[55] If the blithe spirit could have returned to its old haunts in the West, it might have enjoyed

[52] *BHAE*, 333.
[53] *Ibid.*, 327–29.
[54] Unpublished letter, Oct. 2, 1891, BL.
[55] *Life in Letters*, II, 158.

another princely progress. For during the nineties, the name of Bret Harte had taken on new magic in California, and throughout the state it had been freely bestowed on schools, libraries, hospitals, and hotels. The spirit of the man who had never owned a home had acquired in California a broad domain identified on tourist maps as the "Bret Harte Country." And in San Francisco, members of the Bohemian Club (which still wears on one ivy-clad wall a bronze plaque showing Bret Harte's best-known characters) assembled on an October evening to recall ghosts of the past and to "do honor to One who has honored by his genius all Californians—the late Francis Bret Harte."[56]

In September, 1902, the *Overland Monthly* published a Bret Harte Memorial Number. Not all the writers were friendly. But among the contributors were Noah Brooks, John Hay, Charles A. Murdock, Josephine Clifford McCrackin, and Ina Coolbrith, whose loyalty and sincerity can hardly be questioned. Another contributor was Joaquin Miller, one of the staunchest and most enduring of all Harte's friends. The sentimentality of Miller's tribute entitled "Good By, Bret Harte" should not blind us to the substance of his testimony:

> *You loved the lowly, laughed at pride,*
> *We mocked, we mocked and pierced your side;*
> *And yet for all harsh scoffings heard,*
> *You answered not one unkind word,*
> *But went your way, as now.*[57]

From London, Bret Harte had once sent to California a message: "Tell Ina Coolbrith I shall never forget."[58] Ina Coolbrith did not forget either. Her contribution to the *Overland* memorial issue was a poem resembling Harte's tribute to Dickens, whom he acknowledged his master. Eight or nine years after Harte's death Ina Coolbrith wrote

[56] Program—"Bret Harte Jinks," Bohemian Club, San Francisco, Oct. 24, 1903.

[57] *Overland Monthly*, Vol. XL (Sept., 1902), 218. This issue includes no comment from Mark Twain, but in a section devoted to pictures of distinguished contributors, the magazine published an early photograph of "Samuel L. Clemens humorist." The issue also included a Guptill pen sketch of an older Mark Twain. The sketch was followed by a reprint of "The Jumping Frog of Calaveras" with an "introductory and explanatory note by J. G. H." reporting the reminiscences of "a well-known citizen of San Francisco" about the incident in Swain's office when Mark Twain told the story to Bret Harte and Harte urged him to write it. See pages 287–88.

[58] *BHAE*, 169.

Henry Childs Merwin about Harte's assistance to her as a contributor to the *Overland* when Harte was editor. Among other things, Miss Coolbrith said: "I can only speak of him in terms of unqualified praise as author, friend and man."[59]

It may be remembered that before Albert Bigelow Paine became Mark Twain's official biographer, William Dean Howells had been unresponsive to Harper and Brothers' suggestions that he write his friend's biography.[60] After Mark Twain's death, however, Howells wrote the warmly affectionate *My Mark Twain*, which—notwithstanding Howells' love and magnanimity—included some observations which Howells would not have felt free to make while Twain was still living.[61] Mark Twain had announced his original intention of telling the whole truth about himself in his autobiography, and in March, 1907, had given Paine a written recommendation "to any friend or acquaintance" that Paine, "my biographer & particular friend," should be accorded the "fullest trust & confidence."[62] Even so, in 1908, Mark Twain stopped Howells, Twichell, and Mark's nephew Sam Moffett from giving Paine access to Twain's letters before Twain himself had a chance to decide whether he wanted "those privacies exposed." "A man should be dead before his private foolishnesses are risked in print."[63]

Pemberton's devotion to his friend as well as the haste with which *Bret Harte, a Treatise and a Tribute* was compiled weakened that biography. After Harte's death Pemberton set about revising and enlarging the biography published during Harte's lifetime, but he seems not to have been motivated by a desire for greater freedom. His second biography, *The Life of Bret Harte*, published by Dodd, Mead and Company in 1903, shows little more critical detachment than the earlier work. But in relation to Mark Twain's "portrait" of a friendless Bret Harte, it should be noted that Pemberton's admiration and affection color every page of both biographies, and that these had been published in England and America six and three years respectively before Mark Twain re-

---

[59] Merwin, *The Life of Bret Harte*, 49.   [60] *MTH*, II, 724.

[61] I have in mind his account of the collaboration on "Colonel Sellers as a Scientist"; the reception of Mrs. Clemens in England, with its indication of why she did not like England so well as did her husband; and Howells' comments about Twain's failure to return Howells' visits while the two were living some blocks apart in New York.

[62] Paine, *Biography*, frontispiece for Vol. I.

[63] *MTH*, II, 828.

corded his own reminiscences of Bret Harte. Perhaps Mark Twain felt that he should set the record straight. But if Twain looked inside Pemberton's second biography, he must have known that Harte kept more than one friend permanently. For on learning of Pemberton's new work in progress, many individuals who had known Harte in England and in America wrote Pemberton letters, several of which he published. And these letters are far from perfunctory tributes to a dead celebrity.

Most of the letters from personal friends had two elements in common: an affirmation of friendship, and mention of Harte's fundamental kindness and lack of malice. For example, Miss Mary C. Froude, daughter of James Anthony Froude, wrote: "His friends all loved him. I loved him very much, and greatly because he was such a true friend of my father's. He was also more than kind to me, and I always reverenced his high-minded generous self, and his utter aloofness from aught mean or nasty." The Marquis of Northhampton, whom Harte had visited at the historic old estates of Compton Wynyates and Castle Ashby (a smaller, older, and more picturesque edition of Hampton Court), wrote: "I cannot in words say how sad I am and how terribly I feel at the loss of my good friend. I not only loved him, but I respected him and long to let the world know what he really was—very human but with such noble intentions and feelings."[64] The last example I shall cite of friends who wrote to Pemberton was John Hay, who should be remembered not only as secretary of state and American ambassador to England but as the secretary and biographer of Abraham Lincoln. In the *Overland* memorial issue, Hay had called Harte "my dear and honored friend," and had described him as "a great American" and "one of the most attractive and charming figures of the nineteenth century."[65] Hay wrote Pemberton: "His gentle and amiable personality endeared him to all who were admitted to the privilege of his intimacy; his great achievements in literature made his fame a substantial national possession."[66]

Mark Twain could have read those letters. But he could not have known that the most convincing single refutation of his assertion that Bret Harte could not keep a friend permanently was Charles A. Murdock, who had known Harte in Uniontown, California, in 1857, when Harte was a shy and rather inept twenty-one and Murdock was sixteen

---

[64] Pemberton, *The Life of Bret Harte*, 341.   [65] Page 230.   [66] Page 342.

and the son of one of the founders of the *Northern Californian*. Murdock's father had given young Harte his first job as a writer. Before becoming proprietor of the publishing firm of Charles A. Murdock and Company, of San Francisco, young Murdock had worked for a while on the *Morning Call* when Bret Harte was also employed by that periodical. In Murdock's *A Backward Glance at Eighty*, a chapter entitled "The Real Bret Harte" proves that in all the years from 1857 to 1921, Harte had not lost the affection of this friend. "He was sensitive, peace-loving, and indignant at wrong, a scorner of pretense, independent in thought, just in judgment," wrote Murdock. "Whatever his shortcomings and whatever his personal responsibility for them, he deserves to be treated with the consideration and generosity he extended to others. . . . He was quite capable of suffering in silence if defense of self might reflect on others.

"Bret Harte at our hands need not be idealized, but he does deserve to be justly, gratefully, and fittingly realized."[67]

[67] Pages 96–98.

20

THE PLEASANTEST AND THE UNPLEASANTEST MAN
MARK TWAIN EVER KNEW

> There was a happy Bret Harte, a contented Bret Harte, an ambitious
> Bret Harte, a hopeful Bret Harte, a bright, cheerful, easy-laughing
> Bret Harte, a Bret Harte to whom it was a bubbling and effervescent
> joy to be alive. . . .
>
> Bret Harte was one of the pleasantest men I have ever known. He
> was also one of the unpleasantest men I have ever known.
>
> *Mark Twain in Eruption*

THE LIFE OF MARK TWAIN after 1877 is much better known than the
life of Bret Harte. Accounts of Mark Twain's great love and his great
hates, his great tenderness and his great sorrow, his great business failure
which led to his great personal triumph, and—greatest of all—his great
book have been repeated too often to require another summary here.
But a paralleling of some aspects of his life with Harte's affords many
of those dramatic contrasts which played so large a part in the writings
of both authors. Any listing of these contrasts is hazardous, however, for
like every other aspect of Mark Twain's life, the contrasts themselves
include counterpoints and contradictions.

In noting these contrasts, it is by no means my intention to denigrate
Mark Twain's good qualities, which were many, or to minimize his
achievements, which speak for themselves. My purpose is simply to
place Mark Twain's words about Bret Harte in context and to invite
observation from a generally ignored point of view. It seems to me
that this perspective, as a complement to other views, contributes to a
more comprehensive and accurate understanding of both writers.

A basic contrast in the lives of Bret Harte and Mark Twain appears in
their family relations. Mrs. Clemens was the steady half of the compass,
about which her husband's emotional life revolved. When the Clemens

daughters—Susy, Clara, and Jean—were young, they could be enjoyed and entertained in a Hartford house large enough and with servants enough to keep children from becoming too distracting though beloved responsibilities. George, the Negro butler; Patrick McAleer, the coachman; John and Ellen O'Neill, the gardner and his wife; and the ever faithful Katie Leary (who in the days of relative "poverty" accompanied the family to Europe) made it their main business in life to see that Mark Twain was comfortable. Even though the passing years brought many illnesses to Mrs. Clemens and the children, and the time came when the owners of the great Hartford house considered themselves among the dispossessed, always there was the family unit, knit close by Livy's love and care, and here Mark Twain found refuge and succor even in times of turbulence generated by himself.

Also solicitous for Mark Twain's comfort was his sister-in-law, Mrs. Theodore Crane. At Quarry Farm, near Elmira, New York, where the Clemens family spent many summers, Mrs. Crane built for Mark an octagonal, many-windowed workshop at a safe distance from the farmhouse with its bustling servants and playful children. About ten in the morning, Mark Twain would walk across sunlit fields to the pleasant room overlooking the city, a miniature river, and the hazy blue of distant hills. There he remained until about five o'clock, when he returned to his family. And while he was working, "other members of the family did not venture near the place."[1] In this glass-enclosed, carefully protected study, Huckleberry Finn began and ended his picaresque voyage on a raft down the Mississippi River.

Nook Farm was itself an extension of Mark Twain's family. The author of an admirable study of this neighborly community aptly identifies it as "Mark Twain's Hartford Circle." Social acceptance, so slowly and grudgingly yielded Mark Twain by the literary leaders of Cambridge and Boston, was readily given by the Warners, the Hookers, the Twichells, and Harriet Beecher Stowe.[2] From the beginning, Mark had been aware that Hartford was an expensive place to live, and he did not move there until the income from his books and lectures together with his wife's family fortune made it possible for him to compete and excel in this milieu. When he did move there, he built a show place and kept open house for the world. Visitors were sometimes surprised by the

[1] Paine, Biography, 508. [2] Andrews, *Nook Farm*, 18.

bourgeois conservatism in which the author of *The Innocents Abroad* now seemed so much at home.

To live in Hartford as Mark Twain did, to enjoy his family as he did, and to keep open house as he did required money. One significant contrast between the personal lives of Mark Twain and Bret Harte was that Mark had money—lots of money—and Bret did not. As Twain wrote Howells in 1878, it seemed to him that the Clemens family was "fixed at last," that there was more than enough income from investments for the family to live in Harftord on a "generous scale." And live on a generous scale they did. In 1881, Twain paid $12,000 for one hundred feet of land adjoining his own grounds so that he would not be disturbed by too close neighbors.[3] During the summer of the same year the big house—now seven years old—was remodeled and extensively decorated by Tiffany.[4] The walls were ornamented with silver. Although Twain had so bitterly resented what he considered Harte's presumptuous criticism of the original furnishings, apparently Mr. and Mrs. Clemens decided that they did not like them very well either. Mark Twain wrote Charles Warren Stoddard in Hawaii that what the place really needed was an "incendiary." Records assembled at the beginning of 1882 show that during the preceding year, Mark Twain had spent "considerably more" than $100,000.[5] Mr. Paine notes that this "would cramp most authors" and "it was not the best financing, even for Mark Twain. It required all that the books could earn, all the income from the various securities, and a fair sum from their principal."

Mark Twain, like Bret Harte, could spend beyond his means, but Mark had more means to spend beyond. Every year, as the Hartford house grew and living became more lavish, guests were more numerous. Mark Twain had a separate telephone wire from his house to the Western Union telegraph office.[6] In 1884, for a birthday present to his wife, Twain could order from Tiffany's "a diamond solitaire ring . . . to cost $250 or $300."[7] By the time he was fifty, Mark Twain was frightened at the proportions of his own prosperity. It seemed to him that whatever he touched turned to gold. As we have noted, at the age of fifty, Bret Harte lost his consulate in Glasgow and spent many anxious

---

[3] Paine, *Biography*, 661, 714–15.
[4] See Andrews, *Nook Farm*, 81–82.
[5] Paine, *Biography*, 714, 729.
[6] Webster, *Mark Twain: Business Man*, 137.
[7] *LL*, 221n.

hours worrying about whether he would be able to write and sell enough stories to continue to send his wife and children $250 a month.

Unlike Bret Harte at this age, Mark Twain seemed to have boundless energy to invest in a growing number of literary, business, and political enterprises.[8] But Mark was too disorganized to co-ordinate his affairs, and the growing tangle made him increasingly suspicious and irritable. In 1882, Mark left Hartford for a trip down the Mississippi accompanied by the convivial publisher James R. Osgood. Ten years earlier Osgood had been Twain's companion on a sight-seeing tour in England, and four years earlier Osgood had been with Harte when the newly appointed Commercial Agent crossed the Atlantic to take up his duties in Crefeld.[9] It was Osgood, Harte's publisher since 1870, who brought out *The Prince and the Pauper* in 1881 and *Life on the Mississippi* in 1883. Before long, however, Mark Twain became convinced that Osgood was not nearly so good a promoter as Elisha Bliss and that by failing to sell fifty thousand copies of Twain's last book, Osgood had, in fact, injured him.[10] By 1884, Twain was suggesting that if Osgood did not pay up "instantly" a sum of $825 which Mark believed Osgood owed, Charles Webster should sue him "before he gets out of the country." By February, 1885, Twain was writing Webster: "Glad to be rid of Osgood." And when Osgood's publishing house failed three months later, Mark Twain commented: "Osgood's busted at last. It was sure to come."[11]

Mark Twain turned down innumerable invitations to lecture, because, he told Thomas Nast, "traveling alone is so heartbreakingly dreary," and "shouldering the whole show is such a cheer-killing responsibility."[12] But in 1884, Mark Twain went on a lecture tour with George Washington Cable, who not only irritated Twain by his piety and penuriousness but also wore out Twain's patience by having mumps in the Clemenses' home. Guy Cardwell has thoroughly discounted the assumption that tensions developing between Twain and Cable during the tour were

---

[8] Paine, *Biography*, 723–28, 830.

[9] *LL*, 177.

[10] Webster, *Mark Twain: Business Man*, 223, 232; Blair, *Mark Twain & Huck Finn*, 356.

[11] Webster, *Mark Twain: Business Man*, 261, 300, 321. See also *MTE*, 158, and *MTH*, *II*, 527.

[12] Paine, *Biography*, 612.

due to Cable's envy.[13] But more than once Mrs. Clemens felt it necessary to urge her husband not to excoriate Cable in public. She reminded Twain that Cable was a good man, a good friend, and an asset on the lecture tour.[14]

Lecturing with Cable and politicking for Cleveland in 1884 by no means used up all Twain's energy. Neither did his newly established publishing firm which, under the management of Charles L. Webster, helped to make *The Adventures of Huckleberry Finn* one of the great financial successes of the nineteenth century.[15] Like a good many other prosperous Americans of that era, the Clemens family was inclined to regard the possession of property as a moral virtue and the lack of money an embarrassment close to sin.[16] Mark Twain strove manfully for more of this kind of virtue, and even the great affluence which he had already achieved failed to satisfy him. He dreamed of new enterprises which would bring in vast new sums of money. He began to think and talk not in terms of thousands but of millions of dollars.

To win millions, Mark Twain found writing and publishing too slow. Inventions were quicker—or so it seemed. And the most marvelous and intricate of all the inventions which interested him at this time was the Paige typesetting machine. While Bret Harte was struggling to write enough stories to compensate his family for the loss of the consular salary of $3,000 a year, Mark Twain "for 44 consecutive months" was feeding more than $3,000 a month to the Paige invention until the monster consumed about $190,000 in cash.[17] By 1887 money was not flowing so freely in the Hartford household. Plans for a summer trip abroad, which Mrs. Clemens had intended for its educational value to the children, were sacrificed to the Paige typesetting machine. And Mrs. Clemens, worried to see Youth worried, began to "economize." But she never complained that the financial security of her family as well as her inherited fortune had been undermined.[18] Albert Bigelow Paine reports

[13] See *LL*, 219, 223, 232, 234–35, 237; then see Cardwell, *Twins of Genius*, 118n.

[14] Letters from Mrs. Clemens in New York to Samuel L. Clemens, Nov. 21 and Nov. 24, 1884, MTP.

[15] Webster, *Mark Twain: Business Man*, 301.

[16] Brooks, *The Ordeal of Mark Twain*, 68–69, 116; see also Paine, *Biography*, 983.

[17] *MTH*, II, 615. Paine, *Biography*, 914; see also pages 911–12 for Paine's statement that the machine absorbed $4,000 a month.

[18] *LL*, 255–57.

that at this time Mark Twain's life was a "fevered delirium, often a veritable nightmare," and that reporters, "little guessing what he was passing through," believed Mark's fame and fortune had gone to his head and made him "crusty and sour."[19] In 1891 the Hartford house was closed.

To economize, the Clemens family went to Europe. Their frugalities included a villa in Florence with a full staff of servants, including a coachman.[20] From Florence the family moved to Paris, where they economized by transferring from a hotel to a four-bedroom furnished house with rent of $250 a month. Servants for the Clemenses' ménage in Paris included a cook, a manservant, and a chambermaid. This arrangement, costing about $1,000 a month, Twain estimated would save him $200 a month in housekeeping expenses.[21] In addition to household expenses there were, of course, private schools for the girls, health pilgrimages to various spas, and medical bills from which the Clemens family was never free. Thus the family went on "scrimping" for the Paige typesetting machine. To eke out the family income, Mark Twain turned again to his pen. In the depression year of 1893 he sold "The Esquimau Girl's Romance" to *Cosmopolitan* for $800 (which he kept for his own living expenses) and *Pudd'nhead Wilson* to *Century* for $6,500 (which he sent to his wife.)[22]

The Paige typesetting machine devoured not only the earnings of Mark Twain's publications and a large portion of his wife's estate, but also the funds of Charles L. Webster and Company. In 1893 that firm's liabilities approximated $200,000, including about $60,000 of Mrs. Clemens' money.[23] On April 18, 1894, the company failed. This is generally regarded as the lowest point in Mark Twain's financial career. According to Mark Twain, at this time he and his wife had in the bank "but" $9,000.[24] However, in addition to what Mark could earn from his writing, the Clemens family could count on $6,000 a year from Mrs. Clemens' property.[25] At the peak of his financial career Bret Harte had signed a contract which brought him $10,000, probably the largest

---

[19] *Biography*, 912.   [20] *LL*, 263.

[21] Letter of Nov. 6, 1894, to H. H. Rogers, MTP.   [22] *LL*, 267.

[23] Paine, *Biography*, 969. According to the New York *Times* of Sept. 19, 1894, the liabilities of the Webster Company were $94,191, and its net assets, $54,164. See Fatout, *Mark Twain on the Lecture Circuit*, 238.

[24] *MTE*, 193.   [25] Ferguson, *Mark Twain: Man and Legend*, 259.

sum he ever owned at one time in his life. When Bret Harte's finances struck rock bottom just before his Crefeld appointment, he had no money in the bank and $20 in his pocket. Obviously, there are degrees of bankruptcy. But Mark Twain made his bankruptcy legal and official. His copyrights were transferred to Mrs. Clemens, as one of his creditors. He had some difficulty remembering to say "Mrs. Clemens's books," "Mrs. Clemens's copyrights," "Mrs. Clemens's type-setter stock."[26]

Years before, in those desperate days in Washington after the failure of *Ah Sin*, when Bret Harte was worrying that his wife might be left without money in a strange hotel, he had concluded a letter to his "dear, good, patient Nan": "If I could do anything by being *there*, more than I am doing here, I would come. *But I must come with money*."[27] The words Harte underlined in this letter were permanently underscored in his mind. From Crefeld, at the beginning of his long years of separation from his family, Harte had written:

> I have got all your letters. Don't think, Nan, because I have not spoken of them, that they are not anything to me, and that all you tell me of the children and their sayings, and your own thoughts, is not as grateful as the blue sky to me, but I try to stop thinking of you and them and the distance between, and how much yet has to be done, and how I must keep up my strength to do it; for, when I do, I become utterly despondent.[28]

In a letter from Nevada, Mark Twain once declared that he would never see his mother or sister again or revisit his home until he could return a rich man. He could not bear the thought of being "pitied and snubbed" because of failure.[29] In his dark days of 1894, Mark Twain wrote his wife (who for reasons of economy was on the other side of the Atlantic for the better part of four years): "Every night I say to myself 'I *must* see the wife & the children, if only for one day'—but have to follow it with 'Hold your grip & don't be a fool—you've *got* to stay here till this thing is settled.!' "[30]

Mark Twain did not make his fight for financial solvency "single-

[26] *LL*, 301.   [27] *BHL*, 61.   [28] *Ibid.*, 88.
[29] Paine, *Biography*, 199; *Roughing It*, 212.
[30] Clara Clemens, *My Father*, 97; *LL*, 289–90.

handed." He was aided by the very dexterous hands of Henry H. Rogers, multimillionaire and financier of the Standard Oil Company of New Jersey. It was on Rogers' advice and Mrs. Clemens' insistence that Mark Twain set out to pay back dollar for dollar the indebtedness of Charles L. Webster and Company. Mrs. Clemens was in considerable anxiety that Mark Twain might not do right by his creditors, for Twain himself—regarding the settlement of claims as a "tug of war" with his creditors in the game of bankruptcy—urged Mrs. Clemens to leave such matters to him and Rogers, who knew what they were doing.[31]

When Mark Twain made his lecture tour around the world with the highly publicized aim of working himself out of debt, he did not have to suffer the "heartbreaking dreariness" of traveling alone. He was accompanied not only by J. B. Pond, his manager, but also by Mrs. Clemens and their daughter Clara. When, after the death of Susy in 1896, the Clemens family withdrew from the world and secluded themselves in Chelsea, a wild rumor circulated and even gained five-column headlines in a newspaper that Mark Twain's family had deserted him and that he was laboring—ill, alone, and in poverty—to pay his debts. Mark Twain was never really alone, except as every human being is ultimately alone. After his Nevada days, he was never really impoverished. When his financial affairs were plummeting toward bankruptcy, he was able to commute freely between England or France and America. And when he was circling the globe to lecture, Henry Rogers was looking out for Mark Twain's affairs in America, including all complications relating to manuscripts, the Paige typesetting machine, and the failure of Charles L. Webster and Company.[32]

Mark Twain's creditors, with faith in Twain's integrity and the security of his relation with Rogers, were for the most part extraordinarily lenient with him. When one creditor to whom Mark Twain owed $4,500 had him hauled into court for questioning about possible concealed property, there was a storm of editorial protest from newspapers.[33] So great was the sympathy for Mark Twain's dire financial straits that the New York *Herald* solicited contributions to a relief fund to be known as "The American Fund for Mark Twain," and "All Boys

---

[31] *LL*, 298–302, 305–309.   [32] Paine, *Biography*, 1025, 1080–81.

[33] Letter to H. H. Rogers, July 14, 1895. See also the New York *Recorder* (July 15, 1895), MTP.

Who Have Been Entertained" were called upon to "Swell the Amount."[34] One subscriber set about organizing "As Many Ten Cent Clubs as Possible" to supplement other contributions. Mark Twain rather liked the whole idea, but on the cabled advice of Rogers and Bliss, his publisher, as well as the quick and emphatic disapproval of Mrs. Clemens when she learned what was going on, Mark Twain declined the help offered.[35]

Mark Twain estimated that in one lecture season in the United States he could earn $25,000 to $30,000.[36] In his lecture tour around the world he earned considerably more than that. And notwithstanding his professed scorn for the romantic Sir Walter Scott, he had no objection to being compared with Scott in his resolve to pay off debts for which he could not be held legally responsible, for he well knew that this kind of publicity increased attendance at his lectures. It also helped to sell his books.

By January, 1898, Mark Twain had succeeded in paying the last creditor. Before long, with the help of Rogers' investments, he had $50,000 to his credit. He was writing with renewed vigor. Early in 1899 he could inform Howells that Mrs. Clemens had been figuring again and proved to him not only that the Clemens family still owned a house and furniture in Hartford but also that Mark Twain's English and American copyrights brought him an income worth $200,000. Best of all, the family now had $107,000 in the bank. That the Clemens family did not return to the Hartford house was due not to lack of funds but to the fact that after Susy's death, the place had too many painful associations.[37] In 1901, Twain was ready to offer for $60,000 the house, stables, and grounds which he estimated had cost a total of $142,000.[38] After Mrs. Clemens' death, Twain lived in many different places. But wherever he was, he had no need to economize, and Albert Bigelow Paine records that at seventy-five, Mark Twain spent freely, his household expenses alone amounting to more than $50 a day.

Of all the luxuries which Mark Twain enjoyed, perhaps Bret Harte

[34] Meltzer, *Mark Twain Himself*, 201.
[35] Fatout, *Mark Twain on the Lecture Circuit*, 267.
[36] Letter to H. H. Rogers, July 20, 1895, MTP.
[37] Paine, *Biography*, 1056, 1058, 1073, 1112; *MTH*, II, 684.
[38] Letter from Samuel L. Clemens to Frank Whitmore, Oct. 15, 1901, MTP. At a later period his estimate was $167,000. See *MTE*, 192.

found most enviable those periods of not writing, when flagging creative impulses could be given a chance to generate new power. Though once he got started, Mark Twain was capable of intense and steady industry, he could afford to wait for the "call" to work. During the winters, notwithstanding the possibility of retreat to the "third-story remoteness" of the billiard room where *Ah Sin* had been put together, Mark Twain did little writing. More often the billiard room functioned orthodoxly as a place for billiard-playing with billard lovers, though few were so ardent as Mark Twain. Here there was much yarn-spinning with congenial souls who smoked until "the room was blue" and comforted themselves with "hot Scotch and general good-fellowship." Furthermore, Mark Twain reveled in the intensely emotional life of his family and community. He enjoyed games with the children, charades and amateur theatricals with the neighbors' children, the reading aloud of favorite authors (especially Browning), teas, dances, dinner parties, and the extra festivities of Christmas and birthdays. They stimulated him. Also stimulating were the Friday Evening Club, the Saturday Morning Club, and frequent visits to New York, where more and more he was lionized.

Much of Mark Twain's writing was done during the summers in his study at Quarry Farm.[39] But if a year passed when Mark Twain was not inclined to work, he didn't. He could afford to put aside his writing of *Huckleberry Finn* in order to devise a history game for his children.[40] A profitable project of one year was a scrapbook, in which he wrote no words at all. After the collapse of his hopes for the Paige typesetter and the failure of Charles L. Webster and Company, Mark Twain turned again to his pen for a substantial portion of his income. But this dependence on literature for income was for Mark Twain the first in twenty years.

A little more than twenty years earlier Mark Twain had testified that Bret Harte had taught him to write paragraphs and chapters which had won the approval of discriminating readers. Later he had written William Dean Howells: "I owe as much to your training as the rude country job-printer owes to the city boss who takes him in hand and teaches him

[39] Paine, *Biography*, 507, 611, 613–14, 620–21.
[40] Webster, *Mark Twain: Business Man*, 126. See also *MTH*, I, 440n.

the right way to handle his art."[41] Mark Twain, in his turn, once gave Mrs. Fairbanks some excellent advice about the business of writing: "Publish for fame, & you may get money; publish for money & you may get fame: but the true trick is, publish for *love*, & then you don't care . . . whether you get *anything* or not."[42]

A Tramp Abroad (1880), *Tom Sawyer Abroad* (1894), *Pudd'nhead Wilson* (1894), and *Tom Sawyer, Detective* (1896) were written for money. In the *Tom Sawyer* sequels, Mark Twain was—like Bret Harte—reworking a vein already mined. Of the works named, only *Pudd'head Wilson* added to the author's prestige. Although much love went into the writing of some of Mark Twain's books, that love was seldom blind to the possibility of profit. *The Innocents Abroad* (1869), *The Adventures of Tom Sawyer* (1876), *The Prince and the Pauper* (1882), *Life on the Mississippi* (1883), *The Adventures of Huckleberry Finn* (1884), *A Connecticut Yankee in King Arthur's Court* (1889), and *Personal Recollections of Joan of Arc* (1896) secured for Mark Twain a well-earned place among great writers of American literature. Most love went into the writing of *Joan of Arc*.[43] Perhaps the least loved of these books during much of its prolonged gestation was Mark Twain's greatest, *Huckleberry Finn*.

Although Mark Twain's literary significance was long underestimated, and at one time Howells believed that the more refined a reader considered himself, the more that reader doubted the worthiness of Mark Twain's work, Twain lived to see honors, fame, and love almost without parallel heaped upon himself. Bret Harte, Charles H. Webb, and William Dean Howells were no longer the discriminating few who recognized that Mark Twain's best humor was subordinated to the larger purposes of satire. In 1881 the New York *Herald* favorably reviewed *The Prince and the Pauper* as the serious work of a humorist. When *Life on the Mississippi* was published, Thomas Hardy wondered why more people did not recognize that Mark Twain was considerably more than a funny man. Magazines and syndicates pled for manuscripts, sometimes offering as much as a dollar a word. Finally, Mark Twain signed over to Harper and Brothers exclusive serial privileges of "what-

---

[41] Paine, *Biography*, 611, 617. See also Webster, *Mark Twain: Business Man*, 160.
[42] *Mark Twain to Mrs. Fairbanks*, 211–12.   [43] *MTL*, 624.

ever he might write."[44] He turned down several offers to edit magazines.[45] During Bret Harte's lifetime, Yale University and the University of Missouri conferred upon Mark Twain three honorary degrees. After Bret Harte's death came the honor which Mark Twain believed outranked all others: a degree from Oxford. But as Mark Twain used to say, more of that later.

Unlike Bret Harte, who in his years of exile from America saw less of Europe than the most restricted of American tourists, Mark Twain visited all the great countries of Europe and eventually circled the globe. Begun in 1895, Mark Twain's trip around the world to pay off his debts by lecturing brought world acclaim which made Bret Harte's "royal progress" from San Francisco to Boston in 1871 seem a local excursion.

Wherever Mark Twain went, he was acclaimed. Vienna, Berlin, Budapest, London vied with each other in honoring the man from Missouri, who was always ready to be shown. In Vienna, the luxurious suite in the New Krantz Hotel occupied by the Clemens family was known as the "Second Embassy." In Berlin, Mark Twain dined with Emperor William II. He could exchange jokes with the Prince of Wales, autograph a fan for the Princess Hohenloe, and—overwhelmed with the sense that he was on hand at the making of history—mourn the death of Austria's Empress Elizabeth, assassinated in September, 1898. Among Mark Twain's "royal conquests" was the King of Sweden.[46]

William Dean Howells recognized Mark Twain's pleasure at being in titled company but carefully explained that Twain could enjoy dining with the Emperor of Germany because he considered the honor a "delegated recognition from the German people." "Of all the men I have known he was the farthest from a snob," wrote Howells.[47] But when the Clemens family wintered in Berlin, they first settled in No. 7 Kornerstrasse, an apartment which seemed to them very convenient and comfortable until they discovered that, although it was quite reputable, it was not a socially desirable address. Warehouses were visible, women

[44] Paine, *Biography*, 578, 684, 747, 1114; *MTL*, I, 283. See also Pattee, *Mark Twain, Representative Selections*, xxxii.

[45] See note in longhand on letter of Aug. 17, 1900, from *Century Magazine* and forwarded by Mark Twain to H. H. Rogers, MTP.

[46] Paine, *Biography*, 936, 940–41, 951–52, 1070–72, 1083, 1104.

[47] Howells, *My Mark Twain*, 67. Van Wyck Brooks disagrees: *The Ordeal of Mark Twain*, 139.

leaned out of windows to gossip, and not very clean children played noisily in a sand pile near by. "It was eminently not the place for a distinguished man of letters." And so the author of *Huckleberry Finn* lost little time in moving to the Hotel Royal, Unter den Linden, one of the "best" addresses in Berlin.[48]

Throughout the years after their catastrophic collaboration on *Ah Sin*, Mark Twain and Bret Harte continued to have friends in common. Besides Osgood, Howells, and Aldrich, their mutual friends included Charles A. Dana, John Hay, Augustin Daly and his brother Judge Joseph Daly, Edwin Booth, and Lord Houghton. Most of them visited Harte in Glasgow or at Madame Van de Velde's in London. That Mark Twain and Bret Harte continued to have these and other friends in common makes their apparent failure to meet even more surprising. The only record I have found of an American's calling on both Harte and Twain during the same period in London is that of Hamlin Garland.

For Garland's first visit to England, in 1899, he had been given letters of introduction to both Bret Harte and Mark Twain by William Dean Howells, who told him: "I don't know where Clemens is at this moment and I cannot tell you where to find Harte, but if they are in London, I am sure they will be glad to see you."[49] At that time, according to Garland, comparatively little literary fraternizing existed between London and New York. American writers were still inclined to resent the English; and Londoners were apt to patronize American writers except Bret Harte, Joaquin Miller, and Mark Twain. Garland said that these Americans interested Englishmen because of the "tang of the Far-West in their writings."[50] This interest had been awakened by the writings of Bret Harte.[51]

For a long time Harte had been one of Garland's "high admirations" because of Harte's leadership "in point of power as well as of time" in the local-color movement which Garland considered "the most vital development of our literature."[52] In London, Garland discovered that Harte did not frequent places where Americans gathered regularly to eat and drink. The gossip about Harte disturbed Garland. But he was

[48] Paine, *Biography*, 482–83, 929–31.
[49] Hamlin Garland, "Roadside Meetings of a Literary Nomad," *Bookman*, Vol. LXXI (July, 1930), 424.
[50] *Ibid.*, 423.   [51] See Ferguson, *Mark Twain: Man and Legend*, 162.
[52] Garland, "Roadside Meetings," *loc. cit.*, 424.

really shocked when, at a tea at Joseph Hatton's, he was told that a white-haired old figure wearing striped trousers, a cutaway coat over a fancy vest, spats, and—of all things—a monocle was the author of "The Luck of Roaring Camp" and *Two Men of Sandy Bar*. When, at his own request, Garland was introduced to the man who looked to him like a typical English clubman of the American stage, Harte, though courteous, seemed so reserved that Garland hesitated to accept his invitation to call on the following Thursday. But he went.

When shown into Harte's room at 74, Lancaster Gate, Garland found the furnishings "spic and span" and "dainty in coloring" to a degree that seemed to the Middle Westerner effeminate. When his host entered wearing, except for a different tie, the same suit he had worn at the tea, Garland thought the man "almost as aristocratic" as the room. Garland presented his introduction and was invited to be seated while, slowly and silently, Harte read Howells' letter. Then the reserve melted away and Bret Harte in voice and manner seemed to this visitor "wholly American." As Harte hungrily asked for news of Howells, "Tom Aldrich," and "all the rest of the boys," Garland's heart warmed to him. Before long, the two were deep in talk of Americans and America. At the mention of California, Harte showed his awareness that he could never return and, indeed, that *his* California no longer existed. "Sometimes I wish I had never come away," he told Garland. When the visitor finally left, Harte followed him down the steps to the sidewalk, still asking about American friends—Stedman, Charles Dudley Warner,[53] and others. At the corner, when Garland turned for a last look at the house he had left, he saw an old man with white head bowed, standing still and brooding outside his own door. This visit occurred three years before Harte's death.

For several reasons, Hamlin Garland prized Howells' letter of introduction to Mark Twain more than he prized the introduction to Bret Harte. In the first place, he recognized that Mark Twain's fame "was no longer based upon his eccentricities" and that he was now "the largest and most significant figure in American literature."[54] During the past four or five highly successful years as a writer and a lecturer, Mark

[53] In 1892, Harte's letter to Warner about Mrs. Henniker's manuscript was signed "one of your 'lovers and countrymen,' " BL.

[54] Garland, "Roadside Meetings," *loc. cit.*, 425–26.

Twain had been living in Europe, but his royal welcomes had been highly publicized in the United States. Most of all, Garland wanted to meet Twain to talk to him about the publication by Webster and Company of the *Memoirs of General Grant*, for Garland's own biography, *Ulysses S. Grant: His Life and Character*, had been published in 1898, the year before Garland's trip to England. Moreover, *McClure's* had commissioned Garland to write an interview with Mark Twain if he could secure one.

Not long after his interview with Bret Harte, Hamlin Garland found Mark Twain in his small, "exclusive" hotel in Chelsea. The younger man was shocked by the change in the appearance of the famous humorist since he had seen him on the lecture platform in America some years earlier. This old man with his shaggy white hair and a stoop to his shoulders seemed curiously diminished, though the "fine head and rough-hewn features" were more impressive than ever. Mark Twain welcomed the younger writer, pleased him by showing familiarity with his biography of Grant, and then motioned him to a chair. Whereupon Mark Twain began to speak in the "rhythmic drone" with carefully calculated pauses to which Garland attributed much of the success of the lecturer. But there was a "curious aloofness of glance (as though he spoke through a mask)," and Mark Twain's eyes, though surprisingly blue and keen, were so often half-closed behind the bushy brows that they were seldom visible. Garland had difficulty at times in following what Twain was saying.

In answer to Garland's question, Twain said that he had no objection to talking about the publication of Grant's *Memoirs* and no objection to Garland's reporting the interview for *McClure's*, but permission for publication had to be gained from Mrs. Clemens. Then, to Garland's astonishment, Mark Twain began to curse "with heartfelt fervor and oriental magnificence" Charles Webster, who, according to Twain, had "chouselled" him out of fifty thousand dollars and had ruined Twain's publishing house. "With cold malignity" Mark Twain announced "in a level monotone" that he had for many years been writing a "kind of diary" in which he said exactly what he thought about the men and women he had met, and though it could not be published in his or Mrs. Clemens' lifetime, when it *was* published, the "blankety-blank-blank" Webster would turn in his grave. Mark Twain ended with such "deadly hatred in face and voice" that Garland began to share his animosity. That night Garland recorded the scene in his notebook and added the comment: "He has accomplished a tremendous task—a really great soul."

Notwithstanding Mark Twain's repeated assurance that he had no objection to the publication of the interview, it never appeared in *McClure's* because Mrs. Clemens refused her permission. In 1930, when Garland published his account in *Bookman*, he reported as a "most curious sequel" to the whole incident learning from Albert Bigelow Paine that the failure of Charles L. Webster and Company was due to Mark Twain's own unwise investments in a typesetting machine and that, far from "chouselling" Mark Twain out of fifty thousand dollars, Webster had been ill and out of the firm for several years before Twain's publishing house failed.[55]

If Mark Twain did not meet Bret Harte in London, there is substantial evidence that Twain thought about him more than once after Harte lost his Glasgow consulate. In September, 1887, Mark Twain wrote Laurence Hutton a joking letter reporting that both Bret Harte and Thomas Bailey Aldrich were misrepresenting their ages.[56] Mark Twain was right, at least about Bret Harte.[57] But he was mistaken when he told Hutton that Harte was born in 1833 and Aldrich in 1827, for both were born in 1836, one year later than Clemens himself. In 1891, Mark Twain told a correspondent that because he had been a silver miner and knew how to dig, shovel, drill, and blast, he knew "mines and miners interiorly as well as Bret Harte knows them exteriorly."[58] Twain also continued to think of Harte in relation to the Chinese. In January, 1894, attending amateur theatricals in the home of his friend the Reverend Joseph Twichell, Twain had been particularly impressed by one of the little girls participating in a play. In a letter to Mrs. Clemens, Mark described the young actress: "That cunning little devil played Confucius—You should have seen her. She looked just like a Chinaman, & now & then she would work up 'a smile that was childlike & bland' in a most artful & killing way."[59] Apparently Mark Twain still liked

[55] *Ibid.*, 427. It is noteworthy that Garland's article was published after *The Ordeal of Mark Twain* (1920) but before *Mark Twain: Business Man* (1946).
[56] Letters from Hartford, Sept. 22, 1887, MTP.
[57] *BHAE*, 303. [58] Paine, *Biography*, 916.
[59] Letter written from "Joe's Parsonage," Jan. 11, 1894, MTP.

"Plain Language from Truthful James" well enough to quote it.

At the end of this year, Mark Twain wrote a poem called "The Derelict" in which he used an old ship as a symbol for a man whose fame had once filled the world but who was then "friendless," "forlorn," "forgotten," and dying in an almshouse. Written in purple ink in that year of the failure of Charles L. Webster and Company, "The Derelict" concludes that the narrator's shame had ended, his soul was at peace, and he patiently waited for death to free him from life's insults.[60] Here we find another example of the great man fallen which Bernard De Voto noted as an almost obsessive theme in Mark Twain's manuscripts. The sentimentality and pathos of the verses suggest Bret Harte, but Mark Twain was not thinking about his old friend. He was feeling sorry for himself. About the same time, Mark Twain wrote H. H. Rogers a letter in which he referred to himself as an old ship in deep water and commented that never before Rogers had he had a friend who would try to help him when he was in great trouble.[61]

Eighteen hundred and ninety-five was the year when Bret Harte began to suffer from cancer of the throat. It was also the year when Mark Twain began to "follow the Equator." Near the beginning of this famous tour, a reporter for the Minneapolis *Times* gave an interesting description of Mark Twain's appearance:

> There is not the robust figure of the river pilot who could give Carl Schurz points on poker, nor the sunburned skin of the Virginia City editor. The Clemens of today is a rather delicate-looking man, whose cheeks poorly stand the glare of the footlights. Medium in height and in fullness of build he appears as the relic of his former physical self. The quaint character of the '60's and frontier days is lost in the swallow-tail and immaculate shirt-bosom of fin de siecle society.[62]

Oddly the description reminds us of Hamlin Garland's first impression of Bret Harte at a tea in London.

Interviewed by newspaper reporters in Australia, Mark Twain discussed many writers ancient and modern, including Bret Harte. Among

---

[60] See Paine, *Biography*, 1499–1500. All except the last stanza was included in Jervis Langdon's "Samuel Langhorne Clemens: Some Reminiscences and Some Excerpts from Letters and Unpublished Manuscripts," MTP.

[61] *MTL*, II, 619–20.

[62] (July 24, 1895), clipping in MTP.

other things, Mark Twain was quoted as saying: "Bret Harte I consider sham and shoddy, and he has no pathos of the real, true kind."[63] Mark Twain's words aroused a storm of editorial protest. According to the *Argus*, one could recognize that each has a right to his own taste and still be amazed that the author of *A Tramp Abroad* and the "Jumping Frog" should consider the author of "Truthful James" and "The Luck of Roaring Camp" a writer of "shoddy." "To hold the critic guilty of personal animosity for entertaining this frank opinion is to be unjust," but it still seemed to the *Argus* editor that Mark Twain showed a "deplorable Philistinism toward genuine ideals and emotions," and that Twain might be "too ready to find cant where cant does not exist."[64]

Instead of accusing Mark Twain of Philistinism, a writer for the Sydney *Morning Herald* for September 21, 1895, took Mark's words as additional evidence that "authors are perhaps the very worst judges of authors." Citing as parallels some contemptuous words of Johnson about Gray, of Byron about Wordsworth, and of Carlyle about Lamb, the writer believed it all goes to show merely that it is better to read and make your own literary decisions. "Mark Twain has made and earned his reputation, and has good right to be heard in such matters, and yet people with not a thousandth part of his discernment or taste can see how curiously oblique is his view of his brother writer." The editorial concluded: ". . . one would guarantee a long life still for Bret Harte, with his inimitable style, his real humor, and his finely proportioned feeling."

Today Mark Twain would find considerable support for his own appraisal of Bret Harte's fiction, but at that time Twain was aware that all over the world there were people who did not question the Australian critic's guarantee. Before he left Australia, Twain qualified his damnations of Harte by stating flatly that he did not like the man and that this fact should be taken into consideration.

According to reporters, Mark Twain also said: "I am most moderate in my dislikes."[65] But even more surprising and interesting was Twain's statement to reporters that he would probably meet Harte in London.

[63] Sydney *Morning Herald* (Sept. 17, 1895), clipping in MTP.
[64] (Sept. 21, 1895), clipping in MTP.
[65] *Ibid.* (Sept. 17, 1895), clipping in MTP.

These clippings and others with rather severe censures of Mark Twain were all preserved—presumably by Twain himself—and are included among the Mark Twain Papers now in Berkeley.

The pleasantest and the unpleasantest man Mark Twain ever knew was Mark Twain.

21

THE TRIUMPH OF MARK TWAIN

Oxford is healing a secret old sore of mine which has been causing me sharp anguish once a year for many, many years.

MARK TWAIN, 1907

IN 1900, Mark Twain returned to America to be welcomed by paeans of praise from his countrymen. As time passed, the praise did not diminish; rather it swelled in volume. But the adulation was for the superb showman who had repaid his debts rather than for the man of letters who had written one of the greatest American novels. (In 1964 it seems sheer irony that fifty-two years ago two such eminent literary critics as W. P. Trent and John Erskine should have written: "... of late decades it has been pathetically clear that Americans have developed past their taste for Mark Twain's type of fun-making, and if they have remained his ardent and grateful admirers in spite of that change, the tribute has been rather to his manly character than to his writing."[1] The same critics, in a chapter entitled "Bret Harte and Mark Twain," judged that Bret Harte's reputation was best substantiated by his humor, which they believed had less force but greater restraint and delicacy than Mark Twain's.[2] Notwithstanding such critical appraisals, Mark Twain had become a national idol and a prophet with unprecedented honor in his own country.)

Mrs. Clemens' health, never very strong, now began to fail ominously, and in 1902, the year of Bret Harte's death, Mrs. Clemens suffered a particularly severe illness attributed to "organic heart disease and nervous prostration."[3] Much has been written about Mark Twain's devotion to Livy. His devotion was exceeded only by Mrs. Clemens'

[1] *Great American Writers*, 245.   [2] *Ibid.*, 243.
[3] *MTH*, II, 724, 747n.

devotion to her husband. Nevertheless, when Twain was prohibited from entering her sickroom or admitted for not more than five minutes a day during long periods of her illness, Mrs. Clemens found some consolation in the thought that for a while, at least, she would not have to listen to talk about "the damned human race."[4] Mrs. Clemens died in 1904. "The crumbling away of Mark Twain's home life," wrote De-Lancey Ferguson, "left him with little except the sense of public acclaim to serve as a bulkhead between him and the edge of nothing." With all his acclaim, age did not altogether mellow Mark Twain. A few months before his death, Twain wrote: "I am full of malice, saturated with malignity."[5]

Mark Twain had many staunch friends who loved him in spite of— sometimes because of—his rages. His popular acclaim far exceeded Bret Harte's. But during the years, he had turned against a good many friends, and a look at the record shows that here again Bret Harte stands up pretty well in comparison. In the first place, there was a marked difference in the attitudes of these two men toward friends they had lost. Bret Harte could comment as he had in Washington: "It was my own fault, and I cannot blame people for not knowing everything." He rarely criticized even those who spread malicious rumors about him. With Mark Twain, on the other hand, former friends frequently became objects of invective. Noah Brooks and John McComb, who had commissioned him to write the *Quaker City* letters for the *Alta California* became "those Alta thieves" when they claimed certain publication rights to letters they had paid for. And Twain, who complained that Harte concealed a barb in a compliment, would say that Noah Brooks was a good historian "where facts were not essential."[6] Dan Slote, "Mark's splendid immoral room-mate" on the *Quaker City*, one of "the best boys in the world," a man "whose blameless conduct and example will always be an eloquent sermon to all who shall come within their influence," fell, in Mark Twain's estimation, to a position lower than that of a robber, whom Mark could respect for a certain "robust dignity."[7] Not long after Dan Slote's funeral, Mark Twain described

[4] Howells, *My Mark Twain*, 76.

[5] Ferguson, *Mark Twain: Man and Legend*, 308; De Voto, *Portable Mark Twain*, 14.

[6] Neider, *Autobiography*, 148.   [7] Paine, *Biography*, 322, 352.

him as "only a pick-pocker [*sic*], more base than ordinary pick-pockets, who merely filches from strangers."[8] It is astonishing how much abuse Mark Twain's acquaintances accepted and forgave.[9]

Among Mark Twain's friends, however, there were exceptions to those who forgave him everything. Some Westerners who accused Bret Harte of neglect when he went East made similar complaints against Mark Twain. At one time Twain believed that when he departed from San Francisco in the 1860's he left behind more friends than any other newspaperman who sailed beyond the Golden Gate.[10] But after he became established at Hartford, he never returned to California, and when, as a world-famous figure, he lectured around the globe, his itinerary included Portland, Seattle, and Vancouver, but not Virginia City or San Francisco. At least one descendant of pioneers expressed the belief that Mark Twain ought not to forget that the "loyalty of the friends he made in the sagebrush country has helped him very materially in his success." This Californian found in Bret Harte a "straightforwardness and sincerity . . . tinctured with a certain reserve born of good taste," whereas Mark Twain seemed to her "not particularly amiable nor generous personally."[11]

Mark Twain could be caustic about even such close friends and associates as Thomas Bailey Aldrich[12] and Charles Dudley Warner,[13] to whom and for whom he could also express great affection. One suspects

[8] *Mark Twain to Mrs. Fairbanks,* 247.

[9] For example, see *MTH,* II, 865–67.

[10] Webster, *Mark Twain: Business Man,* 89.

[11] Cummins, *The Story of the Files,* 125, 130.

[12] See Neider, *Autobiography,* pages 358–62, regarding Aldrich's prose, and page 359, regarding his vanity and his support of Mrs. Aldrich's ostentatious display of wealth which Twain intimated that the Aldriches had acquired ignobly. Also see Twain's statement that Aldrich was "Mrs. Aldrich's property," page 365. Even John Hay, whom Mark Twain had once admired fervently, did not escape Mark Twain's invective. In 1904, when John Hay became Theodore Roosevelt's secretary of state, Mark Twain wrote the Reverend Joseph Twichell that John Hay had to descend to doing the dirty work because he was "his party's property." Meltzer, *Mark Twain Himself,* 248.

[13] In *Nook Farm,* page 85, Andrews suggests that Twain overcame his dislike of Warner. In 1898, however, Mark's ridicule of Warner's promotional campaign for his *Library of the World's Best Literature* shows more than a grain of malice. See *MTH,* II, 676, 678n. See also Twain's description of Warner's conduct of the "Editor's Study," where Warner had succeeded Howells. *MTH,* II, 686–87 n.

him of cherishing secret grudges.[14] Arlin Turner believed that certain rumors and scurrilous newspaper stories circulated about George Washington Cable after the famous "Twins of Genius" lecture tour may well have emanated from Mark Twain.[15] In 1898, Mark Twain made so severe an attack on a "brother author" that Howells destroyed two pages of Mark Twain's letter. Mark Twain's hostility toward Bret Harte seems to have differed mainly in openness and intensity from his hostility toward several other friends and associates.

Even William Dean Howells, whose devotion to his friend approached the devotion of Mrs. Clemens, did not feel secure in Mark Twain's friendship. For the most part, the association between Howells and Twain was punctuated by expressions of mutual admiration. "I don't wonder you like my literature," Howells once wrote Twain, "It's nearly all about you." When "S. L. Clemens" wrote for *Harper's* a perceptive and discriminating appreciation of the craftsmanship of Howells, Howells in his turn was much moved. In thanking Twain, Howells said he was reminded of earlier compliments paid him by Lowell, Longfellow, and Holmes, whose eminence Mark Twain had now achieved. And in 1906 there was no one living whose praise Howells valued more than Twain's. As for the possible exception of Tolstoy, Howells wrote: "I do not love him as I love you, and the honor he could do me would not reach my heart as the honor you have done me does." The letter concluded: "Dear friend of forty years, thanks!"[16]

But during those forty years there had been strains and lapses. We have observed tensions developing during the collaborations on a play and on the *Library of Humor*. Later Howells refused to write an introduction to Mark Twain's collected works when Twain's publisher Frank E. Bliss would not meet Howells' price of $1,500. (The introductory essay for numerous editions of this twenty-three-volume set was finally written by Brander Matthews.[17]) Other symptoms of tensions can be recognized in the *Mark Twain–Howells Letters*. Howells could write facetiously: "I suppose you consider me worse than Bret

[14] For example, George Washington Cable did not suspect the extent of Mark Twain's animosity toward him. See Cardwell, *Twins of Genius*, 62, 67.

[15] Fatout, *Mark Twain on the Lecture Circuit*, 229.

[16] See *MTH*, II, 676, 678, 680, 769, 813–14.

[17] *Ibid.*, II, 679–80, 682n. See also Frank E. Bliss, in *ibid.*, 906.

Harte, Dan Slote, C. L. Webster and J. T. Raymond and Abby Sage Richardson put together, for getting you down to N. Y. on a holiday."[18] But the playfulness of several references to a rivalry for eminence never completely obscures latent truth. More than once there were long breaks in the correspondence between Howells and Twain. More puzzling than these lapses was the fact that when Twain decided to move his family to Europe in 1891, so close a friend as Howells should not learn of Mark's plans until he read them in newspapers.

Because he knew and loved Mark Twain and because he was more emotionally mature, William Dean Howells was generally forgiving and protective. Thus even as late as 1901, when both authors were awarded honorary degrees from Yale University, Howells took pains to see that Twain was invited to a dinner party which Howells expected to attend. (Howells' correspondent assured him that not only had Twain been invited long before but that he would be treated "like a white man.") After Howells became widely known as the "Dean of American Literature," his humorous reference to a "one-legged Dialogue between two Deans of American Literature" conferred an equal honor on Mark Twain. In 1910, Howells wrote Twain that Oxford University made a mistake when it awarded him a degree three years before it gave one to Mark Twain, a statement with which many critics today would agree.[19]

Yet, though Howells loved, admired, and protected his friend Clemens, he was too independent a thinker not to have reservations. What thoughts were in his mind when, in *A Traveler from Altruria*, he wrote deprecatingly of American humor? When Americans explained to Mr. Homos that "if you have capital in America, you can have individuality; if you haven't you can't" and that, in America, no matter how mighty a genius might be, if he wanted to get rich he must make other men work for him and pay him for the privilege of doing so, was Howells excepting Mark Twain, the mightiest American genius he knew? "The man with the most money . . . now takes the prize in our national cakewalk," Howells said in this work written before the extent of Twain's financial insecurity became known.[20] In *My Mark Twain*, William Dean Howells reported that when he and Mark Twain were elderly men

[18] *Ibid.*, II, 618–19.   [19] *Ibid.*, II, 627, 643–44, 680, 691, 731–32, 755, 851.
[20] See *A Traveler from Altruria*, 23, 26–27, 111, 140, 143.

living some blocks apart in New York City, they seldom saw each other because Twain expected Howells always to come to him and Howells would not do so unless Twain returned the visits. But Howells and Twain never ceased to be friends, Howells said, and good friends "so far as I know."[21] With Mark Twain, one could not be sure. Once when Howells asked how Mark was treating him in the autobiography, Mark Twain jokingly reassured him. In fact, the published *Autobiography* has surprisingly little to say about Howells.

One of the closest and most compassionate of all Mark Twain's friends was the Reverend Joseph Twichell. But finally Mark Twain considered his "strongest and wisest" friend neither Howells nor Twichell but the businessman Henry H. Rogers.[22] "I owe more to Henry Rogers than to any other man whom I have known," said Mark Twain.[23] Once when Mrs. Clemens urged her husband not to fall out with *him*, Mark Twain replied that she had nothing to fear, for Rogers was the kind of man who brought out all the best in him.[24] Bret Harte apparently brought out all the worst.

Laurence Hutton, bibliophile, author, and onetime editor of *Harper's Magazine* as well as a close friend of the Clemens family, tells a story of a strange evening in 1902 when a group of friends had just received news of the death of "a well known and exceedingly popular American author."[25] Mark Twain was present. For an hour or two Mark Twain held forth in a rambling monologue on the "personality of an unknown man" of whom other members of the group had "never heard and in whom they could have no interest." Later when Hutton asked Mark why his usually enjoyable conversation had been so disappointing that evening, Hutton learned with astonishment that the man Mark Twain had been talking about was Bret Harte, whom they all knew well and whose death they were mourning.

This is one of several anecdotes about Mark Twain's reaction to the news of Harte's death. Another—frequently told but seldom printed—is that when reporters asked Mark Twain if he wished to comment on the news, Mark replied: "Oh, yes. Say I *knew* the son of a bitch."[26]

[21] *My Mark Twain*, 93.   [22] See *Mark Twain to Mrs. Fairbanks*, 273.

[23] Paine, *Biography*, 1658.   [24] Letter in MTP.

[25] *Talks in a Library with Laurence Hutton*, 407.

[26] Professor Ferguson reports this anecdote in another context. *Mark Twain: Man and Legend*, 187–88.

Albert Bigelow Paine reports merely that the only time he met Mrs. Clemens was when he visited the Clemens home on the day the news of Harte's death reached America. During the afternoon Twain asked Paine to procure information about the obsequies.[27]

In *Companions on the Trail*, published in 1931, the year following his published account of interviews with Mark Twain and Bret Harte in London, Hamlin Garland tells of attending a luncheon in New York given by William Dean Howells for Henry Harland, novelist and first editor of *The Yellow Book*. The guest list—Mark Twain, Augustus Thomas, George Harvey, James L. Ford, Frank Crowinshield, and John Howells (William Dean Howells' son)—suggests that the luncheon was the one of which Howells reminded Twain in January, 1902.[28] At this time Harte was dying in England, but as Hamlin Garland remembered it, the luncheon occurred after Harte's death. As usual, Mark Twain dominated the conversation, which he directed almost immediately to Bret Harte, whom he "cursed" as a "whelp" and a "blackguard." "His fury of invective was almost comical," wrote Garland.

"Do you know what that blankety-blank two-faced hound did?" asked Mark Twain. "He came to Elmira to get my endorsement of him as consul to Glasgow, and told me with glee that he had secured the support of both parties!"[29] Garland's reaction was: "It was apparent that Twain considered this a case of double-dealing, but to me it appeared an added proof of Harte's popularity."

Howells did not contradict Twain. Instead, when he had a chance to put in a word, he added his own derogatory stories about Harte. Though skeptical of the charges from Twain (whose "drawling intonation conveyed such edge of hate" that he wondered at its cause), Garland had considerable faith in the reliability of Howells. Nevertheless, he found it difficult to reconcile with his image of the "sad exile" whom he had visited in London the picture of Harte drawn by Twain and Howells at the New York luncheon. When these good companions harped on gossip that at the time of his death Harte was "very poor and living with a woman not his wife," Garland remembered the feeble old man

[27] Paine, *Biography*, 1258.   [28] *MTH*, II, 735-36.

[29] Obviously, it is impossible that Bret Harte went to Elmira, New York, to get Mark Twain's endorsement for the consulship at Glasgow. As we have seen, Harte's appointment to Crefeld in 1878 resulted from support of both Democrats and Republicans, and Harte interpreted this bipartisan support as a vote of confidence.

whom he had seen and concluded that "there must have been something finely sympathetic in that woman." Seeing again in his mind's eye the furnishings of the apartment at 74, Lancaster Gate, the Middle Westerner was now convinced that some woman had helped select them and that the woman was a "lady."

On leaving the luncheon during which Harte's former friends thoroughly vivisected his character, the two younger guests—Garland and John Howells—agreed that there was not much left of Harte. "Except his great fame!" said John Howells. "He is still the author of 'The Argonauts.' "[30]

The most direct evidence of Mark Twain's reactions to the news of Bret Harte's death can be found in a letter which Twain wrote Howells in 1903 about Howells' review of Charles Warren Stoddard's recently published book, *Exits and Entrances*. This book includes a rather perfunctory chapter on Mark Twain, whom Stoddard had once served as secretary, and a warmly appreciative chapter about Bret Harte in California. Howells considered the chapter on Harte the best in Stoddard's book and was thereby prompted to add his own recollections of Harte when he came East. Although he paid tribute to Harte's gaiety, his charm, and his dedication to his craft, Howells was considerably more critical than Stoddard. He recalled the Keeler luncheon and a later luncheon in London when Harte, an old man himself, had indulged in railleries about the effects of time on them all. Also, Howells repeated some anecdotes he had told at the luncheon reported by Garland, which rather underscored Harte's irresponsibilities and the limitations of his talent.[31]

Mark Twain professed much pleasure in Howells' essay:

> You have written of Harte most felicitously—most generously, too, & yet at the same time truly; for he *was* all you have said, & although he was more & worse, there is no occasion to remember it & I am often ashamed of myself for doing it. I have had a curious experience. In the bound Blackwood for 1871 I was reading that mag.'s discovery of Harte, & its surprise & [gratification] admiration over the Luck of Roaring Camp, which it reproduced substantially in full. There stood his birth! & I was carried back to it; then the next night came your

[30] Hamlin Garland, *Companions on the Trail*, 181.
[31] Howells, "Editor's Easy Chair," *loc. cit.*, 157.

funeral services over him, in which you brought him in a princely progress across the applauding continent, young & dapper & brown-haired; & by & by laid him to rest, white-headed & half-forgotten, in an alien land. In the one night I saw him born; I saw him flit across the intervening day, as it were, & when night closed down again I saw him buried. It was wierd [*sic*] and impressive.[32]

Howells thanked Twain for his praise. "I am glad that the half-truth of the B.H. didn't quite seem to you a half-lie."[33] He told Mark Twain that he could have written much worse words that would have left "blisters" on Bret Harte's fame. But those words would have been no more sincere, and such things after all had better be left to Judgment Day.

If, as Mark Twain said, Harte was "half-forgotten" at the time of his death, publications about him in 1903 indicate that a good many people were thinking of him again. Besides the reminiscences of Stoddard and Howells and the adulatory biography of Pemberton, also published in 1903 was a critical study of Harte by Henry W. Boynton. Though sometimes caustic about Harte himself, this study praised "The Heathen Chinee": "What is there omitted in this as a study of international relations?" asked Boynton. "The duplicity of Bill Nye, his righteous Occidental indignation at the superior duplicity of his adversary, and the complacent moralizing of Truthful James himself constitute this poem a consummate piece of satire."[34] Although far more thorough and comprehensive than the Pemberton and Boynton books about Bret Harte, Albert Bigelow Paine's three-volume biography of Mark Twain was not published until 1912, two years after Mark Twain's death.

Mark Twain's mellowness toward Harte evoked by Howells' essay did not last. On Sunday, June 17, 1906, in writing Howells about the satisfactory progress of his autobiographical dictations, Mark Twain alluded to the manuscript of "Captain Stormfield's Visit to Heaven," with which he was particularly pleased now that he had made up his mind not to permit its publication during his lifetime. Then he told Howells of his intentions to dictate next day a chapter which would get his "heirs & assigns burnt alive if they venture to print it this side of 2006 A.D." But the following day, after announcing that he would talk

---

[32] *MTH*, II, 774.   [33] *Ibid.*, II, 776.   [34] *Bret Harte*, 114.

about the secret skepticism of Christians, Mark lost little time in getting around to the subject of Bret Harte.[35]

As Bernard De Voto explained, Mark Twain wanted to prove that a good book can be produced by free association of ideas; that is, by dictating any thought that came into his mind regardless of what he had been thinking or talking about a moment before. Actually these dictations prove not that the lack of organization makes a good book but that the "stream of consciousness" reveals a good deal about the author. Mark Twain's dictations about Bret Harte published in *Mark Twain in Eruption* are dated June 13, 1906; June 14, 1906; and February 4, 1907. None is dated June 18, 1906. Bernard De Voto, who selected and edited the autobiographical dictations published in this volume, reported that except for one omission,[36] the dictations about Bret Harte were left intact because "the passage as it stands here is complete in itself, and not only interesting but privileged as a part of the history of American literature."[37] Paine could suggest topics. At the mention of Bret Harte's name, the first idea to enter Mark Twain's mind concerned the inscrutable injustice of Providence. "How wonderful are the ways of Providence!" Twain began. "But I will take that up later." Yet this bitter stream runs underground, seeping into all reminiscences about Bret Harte in 1906 and 1907.

Harte had written about Chinese and become world famous; Mark Twain had written about Chinese and been fired. Like a prince, Bret Harte had made a progress to the East and been lionized in Cambridge, Concord, Boston, New York, and London, while Mark Twain's head was white before he received similar acclaim. At literary luncheons with the Brahmins of Boston, Harte had been the honored guest; Mark Twain "sat below the salt." Even though Mark Twain liked to think his prestige in England greater than Harte's, Harte had been invited to lecture at Oxford and Cambridge and had been sought out—twice—to

[35] *MTH*, II, 812n. The dictations about Mark Twain's skepticism of Christian doctrines have recently been edited by Charles Neider and under the title "Reflections on Religion" published in the *Hudson Review*, Vol. XVI (Autumn, 1963), 350–52.

[36] One passage was restored in Charles Neider's edition of *The Autobiography of Mark Twain*. Another passage, not about Harte but about Harte's daughter Jessamy, who was ill at the time, was rightly omitted, for it is irrelevant.

[37] *MTE*, ix–xi.

respond to the toast "to literature" at the Royal Academy Dinner, a considerably higher honor than being asked to give the toast "to literature" at Guildhall. For the past thirteen years Mark Twain's life had been marked first by financial disaster and then by family tragedy; all the while the "meretricious" Harte was living comfortably in England, hobnobbing with the rich and famous. Or so it seemed to Mark. And from this incredible volcano of bitterness, "the King," "the Belle of New York," "the Belle of London," the holder of degrees from Yale University and the University of Missouri, the very wealthy man whose "royal progress" encompassed the world, erupted. Finally it was Bret Harte's fame and relative poverty that Mark Twain could not forgive.

Like Tom Sawyer expecting that "a clear sky would deliver God's lightnings" on the head of the lying murderer Injun Joe, Twain had looked to Providence to strike Harte down. And when Providence had seemed dilatory about the matter, Mark Twain had been doing what he could to help Providence along. Now Bret Harte was dead. Mark Twain once observed that we say no harsh things of the dead because they cannot be hurt by what we say.[38] But four years after his death Harte's name still lived, and there were still those who spoke of the man with affection.

Mark Twain's eruptions relating to Bret Harte reflect ambivalence, for into the vituperations creep rare reminders of old affection and admiration: the account of Harte's work on "Thankful Blossom"; the report of Harte's telling a joke at his own expense wherein a miner on the Sacramento boat called the author of "The Luck of Roaring Camp" a "Son of a ———!" as a token of great esteem; even parts of Mark Twain's accounts of the abortive attempt at collaboration on *Ah Sin*. Yet Mark Twain insisted that all the good in Bret Harte died in San Francisco, and "it was the corpse of that Bret Harte that swept in splendor across the continent." "I'm in the middle of a history of Bret Harte, but I'll break into that with a newer and hotter interest tomorrow," Twain wrote Howells on June 17, 1906. "The rest of Bret will be postponed—like Orion."

On February 3, 1907, Twain and Howells met and talked about Bret Harte in such a fashion that William Dean Howells' next letter called Mark Twain a "fine old paranoic."[39] At the time of that conversation,

[38] Paine, *Biography*, 618.   [39] *MTH*, II, 811, 823.

did Mark Twain and the Oxonian Howells have any intimation of the possibility of a great event which would occur in June? On the day following that conversation, Mark Twain dictated for his autobiography: "In these days things are happening which bring Bret Harte to my mind again; they rake up memories of him which carry me back thirty and forty years."[40] Howells' letter of February 21 alludes to a welcome which Mark Twain would give the British Ambassador.[41] Early in May, Twain received a cablegram from England.[42] On June 26, 1907, Mark Twain was awarded an Oxford degree, "the highest academic honor which the world has to give."[43]

Mark Twain had come a long way since those New England days when Harte was the favorite and Mrs. Fields pitied Twain because it seemed to her that he was always apologizing. The academic honors of Oxford were preceded by a "spectacular progress across the Atlantic and through England."[44] They were followed by prolonged social honors in London. Paine's list of Mark's engagements in London for the "week following July Fourth" is heavily freighted with titles: Mark Twain dined with Lord and Lady Portsmouth; breakfasted at Lord Avebury's where Lord Kelvin, Sir Charles Lyell, and Sir Archibald Geikie were among the guests; called on Lady Longattock; and lunched with Sir Norman Lockyer.[45] When Clara Clemens in America heard rumors that Mark Twain was walking through the streets of Oxford wearing his bathrobe, and she anxiously cabled him to "Observe the proprieties," Mark cabled back: "They all pattern after me."[46]

Mark Twain's dictations about his Oxford degree have a strange pertinence to the present chronicle.

"Oxford is healing a secret old sore of mine which has been causing me sharp anguish once a year for many, many years," he said. "Privately I am quite well aware that for a generation I have been as widely celebrated a literary person as America has ever produced, and I am also privately aware that in my own peculiar line I have stood at the head of my guild during all that time, with no one to dispute me." (Forty years earlier he had written his mother and sister in St. Louis: "Though I am generally placed at the head of my breed of scribblers in this part

[40] *MTE*, 268.   [41] *MTH*, II, 822.   [42] Neider, *Autobiography*, 348.
[43] Paine, *Biography*, 1393.   [44] *MTH*, II, 826n.
[45] Paine, *Biography*, 1399.   [46] Clara Clemens, *My Father*, 270.

of the country, the place properly belongs to Bret Harte, I think, though he denies it, along with the rest.") Mark Twain's autobiography then alludes to honors paid persons of "local and evanescent notoriety" who drift into obscurity and are forgotten in ten years. He seemed to refer to university degrees for which he whimsically implied that he had been yearning. But he concluded: "Now then, having purged myself of this thirty-five years' accumulation of bile and injured pride, I will drop the matter and smooth my feathers down and talk about something else."[47]

Thirty-five years would take Mark Twain back to 1872, when Bret Harte was the most famous American writer. It was the year following the Keeler luncheon, to which Howells had referred in his 1903 essay on Harte. It was not far from the time when Aldrich had attributed to Twain a "feeble echo" of Harte and Mark Twain had written Orion Clemens his vow to top Bret Harte and stay on top.

In fame and fortune and literature, Mark Twain had topped Bret Harte long ago. Now there could be no doubt that all the world knew it. Harte had never received an honorary degree from a university. But he had been lionized in an American Cambridge whose doors were closed to Mark Twain. "Out of those decorated and forgotten thousands" who had been honored with university degrees, Mark said, "not more than ten have been decorated by Oxford, and I am quite well aware—and so is America, and so is the rest of Christendom—that an Oxford decoration is a loftier distinction than is conferrable by any other university on either side of the ocean, and is worth twenty-five of any other, whether foreign or domestic."[48]

Mark Twain wore his gray and scarlet Oxford gown on every possible occasion, including his daughter's wedding.[49]

Mark Twain's last recorded words about Bret Harte conclude a section in the *Autobiography* expounding Mark Twain's pseudo philosophy of determinism:

> By ancient training and inherited habit, I have been heaping blame after blame, censure after censure, upon Bret Harte, and have felt the things I have said, but when my temper is cool I have no censures for him. The law of his nature was stronger than man's statutes and he had

[47] Neider, *Autobiography*, 349.   [48] *Ibid.*
[49] Howells, *My Mark Twain*, 4; Paine, *Biography*, 1524.

to obey it. It is my conviction that the human race is no proper target for harsh words and bitter criticisms, and that the only justifiable feeling toward it is compassion; it did not invent itself, and it had nothing to do with the planning of its weak and foolish character.[50]

[50] Neider, *Autobiography*, 309.

22

THE QUESTION OF INFLUENCE

I don't believe Harte ever had an idea that he came by honestly.
He is the most abandoned thief that defiles the earth.

MARK TWAIN to WILLIAM DEAN HOWELLS

LITERARY HISTORIANS AND CRITICS of the past thirty years have been
apt to deny emphatically that Bret Harte had any influence on Mark
Twain's work.[1] As we have noted, one exception was the late Van Wyck
Brooks. Another exception is Walter Blair, whose thorough and illuminating study of the genesis and maturation of *The Adventures of
Huckleberry Finn* suggests that Mark Twain's writings about the South
may have been influenced by Bret Harte, that Colonel Grangerford was
a blood relation—almost an identical twin—of Colonel Starbottle, and
that Harte had "prepared the way for Huckleberry Finn as a leading
character." Referring to what is generally regarded as the "Harte
formula" of "good in the heart of an outcast," Professor Blair wrote:
"Twain, eager for acceptance by the literary elite, hardly would have
ventured to make Huck the center of a novel if the trail had not been
broken by Harte."[2]

Although I question some of his conclusions concerning Bret Harte's
influence on Mark Twain's writings about the South, Professor Blair
seems to me to come much closer to the truth than those critics who deny
that Bret Harte had any influence on the writings of Mark Twain.
Most significant is the recognition of Harte's influence on the "sound
heart" of the outcast that won over the "deformed conscience" of the
social conformist in Huck Finn.

As for both authors' writings about the South, I agree that Bret

[1] Ferguson, *Mark Twain: Man and Legend*, 98–99; De Voto, *Mark Twain's
America*, 219.

[2] *Mark Twain & Huck Finn*, 113, 218.

Harte's Colonel Starbottle, a caricature (at times, as in *Two Men of Sandy Bar*, even a buffoon), probably influenced Mark Twain in the humorous portrayal of a Southern colonel, but I believe that Colonel Sellers rather than Colonel Grangerford (a stereotype, not a caricature) bore witness to that influence. Finally Colonel Sherburn and Colonel Grangerford were serious characters with whom the Mark Twain of the white suits could identify. For all the alleged "pathos" of the turnip-eating scene, Colonel Sellers was essentially comic. He was most obviously a caricature in "Colonel Sellers as a Scientist."

Bret Harte and Mark Twain approached their writings about the South from very different perspectives of experience. A fundamental difference between their attitudes toward the sectional conflict and the issues for which it was fought concerns consistency. Born a New Yorker, Bret Harte in California actively, sometimes eloquently, supported abolition and Lincoln before and during the Civil War. It is true that he sympathized with white Southerners after their defeat, and many of Harte's later stories compared Southerners with the dispossessed Spanish Californians, toward whom Harte was also warmly compassionate. But in 1895, Harte was astonished when conservative Southern journals favorably reviewed *Clarence*, a *novella* about the Civil War, for, he said, "I a Northern partisan in will and blood, have made a *partisan* story."[3] We have noted earlier that Bret Harte's support of the principles of Lincoln and the Union never wavered.

In contrast, Mark Twain was as changeable about this subject as about many others. Born and bred in Missouri, he continued to think of himself as a Southerner for some time after he moved to Nevada. By 1879, Mark Twain—who had once enlisted to fight for the Confederacy—was eulogizing General Grant and choking up with the "mere memory" of a "bullet-shredded old battle-flag" of the Union Army "reverently" unfurled to the accompaniment of a thousand Yankee voices singing "When we were marching through Georgia."[4] Before long, however, American fiction reflected or stimulated a neo-Confederate revival emanating nostalgia for the "Old South." By 1901, Mark Twain was referring to himself as a "second lieutenant in the Confederate service" and assuring an audience gathered in Carnegie Hall to honor Lincoln that "We of the South were not ashamed" for "we did our bravest best

[3] *BHL*, 417. [4] *MTH*, I, 279–80.

313

against despairing odds, for the cause which was precious to us and which our conscience approved."[5] Published in *Century Magazine* in December, 1885, within a month of the publication date set by Charles L. Webster and Company for General Grant's *Memoirs*, "The Private History of a Campaign That Failed" admitted but did not fully explain Mark Twain's variability.[6]

Although I can recognize little connection between the two authors' writings about the South, in a study of the relationship between Bret Harte and Mark Twain, the question of influence is a particularly interesting one. Mark Twain himself did not always bother with distinctions between influence, imitation, and plagiarism. Mark Twain's accusation that Bret Harte habitually plagiarized has been given such general credence that a scholar of the stature of the late Dixon Wecter could refer casually to what he called Bret Harte's "flair for plagiarism."[7]

Contrary to any assumption that he freely and cavalierly helped himself to the words and ideas of others, Bret Harte maintained a strong sense of private ownership of literary property. Because of his early prestige and his continued popularity among the mass of readers, Bret Harte's name, without his knowledge or consent, was occasionally added to works not his own. For example, in July, 1877, a story entitled "Joseph's Brother" purportedly by Bret Harte appeared in *Forney's Sunday Chronicle*. Harte's reaction in a letter to the editor of the Washington *Daily Nation* was published in the New York *Times* of July 20, 1877. The first of the letter was terse and to the point: "As I certainly did not write any such story at any time, and, indeed, never saw it until my attention was attracted by my name under its title, I beg you will do justice to the real author as well as myself by contradicting the statement." The rest of the letter was whimsical, including the following paragraph:

> It is a small matter, but as I observe that the careless practice of signing other people's names to checks and drawing the money therefrom appears to be steadily growing into disfavor in commercial circles, it seems to me that the placing of an author's name, without his consent, to an article not written by him should be practiced under some sort of restraint, and only with the greatest delicacy.[8]

[5] *Mark Twain of the* Enterprise, 214–15n.   [6] *MTH*, II, 539.   [7] *LL*, 194.

[8] This letter was called to my attention by Mrs. Elizabeth Woodruff of Redlands, California.

Through a newspaper error, "The Dancing God," by Charles Godfrey Leland, was once attributed to Harte, but the mistake was corrected and the result was nothing more serious than an exchange of cordial and complimentary letters between the two authors.[9] Such incidents Harte could treat lightly.

But Bret Harte reacted very differently when a man named G. T. Lanigan wrote the New York *Tribune* a letter in which he charged Harte with stealing from him in a book recently reviewed in London and New York as "Bret Harte's New Book." "I have heard of wholesale literary piracies," wrote Lanigan, "but there is a sweet, luscious largeness about Mr. Harte's work which reminds one of nothing so much as a mammoth California fruit, ripened in an English hothouse." From Glasgow, Bret Harte (through the columns of the *Tribune*) promptly answered his accuser. The book, he said, bore on its cover the title "Fables by G. Washington Aesop" and upon its title page, "Fables by G. Washington Aesop and Bret Harte." Three of the fables Harte recognized as his own, but he could not remember where or when he had written them. He explained that he had neither authorized the book's publication nor known of its existence until it was publicly sold. "If I have been wantonly or accidentally used as an advertisement for a book which is amusing," wrote Harte, "I do not see that it follows that I should suffer myself to be made an advertisement for Mr. Lanigan, who is certainly not." Charles Meeker Kozlay, a great admirer of Harte and a collector of Harte first editions, discovered that though Bret Harte could not remember when he had written the fables in question, he had contributed them to a publication called *The Chicago Hospital Bazaar* to aid the Homeopathic Hospital Fair held in Chicago, November 19–26, 1874.[10]

Another instance of Harte's name being used for a work not his own can be found in the Gilbert S. Densmore version of Harte's "M'liss," appearing in the *Golden Era* in 1873. This story seemed to have a particular fascination for many writers of the day, and more than one tried to improve the story and exploit the prestige of Harte's name. Jacob Blanck (in "The Question of Bret Harte's Mliss," written for the *Publishers' Weekly* of November 28, 1936), gives an extraordinarily

[9] *BHL*, 53.
[10] See "The Piracy of Bret Harte's Fables," in *The Lectures of Bret Harte*, 51–53.

interesting account of Robert M. DeWitt's piracy of "M'liss" and the resulting lawsuit, which Harte won.

As for Mark Twain's charge that Bret Harte had plagiarized in *Ah Sin*, we have already noted that if Twain had left "hardly a footprint" of Harte, the play could not have remained full of Harte's "deliberate thefts and plagiarisms," and if Twain recognized them, his own "plagiarisms" could hardly remain "unconscious." But more important in relation to Mark Twain's objection that *Ah Sin* lacked originality is a knowledge of the American theater when the Harte-Twain play was written and produced. Stock characters, stock situations, and hackneyed dialogue of "successful" plays on the American stage at that time made application of the term "plagiarism" to any one play almost meaningless. In *The Theater of Augustin Daly*, Marvin Felheim pointed out that since most of the dramas were adaptations or revisions, originality "in the modern sense" was rare. Although he considered Boucicault and Daly both, in a sense, "pirates," Felheim observed that the theater which they helped build prepared audiences for the great innovators: Ibsen, Shaw, and O'Neill.[11] In the days of Boucicault and Daly, and in the early days of Mark Twain, Bret Harte himself was looked upon as the great innovator.

Nevertheless, Mark Twain had some grounds for saying that Harte was imitative. Like Robert Louis Stevenson or Benjamin Franklin, Bret Harte in his earlier years "played the sedulous ape" of such writers as Washington Irving and Charles Dickens, and he continued to experiment with verse forms of earlier and contemporary poets. For example, in "To the Pliocene Skull," he was indebted to Oliver Wendell Holmes.[12] In "Ramon," a poem about a Mexican mining engineer, Harte was clearly experimenting with the metrics of Robert Browning, whom—like Mark Twain—Bret Harte admired. In his *Condensed Novels*, Bret Harte used parody with remarkable skill. One of the best of these novels, *The Haunted Man*, shows Harte an independent and discriminating critic as well as an imitator of Dickens.

For several reasons other than literary criticism, Harte's poetry and fiction frequently include conscious parody. Perhaps the most painful example is Harte's parody of Longfellow's "Excelsior" as an advertisement for Sapolio. Ironically, this work (written in Harte's down-and-

---

[11] *The Theater of Augustin Daly*, 55, 79.   [12] *BHAE*, 142–44.

almost-out phase) has become one of the choicest items for bibliophiles.[13] We have already noted that in "The Willows," Harte burlesqued Poe's "Ulalume" for the purpose of low comedy.[14] An amusing example of Harte's imitation or parody in fiction can be found in Harte's story for children, "The Queen of the Pirate Isle," whose first editions in England and America were charmingly illustrated by Kate Greenaway. Much admired by Ruskin, this story is in many ways a Western version of *Alice in Wonderland*.[15] That Bret Harte deliberately invoked associations of his own stories with earlier works—often relying on the incongruity of this association for humor or irony—is illustrated in his all-too-frequent use of such terms as "Argonauts," "Iliad," and "Idyl" for California characters and incidents. Though more subtle and more serious, James Joyce employed essentially the same technique when he entitled his great novel about Dubliners *Ulysses*.

Harte's practices which I have identified can hardly be interpreted as evidence of intellectual or artistic dishonesty. Similar practices can be observed in the writings of Mark Twain. *Mark Twain in Eruption* scoffed at Harte's "felicitous imitations of Dickens," but Colonel Sellers probably owed something to Mr. Micawber as well as to Colonel Starbottle, and Henry Nash Smith suggests that "Boy's Manuscript," the germ of *Tom Sawyer*, may have been indebted to Dickens' account of David Copperfield's courtship of Dora.[16] Mark Twain frequently employed burlesque. The most obvious use of this technique in *Ah Sin* occurs not in any element attributable to Harte but in the romantic "rhapsody" of Mrs. Plunkett (page 39), which crudely parodies the "In such a night as this . . ." dialogue between Lorenzo and Jessica at the beginning of Act V of *The Merchant of Venice*.

Harte's use of techniques and ideas antedating his own was recognized in a review of Merwin's biography of Bret Harte for *Blackwood's* magazine in April, 1912. But the unknown English reviewer insisted that Harte was an artist "always scrupulous and defiant" who "never lost sight of his vocation." The reviewer scoffed at American prejudice against him and vigorously defended Harte's claims to a place in the greater tradition of world literature:

[13] *Ibid.*, 239. One of these advertisements can be found in the Bancroft Library.
[14] *Writings*, XII, 283–85.
[15] See M. H. Spielmann and G. S. Layard, *Kate Greenaway*, 160.
[16] Smith, *Mark Twain: The Development of a Writer*, 81.

For he brought to the interpretation of the mining camp all the resources of the literary artist. Nor did his attachment to literary tradition ever weaken. The short story was no new artifice. He gave it a turn, which was neither Poe's nor Balzac's. He owed and acknowledged a vast debt in sentiment and workmanship to Dickens and Hood. He borrowed the metre of his "Heathen Chinee" from Swinburne. But this is merely to say that he was a man of letters who refused to cut himself adrift from his moorings. The result was his own and all his own.[17]

Anyone inclined to rely on Mark Twain's testimony that Bret Harte was artistically dishonest should remember that "plagiarism" is an emotionally loaded word which Mark Twain tossed about rather carelessly. Bret Harte was by no means the only collaborator whom Mark Twain accused. While working on *The Gilded Age*, Mark Twain wrote his wife that Charles Dudley Warner had been tempted to copy word for word some of Constance Fenimore Woolson's descriptions until Mark Twain warned him that the plagiarism would have been immediately detected, and, besides, Miss Woolson's language belonged to her.[18] In 1875, Mark Twain gave William Dean Howells an accurate account of the way his mind sometimes worked. After mentioning Bret Harte and Charles Francis Adams as "slovenly" writers, Mark Twain continued:

> The reference to Bret Harte reminds me that I often accuse him of being a deliberate imitator of Dickens; & this in turn reminds me that I have charged unconscious plagiarism upon Charley Warner; & *this* in turn reminds me that I have been delighting my soul for two weeks over a bran new & ingenious way of beginning a novel—& behold, all at once it flashes upon me that *Charley Warner* originated the idea 3 years ago and told me about it! ... I would not wonder if I am the worst literary thief in the world, without knowing it.[19]

But habitually Mark Twain made a careful distinction between "unconscious plagiarism," which he readily admitted in his own writing,

[17] "Bret Harte and the Pioneers of '49," *Blackwood's*, Vol. CXCI (Apr., 1912), 582–84.
[18] *LL*, 182–83. In support of Mark Twain is Wallace Stegner's observation that Charles Dudley Warner "borrowed freely and without enough quotation marks" from descriptions of the Grand Canyon by Clarence E. Dutton. "Western Record and Romance," Spiller *et al.*, *Literary History of the United States*, II, 875.
[19] *MTH*, I, 112.

and "conscious plagiarism," of which he accused Bret Harte. In a letter to a correspondent who thought he had detected another instance of someone plagiarizing Mark Twain, Twain wrote that he had never had an original idea in his life and had never met anybody who *had* had one. "Nothing is ours but our language, our phrasing. If a man takes that from me (knowingly, purposely) he is a thief. If he takes it unconsciously—snaking it out of some secluded corner of his memory, and mistaking it for a new birth instead of a mummy—he is no thief, and no man has a case against him."[20] Notwithstanding his assertion in this letter that "conscious . . . plagiarism is as rare as parricide," Mark Twain accused Bret Harte of this dishonesty.

A well-known principle of modern psychology is that angrily abusive language frequently attributes to the object of abuse deeds and actions which the speaker fears might justifiably be charged to himself. Almost equally well known is the fact that Mark Twain chronically suffered from a sense of guilt.

From the first to the last of his well-known works, Mark Twain on many occasions was accused of plagiarism. His story of "The Celebrated Jumping Frog of Calaveras County" was not and, indeed, did not pretend to be original.[21] In his early lectures in the East, he was accused of plagiarizing Artemus Ward. In his 1870 *Galaxy* article entitled "A Literary Old Offender in Court with Suspicious Property in His Possession," Mark Twain defended himself against accusations of unacknowledged borrowing in his "Story of the Good Little Boy," which had appeared in an earlier issue.[22] In 1881, when a letter to the editor of a New York publication questioned the originality of Mark Twain's account of "A Curious Episode" in *Century Magazine*, Mark Twain launched an angry verbal attack on the New York editor who had published the reader's query, but Twain refused to answer the correspondent publicly.[23] Since Mark Twain had not, in fact, claimed the story as his own, the editor ecknowledged his error and apologized. But Albert Bigelow Paine tells us that when in 1909, "through an oversight due

---

[20] *Robert J. Burdette, His Message,* 136.

[21] De Voto, *Mark Twain's America,* 172–73. See also Lewis, *The Origin of the Celebrated Jumping Frog of Calaveras County,* 23–26.

[22] *Mark Twain to Mrs. Fairbanks,* 147, 149.

[23] Paine, *Biography,* 719–20. As for answering his accuser, Mark Twain said: "I would as soon think of bandying words in public with any *other* prostitute."

to haste in publication," Mark Twain's last work *Is Shakespeare Dead?* had failed to give full credit to George Greenwood, the author of a manuscript from which Mark Twain had quoted "long extracts," and a morning paper carried the sensational headline "IS MARK TWAIN A PLAGIARIST?" Mark protested that he felt no guilt. "The fact that he had been stealing and caught at it," he said, would give Greenwood's book much better advertising than the book would have received if Twain had immediately acknowledged his indebtedness to the source.[24]

At this time, Clemens was seventy-four years old, and it was Paine's impression that his soft answer had turned away wrath. Generally, Mark Twain followed that principle of military strategy which advocates offense as the best form of defense. Nevertheless, though more than one of Mark Twain's works is a "mosaic of materials" read or used earlier, they all bear the indubitable mark of Twain.[25]

Of the innumerable parallels in the personal lives and voluminous writings of Bret Harte and Mark Twain, some are as coincidental as the facts that both men sometimes suffered from gout, both had daughters who studied music in Paris, both detested autograph seekers, and the last novel each read before his death was by Thomas Hardy. (With Bret Harte it was *The Woodlanders*; with Mark Twain it was *Jude the Obscure*.) Parallels in their writings were often nothing more than the agreement of two reporters covering the same story.

Occasionally, elements appearing earlier in the fiction of Mark Twain can be recognized in the fiction of Bret Harte. For example, certain elements of *Huckleberry Finn* are dimly discernible in Harte's "Cressy" and "Three Vagabonds of Trinidad." But these resemblances hardly indicate that Harte had a flair for plagiarism, although they may indicate that Bret Harte was exploiting interest in Mark Twain's themes as Twain in *Roughing It* had exploited interest in Harte's. Harte's little-known story "Ali Baba of the Sierras" seems to owe more to *Tom Sawyer* than to the Forty Thieves. Its small-boy hero and his sweetheart appear shoddy imitations of Tom Sawyer and Becky Thatcher; Spanish Pete was obviously another Injun Joe (who disguised himself as a deaf and dumb Spaniard in a serape) and like Injun Joe was trapped at the mouth of a cave where treasure was hidden. The very title is sus-

[24] *Ibid.*, 1479, 1481, 1497.   [25] Blair, *Native American Humor*, 154.

pect as an elaboration of an allusion to the *Arabian Nights* in *Tom Sawyer*.

But before becoming too sure that Bret Harte was now working a claim staked out by Mark Twain, one should read closely Harte's own revised and lengthened version of the once-popular "M'liss," first appearing in 1860 in shorter form as "The Work on Red Mountain." At the urgent request of the editor, Harte reluctantly tried to expand the story, and the result—which he never liked—was published in serial form in the *Golden Era* in 1863, a year before Mark Twain left Nevada for San Francisco and thirteen years before the publication of *The Adventures of Tom Sawyer*.

> "Now, where on earth can that child be?" said Mrs. Morpher, shading her eyes with her hand, as she stood at the door of the 'Mountain Ranch,' looking down the Wingdam road at sunset. "With his best things on, too. Goodness!—what *were* boys made for?"[26]

Thus begins a chapter entitled "The Trials of Mrs. Morpher," and although the dialogue is much less skillful than the famous beginning of *The Adventures of Tom Sawyer*, Mrs. Morpher's speech as well as her trials are a good deal like Aunt Polly's:

> "Toм!"
> No answer.
> "Tom!"
> No answer.
> "What's gone with that boy, I wonder?
>   You Toм!"
> No answer.
> The old lady pulled her spectacles down and looked over them about the room; then she put them up and looked out under them. She seldom or never looked *through* them for so small a thing as a boy.[27]

The small boy Mrs. Morpher was looking for bore the impossible name of Aristides. He shared Tom Sawyer's resentment against the restraint of new clothes and cleanliness, and with feverish excitement he collected such treasures as a ravished jay's nest and a dead hare. He wore his hat on the back of his head, his trousers were too large for him, and he liked to burrow his bare toes luxuriously in cool, loose dirt. He

---

[26] *Writings*, I, 278.   [27] *The Adventures of Tom Sawyer*, 13.

practiced whistling shrilly between his fingers (instead of whistling melodiously with his tongue tapping the roof of his mouth, as did Tom Sawyer). When he drew a stub of a cigar from his pocket and placed it between his teeth, "it was evident that there was a moral as well as a physical laxity in his conduct."[28] Moreover, he evaded Sunday school when possible. One day when he discovered he was an hour and a half late to school, he played hookey and took refuge in the woods.

> Away from the glare of the red road, how deliciously cool was the damp breath and twilight dimness of the stately pines. How they seemed to welcome him in their deepest recesses, ranging themselves silently around him as he ran, shutting out the world and its schoolhouses, and the pursuit of indignant parents and vindictive teachers.

In "the forest depths the blue jay called to him mockingly, and the kingbird, spreading his tail like a crimson pennant, beckoned him onward. . . . there was recognition and greeting even in the squirrel that scampered past him, mischievously whisking his ridiculous tail within an inch of his outstretched fingers." At last Aristides, "flinging away hat, shoes, and satchel, uttered a shrill whoop and dashed forward like a youthful savage."[29]

Before Tom Sawyer threw off part of his clothes to dash about like Robin Hood, he

> . . . entered a dense wood, picked his pathless way to the center of it, and sat down on a mossy spot under a spreading oak. There was not even a zephyr stirring; the dead noonday heat had even stilled the songs of the birds; nature lay in a trance that was broken by no sound but the occasional far-off hammering of a woodpecker, and this seemed to render the pervading silence and sense of loneliness more profound. It seemed to him that life was but a trouble, at best.[30]

And in the scene on Jackson's Island when Tom wakes before Huck and Joe:

> . . . a catbird, the northern mocker, lit in a tree over Tom's head, and trilled out her imitations of her neighbors in a rapture of enjoyment; then a shrill jay swept down, a flash of blue flame, and stopped on a twig almost within the boy's reach, cocked his head to one side and eyed the

[28] *Writings*, I, 273.   [29] *Ibid.*, I, 246.
[30] Twain, *The Adventures of Tom Sawyer*, 79.

strangers with a consuming curiosity; a gray squirrel and a big fellow of the "fox" kind came scurrying along, sitting up at intervals to inspect and chatter at the boys.[31]

In the margin of Bret Harte's story "A Ghost of the Sierras," in *Drift from Two Shores*, published in 1878, Mark Twain wrote: "When it comes to California scenery, this devil is unsurpassed."[32] Mark Twain's detailed descriptions of American woodland scenes observed by a boy surpass Harte's but were probably influenced by them.[33]

In "M'liss," particularly interesting is an irrelevant interpolation of a small boy's "dream." When Aristides, or Risty, found a secret cave to which he planned to bring a playmate, he imagined the way the other schoolboys would "look up at him with interest as the hero and discoverer of this wonderful cavern." Risty heard the sound of a pick from a second chamber of the cave (an abandoned gold mine where a man had been murdered and a pistol placed in his hand, to prevent detection of the real murderer), and peering down from his vantage point, the boy saw a man working. Later he saw this man (with a red handkerchief tied around his head under his hat) carry from the cave a suspiciously heavy bag. Harte's boy was the first to discover that the man he saw was a murderer, and that this murderer had stored thousands of dollars worth of gold in sacks inside the cave. Like Tom Sawyer, Risty dreamed so feverishly about his experience that he was ill in bed for a time, during which he was haunted by what he had seen and had difficulty deciding whether it was dream or reality.

When he returned to the cave, Risty thought about his sweetheart just before he was trapped inside by a falling tree which blocked the entrance, but—unlike Becky Thatcher—his sweetheart was not trapped with him. In his capacious pocket this boy had, among other treasures, a match with which he lighted a candle stuck in a crevice of the rock inside the cave. Later it was discovered that the cave—like Tom Sawyer's cave—had another entrance on a lower level. Like Aunt Polly and the

---

[31] *Ibid.*, 125.

[32] See Wecter's copy of Mark Twain's Marginalia, MTP. See also *MTE*.

[33] Both paragraphs above find an antecedent in Hawthorne's description of the forest's welcome to Pearl in "A Flood of Sunshine," *The Scarlet Letter*. Bret Harte, who admired Hawthorne, was more apt to be influenced by this paragraph than was Mark Twain, who once wrote of Hawthorne and George Eliot: ". . . they just tire me to death." See Bellamy, *Mark Twain as a Literary Artist*, 44.

citizens of St. Petersburg, Mrs. Morpher and some of the townspeople of Smith's Pocket were alarmed at the boy's absence, and a small search party was sent for him. After a man was killed, the mystery of the cave was at least partly solved. But the schoolmaster marveled that the secret of its great wealth had been known for "three weeks to a penniless orphan girl of twelve and an eccentric schoolboy of ten, and undivulged except when a proper occasion offered."[34]

The "orphan girl" was M'liss, a sibling of Huck Finn. Child of the town drunkard, known as old Bummer Smith, she was a village pariah before being taken in by the respectable Morpher family in an attempt to civilize her. As Tom Sawyer hated Sid, M'liss hated the pink and white Morpher girl held up to her as a model.[35] This character closely resembled those "young ladies clad in lawn and muslin . . . conspicuously conscious of their bare arms" and "their grandmothers' ancient trinkets," who read their trite little compositions in Mark Twain's "Examination Evening" in *Tom Sawyer*.[36] In the "Examination" scene in "M'liss," Clytie Morpher "softly elevated her round white arm," its "seductive curves . . . enhanced by a gorgeous and massive specimen bracelet," and her "low-necked white book-muslin rested softly on Clytie's white, plump shoulders."[37] Contrasting with the orthodox Clytie Morpher, M'liss was, like Huck, a skeptic of orthodox religion, impenitent before a God of wrath. She "did not want to be beholden" to anyone who felt that way about her. Harte's story repeatedly mentions the red hands of M'liss. Perhaps it was a trick of Mark Twain's memory that Tom Sawyer's Gang included "Huck Finn, the Red-Handed."

The supposed murderer in "M'liss" started out as a sinister character but abruptly degenerated to an imbecility like that of Muff Potter. He was imprisoned in a jail even flimsier than the one described in *Tom Sawyer*. Tom and Huck took the prisoner Potter tobacco and matches; M'liss took the prisoner Waters a bottle of brandy. But the brandy,

---

[34] *Writings*, I, 307.

[35] *Writings*, I, 252, 267, 269. Allusions to M'liss's dark skin, her coarse black hair, her "Indian" walk, and her exclamation "that white girl" for her hated rival suggests that Harte's heroine may have had Indian blood in her veins, an interesting contrast to Twain's use of a half-blood as a villain.

[36] *The Adventures of Tom Sawyer*, 176.   [37] *Writings*, I, 269.

like the matches which the boy Sam Clemens gave a drunken tramp in the Hannibal jail, became the means of setting the jail on fire. And though M'liss melodramatically led the prisoner through the flames to safety, the guard suffered a death horrifyingly similar to that of the tramp for whose death the young Clemens blamed himself.[38]

Bret Harte's story includes many other details which find counterparts in *The Adventures of Tom Sawyer* and its sequel, *The Adventures of Huckleberry Finn*. The graveyard in *Tom Sawyer*, identified as the "Western kind," was surrounded by a fence like the graveyard in "M'liss," but (symbolizing emotional differences between the two men as well as characteristic distinctions between the increased realism of Mark Twain's story compared with the romanticism of Harte's) the sunken graves in *Tom Sawyer* were covered with grass and weeds, whereas in "M'liss" the graves were covered in spring with daisies and buttercups. Mrs. Morpher's decorous little parlor with its bright carpet and, on the mantel, its daguerreotypes of the Morpher family in "progressive stages of petrifaction which had the Medusa-like effect of freezing visitors in their chairs" suggests Mark Twain's perspective in the more fully developed and vivid descriptions of the Grangerford parlor and the drawings of Emmeline. More significantly, "M'liss" includes scenes of violence and avid concern with the manner of dying paralleling famous scenes in *Huckleberry Finn*. On the day of the inquest, a fearful boy steals into a room to gaze curiously at the dead body of the murdered man. Citizens of Smith's Pocket discuss with "infinite relish" details of another killing. With morbid curiosity they place their fingers in the bullet holes of the corpse. After a mob gathered, it "pushed and panted, stealthily creeping around the doors and windows of the jail like some strange beast of prey" and planned to lynch.[39]

When, yielding to the insistence of his editor, Harte tried to expand "M'liss," he became so conscious of the absurdity of parts of the narrative that he bogged down in the middle of the story and offered his

[38] Neider, *Autobiography*, 40–41. Tom also smuggled to Muff Potter "such small comforts as he could get hold of," which may well have included whisky, a comfort Mark Twain may have hesitated to mention with approval in a book like *Tom Sawyer*, which he hoped would appeal to boys and girls as well as to adults. See the Preface to *Tom Sawyer*, 11.

[39] *Writings*, I, 289.

readers a chance to suggest conclusions. After a sordid and unconvincing denouement of the affairs of the heroine, Harte's 1863 version ends with the schoolmaster driving away from the village called Smith's Pocket and leaving the boy, Risty, standing in the dust of the highway as if waiting for someone else to come along and do him justice. That boy was a progenitor of Tom Sawyer.

Following his description of the truant schoolboy in the woods, Harte had commented: "Are not these things written in the dog's eared pages of every boy's memory, even though they seemed afterward to the just Aristides a part and parcel of his own strange vision?"[40] What is *Tom Sawyer* but the turning of the "dog's eared pages" of Mark Twain's own boyhood memories? If Harte's sentence was not the seed from which *Tom Sawyer* grew, it may well have been the catalyst for Mark Twain's memories. And the "ghastly stuff" which so impressed Bernard De Voto was also foreshadowed in "M'liss."[41]

Henry Nash Smith says that every reader will recognize in Mark Twain's description of Miss Clapp's school, material which ten years later would go into the "Examination Evening" scene in *Tom Sawyer*.[42] Mark Twain's letter to the Virginia City *Enterprise*, including the account of Miss Clapp's school, was written from Carson City on January 14, 1864. Harte's lengthened version of the already famous "M'liss," with its "Examination" scene, had been running in the *Golden Era* for ten weeks. The last installment appeared on December 20, 1863, less than a month preceding the publication of Mark Twain's letter.

"M'liss" had not been included in the 1867 anthology of Harte's San Francisco prose writings published by G. W. Carleton, but along with "Tennessee's Partner" and "The Idyl of Red Gulch," it reappeared in the volume published by Fields, Osgood and Company early in 1870, the year America and the rest of the world became acutely aware of Bret Harte. In this year Mark Twain probably wrote "Boy's Manuscript," believed to be the "earliest known attempt" at *Tom Sawyer*. When Bernard De Voto explained that this sketch is the embryo of *Tom Sawyer* but "*Tom Sawyer* untouched by greatness," the very weaknesses he noted in Mark Twain's sketch are the weaknesses of

<hr />

[40] *Ibid.*, 246–47. For a close parallel in Booth Tarkington's approval of *Tom Sawyer*, see Blair, *Mark Twain & Huck Finn*, 55.

[41] *The Portable Mark Twain*, 33.

[42] *Mark Twain of the* Enterprise, 22, 29–30, 139–38.

"M'liss." De Voto also noted that "Boy's Manuscript" was Twain's first attempt to write fiction.[43]

Early in the following year Mark Twain wrote Aldrich that Harte had "trimmed and trained and schooled" him. The conclusion of one paragraph of Harte's first version of "M'liss" concerns the futility of Mrs. Morpher's efforts to impose the conventions on the children of her household:

> ... with but one exception, however much the "Prairie Rose" might have *trimmed and pruned and trained* her own matured luxuriance, the little shoots came up defiantly wild and straggling. That one exception was Clytemnestra Morpher, aged fifteen. She was the realisation of her mother's immaculate conception—neat, orderly, and dull.[44]

In relation to Bret Harte's influence on Mark Twain, it should be kept in mind that Harte was generally on the side of the little shoots that came up defiantly wild and straggling, and seldom on the side of the neat, the orderly, and the dull.

It has been suggested that *Tom Sawyer* grew out of Mark Twain's admiration for Thomas Bailey Aldrich's *The Story of a Bad Boy*, published in book form in 1870. Albert E. Stone, Jr., in an interesting study of *The Innocent Eye: Childhood in Mark Twain's Imagination* identifies Tom Bailey as "the immediate ancestor of Tom Sawyer." Mark Twain tried once to mark *The Story of a Bad Boy* for Livy but gave it up because, he said, "for the life of me, I could not admire the volume much."[45] After Mark Twain and Thomas Bailey Aldrich became friends, it was Aldrich's verse for which Twain professed admiration; he seems never to have had a very high opinion of Aldrich's prose.[46] Nevertheless, though the Bad Boy had his beginnings even before 1860, Aldrich's book popularized the term. What Stone chiefly intended to demonstrate was not direct influence on *Tom Sawyer* but the existence among Mark Twain's Nook Farm neighbors and other New England writers of a "tradition of taking childhood seriously as a subject for stories and novels." Stone concluded that the New England pattern "naturally inflenced" Mark Twain's own first efforts in this tradition."[47]

---

[43] *Mark Twain at Work*, 5–8. See also Blair, *Mark Twain & Huck Finn*, 50.

[44] The italics are mine. This version can be found in *Tales of the West: Parodies and Poems by Bret Harte*, 19.

[45] *LL*, 132.   [46] See Neider, *Autobiography*, 358.

[47] Stone, *The Innocent Eye*, 32.

Without disagreeing with this thesis, I should like to point out that for more than ten years Bret Harte had been interested in writing for and about children; that the children in Harte's stories were never the painfully good little creatures of Sunday-school fiction for which Harte himself had developed an early aversion and to which he made satiric reference in "M'liss";[48] that Mark Twain's "The Story of the Bad Little Boy" was written in 1865, when he was closely associated with Bret Harte in San Francisco; and that Mark Twain must have been aware of the practice if not the tradiiton of taking childhood seriously as a subject for fiction before his interest in this subject gained added encouragement by the sanction of New England.

Harte's interest in children as subjects of fiction was probably stimulated by his admiration for Dickens,[49] but Harte's sympathy for children and his understanding of child psychology seemed largely intuitive. Even before "M'liss," whose small boy fought, fell in love, met death, and ran away from home in 1863, such slight journalistic features as "Sufferings of a Small Person" (*Golden Era*, February 3, 1861) and "With 'Buster,' " (*Golden Era*, April 14, 1861) reflect Harte's interest. They demonstrate his awareness of and sympathy with the point of view of a child, his defense of the disorderly small boy, and his condemnation of didactic fiction which falsified life in order to emphasize the horrible retribution in store for the Bad Boy. As editor of the *Overland Monthly*, Harte reviewed with particular attention and discrimination the current books being published for children.[50]

Harte's concern with the theory and practice of writing juvenile fiction was further evidenced by a letter written on May 1, 1874, to Mrs. Mary Mapes Dodge, editor of *St. Nicholas Magazine for Boys and Girls*, which was about to publish Harte's "Baby Sylvester," a bear story. In this letter Harte expressed admiration for the art, "which none values more highly than myself," of writing for children, but on grounds

[48] *BHAE*, 14–15. See also Pemberton, *Bret Harte, A Treatise and a Tribute*, 193. *Writings*, I, 249.

[49] In his editorial on Charles Dickens hurriedly written for the *Overland Monthly* on the day the news of Dickens' death reached him, Harte expressed his admiration for this element in Dickens' work: "No one before him wrote so tenderly of childhood, for no one before him carried into the wisdom of maturity an enthusiasm so youthful— a faith so boy-like." *Writings*, XX, 167.

[50] For example, see Harte's review of Mary Lorimer's *Among the Hills*, *Overland Monthly*, Vol. IV (Jan., 1870), 103.

that it would be writing down to his readers, he rejected the editor's suggestion that he modify his language for childish minds.[51] He insisted that an author should respect a child's taste, his judgment, and his ability to recognize a lie in fiction. Although he continued to try to write stories for children, Bret Harte lacked Mark Twain's ability to *become* the child about whom he was writing. Children often liked his stories, but finally Harte's fiction maintained the point of view of an imaginative and affectionate adult observing the child.[52] Bret Harte's use of this perspective (which obtrudes in less successful passages of *Tom Sawyer*) may partly explain Mark Twain's difficulty in making up his mind whether he intended his first book about boyhood to be read by children or adults. To Mrs. Dodge, Harte professed his own belief that he lacked the art of writing juvenile fiction.

There can be no doubt that Mark Twain was aware of Bret Harte's interest in fiction for and about children. The influence of "M'liss" on Mark Twain's work was, I believe, more specific and detailed than has heretofore been noticed. My hypothesis that the shabby little M'liss with her friend Risty stood, recognized or unrecognized, in the shadowy backgrounds of Mark Twain's mind when he was writing *Tom Sawyer* and *Huckleberry Finn* is altogether compatible with Bernard De Voto's conclusion that with Tom Sawyer, Mark Twain found the theme best suited to his interest, his experience, and his talents.[53] And it does not dim in any way an appreciation of Mark Twain's artistic achievement in writing his two most famous books.[54]

While working on *The Adventures of Tom Sawyer*, Mark Twain gave considerable thought to conscious and unconscious plagiarism. In 1876, the year of the book's publication, he closely annotated a chapter on plagiarism in Henry Breen's *Modern English Literature: Its Blemishes and Defects*. When Breen condemned as a "barefaced plea for literary thievery" a Dumas declaration that "the man of genius does not steal; he conquers; and what he conquers he annexes to his empire," Twain sided with Dumas. In the margin beside Dumas's words, Twain wrote: "Shakespeare took other people's quartz and extracted the gold

[51] Booth, "Unpublished Letters of Bret Harte," *loc. cit.*, 131–42.
[52] See Pemberton, *Bret Harte, A Treatise and a Tribute*, 18–19.
[53] *Mark Twain's America*, 303–304.
[54] Wagenknecht, *Mark Twain: The Man and His Work*, 118–19.

from it—it was a nearly valuless commodity before."[55] The mining metaphor and the sentiment would be peculiarly applicable to a possible adaptation of certain elements in "M'liss" for *The Adventures of Tom Sawyer*.

In 1879, Oliver Wendell Holmes had courteously replied to Mark Twain's apology for inadvertently using the dedication of *Songs in Many Keys* for *The Innocents Abroad* by assuring Mark Twain that he would be "stolen from" a great deal oftener that he would borrow from other writers. Ernest Hemingway's dictum that "all modern American literature comes from one book by Mark Twain called *Huckleberry Finn*" is the best-known testimony to the fulfillment of Dr. Holmes's prophecy. But along with Mark Twain's angry charges that Bret Harte plagiarized should be remembered not only Twain's theories about plagiarism but also the possibility that Harte's influence on Twain continued long after Twain had forgotten his acknowledgment of that influence. In the course of our examination of the relationship between Bret Harte and Mark Twain, we have observed certain or probable influences of (1) Harte's editing on *The Innocents Abroad*, (2) the popularity of Harte's writings about the West on *Roughing It* (particularly the chapters on California, on Chinese, and on Buck Fanshaw's funeral), and (3) Harte's interest in fiction for and about children on *Tom Sawyer* and *Huckleberry Finn*. Professor Stone notes the possible influence of Harte's work on "Huck Finn and Tom Sawyer among the Indians" as late as 1889.[56]

Today the influence of Bret Harte on the development of American literature is underestimated. But in the lifetime of Bret Harte and Mark Twain, it was overestimated. Bret Harte knew it and Mark Twain resented it. The year 1870 was recognized as a turning point in American literature. And 1870 was Bret Harte's year. In the years that followed American critics commented on the deterioration of Harte's work but continued to compare him with Turgenev and to insist that what he had already produced would "always remain a vigorous, brilliant, original contribution to American literature."[57] According to Henry Adams, "the fateful year of 1870" marked the close of a literary epoch, "when

[55] Blair, *Mark Twain & Huck Finn*, 59–60.

[56] *The Innocent Eye*, 174–75.

[57] James Herbert Morse, "The Native Element in American Fiction," *Century Magazine*, Vol. XXVI (July, 1883), 364. See also Charles La Coste Crane, Jr., "The De-

quarterlies gave way to monthlies; letter-press to illustrations; volumes to pages. The outburst was brilliant. Bret Harte led, and Robert Louis Stevenson followed. Guy de Maupassant and Rudyard Kipling brought up the rear, and dazzled the world."[58]

Nineteenth-century critics frequently listed Mark Twain among the followers of Bret Harte. The main reason was that Harte's writing about California stimulated the fictional exploration of other regions so that in 1872, Howells would prophesy that gradually but surely the "whole varied field of American life" would be observable in American fiction."[59] This idea generated Mark Twain's *Atlantic* essays, later expanded and published as *Life on the Mississippi*.[60] But the best of all regional studies in fiction are those marvelous Mississippi Valley scenes in *Huckleberry Finn*: the camp meeting, the Grangerford home, Peter Wilks's funeral, the Arkansas town where loafers laughed as dogs chased an old sow and where a mob gathered for a lynching bee. The fact that the middle chapters of *Huckleberry Finn* are much more than local color does not alter the fact that it was Mark Twain's interest in re-creating the life of the Mississippi River Valley which he knew so well that led him to abandon the idea of taking Jim to freedom.[61] The resulting chapters were not only the greatest in the book but the greatest writing Mark Twain ever produced.

Bret Harte was the first to recognize the effectiveness of Mark Twain's attacks on social ills. Aware of Twain's sensitiveness about assertions that he had imitated Harte, time and again Bret Harte reiterated his own early dictum that Mark Twain stood alone as the most original humorist that America had yet produced: "He alone is inimitable."[62] *Ah Sin*, Mark Twain's bitter words, Mark Twain's triumphs, and Bret Harte's own disappointments and frustrations never changed Harte's critical judgment of Twain's work. In 1899, the year Hamlin Garland interviewed both Harte and Twain in London, Bret Harte was asked to write for *Cornhill Magazine* an essay on "The Rise of the 'Short Story.'" In this essay Harte again rebuked critics who, mistakenly attributing to him the invention of the local-color genre, applied the

cline in the Literary Reputation of Bret Harte," unpublished master's thesis, University of North Carolina.

[58] *The Education of Henry Adams*, 259.
[59] Blair, *Mark Twain & Huck Finn*, 59.
[60] *MTL*, I, 229–30.
[61] *The Adventures of Huckleberry Finn*, viii–xii.
[62] *Writings*, XX, 230.

term "imitators" to such writers as Joel Chandler Harris, George Washington Cable, Mary E. Wilkins Freeman, Constance Fenimore Woolson, and "Mark Twain in 'Huckleberry Finn.' " The term "imitator," Harte said, "could not fairly apply to those who cut loose from conventional methods and sought honestly to describe the life around them." For himself, Harte added, he could claim only "to have shown them that it could be done."[63] Bret Harte had considerable right to that claim.

"Waves of influence run from the man," wrote Henry Seidel Canby in 1926, "and indeed the literary West may be said to have founded itself upon the imagination of Bret Harte."[64] Bret Harte's influence was not nearly so bad as "The Modest Club" would have us believe. That Harte's *Condensed Novels* "brilliantly satirized the falsification of life by sentimental novelists" has been recognized by Everett Carter.[65] But as I have attempted to demonstrate, even Harte's inferior works include seminal elements for better fiction. When Bret Harte, portraying a small town in the wake of the Gold Rush, commented that the teacher who came to "Riches are deceitful" in a pupil's copybook elaborated the noun "with an insincerity of flourish that was quite in the spirit of his text," Harte knew a good deal about Hadleyburg. And when Harte's popular stories exhibited the effects of close observation and detailed reporting of a particular region, with all his romanticism, Harte was encouraging narrative techniques that led to realism.

Instead of attributing to Bret Harte a "flair for plagiarism," it seems more just to accord him a respected place in America's literary history because his techniques and his ideas stimulated the development of superior techniques and the expression of more profound thought.

[63] Vol. VII (July, 1899), 7.

[64] "The Luck of Bret Harte," *Saturday Review of Literature*, Vol. II (Apr. 17, 1926), 717.

[65] *Howells and the Age of Realism*, 69.

23

THE SHOWMAN AND THE SHOW

It warn't funny to me, though; I was all of a tremble to see his danger.

Huckleberry Finn[1]

IF IN THE PRECEDING CHAPTERS I have seemed to overemphasize Bret Harte's virtues and ignore his faults, and at the same time overemphasize Mark Twain's faults and ignore his virtues, the imbalance is due to my belief that for too long a time the scales have been heavily weighted on the side of Harte's damnation. But I have tried to make equally clear my sincere appreciation of the artistic achievements of the author of *Huckleberry Finn* and my interest in the fascinating complexity of the character of Mark Twain, the most original but not the most admirable creation of Samuel L. Clemens. The words of that aggressive and increasingly powerful Twain have given Harte, the man, as well as Harte, the writer, a muscular shove toward oblivion. No one will deny that Bret Harte had deficiencies of character. It is generally understood that human beings without deficiencies are difficult to find. Yet Mark Twain's words—particularly his words uttered in an old and embittered age—should not be taken as evidence of what Bret Harte's deficiencies were.

Even though the late Bernard De Voto warned readers of inaccuracies and distortions in Mark Twain's autobiographical dictations, De Voto accepted Mark Twain's estimate of Bret Harte and at times even attempted to rival his master in invective. The essay in which William Dean Howells expressed a sincere belief that if Bret Harte's temperament was not adapted to the "elder American world," it was possible that Harte's temperament was not altogether in the wrong,[2] De Voto dismissed as "an epitaph to a literary charlatan whose tales have greatly

1 *Adventures of Huckleberry Finn*, 126.
2 Howells, "Editor's Easy Chair," *loc. cit.*, 157.

pleased the second-rate."[3] *Mark Twain's America*, published in 1932, is marked by an anti-intellectual bias which grew frighteningly familiar as a national pattern in the early 1950's. Moving eastward across the wide Missouri, *Mark Twain's America* turns sour. In addition to its particular target, Van Wyck Brooks, the objects of De Voto's scorn include *The Atlantic Monthly* together with *Atlantic* editors James Russell Lowell and William Dean Howells; "the damned shadow of Europe"; that part of Boston where "literature was what the Brahmins wrote and life was dinner with watered madeira on Mt. Vernon Street"; Cambridge, with its "instinctive preference for the second rate"; and "the nightly gatherings of Bostonians before lecture platforms from which incurable schoolmasters read papers on the soul." Although De Voto could hardly have considered Bret Harte an intellectual, he resented the fact that in his day Harte appealed to intellectuals in America as well as in England, and doors in Cambridge, Massachusetts, closed to Mark Twain, swung widely open for Bret Harte. According to De Voto, "Harte was a fraud, as a man, a Westerner, a writer." "His sympathy, embedded in sweet tales, greatly comforted the nice people."[4]

In this book of many sneers which sneered at Harte for sneering, De Voto attributed the break in the friendship between Bret Harte and Mark Twain to Harte's "acetic malice." De Voto reported that after the Keeler luncheon, Harte's "quoted allusions to Mark are sinister."[5] Apparently relying on De Voto's testimony, *The Atlantic Monthly*'s centennial anthology asserted that "As Mark Twain's star rose and Harte's fell, the latter [*sic*] became jealous and vindictive."[6] But neither *Jubilee* nor De Voto quoted any of Harte's "sinister" allusions, and the manuscript for *Mark Twain's America* (deposited in the Abernethy Library of American Literature in Middlebury College, Vermont) includes no documentation of this charge.

In that oddly prophetic story "The Iliad of Sandy Bar," the estranged partners of the Amity Claim became rival candidates in a political campaign. To the "general astonishment" of the comumnity, one of the candidates "launched into bitter denunciation of his rival." "He not only dwelt upon Scott's deeds and example as known to Sandy Bar, but

[3] *Mark Twain's America*, 164.
[4] *Ibid.*, 192.   [5] *Ibid.*, 163.   [6] *Jubilee*, 88.

spoke of facts connected with his previous career hitherto unknown to his auditors. To great precision of epithet and directness of statement, the speaker added the fascination of revelation and exposure."

When the maligned Scott was "dragged, pushed, and pulled" to the speaker's platform, he stood before the crowd and replied in drunken dignity: "There's naught as that man hez said as is n't true. I *was* run outer Cairo; I *did* belong to the Regulators; I *did* desert from the army; I *did* leave a wife in Kansas. But thar's one thing he did n't charge me with, and maybe he's forgotten. For three years, gentlemen, I was that man's pardner!"[7]

Published in an earlier chapter of this book is Bret Harte's letter of March 1, 1877, described by De Voto as "savage." Bret Harte once explained the evolution of a savage: "Take a gentle, trustful man, abuse him, show him the folly of his gentleness and kindness, prove to him that it is weakness, drive him into a corner, and you have a savage."[8] Written after considerable provocation, the March 1 letter shows that Bret Harte was by no means invulnerable to Mark Twain's hostility. It expressed pain and disillusionment that the man Harte turned to as friend responded by offering him a hack writing job which seemed to Harte an attempt to exploit his poverty. But it was a letter *to* Mark Twain, not a letter written about him to other people. Although I have searched for several years, I have been unable to find a record of any "quoted allusion" spoken or written by Bret Harte indicating that in the years after *Ah Sin*, Harte ever forgot that he and Twain had been friends. As far as I can learn, from 1877 to the time of his death in 1902, Bret Harte spoke of Mark Twain only with respect.[9]

[7] *Writings*, II, 9–10.

[8] "Jeff Brigg's Love Story," *Writings*, III, 258. This story was written in 1879. *BHAE*, 263.

[9] Bret Harte's Diary includes notations for October 4, 5, and 8, 1887, about a paragraph in the New York *World* reporting that Mark Twain had taken Buckenham Hall, Norwich, for a year and intended to entertain his "Dutch friends" there. Understandably Madame Van de Velde was not amused by the newspaper paragraph, which reached England. But when she made the mistake of trying to refute the statement, she found herself in the midst of a flurry of letters, newspaper stories, and interviews, from which she withdrew. One newspaper asked Harte to write his reactions, but he merely recorded the incident without comment in his diary. See Paine's account of Mark Twain's reaction to the rumor, *Biography*, 852.

Because it seemed not quite human for a man to remain silent so many years, in November, 1957, I sought out Bret Harte's younger daughter, Miss Ethel Bret Harte, living in Ojai, California. I found her remarkably objective about her father, and by no means uncritical. In answer to my question, however, she said her father seldom talked about Mark Twain and when he did, he merely reminisced, as anyone might, of an old acquaintance. I asked her if her father had ever, in an unguarded moment, spoken about his former friend in a way which, for any reason, she preferred not to discuss with me.

"No," Bret Harte's daughter replied. "He never did. That was not his way. Mark Twain was the genius. But my father was fair. He was understanding. And he was always ready to listen to the other person's side."

"But *why* did he not answer?" I persisted. "*Why* did he remain silent?"

"When they were younger," she said, "the two were always either very close or at swords' points. In the early years, my father thought of Mark Twain as a boy, not yet formed. And when they were old, my father thought Mark Twain was a sick man."

That it is possible to hold this belief and still love the person is indicated by the best of authorities: Mrs. Clemens. "Why always dwell on the evil until those who live beside you are crushed to the earth & you seem almost like a monomaniac," Mrs. Clemens once wrote her husband. "Oh! I love you so & wish you would listen & take heed."[10] Bernard De Voto also recognized that Mark Twain at times came "perilously close to the indefinable line between sanity and madness."[11]

We have seen how Mark Twain's hostility toward Bret Harte continued over a period of thirty years. The obsessive nature of the hostility is obvious. But how and why did it originate? There is, of course, the possibility that Bret Harte committed against Mark Twain some unpardonable sin which neither would mention, but a close scrutiny of available evidence in letters and biographies of both men as well as in testimonials of their friends makes this seem very unlikely. According to Twain's great-nephew, Samuel Charles Webster, "To get away from his own feelings of guilt he sometimes made the injured party the

[10] *LL,* 333. [11] *Mark Twain at Work,* 108.

scapegoat. . . . Mark Twain never forgave anyone he had injured."[12] In defamation of character and in actions relating to *Ah Sin* and *Gabriel Conroy*, it seems to me that Mark Twain injured Bret Harte.

Bret Harte has not been completely without defenders among twentieth-century American scholars. In 1941, George R. Stewart published in *American Literature* an article entitled "Bret Harte upon Mark Twain in 1866," in which Professor Stewart pointed out that Harte was "very far from being that selfish and vicious cad whom Twain in his irresponsible autobiographical meanderings has set up as the essential Bret Harte."[13] In *Bret Harte, Argonaut and Exile*, the same scholar concluded that "from 1878 until his health finally broke," Bret Harte's life was "a constant progression upwards in almost every respect; his early years represented a greater literary triumph, his later years a greater triumph of character."[14] Bradford Booth is another able defender. In 1944 he wrote: "There are still those who believe that in his private as well as in his public life he was a fraud. That is *not* the opinion of those who have read with care his family correspondence. The materials of the Clark Library's collection do much to procure for Harte a belated justice."[15] Much of the truth about Bret Harte has been succinctly summarized in one paragraph of Franklin Walker's *San Francisco's Literary Frontier*:

> Just as the bizarre pioneer society portrayed in Bret Harte's stories came in time to be accepted as more genuine than the real one, so the romantic tradition established by his fiction has created for the world a man who never existed. The public generally has accepted the picture of a wild and wooly Harte, who washed gold in the mines, held off bandits as a gun-guard on the top of stagecoaches, and risked his life fighting Indians. Recently old-timers, jealous of his popularity or annoyed by his picture of themselves, have tried to replace the red-blooded Harte with a yellow-blooded one, a snob, a dilettante, a dude who wore corsets, a deserter of his family, a man who never paid his debts. Few lovers of the dramatic have been interested in the truth: that Harte was primarily a writing man who saw the wilder side of Western life as an artist rather than a hardened participant and then extracted the core of drama from his observations for his writing.[16]

[12] *Mark Twain: Business Man*, viii.   [13] Vol. XIII (Nov., 1941), 264.
[14] Page 332.   [15] Unpublished Letters of Bret Harte," *loc. cit.*, 142.
[16] Walker, *Literary Frontier*, 65.

In the relatively few years when they were on terms of intimate friendship, one reason why Mark Twain and Bret Harte were sometimes "at swords' points" was that temperamentally, the two men were as different as those famous clients of Pudd'nhead Wilson: Angelo and Luigi Capello. Even though he spent his life drudging for it, Bret Harte had no great love for money and, as a romantic idealist, he frequently warned against the dangers of overemphasis on material values. Mark Twain, on the other hand, was frankly materialistic. As Henry Seidel Canby expressed it, Mark Twain "did not give up speculating because he thought it was wrong for the business of America to be business, but because he was a bad speculator and found someone wiser than himself to handle his profits for him."[17] Money—in large amounts—was very important to Mark Twain, and he demanded payment in some coin for everything he did.[18] Although he was lavishly paid with money as well as with other coins he valued—love, literary success, and world fame such as few men have known—Mark Twain came to old age unsatisfied, with a bitter sense of having been cheated.

Bret Harte saw life as a gamble: as far as fame and success were concerned, what was one man's luck today might be another man's luck tomorrow. Like Jack Hamlin, Bret Harte schooled himself to take his gains and his losses with an equanimity often gay. But it is conceivable that the quiet desperation of the day-by-day drudgery when Bret Harte ground out stories to bring in enough money to support his family, pay up old debts, and avoid new ones evidenced more fortitude than Mark Twain himself showed in debts spectacularly contracted and spectacularly repaid. Oddly enough, at the end of life it was not the author of "Tennessee's Partner" but the author of *Huckleberry Finn* who indulged in self-pity.

Mark Twain courted publicity, whereas Bret Harte shunned it. With all his notoriety, Harte remained exceedingly shy. When he was "Poet of the Day" for a California Fourth of July celebration, he was so diffident that Starr King had to read the poem Harte wrote for the occasion. In Cambridge, at the peak of his fame, Harte preferred listening to talking. When he was invited to respond to the toast "to literature" at the Royal Academy Dinner in London, it took the combined efforts of Froude, Leighton, and Mrs. Harte to get him to the scene of

---

[17] *Turn West, Turn East,* 250.   [18] Clara Clemens, *My Father,* 180.

action, and then they succeeded only on the second attempt. Once the proprietor of a hotel in Malvern where Harte had registered sent to his room a basket of hothouse fruit with the manager's compliments. Surprised and pleased, Harte thanked the proprietor for remembering his birthday, but asked how in the world he had found out. The truth was that the proprietor had not known, but on learning it was an anniversary, insisted upon presenting Harte with a bottle of his best champagne, with liqueurs and cigars to follow. Harte's response was typical: "It was awfully embarrassing," he told a friend. "I felt like a fraud."[19] In later life he objected to passing judgment on books and authors either in the literary clubs of which he was a member or in the articles he was asked to write for journals.

In contrast, Mark Twain loved the sound of his own voice and liked to hold forth at great length on all subjects from missionaries to Shakespeare. With his white hair, his white suit, and his calculated drawl, he was much in demand as an after-dinner speaker, and he made his entrances and his exits as dramatic as a prima donna's.[20] Albert Bigelow Paine tells an amusing story of a lobbying expedition to Washington, D.C., when he and Mark in full dress ("fronted and frocked like penguins") started down to dinner in the Willard Hotel. Paine chose a descent by the elevator, which would permit the two of them to enter the dining room without passing through the long hall known as "Peacock Alley." At the dining room door, Mark Twain, with obvious disappointment, asked Paine if there was not another entrance. Paine said there was, but it was very conspicuous. "I don't mind that," Mark Twain said. "Let's go back and try it over."[21] And they did.

To Josh Billings, Mark Twain was a "charming hater."[22] William Dean Howells declared that Mark Twain was "in some respects, and wished to be, the most outrageous creature that ever breathed."[23] Much of the correspondence between the Reverend Joseph Twichell and his friend Mark Twain concerned Twain's bitterness. The minister, like Howells, recognized Mark Twain's need to "spit his spite" but urged him to gain this therapeutic advantage by syphoning off his "secretions" to his minister rather than emptying them into the minds and souls of

[19] *BHL*, 391.   [20] Clara Clemens, *My Father*, 139.
[21] Paine, *Biography*, 1347–48.
[22] "Josh Billings Papers" in Frank Leslie's *Budget of Fun*, clippings, 1871, in MTP.
[23] Paine, *Biography*, 524.

Howells and Rogers or the pages of the *North American Review*.[24] Like others among Mark Twain's friends, Twichell was "fascinated by Mark's tirades." However, the more matter-of-fact Frank Fuller told Mark Twain himself that the extravagance of his words would be called a sin in anybody else, and in Mark Twain, too, except for the "forbearance" of his friends.[25]

Mark Twain has millions of friends today. Like his contemporaries, we admire his power with words. He had a magical way of making them come alive. He could speak with equal effectiveness on opposite sides of the same issue. But if we do as we are sometimes told and enjoy the "magnificent comedy" of Mark Twain in a rage, aren't we behaving like the circus crowd who laughed until they cried at the drunken man clinging to the powerful horse racing wildly around the ring?[26] It was not the clown's skill that the crowd really enjoyed. Huck was all atremble at his danger.

Mark Twain was always much interested in what he called "the duality idea." In parts of the unpublished manuscript of "My Platonic Sweetheart," he expressed admiration for Robert Louis Stevenson's *Dr. Jekyll and Mr. Hyde*, a narrative which reminded Mark Twain that he had played with a similar idea in "The Carnival of Crime in Connecticut." Here his "pigmy conscience" had been portrayed as an entity residing within him in order to plague his soul. Sometimes this conscience left him to go off frolicking with the consciences of his friends, and these truants amused themselves by blackguarding those other selves who were their hosts and victims. With marvelous psychological insight, Mark Twain then proceeded to develop his idea of multiple personality. He believed that within himself existed not only his workaday self and a spiritually somnolent, zombie, self but a third entity, a dream artist, which could sometimes escape and go larking about a world of illimitable time and space, indulging in adventures, escapades, even horrors impossible for the conscious self. Mark Twain liked to think that when this dream artist was away, it got along very well without him and was having a better time.[27]

[24] Andrews, *Nook Farm*, 233–34.

[25] Letter of June 30, 1877, MTP.

[26] De Voto, "The Other Side of Some Mark Twain Stories," *loc. cit.*, 3.

[27] MTP. I am particularly indebted to Harold Eby and Henry Nash Smith for directing me to this manuscript.

Mark Twain was right that Bret Harte had his unpleasant sides. In uncongenial company, he was apt to be reserved and moody. In earlier years, he borrowed money too freely. He sometimes failed to keep appointments, and he could make witty jibes which got under the skins of his acquaintances. Sometimes Harte wielded this rapier-like weapon in his own defense or in retaliation for a wound, and at such times it could be more effective than Mark Twain's verbal bludgeons. But more often, Harte's irony and satire were introduced to forfend his own inclination to sentimentality, which he as well as Mark Twain recognized as a weakness. But there was still another element in Bret Harte—insouciant, gay, a "careless blithe spirit." It was this element which Mark Twain found most exasperating—and most enviable. This spirit in Harte was symbolized for Twain by that maddeningly bright little red necktie, looking "more than usually cheery and contented and conspicuous" during periods of poverty and humiliation such as the time when Bret Harte embarrassed Mark Twain by coming to the St. James Hotel shabbily dressed.[28] Irrationally, Mark Twain suspected that in spite of everything, Bret Harte might be having a better time in life.

If, with all his drudgery, Bret Harte's spirit remained free, Mark Twain's spirit was often imprisoned within him and lashed him with its contempt.[29] Mark Twain is the poet of the Great River; he is the funny man, the clown; but for many critics he is most impressive as the living symbol and voice of a disillusioned, angry, frustrated, soul-sick humanity. Full recognition of Mark Twain's bitterness came only after the posthumous publication of "The Mysterious Stranger," with its desolate cry that a human being is only a vagrant, useless, homeless thought wandering "forlorn among empty eternities."

Bret Harte found love in the heart of the outcast; Mark Twain found malevolence at the heart of Nature.[30] It was this essential quality of love which Sir Frederick Leighton, at the Royal Academy Dinner in London in 1880, identified as the basis of the appeal of Harte's fiction. Although sometimes clothed in sentimentality, this quality was more than sweet sentiment. Henry Adams considered it an allegiance to Eros. The bitterness and depression of Mark Twain's last years resulted less from financial failure and family tragedies than from anger turned

---

[28] *MTE*, 285.   [29] Paine, *Biography*, 323.
[30] Bellamy, *Mark Twain as a Literary Artist*, 187.

inward upon himself. Ultimately, it was this anger that consumed and destroyed Mark Twain as a writer.[31] His recent publication, "Reflections on Religion," demonstrates that finally the satirist's savage indignation from a lacerated heart had become little more than a reflex action.

It may be remembered that Mark Twain's last words about Bret Harte attempted to fit his final judgment to the Procrustean bed of Mark Twain's theory of determinism. Bret Harte was part of the damned human race which provided no proper traget for harsh words and criticisms because it had nothing to do with planning its weak and foolish character. Thus Mark Twain tried to free himself from responsibility for his own guilt. But his words should be complemented by Mark Twain's marginalia for Greville's assertion that Byron despised pretenders and charlatans while Byron himself was a pretender, "as all men are who assume a character which does not belong to them and affect to be something which they are all the time conscious they are not in reality."

"But, dear sir," Mark Twain wrote on the margin, "you are forgetting that what a man sees in the human race is merely himself in the deep and honest privacy of his own heart. Byron despised the race because he despised himself. I feel as Byron did, and for the same reason."[32]

William Dean Howells sometimes wanted "to get rid of Mark Twain" because the public figure seemed always to mask the man and keep him from Howells' "personal sense."[33] As we have seen, Bret Harte was the first to insist upon the duality of the individual who signed himself Mark Twain and to urge that Samuel Clemens not be held responsible for the verbal slings and arrows of Mark Twain. In that 1870 review which praised *The Innocents Abroad* as a "joyous revelation—an Indian spring in an alkaline literary desert," Bret Harte had noted that Mark Twain "worked himself into a grotesque rage at everything and everybody." This "very eccentric creation of Mr. Clemens" enabled him to say his "most deliberately funny things with all the haste and exaggeration of rage." It gave him an opportunity "to invent epithets and apply them with no sense of personal responsibility on the

[31] Smith, *Mark Twain: The Development of a Writer*, 186–88.
[32] Paine, *Biography*, 1539.
[33] *MTH*, II, 838–39. See also Howells, *My Mark Twain*, 4.

part of the reader or writer. And the rage is always ludicrously disproportionate to the cause."[34]

But in the years that followed, something happened to the dual personality. Sometimes on lecture platforms where the great American humorist was scheduled to speak, a man dressed in the conventional stage manager's black suit and tie appeared and announced that Mr. Clemens had fully expected to be present but had been unavoidably detained. At this, there were murmurs of protest from the audience. Then, holding up his hand for silence, the showman announced that although Mr. Clemens could not come, Mr. Twain would appear and give his lecture. "Whereupon the audience roared its approval."[35] The showman was, of course, Mark Twain.

Whatever became of Mr. Clemens? He fully expected to be present. But after Mrs. Clemens died, nobody could persuade him to appear.

Although the words of Mark Twain about Bret Harte are not very reliable, Bret Harte's judgments of Mark Twain as a man and a writer are as valid today as they were in 1866 and 1870 when they were written. If Bret Harte recognized the duality of Samuel Clemens and Mark Twain, he also foresaw its dangers. In that early review of *The Genial Showman*, Harte noted that Mark Twain had mastered and improved the techniques of Artemus Ward. But Harte warned the younger showman crowding the footsteps of the old master: "It is possible . . . that the 'showman' may become in time part of the show—may yield his individuality and his intellectual integrity to that necessity that drives and controls him."[36] This is what happened to Samuel Clemens, who was once the friend of Bret Harte.

Mark Twain, the showman, became part of the show, and this Mark Twain is very much alive today. But in the persona, also, exists a fascinating complexity. Dominated by Tom Sawyer, the "impresario of the gimmick,"[37] Mark Twain can aspire only to a Parnassus as limited and conventional as the concept of heaven about which Satan wrote such disparaging *Letters from Earth*. However, once by way of a raft on the Mississippi River that "mysterious stranger," the "dream artist," escaped from the showman. For salvation and immortality as one of the

---

[34] *Overland Monthly*, Vol. IV (Jan., 1870), 100–101.
[35] Paine, *Biography*, 492.   [36] *Loc. cit.*, 388–89.
[37] See Marcus Cunliffe, "A Lost Masterpiece?" *Encounter*, Vol. XV (Oct., 1960), 73.

world's great writers, Mark Twain can rely on Huck Finn, whose very existence contradicted all Mark Twain's pseudophilosophical theories of determinism and who lived by the highest moral code of responsibility, compassion, and love.

And Huck said: "I would n't 'a' been in that ringmaster's place, not for a thousand dollars."

SELECTED BIBLIOGRAPHY

1. Manuscript Materials

Crane, Charles La Coste, Jr. "The Decline in the Literary Reputation of Bret Harte." Unpublished M.A. thesis, University of North Carolina, 1939.

Harte, Bret. "Things That Happened 1881 . . . 1888." In the handwriting of Madame Van de Velde. Berg Collection, The New York Public Library.

Langdon, Jervis. "Samuel Langhorne Clemens: Some Reminiscences and Some Excerpts from Letters and Unpublished Manuscripts." Mark Twain Papers, University of California Library, Berkeley.

Lauterbach, Edward S. "Forty Years of Fun: The History of Victorian Humor Magazines." Unpublished Ph.D. dissertation, University of Illinois, 1958.

2. Books

Adams, Henry. *The Education of Henry Adams*. New York, The Modern Library, 1931.

Aldrich, Mrs. Thomas Bailey. *Crowding Memories*. Boston, Houghton Mifflin Company, 1920.

Andrews, Kenneth R. *Nook Farm: Mark Twain's Hartford Circle*. Cambridge, Massachusetts, Harvard University Press, 1950.

Bancroft, Hubert Howe. *History of California, 1860–1890*. Vol. VII. San Francisco, The History Company, 1890.

Bellamy, Gladys Carmen. *Mark Twain as a Literary Artist*. Norman, University of Oklahoma Press, 1950.

Benson, Ivan. *Mark Twain's Western Years*. Palo Alto, Stanford University Press, 1938.

Blair, Walter. *Mark Twain & Huck Finn*. Berkeley, University of California Press, 1960.

———. *Native American Humor, 1800–1900*. New York, American Book Company, 1937.

Blanck, Jacob, compiler. *Bibliography of American Literature.* 4 vols. New Haven, Yale University Press, 1955–63.

Boynton, Henry W. *Bret Harte.* New York, McLure, Phillips, and Company, 1903.

Brooks, Van Wyck. *Howells: His Life and World.* New York, E. P. Dutton & Co., Inc., 1959.

———. *The Ordeal of Mark Twain.* With an introduction by Malcolm Cowley. New York, Meridian Books, 1955.

———. *The Times of Melville and Whitman.* New York, E. P. Dutton & Co., Inc., 1947.

Burdette, Robert J. *Robert J. Burdette, His Message.* Pasadena, California, Burdette, 1922.

Calendar of the Francis Bret Harte Letters in the William Andrews Clark Memorial Library. Los Angeles, The Southern California Historical Records Survey Project, 1942.

Canby, Henry Seidel. *Turn West, Turn East: Mark Twain and Henry James.* Boston, Houghton Mifflin Company, 1951.

Cardwell, Guy A. *Twins of Genius.* East Lansing, The Michigan State College Press, 1953.

Carter, Everett. *Howells and the Age of Realism.* Philadelphia, J. P. Lippincott Company, 1950.

Caughey, John Walton. *California.* New York, Prentice-Hall, Inc., 1952.

Clappe, Louise Amelia Knapp Smith. *The Shirley Letters from the California Mines, 1851–1852.* Edited by Carl I. Wheat. New York, Alfred A. Knopf, 1949.

Clemens, Clara. *My Father, Mark Twain.* New York, Harper & Brothers, 1931.

Clemens, Samuel L. *The Curious Republic of Gondour and Other Whimsical Sketches.* New York, Boni and Liveright, 1919.

Crane, Stephen. *Stephen Crane: Letters.* Edited by R. W. Stallman and Lillian Gilkes. New York, New York University Press, 1960.

Cummins, Ella Sterling (Mrs. Mighels). *The Story of the Files.* San Francisco, World's Fair Commission of California, Columbian Exposition, 1893.

Daly, Joseph Frances. *The Life of Augustin Daly.* New York, The Macmillan Company, 1917.

De Voto, Bernard. *Mark Twain at Work.* Cambridge, Massachusetts, Harvard University Press, 1942.

———. *Mark Twain's America.* Boston, Houghton Mifflin Company, 1932.

346

Eighteenth Year Book, 1919. Boston, The Bibliophile Society, 1919.

Erskine, John. *Leading American Novelists.* New York, Henry Holt and Company, 1910.

Fatout, Paul. *Ambrose Bierce, the Devil's Lexicographer.* Norman, University of Oklahoma Press, 1951.

———. *Mark Twain on the Lecture Circuit.* Bloomington, Indiana University Press, 1960.

Felheim, Marvin. *The Theater of Augustin Daly.* Cambridge, Massachusetts, Harvard University Press, 1956.

Fenn, William Purviance. *Ah Sin and His Brethren in American Literature.* Peking, China, College of Chinese Studies, Co-operating with California College in China, 1933.

Ferguson, DeLancey. *Mark Twain: Man and Legend.* Indianapolis, The Bobbs, Merrill Company, 1943.

Foner, Philip S. *Mark Twain: Social Critic.* New York, International Publishers, 1958.

Gaer, Joseph, editor. *Bret Harte: Bibliography and Biographical Data.* N. p., 1935.

Garland, Hamlin. *Companions on the Trail: A Literary Chronicle.* New York, The Macmillan Company, 1931.

———. *Roadside Meetings.* New York, The Macmillan Company, 1930.

Greene, Laurence. *The Filibuster.* Indianapolis, The Bobbs, Merrill Company, 1927.

Greenslet, Ferris. *The Life of Thomas Bailey Aldrich.* Boston, The Riverside Press, 1908.

Hart, James D. *The Oxford Companion to American Literature.* New York, Oxford University Press, 1948.

Harte, Bret. *The Lectures of Bret Harte.* Edited by Charles Meeker Kozlay. Brooklyn, New York, Charles Meeker Kozlay, 1909.

———. *The Letters of Bret Harte.* Edited by Geoffrey Bret Harte. Boston, Houghton Mifflin Company, 1926.

———. *Bret Harte: Representative Selections.* Edited by Joseph B. Harrison. New York, American Book Company, 1941.

———. *San Francisco in 1866 by Bret Harte, Being Letters to the Springfield Republican.* Edited by George R. Stewart and Edwin S. Fussell. San Francisco, The Book Club of California, 1951.

———. *Tales of the West: Parodies and Poems by Bret Harte.* London, Thomas Nelson and Sons, Ltd., n.d.

———. *The Writings of Bret Harte.* 20 vols. Boston, Houghton Mifflin Company, 1896–1914.

————. and Mark Twain. *Sketches of the Sixties by Bret Harte and Mark Twain.* Edited by John Howell. San Francisco, John Howell, 1926.

Hemminghaus, Edgar H. *Mark Twain in Germany.* New York, Columbia University Press, 1939.

Hittell, John S. *California as a Home for the Emigrant: A Brief Statement of Its Public Lands, Wages, Climate, Agriculture, Manufacturers, Attraction, and General Business.* San Francisco, The California Immigrant Union, 1870.

Howells, William Dean. *The Complete Plays of W. D. Howells.* Edited by Walter J. Meserve. New York, New York University Press, 1960.

————. *Life in Letters of William Dean Howells.* Edited by Mildred Howells. Garden City, New York, Doubleday Doran & Company, Inc., 1928.

————. *Literary Friends and Acquaintances.* New York, Harper & Brothers, 1901.

————. *A Modern Instance.* Edited by William M. Gibson. Boston, Houghton Mifflin Company, 1957.

————. *My Mark Twain: Reminiscences and Criticism.* New York, Harper & Brothers, 1910.

————. *A Traveler from Altruria.* New York, Harper & Brothers, 1908.

Hutton, Laurence. *Talks in a Library with Laurence Hutton, Recorded by Isabel Moore.* New York, G. P. Putnam's Sons, 1909.

Johnson, Merle, compiler. *Bibliography of the Works of Mark Twain, Samuel L. Clemens.* New York, Harper & Brothers, 1935.

Lewis, Oscar. *The Origin of the Celebrated Jumping Frog of Calaveras County.* San Francisco, The Book Club of California, 1931.

McWilliams, Carey. *Ambrose Bierce: A Biography.* New York, Albert and Charles Boni, 1929.

Magarshack, David. *Chekov: A Life.* New York, The Grove Press, 1955.

Marberry, M. M. *Splendid Poseur: Joaquin Miller—American Poet.* New York, Thomas Y. Crowell Company, 1953.

Mark Twain. *Adventures of Huckleberry Finn.* Edited by Henry Nash Smith. Boston, Houghton Mifflin Company, 1958.

————. *Adventures of Tom Sawyer.* New York, The Heritage Club, 1937.

————. *The Autobiography of Mark Twain.* Edited by Charles Neider. New York, Harper & Brothers, 1959.

————. *Contributions to* The Galaxy *by Mark Twain.* Edited by Bruce R. McElderry, Jr. Gainesville, Florida, Scholars Facsimiles & Reprints, 1961.

————. *The Forgotten Writings of Mark Twain.* Edited by Henry Duskis. New York, The Citadel Press, 1963.

————. *Letters from the Earth.* Edited by Bernard De Voto, with a Preface by Henry Nash Smith. New York, Harper & Row, 1962.

————. *Mark Twain to Mrs. Fairbanks.* Edited by Dixon Wecter. San Marino, California, Huntington Library, 1949.

————. *The Love Letters of Mark Twain.* Edited by Dixon Wecter. New York, Harper & Brothers, 1949.

————. *Mark Twain–Howells Letters.* Edited by Henry Nash Smith and William M. Gibson with the assistance of Frederick Anderson. Cambridge, Massachusetts, The Belknap Press of Harvard University Press, 1960.

————. *Mark Twain in Eruption.* Edited by Bernard De Voto. New York, Harper & Brothers, 1940.

————. *Mark Twain of the* Enterprise. Edited by Henry Nash Smith with the assistance of Frederick Anderson. Berkeley and Los Angeles, University of California Press, 1957.

————. *Mark Twain: Representative Selections.* Edited by Fred Lewis Pattee. New York, American Book Company, 1935.

————. *Mark Twain: San Francisco Correspondent.* Edited by Henry Nash Smith and Frederick Anderson. San Francisco, The Book Club of California, 1957.

————. *Mark Twain's Autobiography.* Edited by Albert Bigelow Paine. 2 vols. New York, Harper & Brothers, 1924.

————. *Mark Twain's Letters.* Edited by Albert Bigelow Paine. New York, Harper & Brothers, 1917.

————. *Mark Twain's Notebook.* Edited by Albert Bigelow Paine. New York, Harper & Brothers, 1935.

————. *"My Dear Bro": A Letter from Samuel Clemens to His Brother Orion.* With a Foreword by Frederick Anderson. Berkeley, The Berkeley Albion, 1961.

————. *"My Platonic Sweetheart," "The Mysterious Stranger," and Other Stories by Mark Twain.* New York, Gabriel Wells, 1923.

————. *The Portable Mark Twain.* Edited by Bernard De Voto. New York, The Viking Press, 1946.

————. *Pudd'nhead Wilson and Those Extraordinary Twins.* New York, Harper & Brothers, 1893–94.

————. *Roughing It.* Hartford, American Publishing Company, 1872.

————. *The Writings of Mark Twain.* Author's National Edition. 22 vols. New York, Harper & Brothers, 1899–1900.

————. and Bret Harte. *"Ah Sin," A Dramatic Work by Mark Twain and Bret Harte.* Edited by Frederick Anderson. San Francisco, The Book Club of California, 1961.

Meltzer, Milton. *Mark Twain Himself, A Pictorial Biography.* New York, Thomas Y. Crowell Company, 1960.

Melville, Herman. *The Portable Melville.* Edited by Jay Leyda. New York, The Viking Press, 1952.

Merwin, Henry Childs. *The Life of Bret Harte, with Some Account of the California Pioneers.* Boston, Houghton Mifflin Company, 1911.

Mott, Frank Luther. *A History of American Magazines, 1865–1885.* 3 vols. Cambridge, Massachusetts, Harvard University Press, 1938.

Murdock, Charles A. *A Backward Glance at Eighty.* San Francisco, Paul Elder and Company, 1921.

Paine, Albert Bigelow. *Mark Twain: A Biography. The Personal and Literary Life of Samuel Langhorne Clemens.* 2 vols. New York, Harper & Brothers, 1912.

Pemberton, T. Edgar. *Bret Harte, A Treatise and a Tribute.* London, Greening & Co., Ltd., 1900.

———. *The Life of Bret Harte.* New York, Dodd, Mead & Company, 1903.

Quinn, Arthur Hobson. *A History of the American Drama from the Civil War to the Present Day.* 2 vols. New York, Harper & Brothers, 1927.

Royce, Josiah. *California, from the Conquest in 1846 to the Second Vigilance Committee in San Francisco: A Study of American Character.* New York, Alfred A. Knopf. 1948.

Scott, Arthur L., editor. *Mark Twain: Selected Criticism.* Dallas, Southern Methodist University Press, 1955.

Smith, Henry Nash. *Mark Twain: The Development of a Writer.* Cambridge, Massachusetts, The Belknap Press, 1962.

———. *Virgin Land: The American West as Symbol and Myth.* Cambridge, Massachusetts, Harvard University Press, 1950.

Spielmann, M. H., and G. S. Layard. *Kate Greenaway.* New York, G. P. Putnam's Sons, 1905.

Spiller, Robert E., *et al.,* editors. *Literary History of the United States.* 3 vols. New York, The Macmillan Company, 1948.

Stewart, George R., compiler. *A Bibliography of the Writings of Bret Harte in the Magazines and Newspapers of California, 1857–1871.* Berkeley, University of California Press, 1933.

———. *Bret Harte, Argonaut and Exile.* Boston, Houghton Mifflin Company, 1931.

Stoddard, Charles Warren. *Exits and Entrances*. Boston, Lothrop Publishing Company, 1903.

Stone, Albert E., Jr. *The Innocent Eye: Childhood in Mark Twain's Imagination*. New Haven, Yale University Press, 1961.

Thayer, William Roscoe. *The Life and Letters of John Hay*. 2 vols. Boston, Houghton Mifflin Company, 1915.

Trent, W. P., and John Erskine. *Great American Writers*. New York, Henry Holt and Company, 1912.

Trilling, Lionel. *The Liberal Imagination*. Garden City, New York, Doubleday & Company, 1953.

Wagenknecht, Edward. *Mark Twain: The Man and His Work*. New Haven, Yale University Press, 1935.

Walker, Franklin. *San Francisco's Literary Frontier*. New York, Alfred A. Knopf, 1939.

Wallace, Edward S. *Destiny and Glory*. New York, Coward, McCann, Inc., 1957.

Walterhouse, Roger Rilus. *Bret Harte, Joaquin Miller, and the Western Local Color Story*. Chicago, The University Libraries, 1939.

Weber, Carl J. *The Rise and Fall of James Ripley Osgood: A Biography*. Waterville, Maine, Colby College Press, 1959.

Webster, Samuel Charles, editor. *Mark Twain: Business Man*. Boston, Little, Brown and Company, 1946.

Weeks, Edward, and Emily Flint, editors. *Jubilee: One Hundred Years of the Atlantic*. Boston, Little, Brown and Company, 1957.

Williams, Stanley T. *The Spanish Background of American Literature*. 2 vols. New Haven, Yale University Press, 1955.

Winter, William. *The Life of David Belasco*. 2 vols. New York, Moffat, Yard and Company, 1918.

3. Articles

Blair, Walter. "On the Structure of Tom Sawyer," *Modern Philology*, Vol. XXXVII (August, 1939), 75–88.

Blanck, Jacob. "The Question of Bret Harte's Mliss," *Publishers' Weekly*, Vol. CXXX, Pt. 2 (November 28, 1936), 2102–2103.

Booth, Bradford A. "Mark Twain's Comments on Bret Harte's Stories," *American Literature*, Vol. XXV (January, 1954), 492–95.

———. "Unpublished Letters of Bret Harte," *American Literature*, Vol. XVI (May, 1944), 131–42.

"Bret Harte and the Pioneers of '49," *Blackwood's*, Vol. CXCI (April, 1912), 582–84.

Brooks, Noah. "Bret Harte: A Biographical and Critical Sketch," *Over-land Monthly* (Bret Harte Memorial Number), Vol XL (September, 1902), 201–207.

———. "Bret Harte in California," *Century Magazine*, Vol. LVIII (July, 1899), 447–51.

———. "Reminiscences of Bret Harte," *Overland Monthly*, Vol. XL (September, 1902), 225.

Canby, Henry Seidel. "The Luck of Bret Harte," *Saturday Review of Literature*, Vol. II (April 17, 1926), 717–18.

Childs, Marquis. "The Home of Mark Twain," *American Mercury*, Vol. IX (September, 1926), 101–105.

Clark, George Peirce. "Mark Twain on Bret Harte," *Mark Twain Journal* (Spring and Summer, 1958), 12–13.

Cunliffe, Marcus. "A Lost Masterpiece"? *Encounter*, Vol. XV (October, 1960), 71–74.

De Voto, Bernard. "The Other Side of Some Mark Twain Stories," *The New York Herald Tribune Weekly Book Review* (February 10, 1946), 3.

Duckett, Margaret. "Bret Harte and the Indians of Northern California," *Huntington Library Quarterly*, Vol. XVIII (November, 1954), 59–83.

———. "The 'Crusade' of a Nineteenth-Century Liberal," *Tennessee Studies in Literature*, Vol. IV (1959), 109–20.

———. "Plain Language from Bret Harte," *Nineteenth-Century Fiction*, Vol. XI (March, 1957), 241–60.

Evans, Taliesen. "Reminiscences of Bret Harte," *Overland Monthly*, Vol. XL (September, 1902), 229.

Fatout, Paul. "Mark Twain's Nom de Plume," *American Literature*, Vol. XXXIV (March, 1962), 6–7.

Ferguson, DeLancey. "Mark Twain's Lost Curtain Speeches," *South Atlantic Quarterly*, Vol. XLII (July, 1943), 262–69.

Fields, Mrs. James T. "Bret Harte and Mark Twain in the 'Seventies,' Passages from the Diaries of Mrs. James T. Fields," edited by M. A. DeWolfe Howe, *The Atlantic Monthly*, Vol. CXXX (September, 1922), 342–48.

Garland, Hamlin. "Roadside Meetings of a Literary Nomad," *Bookman*, Vol. LXXI (July, 1930), 423–24.

Harte, Bret. "The Genial Showman. By Edward P. Hingston. New York, Harper & Bros.," *Overland Monthly*, Vol. V (October, 1870), 388–89.

———. "The Rise of the 'Short Story,'" *Cornhill Magazine*, Vol. VII (July, 1899), 1–8.

Hill, Hamlin. "Mark Twain's Quarrels with Elisha Bliss," *American Literature*, Vol. XXXIII (January, 1962), 442–56.

Howells, William Dean. "Editor's Easy Chair," *Harper's Magazine*, Vol. CVIII (December, 1903).

———— "The Pilot's Story," *The Atlantic Monthly*, Vol. VI (September, 1860), 323–25.

McCrackin, Josephine Clifford. "Reminiscences of Bret Harte," *Overland Monthly*, Vol. XL (September, 1902), 223–24.

Mark Twain. "The Jumping Frog of Calaveras, by Mark Twain. With an Introductory and Explanatory Note by J. G. H.," *Overland Monthly*, Vol. XL (September, 1902), 287–88.

————. "Reflections on Religion," *Hudson Review*, Vol. XVI (Autumn, 1963), 330–52.

Morse, James Herbert. "The Native Element in American Fiction," *Century Magazine*, Vol. XXVI (July, 1883), 362–75.

Overland Monthly (Bret Harte Memorial Number), Vol. XL (September, 1902).

Smith, Henry Nash. "That Hideous Mistake of Poor Clemens's!" *Harvard Library Bulletin*, Vol. IX (Spring, 1955), 145–80.

Stewart, George R. "Bret Harte upon Mark Twain in 1866," *American Literature*, Vol. XIII (November, 1941), 264.

————. "Some Bret Harte Satires," *Frontier*, Vol. XIII (January, 1922), 93–101.

"Three Lost Years in the Life of Bret Harte," San Francisco *Examiner*, Pt. II (January 24, 1926), 1.

Twainian, Vol. VIII (July–August, 1949).

Young, James H. "Anna Dickinson, Mark Twain, and Bret Harte," *Pennsylvania Magazine of History and Biography*, Vol. LXXVI, January, 1952), 39–45.

INDEX

Harte, Bret (herein cited as BH): finances,
8, 28, 94, 96, 133, 139, 160, 168–70,
175, 178, 184, 218, 228–29, 250,
285, 338; appearance, 10, 15, 66, 71,
89, 187, 226, 292; charges of Bohemianism, 10; character, 11, 67, 72, 268,
278, 341; political stands, 12; friends,
13, 23, 226, 238, 269, 271, 276, 291;
treatment of wife and family, 14, 132,
185, 200, 204, 227, 239, 241; as an
editor, 14, 24, 31, 245, 328, 330; sentimentality, 61, 79, 111, 295, 312, 341;
lecturing, 88–89, 183, 185–86, 199;
literary craftsmanship, 96, 245, 252–
53, 256; scenic descriptions, 108; affection for children, 108, 125, 181,
328–30; translation of, 109, 118, 252;
influence on American drama, 116;
health, 132, 161, 187, 198, 200, 202,
221, 225, 268, 273, 295; Jewish blood,
173; charges of drunkenness and im-
morality, 188, 219; treatment of sex,
234, 236–37; attitude toward women,
237–38; attitude toward divorce, 241;
patriotism, 259, 267; views on class
distinctions, 266; views on poor, 266;
dislike of publicity, 338–39
———, collaboration:
with MT, 5, 26, 47, 52, 61, 98, 107,
115, 119, 122–23, 131, 136;
with Boucicault, 110, 117;
with Pemberton, 230, 245;
with Hatton, 246
———, prejudices (racial, religious, national), 12, 19, 38 f., 53, 114, 252:
Indians, 11, 22, 79, 117, 252;
Spanish culture in the United States, 22,
237, 251;
Chinese, 23, 52, 108, 114, 150, 252,
294, 307;
Catholic church, 237
———, as a critic, 15, 28, 33, 47, 65,
246, 255, 316, 342–43:
critical opinions of MT, 27–30, 73,
195, 331
———, literary forms:
satire, 29, 149, 263, 306, 332;
parody, 32, 37–38, 55, 78, 167, 316–17

———, government appointments:
Crefeld, 163 ff.;
Glasgow, 197 ff.
Harte, Ethel Bret: 82, 182, 204, 236,
240, 270–71
Harte, Francis King (Frank): 12, 48,
76, 182–83, 188, 204–207, 211, 230,
232, 240, 263, 269, 271
Harte, Geoffrey Bret: 132, 232, 240
Harte, Griswold: 12, 180, 204, 207, 271
Harte, Jessamy: *see* Steele, Jessamy
Harte, Margaret: *see* Wyman, Margaret
Harte, Richard: 240
Hartford *Courant:* 105, 215
Hartford *Post:* 121
Harvard University: 90
Harvey, George: 304
Hatton, Joseph: 246–47, 254, 292
Haunted Man: 316
Hawthorne, Nathaniel: 109, 203
Hay, Clara S. (Mrs. John Hay): 204
Hay, John: 87, 172, 178, 196–97, 199,
200, 203 f., 210, 221, 241, 254, 275,
277, 291
Hayes, Rutherford B.: 129, 144, 162,
169, 176, 197, 223, 260
Hazard of New Fortunes, A: 67
Hearth and Home: 77
"Heathen Chinee, The": 5, 32, 34, 37, 39,
49, 52, 56 f., 80, 113, 115, 117, 149,
219, 306, 318; *see also* "Plain Lan-
guage from Truthful James"
"Heiress of Red Dog": 189, 191
Hemingway, Ernest: 330
Henniker, Mrs.: 238, 254, 256 f., 267,
274
Herschel, Herman: 118
Hesse, Fanny C.: 125
Higginson, Thomas Wentworth: 168
Hill, Hamlin: 137–39
Hiner, Cincinnatus: *see* Miller, Joaquin
Hingston, Edward P.: 33, 84
Hohenloe, Princess: 290
H. O. Houghton and Company: 70, 85
Holmes, Oliver Wendell: 66, 77, 107,
164–65, 170f., 301, 316, 330
Holy Land: 29
Homeopathic Hospital, Chicago: 315

The paper on which *Mark Twain and Bret Harte* has been printed bears the watermark of the University of Oklahoma Press and is expected to have an effective life of at least three hundred years. The type chosen is Caslon Old Face, a machine casting of one of the most popular type designs used for English language composition.

UNIVERSITY OF OKLAHOMA PRESS

NORMAN